Management Divided

Management Divided

Contradictions of Labor Management

Matt Vidal

OXFORD
UNIVERSITY PRESS

OXFORD
UNIVERSITY PRESS

Great Clarendon Street, Oxford, OX2 6DP,
United Kingdom

Oxford University Press is a department of the University of Oxford.
It furthers the University's objective of excellence in research, scholarship,
and education by publishing worldwide. Oxford is a registered trade mark of
Oxford University Press in the UK and in certain other countries

Impression: 1

Published in the United States of America by Oxford University Press
198 Madison Avenue, New York, NY 10016, United States of America

British Library Cataloguing in Publication Data
Data available

Library of Congress Control Number: 2021947706

ISBN 978–0–19–879527–8

DOI: 10.1093/oso/9780198795278.001.0001

Printed and bound by
CPI Group (UK) Ltd, Croydon, CR0 4YY

For Ellen, with love and thanks

Preface

This book had a long gestation period. From 2002 through early 2005, I conducted a field research project on labor management and supplier development in American manufacturing, including in-depth interviews with over 100 people in 31 manufacturing firms across Wisconsin, Michigan and Illinois. I also conducted over 150 hours of direct observation. Over several months I followed two unionized component suppliers (one for 15 months, one for seven) whose management agreed to implement a Labor-Management Partnership with support from the Wisconsin Regional Training Partnership (WRTP), one being a High-Performance Work Organization framework supported by the International Association of Machinists. I followed a nonunion component supplier for 16 months, observing a supplier development project run by a Fortune 500 household-name company with support from the Wisconsin Manufacturing Extension Partnership (WMEP), and participated in a day-long Lean 101 training session along with shopfloor workers.

I observed two half-day meetings of the Wisconsin Manufacturers Development Consortium, a group of seven large, brand-name corporations who worked together with the WMEP and technical colleges to develop a curriculum and deliver training (primarily lean production) to local suppliers, one meeting of 14 supplier firms and the WMEP discussing the problems they experienced trying to implement just-in-time production and the training they needed to help them with it, and six meetings of a network of unions representing workers at six large, brand-name corporations (three of which were in the WMDC) strategizing on how to fight outsourcing and organize the domestic supply chain.

I received my PhD from the University of Wisconsin-Madison in 2007, the same year that the first two journal articles based on this research were published. In the intervening years, while also working on several other research projects, I continued analyzing the data for this book and inductively developing the theory. I started reading Marx during my undergraduate years but only found the contemporary labor process literature during graduate school. The most influential contributions of the contemporary literature deptict the workplace is a battleground of class struggle. Harry Braverman argued that the degradation of work is inherent to capitalist management. David Gordon and Richard Edwards portrayed managers as preoccupied with controlling labor to maximize the extraction of surplus value and minimize the power of labor. Michael Burawoy theorized the workplace as the crucible in which class consciousness is formed and the contemporary American workplace as effectively subverting working-class consciousness. These arguments and images did not resonate with my own experiences as a worker—from several positions in kitchens, restaurants and supermarkets to janitorial work, call center work and jobs in two factories (light electronics assembly; machine operator in a metalfab shop)—other than the part about semiskilled manual labor being incredibly boring. Yet, critical studies of lean production seemed to confirm the predictions from labor process theory: the rhetoric promised teamwork and empowerment but the reality was degraded, intensified work and increased managerial control.

As with my own personal work experience, my interviews and observations in American manufacturing firms were hard to reconcile with the picture painted by contemporary labor process theory and the critical scholarship on lean. Workers were generally interested in the success of their organizations and in doing their part to ensure that success (though often deeply skeptical of management). Managers in general were not focused on—let alone preoccupied with—labor control or work speedup, and in many cases were focused on cross training their workers and including them in problem solving and decision making around process improvement. To be sure, there was labor-management conflict, but this was generally about competing visions of efficiency and contestation over changing workplace routines, not about control, autonomy, or the pace of work.

As I continued reading Marx, I found much that was not reflected in the contributions of Braverman, Gordon, Edwards, and Burawoy and I developed an interpretation different from theirs. I learned much from contemporary labor process theory, including the work of Peter Armstrong, Rick Delbridge, Tony Elger, Andrew Friedman, Theo Nichols, Chris Smith, Vicki Smith, Phil Taylor, Paul Thompson, Steve Vallas, and Chris Warhurst, but continued to find its theoretical core—the control-resistance framework—of limited use for understanding my observations. In my search for relevant theory to understand and analyze my findings, I read widely across the sociology of work, human resource management and employment relations; organization theory, institutional theory, and social psychology; economics, economic sociology, and comparative political economy.

I am delighted to present this book, which offers a synthetic theoretical framework and research program for the analysis of labor management and work organization. Although my case study is on contemporary American manufacturing, the framework, which I call organizational political economy, is explicitly developed for comparative and historical research on organizations across sectors and countries. The foundation is historical materialism, including a classical marxist labor process theory and a stage theory of capitalist development informed by regulation theory, into which I integrate the organization theoretic concepts of institutional logics and organizational fields, managerial satisficing, and operational routines.

The theory proposes that the western world entered a postfordist stage in the 1990s, after more than two decades of organizational experimentation and institutional change. Within this stage, lean management and worker empowerment have been institutionalized as logics of best practice in the manufacturing field and beyond. However, managers face contradictory pressures between ensuring labor discipline (so workers produce output of sufficient quantity and quality) versus empowering labor (so workers can contribute to problem solving and decision making in service of flexibility, continuous improvement, and organizational learning).

In the fifteen years since the data were collected, the core theoretical propositions have been corroborated: lean production remains the undisputed model of global best practice in manufacturing and has spread to a range of service sectors. Conflicting strategies emphasizing standardization or discretion, deskilling or upskilling, manual or cognitive labor are observed in a broad range of occupations, including production, social services, education, healthcare, administrative support, and software. The book presents evidence that within manufacturing, the common strategy of using workers exclusively for routine manual labor is a satisficing approach, inferior—in terms of achieving dynamic efficiency, including low costs with high levels of quality, flexibility, and organizational learning—to a strategy of enlisting workers in abstract cognitive labor.

As would be expected, my debts are many. I would like to thank all of the organizations that participated in my research and all of the individuals who gave their time to be interviewed, provided me with access to their organizations, facilitated access to other organizations or individuals, or otherwise allowed me to observe their working lives. Rhandi Berth,

Dawn Schaefer, and Bob Bergmann of the Wisconsin Regional Training Partnership, and Mike Klonsinski and Steve Straub of the Wisconsin Manufacturing Extension Partnership, facilitated access to several companies and were gracious with their time and support. Steve provided helpful written feedback on one draft paper. Four managers were especially supportive. The plant managers at Second Tier Specialist, Metalfab Plus, and Mini OE were particularly generous with their time and providing access to their companies and personnel. Paul Ericksen facilitated many introductions, opening many doors within his own organization and others, and remains a good friend today.

The research for this book was made possible by a grant from the Alfred P. Sloan Foundation for the Advanced Manufacturing Project (AMP) research consortium. Sue Helper, Gary Herrigel, Dan Luria, Joel Rogers, and Jonathan Zeitlin were the principal investigators on that project and Josh Whitford was a fellow research assistant. All of these colleagues provided guidance and feedback on my earliest papers, including the two publications from 2007, which developed some parts of the analysis presented in this book. At the University of Wisconsin-Madison, the Sociology department, the Center on Wisconsin Strategy (COWS), and the Economic Sociology brownbag seminar provided an intellectually rich and stimulating environment, and I received feedback on the earliest papers from several colleagues at Madison including Ivan Ermakoff, Jennifer Farnham, Michael Handel, Chip Hunter, Pablo Mitnik, Matt Nichter, Jamie Peck, Jeff Rothstein, Rob White, and Erik Wright. Other Madison friends who helped shape my thinking in one way or another include Laura Dresser, Mark Harvey, Brent Kaup, Shamus Khan, Monica Erling (née Willemsen), Brad Manzolillo, Arthur Scarritt, Amy Quark, Matías Scaglione, Matt Zeidenberg, and Jeff Rickert, a dear friend who passed far too soon. I also received constructive comments on an early paper from Nina Bandelj.

The Institute for Research on Labor and Employment (IRLE) at UCLA provided me with a postdoctoral fellowship and dedicated time to work on further analysis and drafts of my first paper drawing from the entire dataset and developing the synthesis of labor process and institutional theory. UCLA was another stimulating place to be, including the IRLE and the Comparative Social Analysis seminar. I am particularly grateful for the support and guidance I received from Ruth Milkman, then director of the IRLE, who continues to be a mentor and friend. Michael Mann and Lynne Zucker also provided constructive feedback on a draft paper.

After moving to King's College London, I received written comments on a draft of that paper from Howard Gospel and Jon Hindmarsh. I was fortunate to receive additional written comments from Mike Lounsbury, Adam Slez, and Steve Vallas. During my time at King's I formed friendships with colleagues who have shaped my thinking in one way or another: Juan Baeza, Chiara Benassi, Ginny Doellgast, Ian Hill, Martin Edwards, Tony Edwards, Andreas Kornelakis, Dirk vom Lehn, Thomas Roulet, Gerhard Schynder, and Sotiris Vandoros.

King's provided me with a short sabbatical, during which the Max Planck Institute for the Study of Societies, in Cologne, generously allowed me to be a visiting researcher. During that time I wrote drafts of the first two chapters of this book. I am grateful to Wolfgang Streeck, Jens Beckert, and the MPIfG.

Loughborough University London has provided a convivial workplace and excellent new colleagues. It is only during these years that I found the time to complete this book. I have been fortunate to receive written feedback on drafts of the book chapters from Chiara Benassi, Gregor Bouville, Joseph Choonara, Ginny Doellgast, Paul Erickson, Ian Greer, Simon Joyce, Nick Krachler, Martin Krzywdzinski, Mike McCarthy, Jeff Rothstein, Chris Ryan, Gerhard Schnyder, Chris Smith, Paul Thompson, and Chris Warhurst.

I owe particular thanks to my mentors at UW-Madison. Jamie Peck inspired and continues to inspire me in terms of both substance and style. Joel Rogers taught and nurtured me as my advisor, employer, and advocate. My views on the labor movement and labor-management partnership have been shaped by his level-headed political pragmatism. Erik Wright was a model advisor and good friend until his untimely passing, even though we had serious theoretical disagreements on some core issues. Such disagreements notwithstanding, my intellectual debt to Erik cannot be overstated, and I hope that his demands for analytical rigor and conceptual clarity have made a noticeable impact on my own thinking and writing.

Other scholars have provided ongoing feedback on my work over several years along with inspiration and friendship: Paul Adler, Paul Thompson, Chris Smith, Tony Smith, and Steve Vallas. Tony read and provided written feedback on drafts of all ten chapters. One is fortunate to have a philosopher go through 130,000 words with a fine-tooth comb. Steve has been a mentor and was among the first scholars from outside UW-Madison that I developed a close friendship with. Paul Adler has been an unlimited source of ideas, feedback, and camaraderie. We share a broadly similar reading of

Marx, of the deficiencies of neomarxism, the problems with contemporary labor process theory, and the importance of straddling the worlds of marxism and mainstream theory, writing marxist analysis with the skeptical mainstream in mind while taking what is useful from mainstream theory for critical analysis and marxist theory.

Several friends have influenced my thinking while providing emotional nourishment. Four of these are dear friends from Madison: Monica Erling (née Willemsen), Matt Nichter, Jeff Rothstein, and Josh Whitford. Others I have met since leaving Madison: Olivier Butzbach, Ginny Doellgast, Tony Edwards, Doug Fuller, Ian Greer, Marco Hauptmeier, Hyunji Kwon, and Gerhard Schnyder.

Finally, my family. My parents, Judy and Brent, Connie and Lou, Kay and Ron, have supported me in all the ways good parents do. My kids, Remy and Axel, have become the lights of my life. Most of all, my partner Ellen Christensen has been everything to me for more than twenty years. She is my best friend and source of stability. She has served as a sounding board for an endless stream of ideas and always provided thoughtful feedback. And she has picked up more than her share of the household labor while I have been preoccupied with work. I dedicate this book to Ellen.

Contents

List of Figures

List of Tables

PART I

THE PROBLEM

1

The Problem of Labor Management

Across a wide range of sectors, managers today face conflicting pressures on how to utilize their employees.[1] On the one hand, they need to ensure that workers produce output, whether in goods or services, of sufficient quantity and quality. To this end, managers ensure workforce discipline through work simplification and standardization, automation and machine-paced work, rules and procedures, threats and rewards. On the other hand, organizational success increasingly depends on the ability of managers to harness the creativity and initiative of workers. To this end, managers empower the workforce through job enlargement and enrichment, cross training and multiskilling, and opportunities to participate in problem solving and decision making.

It is possible—if a manager or management team is sufficiently competent and has sufficiently high aspiration levels—to forge a configuration of routines and practices that establishes a balance including empowerment (via multiskilling, problem solving and decision-making authority) and discipline (via standards, process and quality control tools, and incentives). Such organizations are celebrated in the business and academic press, the likes of Toyota, AT&T, Xerox, IBM, Hewlett-Packard, and Kaiser Permanente. But establishing a balance that includes some degree of both does not eliminate the underlying conflict managers face between ensuring discipline and harnessing creativity. Consider Toyota, whose production system is widely celebrated for its productivity, quality, and flexibility performance, based in part on harnessing ideas from workers, but where employee involvement for production workers is more consultative than substantive (Marsh 1992; Masami 1994) and assembly line work remains simple, boring, and intense (Ilhara 2007; Kamata 1982 [1973]).

More commonly, managers strive but struggle to achieve any sort of balance between these competing pressures. Some deploy limited forms of employee involvement (e.g. suggestion programs and other channels

[1] This chapter draws on parts of Vidal (2015) and Vidal (2019c) but contains a substantial amount of new material.

Management Divided. Matt Vidal, Oxford University Press. © Matt Vidal (2022).
DOI: 10.1093/oso/9780198795278.003.0001

for workers to suggest ideas) or isolated islands of genuine empowerment (worker participation in problem solving and decision making) within otherwise traditional labor-management relations. Others, in the face of intense competition and conflicting pressures, do not even attempt to strike a balance, sacrificing empowerment entirely in favor of discipline, taking the easier path and *settling for good enough*, to the detriment of organizational performance and worker well-being.

The thesis of this book is that the tension between ensuring worker discipline and harnessing worker creativity is one of the central dynamics shaping organizations today. This tension is the inevitable expression of a material contradiction inherent to the labor-management relation. As employee involvement has become increasingly important over the last four decades in response to rapid technical change, and demands for flexibility and continuous improvement, this contradiction has been intensifying. Management is divided: individual managers face irreconcilable, conflicting pressures; and management as a whole is divided based on competing visions of how to manage labor and organize the division of labor in the workplace.

If mainstream management scholars tend to emphasize celebrity cases, sociologists and critical management scholars tend to focus on more typical cases, often finding deskilling and work intensification. While the latter have been pronounced tendencies for much of the history of capitalism and remain all too common today, neither sociological theory nor organization theory has grasped the conflicting pressures that managers increasingly face regarding their workforce. Most organizations stumble forward, ever-unable to resolve this underlying tension. By focusing on this contradiction, I develop a theory of organizational political economy that explains variation in labor-management regimes—from high-involvement, world-class organizations to low-involvement, good-enough establishments that are muddling through—and shows how the capitalist employment relation as such, due to its inherently contradictory nature, makes the typical organization a relatively inefficient imitator rather than a high-efficiency innovator.

Among the most widely adopted labor management systems today, which is successful because it provides tools for achieving a balance between discipline and empowerment, is the Toyota production system, also known as lean production. Although lean began in manufacturing, it has always been seen as a management system applicable to a wide range of organizational contexts. In the words of its founder, Taiichi Ohno, "The

Toyota production system . . . is not just a production system. I am confident it will reveal its strength as a management system adapted to today's era of global markets and high-level computerized information systems" (1988: xv). Ohno had good reason to be confident: Today lean is increasingly being adopted in healthcare, banking, insurance, civil service, education, software, airline services, legal services, telecom, mass merchandising, and restaurants (for chapters on lean in many of these sectors, see Janoski and Lepadatu 2021). Wherever the creation of a product of delivery of a service involves a multi-step process, lean can be applied.

Lean ultimately emerged as the preeminent manufacturing model following the crisis of traditional manufacturing (aka fordism) in the 1970s, when the rigidities of the latter became increasingly uncompetitive under competition from emergent, more flexible production models. In Germany, Japan, and Sweden, new production models included varying degrees of worker participation in problem solving and decision making. The most radical departure from traditional mass production was tried by Volvo in the 1970s and 1980s. At the Uddevalla factory, the assembly line was eliminated and truly self-directed teams would assemble an entire car in-dock, each team deciding how to organize and execute the work.

By the mid-1990s, however, both Volvo and leading German manufacturers had adopted lean. The reason why lean surpassed other contenders to become widely seen by practitioners as best practice is because, as Paul Adler and Robert Cole (1993) first observed, it combines various tools for process control and standardization with teamwork and other employee involvement practices; the latter function (however problematically) to solicit ideas for process improvement from front-line workers while the focus on process standardization (ideally) ensures that best practice is diffused throughout the organization.

In this book, I present a study of lean management in American manufacturing during the early 2000s. I did not set out to study lean, but rather to examine questions of labor management, organizational decision making and institutional change in the manufacturing sector, where taylorist scientific management and fordism were born and where various ideas and practices around work humanization, employee involvement, and self-directed teams have promised to fundamentally transform capitalist employment. For example, in characterizing the adoption of job enrichment, multiskilling, and teamwork in German manufacturing, Horst Kern and Michael Schumann (1992: 111) claimed that "the project of liberated, fulfilling work, originally interpreted as an anticapitalist project" was being "staged by capitalist management itself . . . in the name of efficiency."

While my empirical case is the manufacturing sector in the US Midwest, my argument is not limited to manufacturing or to lean production. The focus of my analysis is on the contradictory pressures managers face between ensuring labor discipline (so workers produce sufficient levels of output) versus empowering labor. This contradiction is manifest in conflicting pressures to use workers for routine manual versus abstract cognitive labor power; to provide minimal training versus substantial training (e.g. training in a single skill versus multiple skills or training in narrow skills versus broad skills); or to standardize work versus allowing discretion and autonomy.

This contradiction exists across a wide range of occupations. Just as occupations typically associated with routine work (e.g. production occupations) are increasingly subject to pressures for multiskilling and substantive employee involvement, occupations that offer high levels of discretion and autonomy are experiencing increasing pressures for standardization, from healthcare occupations, including the work of doctors (Timmermans 2005), to teaching (Au 2011) to software development (Trusson et al. 2018). Managers experience conflicting pressures for standardization versus discretion, deskilling versus upskilling, and routine manual versus abstract cognitive labor in a wide range of occupations, including social service occupations, educational occupations, healthcare occupations, office and administrative support occupations, computer occupations (e.g. software development), and of course production occupations.

Lean Management: Boosters, Critics, and Beyond

When I entered the field in 2002 to study these questions, the received wisdom among sociologists, employment relations scholars, and comparative political economists was—and perhaps still is—that there is no one best way to organize production. In the literature on "models of production," reviewed in Chapter 2, three models were still presented as viable competitors to the Toyota Production System: Volvo's radical experiment at Uddevalla, which eliminated the assembly line and introduced self-directed teams; the German model; and the "flexible specialization" model of the Italian industrial districts. The fact that lean had prevailed in the Swedish, German, and American auto industries by the mid-1990s did not seem to dampen enthusiasm for the vanquished models. In the factories I studied, lean was everywhere I looked, on the lips of everyone I interviewed. When discussing best practice, managers referred only to Japan, not to Sweden, Germany, or Italy. Nearly twenty years later, lean remains synonymous with world-class manufacturing.

Although there is consensus among managers that lean is the one best way, lean has been divisive and contested. Its boosters tout it as a work system whose efficiency and flexibility advantages are *based on* empowered workers engaged in decision making and problem solving. In the words of Martin Kenney and Richard Florida (1993: 1), lean is "a revolutionary method of organizing production" based on "a powerful synthesis of intellectual and physical labor," heralding a new era of capitalism in which labor at all levels is engaged in intellectually rewarding work. According to Toyota Production System gurus Jeffrey Liker and David Meier (2007: 24, 26):

> Training and development of team members (all employees) at Toyota is part of the broader "Human System." At the core of Toyota's Human System is the development of people, including the ability to attract capable people, engage them, and enroll them as full-fledged members of the Toyota culture. . . . The Toyota Production System is designed to identify and highlight problems, while the Human System model is designed to engage people who are able and willing to solve them.

And according to engineer-consultant Pascal Dennis (2015: 34, 143), author of the how-to manual, *Lean Production Simplified*, now in its third edition, "total involvement animates the Toyota system . . . we seek to involve our team members in all these activities because they are the wellspring of continuous improvement."

By contrast, many critics charge that the performance benefits of lean come not from harnessing the skill and knowledge of workers but from work intensification and improved process control, within a neotaylorist context of rotation among semiskilled tasks (Carter et al. 2013; Danford 1999; Fucini and Fucini 1990; Graham 1995; Parker and Slaughter 1995; Rinehart et al. 1997; Stewart et al. 2009). Paul Stewart and collaborators (2009: x) argue that "lean production demands labor subordination" and that it is "the reason for the deterioration in the employment experience for many millions of workers." These scholars do important work showing that lean can be used in a way that increases work intensification via speedup and reducing or eliminating production buffers, hence reducing downtime workers have for rest and recuperation, often with negative health consequences for workers. Bob Carter and colleagues (2013) documented increased work volume, pace, and intensity under lean being associated with fatigue, musculoskeletal disorders, and stress (see also Bouville and Alis 2014).

But my research demonstrates that lean is a management model which can be implemented in distinct ways, with distinct emphases, depending on the orientation of management and the power and orientation of labor. Here I present extensive evidence from supplier factories of managers who prioritize qualitative process improvement over quantitative work intensification, including a majority of workers who did not experience any work intensification or who experienced qualitative work intensification but found it to be a positive change that made their work less boring and more interesting.

It must be remembered that the main tools used for speedup and downtime reduction under lean have existed for a century or more: time study was developed by Frederick Winslow Taylor in the 1880s, motion study by Frank and Lillian Gilbreth in the 1910s, and process mapping (the forerunner of lean value-stream mapping) by Frank Gilbreth in the 1920s. Fordist mass production moderated pressures for work intensification, in part due to its batch-and-queue approach, which necessarily adds buffers in between long production runs in a push production system driven by forecasts. But more fundamentally, work intensification pressures were moderated because the institutional growth regime of the fordist period (roughly from the 1920s through the early 1970s) was based in oligopolistic competition.

A marked increase in work intensification has occurred over the last thirty-plus years across sectors and occupations (Crowley et al. 2010; F. Green 2006; V. Smith 1997), occurring far more widely than the diffusion of lean production. The fundamental source of this work intensification has been the intensification of competitive pressures in both product markets and financial markets. A general rise in work intensification is a background condition of the postfordist era.

To be sure, the lean focus on reducing production buffers reduces downtime for workers. But the impact of lean management on work intensity depends on the orientation of management and the total package of practices adopted. While a logic of work intensification seems to dominate in subsectors like auto assembly, in the upper tiers of the component supplier sector, some managers adopt logics of process improvement and worker empowerment. Lean tools and practices can generate performance improvements that are not based on speedup or reduction of worker downtime: streamlined process flows, better inventory management, and faster tool changeovers; reduction of bottlenecks and unnecessary movements; visual management with worker empowerment to stop production and engage in problem solving.

In my analysis, lean reflects and intensifies a material contradiction that is inherent to the capitalist employment relation: the need to ensure discipline versus the need to harness the creativity of workers. The core argument of this book is that in facing the conflicting pressures generated by this contradiction, managers often satisfice—settle for good enough—rather than maximize profit, efficiency, labor control, or anything else. World-class manufacturing practice involves adopting a complementary package of lean practices, including the substantive empowerment of workers. The leanest systems are highly fragile due to their lack of buffers (a stoppage anywhere in a continuous flow system will shut the whole system down). Empowered workers can both manage these highly fragile systems, via problem solving on the line, and drive continuous improvement in online and offline teams. Because this is exceedingly difficult to implement on a sustainable basis, particularly in the face of resistance and reticence from alienated workers, managers often satisfice. Concerned with securing sufficient output from workers, they fail to adopt best practice by devolving real decision-making and problem-solving power to workers or by adopting the leanest—hence most fragile—organizational practices.

This book presents a case study of Midwestern American manufacturing conducted over 2002–05. The present chapter presents key theoretical concepts and a brief historical sketch of labor management in American manufacturing, followed by an overview of my argument.

To preview the historical argument, from roughly the 1920s through the 1960s, there was widespread agreement within American industry that fordist mass production with a taylorist division of labor constituted best practice. Although there have been proposals and experiments with limiting or abandoning taylorist task fragmentation, standardization, and managerial hierarchy since it became dominant in the early twentieth century, fordism and taylorism remained institutionalized as best practice through the 1960s. During the 1970s and 1980s, as the challenge to fordism from more flexible forms of production developed in Germany, Japan, and

Sweden became apparent, there was widespread experimentation with new organizational models. From the 1990s through to the present, lean production with substantive worker empowerment has been institutionalized as best practice in American manufacturing.

Although lean is often contested by workers and unions, there is widespread agreement among senior managers, middle managers, engineers, industry associations, and consultants that it constitutes best practice. Lean has been codified into a package of well-defined, complementary practices intended to be implemented as a system. The core practices include just-in-time production (demand-driven production with low inventories), continuous flow organization, waste elimination, teamwork, and continuous improvement. In American manufacturing, the best practice for teamwork and employee involvement is widely understood to include empowerment, that is, cross training workers and involving them in problem solving and decision making. However, because many managers satisfice in the face of conflicting pressures, they are adopting basic lean practices to improve performance but failing to substantively empower their workers or implement the whole package of complementary lean practices.

Theoretical Framework and Historical Background: A Sketch

Why do some managers substantively empower their workers to engage in decision making (regarding work organization and process design) while others in the same sector do not? To answer this question—to explain variation in labor-management regimes across organizations competing in the same sector—this book presents a synthetic theory, which I call organizational political economy. The foundation of the theory is Marx's historical materialism, into which I integrate concepts and propositions from organization theory. In this section I briefly outline the theoretical framework, focusing on structural contradictions, institutional logics, and the transformation of contradictions and logics across stages of growth. This is followed by a brief outline of the fordist and postfordist stages of American socioeconomic development. The full theory is developed in Chapter 3.

I draw on and develop labor process theory, but I diverge significantly from the most well-known version of it—that initiated by Harry Braverman (1974: 40)—which emphasizes deskilling and the degradation of work as *overriding imperatives* of capitalist management. Braverman's contribution was monumental, inaugurating an important new research program, which has indeed documented widespread deskilling and intensification under capitalist management, past and present. But Braverman presented a narrow reading of Marx, abandoning any notion of contradictory development in favor of theory in which the problem of management is conceived to turn exclusively on the question of extracting effort from workers, where workers are theorized to have clear interests in exerting as little effort as possible, and deskilling plus standardization is seen to be a universal solution to the management problem.

My goal is to present a broad interpretation of Marx, reasserting the dialectical and contradictory character of capitalist development, against one-sided Bravermanian interpretations. I build on two alternative traditions of labor process scholarship: one that explicitly theorizes the capitalist labor process as inherently contradictory (Adler 2007; Cressey and MacInnes 1980; Elger 1979; Littler 1982; C. Smith 1987; Thompson 1983, 2003) and another that emphasizes how the overriding focus on profits leads to a relatively inefficient use of labor (Edwards 1979; D. M. Gordon 1976; D. Gordon et al. 1982; Noble 1986).

Before turning to Marx, however, I make a few preliminary comments on the relation between profits and organizational efficiency within capitalism. The primary goal of capitalist production is profit. Efficiency is a means to make profit but maximizing efficiency is generally not necessary to make profit. Within manufacturing there is wide variation in productivity levels, with only a small proportion of firms achieving the highest levels (Angeriz et al. 2006; Caves and Barton 1990; Frantz 1988; A. Green and Mayes 1991; Luria 1996). The average firm is a mediocre performer compared with leading firms.

Even more fundamentally, the profit motive within capitalism can conflict with what we might call the efficiency motive. This argument was central to Thorstein Veblen's *Theory of Business Enterprise* (1904), which distinguished "business enterprise" (investment for profit) from "the industrial system" (engineering to produce goods and services). In Veblen's analysis, business and industry are distinct interests that are often in conflict, as the profit motive often overrides concerns with efficiency, for example through wasteful spending on advertising in an attempt to capture market share or collaboration with competitors in curtailing production to keep prices high.

There is a clear and direct conflict between profit and efficiency in the case of negative externalities of production, for example, environmental degradation or costs absorbed by workers in the case of sweatshops, whether in manufacturing (Bonacich and Appelbaum 2000) or labor-intensive services (Bernhardt et al. 2008). Low-cost strategies of "bloody Taylorism" (Lipietz 1987) can produce cheap goods or services, but they often entail sacrificing product or service quality and worker health and safety. The resulting shoddy products, poor services, injured workers, and high turnover rates raise serious questions about the efficient use of resources.

More broadly, the package of human resource management practices that would utilize labor to its fullest potential is often not adopted. To be sure, high levels of productivity can be achieved with a simple division of labor, basic managerial competence, and sufficient financial capital. Those levels, however, are far below world-class performance levels for any given sector and strategy, whether a low-cost approach or a differentiation/quality/flexibility approach. And world-class, lean establishments with substantively empowered workers are able to reduce the tradeoff between static input/output efficiency and flexibility, achieving low cost, high quality, high flexibility and continuous improvement (Adler et al. 1999). But developing organizational capabilities for consistently achieving such a combination is exceptionally difficult.

Echoes of this difficulty can be heard in the human resource management literature. In the 1980s, human resource management emerged as a distinct discipline within management theory, with scholars championing it as a strategic business function and advocating a "high-performance" or high-involvement model of extensive training and empowerment of labor as best practice (Beer et al. 1985; Lawler 1992; Pfeffer 1998). Robust evidence demonstrates that the high-involvement model improves productivity and performance (Huselid 1995; Ichniowski et al. 1996; Ichniowski et al. 1997; MacDuffie 1995; Pil and MacDuffie 1996). Yet, its diffusion has been uneven and limited (Bacon and Blyton 2000; Boxall and Winterton 2018; Eurofound 2013; Osterman 1994). Small organizations are less likely to provide formal training or have a formal human resource management program (Barron et al. 1987; Knoke and Kalleberg 1994; Osterman 1995). And even large organizations vary substantially in their human resource management approaches. Limited training in narrow tasks is often sufficient to generate performance and profits that are good enough for managers and owners, even where more extensive training in broader skills would develop more productive workers.

In this book I demonstrate that many managers prioritize manual labor, narrow skills, and standardization to achieve good-enough performance, while managers in comparable organizations prioritize using workers for manual *and* cognitive labor, cross-training them in broader skills. I argue that these divergent approaches result from distinct managerial responses to the same contradictory pressures, which I theorize as reflecting an underlying contradiction between the forces of production and relations of production. I discuss this more in Chapter 3. For now, I provide a few brief definitions and comments.

The forces of production are, at root, human ingenuity and capability. The primary productive forces are labor power, codified knowledge (science), and its practical applications (technology), which may take the form of machines and physical processes (electrification, digitalization) or of organizational procedures (divisions of labor, management models, operational routines). Marx ([1867] 1990: 468) saw labor power, human cooperation, and the division of labor as the primary forces of production, oriented toward the harnessing and transformation of nature. The productive forces are fundamentally social, based in human labor (cognitive and manual): Marx referred to them variously as the "forces of social production" ([1857–8] 1993: 540, 706) or the "forces of social labor" (Marx [1867] 1990: 508).[2]

The relations of production refer to the class structure of society, that is, the nature of the relation by which a class who owns or controls the means of production appropriates the surplus product from a class of direct producers. Veblen (1904: 1) adopted a similar distinction to that between the forces and relations of production, but without the marxist class analysis, in his distinction between the industrial system (the efficiency motive of engineering) and business enterprise (the profit motive): "The material framework of modern civilization is the industrial system, and the directing force which animates this framework is business enterprise."

In the historical materialist analysis, while the details are beyond the scope of this chapter, the class structure of feudal society blocked the development of the productive forces by discouraging: concentration of the means of production necessary for economies of scale (Marx [1867] 1990: 447–8); the use of finance capital to achieve this concentration (915); and the detail division of labor to achieve economies of scale via specialization

[2] Marx ([1857–8] 1993: 704, 706) speculated on how "general social knowledge" or "the general intellect" will eventually become a "direct force of production." When this happens "the creation of real wealth" will depend less on labor and more on science and technology.

(Ch 14).[3] Such breakthroughs were achieved only with the emergence of capitalist tenant farmers and capitalist manufacturers. With the full transformation to the capitalist mode of production, the profit motive became institutionalized and legitimized as the unassailable goal of the economy.

While the profit motive unleashed a radical breakthrough in the development of the productive forces, Marx expected that as the forces continue to develop, at some point the relations of production would begin to fetter their further development. More broadly, he theorized the forces and relations of production as existing in a contradictory relation, giving rise to contradictions within the capitalist labor process.

Here I seek to develop this historical materialist analysis in two ways: elaborating a theoretical framework for the analysis of the contradictions of labor management and articulating an institutionalist theory of growth stages within capitalism.

Marx ([1867] 1990: 450) theorized the production process within capitalism as reflecting the contradiction between the forces and relations of production, being "on the one hand a social labor process for the creation of a product, and on the other hand capital's process of valorization." Valorization refers to the process of producing surplus value, that is, the creation of new value in the labor process, above and beyond the cost of wages and salaries.

The labor process—human cooperation, techniques, and tools to produce useful goods and services—is part and parcel of the forces of production, taking distinct forms under different relations of production.[4] The productive forces are the productive capabilities of humans and we may say, with Veblen, that there is an engineering motive—distinct from the profit motive—underlying their transhistorical growth: creativity and efficiency. The valorization process concerns ensuring that workers produce sufficient levels of output that can be sold on the market for profit. The valorization process is specific to capitalist relations of production, driven by the profit motive. The emergence of the profit motive and capitalist production relations gave a steroidal boost to the engineering motive and the productive forces, and the former sometimes warps the latter, but

[3] For analyses of relations of production fettering the development of the productive forces, see Robert Brenner ([1976] 1985) on western feudalism; Chris Wickham (1985) and Neil Davidson (2004) on the eastern tributary mode of production; and Perry Anderson (1974) and Wickham (1984) on the slave mode of production (classical antiquity).

[4] "In so far as the labor process is solely a process between man and nature, its simple elements remain common to all social forms of its development. But each particular historical form of this process further develops the material foundations and social forms" (Marx [1894] 1981: 1023).

the underlying processes and motivations remain distinct, even if they are entwined in ways we need to unpack.

Within capitalism the labor process contains a valorization process, but these are in a contradictory relation. This relation is expressed in the dual role of managers (Marx [1867] 1990): on the one hand, they play a productive role in coordination and planning; on the other hand, they play an unproductive role in ensuring discipline within the workforce, so that workers follow the rules and produce sufficient levels of output. These roles often conflict. I develop Marx's insights here with the concept of satisficing (March and Simon [1958] 1993; Simon 1955), where managers with moderate aspiration levels respond to conflicting pressures by opting for discipline (e.g. restricting workers to routine manual labor to ensure sufficient output) over coordination (e.g. cross training and empowering workers so they can contribute abstract cognitive labor with a goal of increasing organizational flexibility and continuous improvement).

Marx's theory of the labor process was part of a broader stage-model of capitalist growth, in which stages are based in a dominant model of production. Capitalism develops through stages, and across those stages we see evolution in the nature of the tension between managers' coordinative (productive) and disciplinary (unproductive) roles. Each stage has a distinct set of structural and ideological dynamics that condition the precise pressures felt by capitalist managers, the orientations of workers, and the strategies pursued by each within the labor process.

To flesh out a mid-range theory of Marx's growth stages, I draw from organization theory. Institutional logics are socially constructed beliefs, goals, and practices based in the material practice and symbolic discourse of influential actors (Friedland and Alford 1991; Scott 2008). Some logics are "cornerstone institutions" of a given social order (Thornton et al. 2012: 53). The logics of the capitalist market, capitalist firm, bureaucratic state, and political democracy are cornerstone logics of the core of the capitalist world system, emanating out into the semi-periphery and periphery. These basic logics get elaborated, internally differentiated, and hybridized within growth stages and organizational fields.

I theorize growth stages as accumulation regimes, in a broadly regulation theoretic sense (Aglietta [1976] 2000; Boyer 1988; Boyer and Saillard 2002b, 2002a; Lipietz 1987, 1988).[5] In my analysis (Vidal 2012, 2013, 2015,

[5] In other work, I have developed a regulation theoretic approach without the functionalist concept of a (complementary) mode of regulation For an extended criticism of this concept, as reproducing the

2019a), growth stages are based in an institutional settlement across three domains: (i) the dominant model of production, understood in broad terms to include employment relations, interfirm relations, and the articulation between sectors; (ii) the form of competition; (iii) the form of state. Growth regimes are geographically nested at the regional, national, and international scales, each regime having a particular location within the capitalist world-system.

Each of the broad institutional domains within regions and states (i–iii) is based in a dominant institutional logic. The cornerstone logics of the capitalist world system get elaborated in distinct ways within growth stages. In addition, various organizational fields emerge and typically become settled within each growth stage. Fields consist of shared meaning systems based around a focal population of organizations (typically an economic sector) along with other organizations that influence or interact with the core population (suppliers, regulators, funding sources, etc.). The influence of cornerstone logics within a growth stage is broad, spanning multiple organizational fields, although some fields will develop *sui generis* dominant logics. Both the cornerstone logics of the growth regime and its various organizational fields include institutional contradictions, as discussed in more detail below.

Schematically, the fordist growth regime (stage) in the US (roughly from the 1930s through the 1970s), was based in (i) a production model consisting of vertically integrated, forecast-driven mass production, with giant manufacturing firms being dominant players in the overall economy and controlling supply chains, with the wholesale, retail, and finance sectors playing a subordinate, intermediary role (Boyer 2000; Jessop 2012). Based on this dominant role in the economy and its prominence as a growing and thriving employment sector, manufacturing was the leading sector informing labor management and employment relations, with the logics of fordist production and taylorist labor management exerting influence across organizational fields, and the Big Three auto producers setting employment standards. These standards endorsed an internalization model of employment that partially decommodified labor: commitment to providing good jobs, internal labor markets, administratively determined wages, and acceptance of unions. The (ii) form of competition was oligopolistic,

problematic distinction between the economic and the institutional, and an alternative, constructionist approach to accumulation regimes that does not assume institutional coherence or complementarity, see Vidal (2014).

domestically oriented markets. The (iii) form of state was Keynesian. The location in the world-system was that of global hegemon.

The postfordist stage, roughly from the 1980s to the present, is based in (1) a production model consisting of vertically disintegrated, demand-driven, domestic lean producers of mass customized products combined with extensive sourcing of parts from producers in low-wage countries. While lean production and worker empowerment exert influence on labor management across a range of organizational fields, the manufacturing sector has taken on a subordinate role under the rising power of retail and finance capital. Retail now controls supply chains and is the leading employment sector. Walmart popularized an externalization employment model that increases labor commodification: minimal commitment to the workforce; low, market-determined wages; limited opportunities for training and promotion; vehement antiunionism (Vidal 2012). Finance plays an increasingly powerful but parasitic role, with financial logics and actors dominating markets (Fligstein and Goldstein 2010; Lapavitsas 2009), corporations (Fligstein 1990), employment relations (Lazonick and O'Sullivan 2000), and households (Lapavitsas 2009, 2011). The (2) form of competition is highly competitive, internationalized markets. The (3) form of state is neoliberal. The location in the world system is that of declining hegemon under competition from the European Union and China.

On the influence of cornerstone logics across fields, during the fordist era organizational practice and employment relations in retail sales were shaped by the logic of mass production with internalized, decommodified employment relations (see Jacoby 1997). Neotaylorism continues to be influential across occupations, extending even into the professions (Crowley et al. 2010), and across sectors such as construction, food services, and the public sector. As noted above, lean has been influential across a broad range of sectors. Just as retailing organization and employment was shaped by fordist mass production, in the postfordist stage it has been transformed into "lean retailing" pioneered by Walmart (Abernathy et al. 1999; Vidal 2012). Institutional logics can be hybridized within organizational fields, resulting in new logics, such as agile software development, which is based partly in lean principles. But fields may be dominated by distinctive logics that are *sui generis* and not connected to cornerstone logics.

Fields can become settled around dominant logics of best practice for an extended period until they become destabilized by some force, such as an economic crisis or the emergence of a new, competing practice (Fligstein 1990). However, even where a logic has become dominant within a field or subfield, formerly dominant logics may continue to hold some influence in a field: alternative visions, goals, templates, or understandings persist, albeit outside of mainstream practice and discourse. Formerly dominant logics may continue to influence action, either via deliberate, conscious cognition (DiMaggio 1997; Schneiberg 2007) or via more automatic cognition, in the form of a taken-for-granted conceptual schema associated with a formerly dominant logic (DiMaggio 1997; Thornton et al. 2012).

Thus, even in settled fields with dominant logics of best practice, managers experience competing pressures at multiple levels: contradictory pressures inherent to the capitalist labor process; contradictions between management goals in the labor process and pressures on the employment relation due to financialization and intensified competition (Thompson 2003); contradictory institutional logics and competing organizational goals; and contradictory demands from influential organizations in the field (Whitford 2005). All of these competing pressures encourage satisficing and lead organizations to deviate from best practice.

In the following sections I propose that the contradiction between discipline and empowerment has been intensified in the postfordist era under increasing demands for flexibility and innovation. Specifically, strategies to ensure sufficiently profitable labor valorization are increasingly conflicting with and taking priority over adopting the most productive labor process. To the extent that managers are facing more intense contradictions, and (as will be argued below and throughout the book) that best practice is difficult and requires high aspiration levels, deviation from best practice has likely become more common in the postfordist era.

From Craft Production to Fordism

According to Marx ([1867] 1990: 455), a period of *petty craft production* (handicraft production within guilds) during the late middle ages consisted of self-employed, multiskilled workers owning and using all tools necessary to build a complete product. He dated the stage of *manufacture*, "roughly speaking," from the sixteenth to the eighteenth centuries, during which skilled, self-employed labor was replaced with semiskilled, wage-labor working in households or small workshops, using a single tool and responsible for a single operation under a detailed division of labor. This was followed by the period of *large-scale industry*, beginning in the late eighteenth century, under which semiskilled workers in factories used independently powered machines, rather than hand tools, but still under a detailed division of labor.[6]

Marx's analysis was prophetic insofar as he highlighted deskilling as a major tendency, forecasting the coming dominance of scientific management. However, Marx was emphasizing the dominant tendency across particular growth stages and not positing a singular, timeless imperative à la Braverman. Rather, he suggested that there will always remain a need for some skilled workers, that "Modern industry . . . is continually transforming not only the technical basis of production, but also in the functions of the worker and the social combinations of the labor process," and that eventually, as technical progress continues apace, "the partially developed individual, who is merely the bearer of one specialised social function, must be replaced by the totally developed individual" (Marx [1867] 1990: 617–18).

Marx's periodization was extended by Michel Aglietta ([1976] 2000), who analyzed the development of mass production in the US. He divided large-scale manufacture into two stages, extensive and intensive. The *extensive* period unfolded over the nineteenth century as capitalist production spread to new branches of the economy. In this stage, productivity increases occurred through the extension of wage labor and mechanization to new areas, without altering the organization of work to increase efficiency. Large-scale industry developed first in capital goods sectors, most importantly agriculture, armaments, mining, and railroads, and in the non-durable consumer goods sector, primarily food and clothing. The stage of *intensive*, large-scale production, which Aglietta labeled "fordism," began in the twentieth century with the development of mass production of standardized consumer durable goods for a mass market. Fordist production achieved efficiency primarily through transformations in the organization of work.

The origins of fordist mass production are found in standardization, which was pioneered in the arms industry under the initiative and funding of the US government. At the direction of Thomas Jefferson, who had observed visionary but unsuccessful French military experiments with standardization, beginning in the 1790s the US War Department

[6] According to William Lazonick (1990: 36), Marx was correct about the timing of the factory system (large-scale production), but "historical research does not support Marx's claim" that the manufacturing workshop "constituted a significant form of work organization prior to the rise of the factory system"; the main form preceding the factory system was the household-based putting-out system.

funded the Federal Armory at Springfield and private contractors, most notably Simeon North and Eli Whitney, to develop standardized arms. Three decades later, in 1826, the engineer Thomas Blanchard perfected an assembly-line style operation with thirteen single-purpose machines that, together with his custom-made lathe, produced rifle stocks without the need for skilled labor (Hounshell 1984).

Standardized production and mechanization spread slowly over the following decades, touching only a few industries outside of arms such as nails and spikes, cutlery, clocks, steam engines, and machine tools. Over the 1850s and 1860s, the use of semiskilled workers to produce standardized durable goods spread to sewing machines, mechanical reapers, and bicycles. However, these early adopters of standardization developed hybrid systems, including the use of skilled machinists and fitters. And they marketed their products in the top price range. It was not until Henry Ford, in the 1910s, that a commercial company pursued complete standardization as a strategy to produce *low-cost* goods for a *mass* market (Hounshell 1984).

In 1916 the Ford Motor Company produced half a million Model T cars and by 1921 it controlled 55% of the US market. Due to the extremely demanding environment of machine-paced, standardized work, Ford's turnover rate reached 380% by 1913. Following this, Ford famously introduced the five-dollar day in 1914, effectively doubling the wage of his workers.

The term *fordism* came to be used in popular discourse during Henry Ford's lifetime. Fordism, as the mass production of standardized products using semiskilled workers in pursuit of a low-cost strategy, has been widely accepted as a good characterization of the dominant model of production in the US from the 1920s through the 1970s. Taylorist scientific management is often said to be a core element of fordism. In fact, there were many versions of scientific management being developed at the turn of the century, and Ford developed his own form independent from the work of Taylor.

Contrary to the common mythology, Taylor emphasized training and two-way communication (Nyland 1998). However, for simplicity I continue to follow convention in using taylorism and scientific management interchangeably to refer to the model in which: engineers break down work tasks into their simplest components and conduct job analysis to determine and standardize the best way to do a task, while workers focus on executing single, narrow, standardized tasks.

Critics have argued that fordism did not become a universal model of best practice in the west. Indeed, some scholars have questioned whether Ford's system was widely replicated in the US economy after the 1920s, and hence questioned the concept of fordism as such (Clarke 1992; Williams et al. 1992). What is at stake here is not simply semantics, but our understanding of the nature of economic development. The debate over fordism is not simply about whether it accurately describes a historically prominent production model. Rather, it is about whether the stage-theory of economic development is defensible.

The first question, then, is whether fordism functioned as a dominant logic of production within a settled growth regime. Perhaps the most widely known conceptualization of fordism is Michael Piore and Charles Sabel's (1984: 5). They see mass production as the use of special-purpose machines to produce high volumes of standardized goods. In their analysis, in the late nineteenth century rigid mass production technologies and semiskilled work replaced an earlier, craft system of "skilled workers using sophisticated general-purpose machinery to turn out a wide and constantly changing assortment of goods." Mass production using special-purpose machinery persisted in America into the 1980s—they argued—but was unable to respond to changing markets, and its persistence was the source of stagnation. A return to general-purpose machines run by multiskilled, autonomous workers—what they called flexible specialization—would revive growth and prosperity.

This hopeful vision was compelling to many, but it greatly oversimplified the evolutionary process as one of a clean break from fordism to flexible specialization. Based on this notion of fordism as the use of special-purpose machines used to produce a single product (the Model T), Simon Clarke (1992) argued that Ford's system failed, ultimately conceding product diversification under competitive pressure from General Motors (GM). Clarke is correct that Ford's Model-T system failed, but this failure did not signal the demise of fordism. Rather, as I have argued in detail elsewhere (Vidal 2015), the fordist model was refined and generalized by GM.

The Model-T system of largely single-purpose machinery dedicated to making a single product was never going to have a long life. It was simply not feasible to have such a high level of dedicated, extremely expensive capital equipment in an ever-changing market economy. When making annual model changes—and later, variations on the same model—flow production with dedicated machinery was impossible. It was GM that made the refinements in these areas, which generalized the model of high-volume, low-cost production.

The standard distinction between special- and general-purpose machine tools is too basic. It is possible to distinguish three types of machine tool: single-purpose (dedicated to a single operation), special-purpose (presses that can be retooled with new jigs and fixtures) and general-purpose (lathes, mills, etc.). The Model-T system primarily used single-purpose machines supported by a smaller number of special- and general-purpose machines. In its move to annual model changes in 1927, GM shifted the balance toward primarily retoolable special-purpose machines supported by general-purpose machines.

In terms of workflow, the use of retoolable special-purpose and general-purpose machines to produce more varied products made flow production extremely difficult—a problem not fully solved until the development of the Toyota production system. GM thus introduced a decentralized but still vertically integrated structure, in which there was functional differentiation between plants owned by GM but autonomously run by local management: motors and body stampings in Flint, forgings and axles in Detroit, transmissions in Toledo, carburetors in Bay City, and seven assembly plants located in large cities. This development initiated a shift from the flow production system of the Model T to a batch production system. The combination of a wider range of parts required for multiple models and production decentralized across multiple plants led to the development of batch production with large buffer stocks, which ensured continuity of production (Tolliday and Zeitlin 1992).

Some scholars speak of a transition from fordism to sloanism, after GM president and CEO Alfred Sloan (e.g. Boyer 1998; Hounshell 1984). However, I propose that the GM model is best conceived as a refined, generalization of fordism. Similarly, Toyota implemented its first complete just-in-time system in 1958, but was not able to fully debug the *kanban* system for demand-driven, continuous-flow production until 1962, after which it was adopted companywide (Tolliday 1998). These are similar periods of time from the development of an initial system that works in a single factory to its generalization into a transferable model. The fordist period of consolidation was slightly longer (and occurred across two firms operating in an oligopoly), but this must be considered against the background of its truly revolutionary origin as the first system of mass production in 1913.

In sum, Ford's Model T system is best conceived as a transitional model on the way to fully fledged classical fordism. The latter combines mass production of standardized products, using semiskilled workers, with two refinements made by GM: retoolable special-purpose machines and batch production. This model was codified into a set of core principles and practices that became a deeply institutionalized logic guiding manufacturing practice across the Organisation for Economic Co-operation and Development (OECD). It was first widely emulated in the United States and "was constructed after 1945 as a universal model for the Western world" (Djelic 1998: 2).

Taylorism and the Suppression of the Contradiction between Discipline and Empowerment

At the turn of the twentieth century, empowering labor was not even a consideration of managers. Scientific management was ascendant with taylorism emerging as the first coherent, fully articulated theory of labor management. The institutional logic of taylorism, which presented labor specialization focused on simplified tasks as the one best way to maximize efficiency, was not just the dominant logic of labor management; it was the *only* logic of labor management. As noted above, and discussed in more detail in Chapter 4, progressive taylorists and other reformers who advocated worker participation saw it as a means to stop management abuses and increase commitment, not as a way to directly increase efficiency (concepts such as organizational flexibility and learning were decades from being articulated). When fordism emerged as an influential production model in the 1910s, it reinforced the scientific management model, focusing managerial concerns with productive efficiency on economies of scale, mechanization, task simplification, and process standardization. These became the efficiency basis of the fordist era, where the overriding focus was on capacity utilization and task specialization in service of cost reduction.

To be sure, before the scientific management movement took off, American workers had engaged in large-scale, coordinated actions aimed at challenging managerial authority and wage cuts, and pressing for the eight-hour day, beginning with the first mass strike in 1877 (Brecher 1997). These struggles often occurred against the wishes of the leaders of the union bureaucracies, who were mostly committed to accommodation with employers and limiting union action to collective bargaining. The late nineteenth-century craft unions attempted to maintain their functional autonomy and impose their work rules on management, including mandatory fixed apprenticeships, standard wage classifications, and prohibitions on workers running more than one machine (Montgomery 1979). Following the rise of the scientific management movement, another workers' control movement emerged in the first decades of the twentieth century, aimed, with little success, at imposing work rules on management. These battles over control were driven by concerns with wages and dignity at work, not with efficiency.

There were a small number of noteworthy experiments during the 1920s in labor-management cooperation, focusing on enlisting unions in the development of taylorist work standards and methods. But as with the progressive taylorists and the Human Relations school, worker participation was seen by management as a way to make work less alienating and improve morale, not as a means to improve efficiency and flexibility. Such labor movements notwithstanding, and with the exception of a very few experiments in joint management, mainly where employers were facing a crisis and too weak to resist, American management during the fordist period never seriously considered empowering workers and did not face any technological pressures to do so.

Against the common caricature of taylorism as inherently anti-worker and anti-union, following Taylor's death in 1915, the Taylor Society began advocating alongside unions for worker participation in production decisions and, indeed, forged an alliance with the American Federation of Labor (AFL) (Jacoby 1983; Nyland 1998). Following an intense backlash against scientific management by unions and progressive reformers, including the damning 1915 Hoxie Report to the Commission on Industrial Relations, key disciples of Taylor, including Morris Cooke, Mary Van Kleeck, and Ordway Tead, sought rapprochement with organized labor.

These progressive taylorists argued for joint standard setting and union involvement in production decisions. It is important to note that such worker participation was seen as a way to increase worker commitment to scientific management and stop management abuses of the system, leading to mutual gains for workers and managers. It was not seen as a means to directly increase efficiency or organizational learning, in the way that employee involvement came to be seen decades later by advocates of the sociotechnical systems approach in the UK and the quality control movement in Japan.

The rapprochement between the Taylor Society and organized labor happened in many fora: "The Taylor Society *Bulletin* regularly carried articles on AFL experiments in union-management cooperation, and the AFLs

Federationist published articles by well-known Taylorists" (Jacoby 1983: 24). Cooke, who advocated collective bargaining, the eight-hour day, minimum wages, and health and safety standards, become friends with Samuel Gompers, founder of the AFL. While the latter never advocated time studies and production standards, it worked with the Taylor Society in support of union involvement in production decisions and it even passed a resolution in 1919 supporting the application of science to industry. In 1929, the Taylor Society postponed its annual meeting in support of striking textile workers.

The liberal taylorist vision of mutual gains was not unproblematic, tending to emphasize the need for the independent, professional technicians and "responsible leadership" of unions. But it did increasingly acknowledge the problems of scientific management in practice, including negative effects on worker health and a tendency to concentrate power in the hands of managers. There were other management theorists advocating more conservative, authoritarian versions of job analysis and time study, including Henry Ford. Despite the received caricature of taylorism, Taylor wrote that managers should encourage workers to give their ideas and that managers should seriously and systematically consider these ideas (Crowley et al. 2010), while his key disciples were more progressive, advocating and working with unions to expand worker involvement in production decisions, including standard setting, layout, materials, and personnel issues (Nyland 1998).

Critically, however, in these experiments management never considered any alternative to simplified, standardized work. And it is important to note the limited reach of these efforts. Jacoby counted only five experiments during the 1920s, four in textiles and one in the railroads (nearly all of which the Taylor Society was involved in). They experienced strong opposition from union rank-and-file and most of these experiments collapsed, along with the broader labor movements for workers' control, in the face of the Great Depression, the institutionalization of collective bargaining under the National Labor Relations Act of 1935, and the consolidation of managerial authority by corporate America (with the support of the state).

As the economy ramped up production for the Second World War, the Congress of Industrial Organizations (CIO) joined with the Taylor Society to revive demands for union participation in production decisions (Nyland 1998). However, GM rejected joint management and its anemic system of union-management cooperation—with unions contributing to productivity improvements in exchange for wages being indexed to productivity, but with managerial prerogative over production decisions—became institutionalized.

Despite these noteworthy attempts at increasing worker and union participation in production decisions, the commitment of American management and the engineering profession to mechanization and an authoritarian form of scientific management was remarkable in its near unanimity (Braverman 1974; Noble 1986). This near universal agreement among American management on economies of scale as the exclusive basis of efficiency and authoritarian scientific management as the one best way to utilize shopfloor labor suggests that they constituted a dominant institutional logic of labor management. Culture, in the form of the dominant institutional logic embedded in practice and discourse, and technology, in the form of sufficient productivity growth under this practice, thus reinforced each other in making authoritarian scientific management the only game in town. In this respect, the contradiction between discipline and empowerment was effectively dormant.

Some marxists and fellow travelers have argued that the division of labor with detail workers responsible only for a single task, within a rigid authority hierarchy where managers monopolize conception and planning, was technically unnecessary (Braverman 1974; Marglin 1974; Montgomery 1979). Marglin (1974: 62) famously argued that capitalist management does not play any productive role. Authority hierarchies are the result of capitalists inserting themselves into the labor process to extract income, "at the expense of workers," without increasing the efficiency of production. Both Marglin and Braverman maintained that the Babbage principle—breaking tasks into their basic elements so that the simplest tasks can be performed by unskilled workers—is about profit, not efficiency as such.

It is noteworthy that both Marglin and Braverman agreed that task simplification does increase efficiency. But they contended that workers could do the efficiency analysis themselves and then rotate among the various tasks, without the need for a managerial hierarchy. It is only capitalists that would have each individual task carried out by a detail worker, who only had to learn a single, simple operation, increasing profits by only having to pay semiskilled or unskilled workers.

I sympathize with the intuition that workers can self-organize and hence authority hierarchies are unnecessary from an efficiency perspective. If, however, large-scale production and mass production were necessary stages in the development of the forces of production—necessary for providing the productive capacity to increase living standards for national populations of tens or hundreds of millions of people—then a highly detailed division of labor was necessary. Marx agreed, arguing not only that the financial capital and authority of the capitalist were necessary for cooperation in commodity production, but that the use of detail workers was efficiency increasing (Marx [1867] 1990: Chs 13–14; for an extended discussion see Vidal 2020).[7]

The dramatic growth of productivity over the fordist era was driven by economies of scale based on simplified tasks and a detail division of labor, along with automation. When product volumes are in the thousands, there is a productivity advantage to a detailed division of labor. This productivity—in combination with a class compromise rooted in collective bargaining and indexing wages to productivity—was responsible for radical expansion of the American middle class over the twentieth century. It surely could have been achieved in ways that were less damaging to the health of workers, and just as surely with less authoritarian and more cooperative forms of labor-management. But it could not have been achieved without task simplification, a detail division of labor and managerial hierarchy.

In response to Marglin, David Landes (1986) countered, correctly in my view, that the strategy of increasing profit by decreasing prices via the use of semiskilled labor was the motive behind centralization of production and economies of scale in the first place. The typical craft worker simply did not have these goals in mind, and where he did, he became a protocapitalist by subcontracting work to others. In short, the profit motive, a peculiarly capitalist logic, was necessary for transforming craft production into large-scale production to realize economies of scale.

Likewise, to drive increasing productivity under fordist mass production, the continued division of labor and simplification of tasks was necessary. Even the historian David Montgomery (1979: 2, 106), who decried the "single-minded cult of productivity and expertise" was forced to agree that "the progress of scientific management had ruled out the possibility of" workers "restoring control in its traditional form (the journeyman apprentice, pledged to union rules, making the product his way)." To be sure, the capitalist pursuit of profit has generated injurious work intensification, arbitrary and often ruthless management that are not only wholly

[7] "Through the co-operation of numerous wage-labourers, the command of capital develops into a requirement for carrying on the labour-process itself, into a real condition of production. That a capitalist should command on the field of production, is now as indispensable as that a general should command on the field of battle" (Marx [1867] 1990: 448).

unnecessary for efficiency growth but also introduce their own forms of waste and inefficiency. But economies of scale, and hence a detail division of labor, were necessary. And to the extent that the primary basis of efficiency is scale economies, having multiskilled workers able to rotate among tasks would mainly add costs, and little by way of efficiency.

In sum, in pursuit of profit, capitalists and their managers drove the increasing division of labor, generating a bitter class struggle over the control of production knowledge. Despite contestation from workers, managers and engineers were virtually united in their agreement with Taylor that the detail division of labor based on simplified tasks was the one best way to organize production. This agreement has a strong technical basis insofar as mass production was a necessary stage in the development of American capitalism, given the state of technical knowledge at the time, and task simplification and a detail division of labor were technological requirements for mass production.

Postfordism, Lean Production, and the Activation of the Contradiction between Discipline and Empowerment

In the late 1960s and early 1970s, fordist production went into crisis. Across the OECD on a range of indices, "the year 1973 marked the watershed between the golden age years of rapid growth and the stagnation which followed" (Glyn et al. 2007: 72). Within the US, hourly labor productivity, profits, and output began to decline in the late 1960s. The macroeconomic factors driving the profit-rate crisis included overproduction due to intensified international competition (Brenner [1998] 2006), a profit squeeze due to a powerful labor movement able to claim a rising share of GDP (Wolff 2003), and declining surplus-value production due to a rising ratio of fixed capital to wages (Shaikh 1987). At the organizational level, there were two main factors behind the crisis of fordist production.

First, the vertically integrated, forecast-driven, batch production orientation of fordism made it rigid and unresponsive. Under fordist production, firms held large inventories and depended on full-capacity utilization, which proved a competitive disadvantage in the face of a rapidly changing economy, including emerging organizational forms that were more flexible, alongside the fragmentation of demand.

Second, there was growing resistance to semiskilled work under fordist mass production. While strikes and resistance had waned during the depression decade of the 1930s, with the ramping up of production and labor shortages during the Second World War, workers again began to assert their dissatisfaction in organized ways. In exchange for a no-strike pledge, the War Labor Board instituted maintenance-of-membership provisions, which combined with war production to boost membership levels (Brecher 1997). By 1942, unsanctioned wildcat strikes began to increase and in 1946 nearly three million workers were involved in strikes. In all but seven of the thirty-three years from 1947 and 1979, more than one million workers went on strike per year. Following President Ronald Reagan's firing of the striking air traffic controllers in 1981—and after years of union decline—strikes dropped precipitously and have never reached anywhere near the level of the preceding three decades.

The 1970s and 1980s were a transition period from the fordist era, which may be stylistically bounded from 1927 (when GM refined and generalized the fordist model) to the 1973 watershed. In the US, there was widespread experimentation. Job enlargement – the horizontal augmentation of tasks – which was developed in the 1940s at IBM and other American corporations, was only widely adopted beginning in the 1970s. Job enrichment – restructuring work to make it more challenging – developed at IBM, AT&T and others in the late 1960s, saw wider diffusion in the 1970s (Guillèn 1994). But these practices were exclusively focused on job redesign to improve worker motivation.

The roots of more fundamental changes that ultimately transformed the production model, focusing on work system redesign with primary goals of harnessing the knowledge and abstract cognitive capabilities of workers, developed outside the USA in the 1950s: experiments with autonomous teams in British coal mining, which gave rise to sociotechnical systems theory (Trist 1981), and the quality control movement in Japan (Deming 1982; Juran and Gryna [1970] 1993), which produced the concepts of Total Quality Management, statistical process control, and quality circles (as part of a broader rethinking of the production model by Toyota engineers). All of these sources fed into the movements for the humanization of work and Quality of Working Life that emerged in the US in the late 1970s and 1980s, including an emphasis on quality circles and teamwork (Parker 1985). Teamwork came to be widely championed in American management discourse and the practice of leading companies (Fantasia et al. 1988).

Braverman and Aglietta correctly saw job enrichment and enlargement programs as largely superficial forms of employee involvement driven by problems with labor control, in particular labor unrest, absenteeism, and sabotage under increasing work intensification. But

Andre Gorz (1968, 1976) and Serge Mallet (1975), were also correct to perceive a more fundamental shift toward worker empowerment as a substantive development driven by technical change. Automation and ever-increasing technical change were rendering obsolete narrow specializations. Technical complexity was increasing, thus raising the demand for highly skilled, technical workers. Gorz and Mallet both saw workers' control of production via self-directed teams of multiskilled workers as the technological frontier, but thought the need of capitalists to maintain control would result in the continuation of a detailed division of labor and managerial hierarchy.

During the late 1970s and early 1980s, when there was much buzz about self-directed work teams, the Toyota Production System—which prioritizes standardization over autonomy—was introduced to the American manufacturing community. Japanese producers were dominating American producers on cost and quality, and popular books and articles on the Toyota production system were published, both by leading Japanese engineers in English (Monden 1983; Ohno 1988; Shingo 1988; Sugimori et al. 1977) and by American academic-consultants (Krafcik 1988; Schonberger 1982; Womack et al. 1990).

By 1990 Japan was the second largest foreign direct investor in the US, behind only the UK (Milkman 1991: 77). As of 1987, there were 185 Japanese-owned factories in California alone. Surprisingly, many of these plants were not doing just-in-time or quality circles. Ruth Milkman suggested perhaps this was because they were operating a branch-plant strategy, which does low-skill assembly on traditional fordist lines, with just-in-time and empowerment saved for more complex work in home factories. However, her discussion suggested the issue was managerial satisficing. Where managers tried to set up quality circles, they stopped because "the workers didn't really understand the techniques," due to low education levels and lack of technical knowledge. Milkman noted, correctly, that such problems could be overcome with training, but that there was "little effort" to do so. I theorize more fully the satisficing explanation in Chapter 3 and demonstrate it empirically throughout the other chapters.

In their exhaustive review of American industrial experimentation with various models of flexible production in the 1980s, Eileen Appelbaum and Rosemary Batt (1994: 7) concluded that although change was piecemeal and did not add up to a coherent alternative to fordism, two distinct models of high performance could be discerned: lean production and team production. The latter combined self-directed teams, based on "the principles of Swedish sociotechnical systems with those of quality engineering," although in practice teams were typically often semi-autonomous, with supervisor-coaches, rather than truly self-managing, as at the Volvo Uddevalla plant.

This contrast of lean and team, however, was exaggerated. Appelbaum and Batt (1994: 125–6, 134) noted the team system incorporates just-in-time, total quality maintenance, and statistical process control, all of which are lean practices. The main difference is that the team system is "decentralized" while the lean system is "top-management-driven." I read their evidence to show not two distinct systems but two variants of an emerging single system: both are lean, but one is a low-involvement variant and the other a high-involvement variant.

By the 2000s lean had become synonymous with modern manufacturing best practice the world over. In America, early adopters included the Big Three auto companies, but lean has subsequently been adopted—in whole or in part—by a diverse range of high-profile companies including Boeing, Lockheed Martin, General Electric; John Deere, Caterpillar, and Harley-Davidson; Nike and New Balance; IBM, Dell, HP, and Intel. Lean has diffused through the supply chains of these prime contractors and their competitors by coercive means—get lean or lose the business. Lean has been endorsed by major business and occupational associations throughout the sector including the National Association of Manufacturers, Society of Manufacturing Engineers, National Association for Job Shops and Small Manufacturers, Institute of Industrial Engineers, and Association for Manufacturing Excellence.

An American manufacturer would be hard pressed to find a manufacturing consultant that did not have lean as its core strategy. McKinsey & Company uses lean as its core operations management model for both manufacturing and services. According to an article in the *McKinsey Quarterly* written by two McKinsey principals, "Lean is one of the biggest management ideas of the past 50 years" (Duncan and Ritter 2014). The McKinsey webpage on "Lean Management" states: "McKinsey believes that lean is much more than a 'toolkit' or a methodology for removing waste. We completely transform how companies operate, focusing in particular on creating a culture of continuous improvement and a new leadership approach."[8]

[8] https://www.mckinsey.com/business-functions/operations/how-we-help-clients/service-operations/lean-management. Last visited on October 7, 2020.

Table 1.1 Models of production: Fordism versus lean

Fordism	Lean
Continuities in the production model	
Mass production	Mass production
Process standardization	Process standardization
Mix of special- & general-purpose machinery	Mix of special- & general-purpose machinery
Changes in the production model	
Forecast-driven, batch production	Demand-driven, flow production
Economies of scale	Economies of scale, flexibility, & continuous improvement
Individual work on fmented tasks	Teamwork & cross training on fragmented, enlarged, or enriched tasks
	Participation in problem solving & decision making
Changes in the model of the firm	
Vertical integration	Vertical disintegration
Oligopolistic competition	Cutthroat competition

Likewise, lean is the primary operations management program offered by the Manufacturing Extension Partnership (MEP), a national network of public-private partnerships dedicated to helping small and mid-sized manufacturers.[9] The MEP system is partially funded by the National Institute of Standards and Technology, with centers in all fifty states.

We can now specify the production models in detail (Table 1.1). Against the paradigm break argument, it is important to begin with continuities. Both fordism and lean emphasize process standardization, use a mix of special- and general-purpose machines, and are forms of mass production. Given that lean emphasizes smaller production runs and demand-driven production, it has been called mass customization rather than mass production (T. Smith 2000). This is surely an accurate characterization, but it is important to recognize continuity, and mass customization is a form of mass production.

Now the differences. The fordist logic of production includes (1) forecast-driven, batch production, (2) economies of scale, and (3) and traditional taylorism. In contrast, lean production includes

[9] https://www.nist.gov/mep/lean-and-process-improvement. Last visited on October 7, 2020.

(1) demand-driven, flow production, (2) economies of flexibility and continuous improvement (with economies of scale), and (3) neotaylorism with worker empowerment, consisting of (3a) teamwork and cross training on fragmented tasks and (3b) employee involvement.

It is important to note that while lean shifts the emphasis toward economies of flexibility and continuous improvement, it does not dispense with economies of scale. Despite much rhetoric to the contrary, lean is still a form of mass production. But instead of emphasizing machine uptime and capacity utilization, the focus should be on producing only what there is demand for, with efficiencies coming from economies of scope and flexibility (e.g. quick changeover and rapid response to deal with shifting demand) along with continuous improvement. Lean is neotaylorist insofar as a primary emphasis is on standardization and, indeed, on finding the one best way to organize production. But it differs because workers are engaged in cross training and teamwork, and because they are expected to contribute their ideas for process improvement and, in some cases, to contribute to decision making about process improvement and work design.

Finally, two additional elements must be added to the core production model. The fordist logic of the firm included (i) vertical integration and (ii) oligopolistic competition. In the prefordist stage of extensive growth and competitive capitalism, firms engaged either in predatory price competition or in cartelization (Fligstein 1990). With the former being ruinous and the latter having been outlawed, the turn to vertical integration was accompanied by mergers and general agreement on oligopolistic competition. Until the late 1960s, the large American market provided space for a small number of giant firms to all attain strong and stable profits. Trade between countries was complementary, with little head-to-head trade in competing product lines. Only after markets became saturated at the end of the 1960s, as part of the crisis of fordism, did large producers begin to enter into direct international competition with each other, pressured by reduced demand and overcapacity (Tolliday and Zeitlin 1992). Vertical disintegration and intensified competition were thus central to the postfordist growth regime from its beginning.

Oligopoly in the core of the national fordist growth regime—in conjunction with low levels of international trade—allowed wages to be taken out of competition and moderated the pressure to intensify labor, allowing the existence of buffers in production (Vidal 2015). The postfordist regime brought wages back into competition and ushered in the return of work intensification.

Overview of the Argument

Chapter 2 presents a review of the literature on lean production covering the key debates. I make an extended argument that, across a range of manufacturing and service sectors—generally, where the repeated production of a good or service entails a sequence of steps—lean with substantive empowerment is the one best way to achieve a combination of high productivity, quality, flexibility, and continuous improvement. Chapter 3 presents a theory of organizational political economy for the analysis of the diffusion and incomplete, contested implementation of best practice. It is political economy because it is based on a classical marxist foundation; it is organizational because it draws from organization theory. I theorize growth stages as accumulation regimes constituted by cornerstone institutional logics and a web of mostly settled organizational fields. I develop a labor process theory focusing on contradictory pressures and conflict over routines. And I articulate a cultural-satisficing theory of agency, in which decision making is shaped by institutional logics (Ocasio 2011; Thornton et al. 2012) and aspiration levels (March and Simon [1958] 1993).

Chapters 4 through 9 are empirical chapters. Chapter 4 describes my case study and methods in detail. Over three years in the field, I interacted with 486 people from fifty-nine organizations over a total of 332 hours. I conducted in-depth interviews with 109 individuals in thirty-one manufacturing firms across Wisconsin, Michigan, and Illinois (totaling 163 hours). I also conducted 169 hours of direct observation on fifty-nine occasions. Chapter 4 presents a field-level analysis of the diffusion and implementation of lean production in American manufacturing. It demonstrates that lean production and worker empowerment are institutionalized as best practice in the American manufacturing field.

Chapter 5 presents a high-level overview of labor management and work organization in twenty-two component suppliers, developing a typology of four approaches to lean. The high-involvement lean approach, which includes adopting lean as a complete package of complementary practices, including substantive empowerment, is the most efficient and flexible regime, being the most likely to institutionalize learning routines for true continuous improvement. It was adopted by eight factories. The three other approaches (which I call lean standardization, autonomous lean, and lean enough) are less efficient and less flexible with limited or no learning capability.

High-involvement lean was adopted by factories spanning a range of structural characteristics, being adopted in establishments ranging from 35 to 500 shopfloor workers, across key production technologies (fabrication, machining, casting, assembly, sewing) and levels in the supply chain (from first-tier, strategic suppliers to lower-tier suppliers of basic parts). Only two patterns regarding structure could be discerned: one regarding product complexity and one regarding union power. On complexity, factories where the product can be produced in a single operation (here: thermoformed plastic containers and injection-molded parts) have less need for a comprehensive package of complementary lean practices regarding workflow and employee involvement.

On union power, of the eight union plants in my sample, four are among the eight high-involvement lean regimes. Unions may push to increase training, employee involvement, and labor-management partnership. Comparative research has demonstrated that the form and strength of employee interest representation, including broader employment relations institutions such as works councils and corporatist vocational training systems, can play a key role in shaping workplace outcomes (Doellgast 2012; Krzywdzinski 2017; Maurice et al. 1986; Turner 1991). Within the US, the main form of variation is in local union orientation. In my study, some unions adopted confrontational stances toward restructuring while others sought to increase worker empowerment. Union demands for training and empowerment may not only force or facilitate more substantive forms of empowerment but also encourage the adoption of a comprehensive package of lean practices to utilize the empowered employees.

Chapters 6 through 8 are a triplet, documenting and analyzing what I call *routine* politics of production. The term politics of production is associated with Michael Burawoy (1982, 1987), but my usage is more general and in some ways opposed to his. For Burawoy, production politics refer to the ideological effects of the workplace. In the fordist factories he studied, he argued, the organization of work generated worker consent to capitalist exploitation by individualizing the workforce and encouraging game playing around output, in a context where internal labor markets concretely coordinate the interests of workers and the organization.

I use the term production politics more broadly to refer to workplace conflict and culture within the workplace. I adopt a broader usage for two reasons. First, Burawoy's conceptualization of production politics and workplace regimes effectively theorizes consent as the inevitable outcome of working within the monopoly capitalist firm, thus missing the most interesting points about contradictory pressures, the problems of managerial strategy, and the forms of worker resistance (Thompson 1983; Vallas 1993).

Second, I find wholly unconvincing Burawoy's (1982: xii, 135) argument that "Whatever consent is necessary for the obscuring and securing of surplus value is generated at the point of production rather than imported into the workplace from outside," a process that occurs entirely "independent of schooling, family life, mass media, the state, and so forth" (for an extended critique of Burawoy, see Vidal 2019b). My findings align with those of Theo Nichols and Peter Armstrong (1976), that workers come to work already having consented to capitalism before entering the workplace, based on their socialization via the families, schools, and mass media that Burawoy discounted as irrelevant.

Chapter 6 begins the argument, which extends across Chapters 6 through 8, that postfordist American supplier factories are characterized by *routine* politics of production, in which the primary focus of managers is making qualitative changes to routines to realize continuous improvement in productivity, flexibility, and learning capability (quality), not with increasing effort levels as such (quantity). My qualitative analysis led me to distinguish types of work intensification (quantitative and qualitative) and impacts of intensification (positive or negative), resulting in a fourfold typology.

Quantitative work intensification refers to increasing the pace of work or reducing downtime. Qualitative work intensification refers to increasing demands for mental focus and concentration at work (e.g. new responsibilities for quality control) or cognitive labor (problem solving and decision making). In terms of impacts, moderate levels of quantitative and qualitative intensification can be experienced by workers as an improvement in their work experience by reducing monotony and boredom, which are central complaints about fordist/taylorist work organization. I thus focus on the subjective experience of work intensification.

Based on in-depth interviews with fifty-two workers across twelve companies, I find thirty-seven workers reporting no work intensification, thirteen reporting positive work intensification (nine on qualitative aspects, three on quantitative, and one on both), and only two reporting negative work intensification (both quantitative). I did hear from some workers who said they found or would find demands for cognitive labor stressful, but these workers were able to avoid being forced to work in intellectually demanding jobs, either by not transferring into particular jobs or by transferring out of them.

Chapter 7 focuses on what I call the workforce contradiction: management attempts empower workers through cross training and responsibilities or opportunities for problem-solving and decision-making authority are often met with resistance or reticence. I present evidence that such resistance and reticence are driven by two concrete manifestations of alienation, concretely rooted in their labor process experience. First, workers have long experience of management refusal to consider their suggestions and, when management does invite suggestions or involve them in problem solving, it often considers but ultimately rejects their suggestions, asserting managerial prerogative. This experience generates skepticism toward managerial aims and initiatives, and becomes institutionalized in local workplace culture.

Second, my findings confirm those of Randy Hodson (2001), that the alienating nature of the capitalist labor process encourages workers to attempt to make work meaningful, realize a purpose, or feel pride in their work. Drawing from local workplace culture, custom, and practice, many workers embrace fordist notions of efficiency and the proper ownership of responsibilities. I document how workers often express concern with the success of the company and see managerial initiatives as harmful to the firm's competitiveness. They reject, resist, or respond with apathy to managerial initiatives that they think are harming efficiency and quality.

Chapter 8 focuses on what I call the management contradiction: managers face conflicting pressures to use workers exclusively or primarily for simple, manual labor, emphasizing standardization and task specialization, versus using them for more complex, abstract cognitive labor as well, emphasizing cross training, problem solving, and decision making. I conceive the underlying issue of ensuring sufficient effort—including the question of whether to engage workers in intellectual labor or not—as the valorization problem. This chapter documents two processes by which the management contradiction operates. First, the contradiction as such is expressed in two competing logics of valorization: substantive empowerment versus traditional taylorism. I theorize this as a top-down process, in which managerial behavior is shaped by institutional logics, with some managers continuing to be influenced by the logic of traditional taylorism.

Second, in a bottom-up process, some managers respond to their local situation by satisficing: settling for good enough by failing to devolve responsibility for—and train workers to provide skills for and facilitate contributions to—problem solving and decision making. The managers I interviewed did not resist empowering workers because it was a threat to their own power. Rather, managers with moderate aspirations responded to the contradictory pressures to discipline or empower labor by emphasizing the former because it is the easier course of action, in large part due to the reticence and resistance generated by alienation and the workforce contradiction.

It is a standard finding from the comparative employment relations literature (Doellgast 2012; Krzywdzinski 2017; Turner 1991; Wever et al. 1996) that empowerment-based strategies are difficult to implement on a sustainable basis in countries such as the US where most workplaces are nonunion and there are no other institutional sources of worker power to hold management to these practices. Consistent with this, my research found that where a local union is focused on increasing worker empowerment rather than resisting managerial restructuring altogether, union power is an important factor that can increase the likelihood, extent, depth, and stability of worker empowerment. But my findings also demonstrate the critical role of low or moderate managerial aspiration levels in limiting the diffusion of best practice, including the substantive empowerment of labor, in the face of the management and workforce contradictions.

Chapter 9 expands from the valorization problem to the broader question of work organization, presenting holistic analysis of workplace regimes. As in Chapter 8, this chapter documents two factors leading some managers to settle for relatively inefficient organizational forms. First, in a schema driven (top-down) process, managers continue to be influenced by fordist logics, such as maximizing machine uptime, resulting in a hybrid logic of practice I call lean-as-toolbox. Second, in an aspiration-driven (bottom-up) process, managers who have achieved satisfactory performance with a lean-as-toolbox approach fail to adopt the lean practices that are most difficult to implement and sustain: true continuous flow production and worker-driven continuous improvement.

The valorization approach and the organizational approach are relatively independent insofar as a manager can make an independent decision on each and then combine them (as demonstrated in Chapter 5). But Chapter 9 illustrates how this dependence is only partial. Specifically, implementing lean-as-system—true continuous flow and regular use of value-stream mapping to drive continuous improvement—is exceptionally difficult without a substantively empowered workforce with formal channels for input into problem solving and decision making.

The general picture that emerges is not one of managers serving as passive conduits of an overriding capitalist drive to maximize labor control, deskill workers, or intensify work, but of managers muddling through while facing competing pressures and acting according to distinct logics. As a result of contradictory pressures and competing logics, and in response to alienated workers, the capitalist management of these firms systematically limited the efficiency, flexibility, and innovative capability of the organization.

Capitalist Management and Routine Inefficiency

In the concluding chapter I reflect on the implications of my analysis for our understanding of labor management, organizations, and markets. Broadly, for the sociology of work and human resource management, my findings suggest that the orientations of both managers and workers are far more variable than existing theory assumes. Institutional theory has demonstrated how people interpret the world through culturally constituted conceptual frameworks, but such insights have not been incorporated into the sociology of work or human resource management theory. In addition to systematically theorizing and empirically documenting such cultural sources of variation in individual orientations, I demonstrate the centrality of contradictory pressures and experiences within the labor process.

Managers face contradictory pressures to empower labor and to ensure discipline, meaning that capitalist management is divided between those who pursue the more dynamically efficient, but also more difficult, strategy of substantive empowerment and those who settle for good enough by focusing on standardization, limited training, and consultative worker participation (or no employee involvement). This leads to contradictory practice (such as management fads of the month, aborted initiatives, disconnection between rhetoric and action) and satisficing. Workforces are often divided into competing factions, based around alternate interpretations of their contradictory experience.

With regard to labor process theory in particular, a central goal of this book is to shift the focus from the control/resistance framework in three ways. First, managers have a broader range of concerns than controlling labor. Managers in postfordist American component manufacturing are more concerned with the qualitative improvement of operational routines than with the quantitative intensification of physical effort. The distinction between the valorization process and the labor process highlights this broader concern: the former is about effort (intensity *and* form: simple, routine manual labor versus complex, abstract cognitive labor) while the latter concerns the overall production process, including routines for co-operation, process control, quality control, and continuous improvement.

Second, workers are not necessarily preoccupied with resisting managerial control or with minimizing their effort. Rather, they are interested in making work meaningful and in helping their organization be successful but are skeptical due to their alienation under capitalism management. They respond to managerial practice in divergent ways depending on individual dispositions and culturally shaped orientations.

Third, I am advocating a return to a focus on the capitalist production of inefficiency, picking up on a largely abandoned research program initiated by David Gordon and Richard Edwards (Edwards 1979; D. M. Gordon 1976; D. Gordon et al. 1982). But these authors presented a rational choice analysis, which I reject on theoretical grounds (see Chapter 3) and empirical grounds (Chapters 6 through 9). I sketch an alternative approach to this problem, focused on managerial satisficing in response to contradictory pressures.

Based on the foregoing, I suggest that the sociologies of work, organizations, and markets need to take inefficiency seriously as a core topic of analysis. If mainstream economics assumes that capitalist firms and markets normally increase efficiency, sociology should question this assumption. The analytical tools assembled into my theory of organizational political economy provide the foundation for a more realistic theory of markets that does not assume they generate efficiency, but instead takes efficiency as an empirical question.

Drawing on organization theory, I develop a model of information processing that incorporates both competing institutional logics and satisficing. This, in turn, gives rise to a theory of permissive competition: markets are constituted by organizations, which produce and permit inefficiency due to internal factors (contradictory pressures, conflict over routines, and managerial satisficing) and external factors (embeddedness and satisficing within the customer-supplier relation).

In the dominant narrative of capitalism and free markets, efficiency is apolitical: technical efficiency is simply the maximization of outputs given inputs; allocative efficiency is simply when production output matches consumer preferences. The theory holds that both forms of efficiency are natural outcomes of private ownership and free markets; any inefficiencies are aberrations caused by misaligned incentives, market imperfections, or market interference.

The traditional critical perspective highlights the cost of technical efficiency for workers who are often its victims. Without denying the importance of this critique, my book aims to ground a critique that goes much further in attacking the legitimacy of capitalism, which rests on the assumption that private, for-profit firms maximize technical efficiency and that markets maximize allocative efficiency while ensuring technical efficiency through competitive discipline. My analysis suggests that inefficiency is increasingly produced by capitalist management and permitted by markets as part of their normal operation. Capitalist managers satisfice in response to contradictory pressures and conflict over routines, settling for good enough and failing to adopt the best practice of substantively empowered workers operating a lean system of continuous flow production with continuous improvement.

The underlying source of efficiency improvements and innovation is not the market or the profit motive but human intellect and creativity. To be sure, rates of growth in productivity and innovation rose by orders of magnitude under the capitalist mode of production, specifically the pursuit of private profit under market competition. But the forces of production did grow in pre-capitalist modes of production, however slowly. The foundation of such growth, and of innovation more broadly, is the natural capacity of humans to ponder, reflect, and plan to reduce toil, improve their situation, and express themselves creatively. Capitalist production relations amplified human innovation by facilitating the concentration of wealth necessary for investment, radically increasing the rate of development of the productive forces (Marx [1867] 1990) and the productive capabilities and structural capacities of society, as extensions of natural human capabilities and capacities (Callinicos 2009; Wright 1978).

My argument is that in the postfordist stage, capitalist relations of production are precluding the full realization of organizational capabilities within the economy. Specifically, I aim to demonstrate that capitalist management systematically obstructs adoption of the most efficient operational practice. If I am correct, then we have an even stronger argument for the need to transcend the limitations of the capitalist system.

2

Lean Management and Employee Involvement

This chapter examines arguments of the lean boosters that its performance effects are based in worker empowerment and those of its critics that it is a system of deskilling whose effects flow mainly from work intensification. I conclude that lean is not inherently one or the other. Lean tools can be highly effective for intensifying work, but the intensification of work is neither specific to lean nor is it what makes lean such an effective production model. Rather, lean has become the undisputed model of production in manufacturing, and is increasingly prominent in other sectors, because it is a system that combines tools for flexible production, process control, and continuous improvement. These basic tools can be implemented with or without work intensification. They are most effective when implemented as a system of complementary practices managed by workers who are substantively empowered to engage in decision making regarding process and product improvement.

Following a discussion of empowerment and intensification, I briefly revisit debates about whether lean is best characterized as neofordist or postfordist. I reject formulations which see postfordism as a radical break from the past. Nonetheless, I suggest that since the institutional growth regime of fordism—oligopolistic competition among vertically integrated firms producing for domestic markets—has crumbled, we are living in a postfordist era. The dominant production model in the postfordist era is lean production. While there are continuities between fordist production and lean—both are forms of mass production that adopt taylorist standardization—lean includes a suite of principles and practices that mark it as a distinct model for a distinct era: demand-driven, just-in-time production based on economies of scope and flexibility.[1]

[1] I define economies of flexibility as a reduction in total production costs resulting from increases in the capacity to adjust production to meet demand. Examples include the capacities to reduce overproduction, machine changeover times, and the costs of redeploying labor, and to increase the scope of production.

Management Divided. Matt Vidal, Oxford University Press. © Matt Vidal (2022).
DOI: 10.1093/oso/9780198795278.003.0002

I then briefly revisit debates over whether, as lean travels from Japan, it is inevitably hybridized with local practices. At issue here is whether the concept of global best practice is tenable. I show that a model of core lean practices from the Toyota Production System had diffused across North America and Western Europe by the end of the 1990s and continues to be the dominant model of production. While hybridization is common, it is either the combination of different human resource management practices with a core package of lean production practices or, more relevant to the argument of this book, a result of satisficing rather than strategic adaptation and innovation.

Finally, I argue that not only is lean the preeminent model of production under postfordism—a dominant institutional logic—but that lean with substantive empowerment constitutes global best practice for a range of manufacturing and service contexts, generally wherever the production of a product or service consists of a sequence of multiple steps. To make my case, I review the performance data on lean and employee involvement.

Lean Management and Workers

The Boosters and the Critics

In their influential book, *The Second Industrial Divide*, Michael Piore and Charles Sabel (1984: 6) theorized a paradigm break in production models. The first industrial divide occurred in the late nineteenth century, when standardized mass production emerged as an alternative to craft production, becoming the main production model in western economies after the First World War. There was a complete break from the old model to the new: from skilled workers producing custom products using general-purpose machinery to unskilled workers mass producing standardized products using special-purpose machinery. The second industrial divide began in the 1980s, based on an emerging system they termed flexible specialization: "a strategy of permanent innovation" combining flexible firm structures, flexible machinery, and multiskilled workers in self-directed teams. The canonical case of flexible specialization was the industrial districts of northern and central Italy, where small craft firms alternately cooperate and compete.

The second paradigm break was said to include a shift from taylorism to post-taylorism. Gary Herrigel and Charles Sabel included the

Toyota Production System and the German model as large-scale versions of flexible specialization (Herrigel and Sabel 1999: 79–80, 89). In both systems, the key is "reuniting conception and execution at various levels: above all in the person of the skilled worker in a batch production process and in close, cooperative subcontracting relations." However, the German model retained "considerable hierarchy and fragmentation" based on "clearly bounded skill identities" and distinctions, while the Toyota model realized a "more thoroughgoing integration of conception and execution." As a result, during the 1990s German manufacturers adopted lean production.

Herrigel and Sabel greatly overestimated the extent to which the Toyota Production System reunites conception and execution. Sabel's analysis was influential on subsequent interpretations of lean production, which saw the latter as a complete renunciation of taylorism based on the full reintegration of conception and execution. Thus, Martin Kenney and Richard Florida (1993: 16, emphasis added) concluded that "The underlying organizational feature is the *self-managing* work team." They exclaimed:

> Japan is at the center of *an epoch-making new model* of technology, work, and production organization . . .. This *revolutionary method of organizing production* integrates the knowledge and intelligence of a far wider spectrum of workers, from R&D (research and development) scientists and engineers who create new technologies and product ideas to shop-floor workers who turn those innovations into products. It . . . results in *a powerful synthesis* of intellectual and physical labor" (1993: 1, emphasis added).

Kenney and Florida did acknowledge that "Life on the Japanese assembly line is stressful, difficult, and at times even unhealthy." However, their emphasis was overwhelmingly on the centrality of problem-solving skills required by the system: "Among *all workers*, narrow skills *must* be accompanied by broad knowledge and an ability to understand and think abstractly and to continually grasp new concepts" (Kenney and Florida 1993: 10, 15, emphasis added).

Similarly, John Paul MacDuffie and Frits K. Pil (1997: 11) asserted that the four principles of mass production (specialized resources, standard products, centralized hierarchy, and separation of conception from execution) are "inverted" by lean. Worker empowerment is "required" because of the highly fragile nature of a lean system. Likewise, Thomas Kochan and collaborators (1997: 306) claimed that "the delegation of decision making authority" is central to lean, which is "incompatible with" an "authoritarian style" of management.

Paradigm-break models were influential precisely because they posited a radical new model that had completely inverted all past organizational principles, resulting in a more progressive, win-win outcome for firms and workers. The mind-numbing, arduous world of taylorist work was a relic of the past, soon to be extinct.

Against this vision of a paradigm break in work organization, as this chapter will demonstrate in detail, Toyota built on and maintained key mass production principles, most notably high-volume, standardized production and, indeed, a rigid authority hierarchy. There is extensive evidence that lean can be implemented as a form of work intensification without substantive worker empowerment. That being said, other lean advocates have correctly argued that the Toyota system does—in principle, at least—include important increases in worker empowerment, subject to the constraints of standardization.

In the bestselling *The Machine that Changed the World* (1990: 225), James Womack and colleagues wrote that "[l]ean production is a superior way for humans to make things. . . . It provides more challenging and fulfilling work for employees at every level, from the factory to the headquarters." They noted cross training and the devolution of quality control responsibilities to shopfloor workers so they could engage in team-based problem solving.

In *The Toyota Way*, Jeffrey Liker (2004) included among his fourteen principles four that relate to "worker empowerment." First, "develop exceptional people and teams," refers to training shopfloor workers in problem-solving techniques and providing them with knowledge of the entire production system so they can drive continuous improvement. Second, "build a culture of stopping to fix problems," recommends that any problem should be immediately diagnosed and fixed. Workers are supposed to immediately stop production if they detect an error and then convene a team to solve the problem.

Third, "standardized tasks are the foundation for continuous improvement and employee empowerment." This is what differentiates lean systems from those with high levels of individual autonomy, such as the Volvo Uddevalla system. Individual autonomy limits the ability to diffuse improvements across the organization to standardize best practice. Under a highly lean system, autonomy will be limited to the "collective autonomy" of contributing to team decision making (Klein 1991). Groups of workers may develop solutions within problem-solving teams and if the new practices are found to be robust improvements, they are adopted throughout the establishment. It is this emphasis on worker-driven continuous improvement *with* standardization that makes lean more effective than models based on individual autonomy, because the former creates a context highly conducive to organizational rather than exclusively individual learning (P. S. Adler and Cole 1993).

Finally, "make decisions slowly by consensus" (Liker 2004). It is important to understand this principle in context and not exaggerate its reach. Toyota maintains an extended managerial hierarchy and its consensus building process (*nemawashi*) largely excludes shopfloor workers: supervisors and middle managers informally discuss their proposals with higher-level managers to obtain feedback and consent before formal meetings take place. While workers can propose ideas to supervisors via quality circles, it is only supervisors or higher managers who can formally submit proposals for refinement and approval (the *ringi* procedure). Decisions are made above the rank-and-file level, at the highest levels for organization-wide proposals and at lower levels for proposals informed by shopfloor knowledge and skills (Marsh 1992; Misumi 1984). However, the system does effectively harness some knowledge and ideas of shopfloor workers via problem-solving activities such as quality circles.

What, then, do the critics say? One of the earliest criticisms was articulated by the union activist and author, Mike Parker (1985). The first lean practice to be implemented in American industry was quality circles, in which teams are trained in problem-solving, statistical, and management skills. Quality circles were first introduced in the late 1970s as part of Quality of Working Life (QWL) programs, which were based on Japanese practice and championed by leaders in corporate America and the labor movement, most notably United Auto Worker vice-president Irving Bluestone, who saw circles as an extension of democracy into the workplace.

For Parker, because labor and management have fundamentally diverging interests, any attempt to build cooperation is an assault on the union. This line follows a venerable union tradition in which any engagement with productivity improvement is seen as contributing to the reduction of jobs and therefore should be resisted on principle. Now, I do not dispute that QWL programs were used by some, perhaps many companies as part of a broader set of union-busting strategies. When they were introduced in the late 1970s and early 1980s, capital was suffering a profitability crisis and was in the middle of dismantling the fordist class compromise via a frontal assault on labor in the form of deunionization, outsourcing, downsizing, and reducing employment security (Vidal 2012, 2013).

But Parker's basic critique is that managerial efforts to increase employee involvement are done to advance managerial goals, namely, improving productivity. That is true as far as it goes, but it does not go very far. Union busting is a reprehensible assault on democracy in the workplace, but it is simply untrue that all management initiatives to increase worker participation are attempts to bust unions. The fact that such initiatives are implemented to increase productivity simply does not, on its face, suggest a compelling reason why unions and workers should resist them.

By the early 1990s, the Toyota Production System was recognized as global best practice by American auto companies. The emphasis is on eliminating buffers and waste, that is, all unnecessary, non-value adding time. In practice, this is often defined to include any "idle time" that workers may have had for brief bouts of rest and recuperation. Parker and Slaughter (1995) dubbed this management-by-stress because it continually stresses the system—and the workers—by the emphasizing waste reduction and continuous flow production.

Others have argued more directly that lean is simply a system of work intensification. Indeed, in automotive assembly, a common goal is to increase the amount of time workers are working to 57 seconds of every minute, up from 40–50 seconds of every minute in traditional American manufacturing (P. Adler 1993; Fucini and Fucini 1990). In her ethnography of a Subaru-Isuzu transplant in Indiana, Laurie Graham (1995: 62) found that after attempting to increase working time to 57 seconds of every minute, there was a substantial rise in workplace injuries. She found that although "the model does attempt to capture workers' knowledge . . . the overriding daily experience was one of demanding, physical labor." Graham concluded that "a key feature of the Japanese model is speedup and work intensification."

Similar findings were reported in a study of CAMI Automotive, a Canadian joint venture between GM and Suzuki, by James Rinehart, Christopher Huxley, and David Robertson (1997: 62, 129). They posed an either/or question: Does lean empower workers "or is it a process whose parameters of participation preclude genuine worker empowerment?" They describe job rotation among narrow and standardized jobs as multitasking rather than multiskilling, arguing that enlarging jobs to include Total Productive Maintenance, quality monitoring, etc. "is more a matter of work intensification . . . than of skill." There were other sources of work intensification too, including a systematic focus on eliminating idle time and non-value added labor, and increasing line speeds in order to stress the system to highlight problems. Workers were encouraged to give input and ideas, but the process was controlled by management, with only the latter making decisions regarding worker suggestions.

Andy Danford's (1999: 34–5, 42) study of lean included a survey of fifteen Japanese transplants in South Wales, UK, mainly in electronics and chemicals, and an in-depth case study of an auto parts factory. In addition to extensive work intensification, he found "no evidence . . . that the organization of workers into teams, in whatever form, acted to enrich the labor process . . . 'empowerment' just did not come into the equation." While I don't question his findings regarding the extent of work intensification, a general lack of empowerment and the fact that *kaizen* (continuous improvement) was management-driven, I do note that his description of a *kaizen* event appears to include genuine opportunities for problem solving and some role in decision making by shopfloor workers, even if both are highly limited:

> Once ideas were "thrown up into the air" and recorded, each group went through a "democratic" voting process to prioritize the most practical suggestions. The groups met in company time, but once suggested improvements were prioritized members often work in their own time to collect and analyze data and to formulate countermeasures to each problem. . . . The end results of this kaizen activity would be presented to senior management and, if approved, implemented and proceduralized.

Despite this description of apparent worker participation in problem solving and decision making, Danford concluded that "teamworking and kaizen" constitute attempts to return "to the days of full managerial prerogative" (1999: 35, 123).

I think Danford's findings leave the question of empowerment open and I find his interpretation to be too broad brush. First, given contradictory pressures, different managerial orientations and competing strategies, it is implausible that all managers everywhere use teams and lean to restore managerial control and disempower workers. Second, I agree with Larry Hirschhorn (1990) that in the age of computer-based machines and information systems, which are prone to errors, substantive empowerment is at the technological frontier. To the extent that such empowerment does encroach on managerial prerogative, it is not terribly surprising that some managers resist or limit it.

More recently, Paul Stewart and collaborators (2009: x–xi, 9) published a book on the British car industry covering decades of research by the Auto Workers' Research Network and including in-depth case study research at GM-Vauxhall and Rover-BMW. They argued that "lean production demands labor subordination" and is "the reason for the deterioration in the employment experience for many millions of workers." The central reason is the lean emphasis on reducing waste, which "invariably means, in large measure, workers' time . . . the space people utilize at work for respite and regeneration . . . . The high cost to labor is an inherent, necessary part of . . . lean production."

Again, I do not question the findings of Stewart and colleagues regarding how workers experience lean in the factories they studied. But, as argued in detail in Chapter 1, I do reject the argument that labor subordination, degradation, and intensification are inherent, necessary elements of lean. In my analysis, the source of intensification and degradation of work in auto assembly is extreme competitive pressures, including extremely low profit margins and exceptionally high costs of downtime.

The pressure to intensify work is most acute in auto assembly, which is subject to the harshest cost competition of any major durable goods sector and—not coincidentally—the only context I have ever heard of the 57-second benchmark being used. Profit margins are razor thin and the costs of assembly line downtime are astronomical. According to a 2006 survey of the auto industry, the average cost of downtime was US$22,000 per minute (Warner Communications 2006). In this context, managers face powerful pressures to prioritize uptime and intensify work; the 57-second benchmark has become an industry norm. There is some support for my interpretation in Stewart et al. (2009: 122), which quotes a union branch secretary at Vauxhall Motors: "I'm sure that in some workplaces, teamwork was something that took off and there were some benefits for workers. But in a car plant, this is nigh on impossible. The pace of work and the relentless push for more with less is mind-blowing."

Work intensification in global auto assembly preceded the global diffusion of lean, rising in the late 1960s following the intensification of global competition and declining profits. In Ruth Milkman's (1997: 12) case study of the GM assembly plant in Linden, New Jersey, the workers did not defend traditional, fordist arrangements, which they experienced as "relentless and dehumanizing." The primary complaints of these workers were that management treated them in a degrading manner and did not follow through on its promises of increased participation under lean. These workers embraced management's rhetoric of participation but this was never delivered, as managers continued to emphasize uninterrupted production in the face of severe pressures for output.

Similarly, in Rick Delbridge's (2003) ethnography of an electronics plant and an auto parts supplier, although the lean regimes were demanding, the primary complaints of workers did not concern quantitative work intensification but rather unfair treatment by management and qualitative intensification: stress due to increased responsibilities within a highly interdependent and fragile system.

Summing up, then, on the one hand, the critics are correct that lean can be used as a tool for intensifying work and that a generation of auto workers experienced job degradation under lean. But they mistakenly see the way lean has been implemented in auto assembly for an outcome inherent to lean as such. On the other hand, the advocates are correct that lean does contain the potential for genuine forms of worker empowerment. But they fail to appreciate the inherently contradictory nature of capitalist labor management and the resulting outcome that, under pressure to get products out the door, movements toward worker empowerment have been consistently limited.

Factors Producing Variation in Lean Regimes

Some scholars have avoided the trap of attempting to characterize lean as a system based on either intensification or empowerment. In Lowell Turner's (1991. 22) comparison of auto assembly plants in Germany and the USA, unions played a decisive role in whether teamwork was adopted in a meaningful way so that workers were involved in decision making. Having been battered by Japanese automakers in the late 1970s and early 1980s, managers in both countries were attempting to introduce Japanese production methods including forms of teamwork. In the USA, despite a broad pattern of "authoritarian shop-floor approaches" and "adversarial management," in a small number of plants the United Auto Workers succeeded in securing a role in managerial decision making, including more flexible teamworking with genuine forms of worker participation in decision making.

In Germany and Scandinavia, where worker representation is institutionalized via corporatist codetermination arrangements alongside powerful movements, there tends to be high levels of training and worker participation in decision making, although even within these countries there is wide variation across firms (Benders and Van Bijsterveld 2000; Benders et al. 2018; Gustavsen 2007; Jürgens 2004).

In a study of GM assembly plants, Jeff Rothstein (2016) found that the incessant drive for productivity improvements led to work intensification and a focus on standardization limited worker discretion on the line. Rather than attributing this work intensification to lean as such, however, Rothstein argued, correctly, that the underlying factor is increased competitive pressure under globalization.

Other scholars have argued that the role of workers in lean will depend on the priorities and orientations of management. Eileen Appelbaum and Rosemary Batt (1994) suggested that some managers may prioritize technically oriented changes over worker empowerment. Thomas Kochan and collaborators (1997: 303) referred to existing organizational "values and traditions" and competing strategic orientations, such as maximizing production of popular models. They suggested further that some firms "have placed cost reduction and minimization ahead of lean production as an objective." Vagelis Dedoussis and Craig Littler (1994) made a similar claim.

These authors are surely correct in focusing on different managerial orientations and priorities. But the suggestion that technical changes are prioritized over worker empowerment, and cost reduction over more thorough adoption of complementary lean practices, implies either an equifinality of approaches (Applebaum and Batt's position) or, more incoherently, that lean and empowerment are is not about cost minimization. There is clearly equifinality in terms of profitable strategies. But there is no equifinality in terms of maximizing efficiency of any kind, let alone achieving world-class dynamic efficiency with high levels of flexibility. According to its designers, and confirmed by the experience of world-class organizations, lean *is* a form of cost minimization that is achieved *through* the empowerment of workers to engage in continuous improvement; any and all forms of training and employee involvement should be investments that pay off in lower overall costs.

In my analysis, prioritizing technical changes or not adopting the full package of complementary lean practices is a form of satisficing: Emphasizing easier methods of reducing costs—technical practices such as improving workflow and reducing batch size, while limiting investments in training and empowerment—rather than pursuing a full-spectrum approach to work design, training, and quality management, which is more effective in reducing overall costs and generating continuous improvement, but much more difficult to implement.

More in line with my analysis, Rick Delbridge (2003) and Tony Elger and Chris Smith (2005) noted that although lean may involve the empowerment of workers, in practice the pressure to maintain tight process control and get products out the door makes it difficult for managers to find time to train workers and devolve responsibility. Further, an emphasis on speed at the expense of quality and failure to open two-way communication channels lead workers to withdraw discretionary effort. Both noted that managerial satisficing is likely behind these outcomes.

My theory to explain variation in which set of lean practices are implemented across firms, including the role of worker empowerment, is presented in Chapter 3. The theory locates the source of variation in distinct managerial orientations, themselves rooted in competing institutional logics, and in managerial satisficing. For the remainder of this chapter, I address key theoretical debates that have emerged in the literature on production models and lean.

Theoretical Debates Over Lean

Neofordism or Postfordism?

Antonio Gramsci ([1929–35] 1999) argued that fordism—as a model of high-wage mass production—was a form of material class compromise between capital and labor in the workplace. Michel Aglietta ([1976] 2000) extended the notion of fordism as an institutional basis for class compromise from the workplace to the macroeconomy. Fordism was not just a production system but a regime of accumulation, or national growth regime, characterized by mass production combined with institutions supporting mass consumption, including a system of collective bargaining which generalized the class compromise of relatively high and growing wages in return for union cooperation in productivity improvements.

Aglietta followed Christian Palloix (1976) in arguing that increasing work intensification under fordism was the source of a wave of strikes, absenteeism, work injuries, and defects during the late 1960s. The response of capital was a turn to neofordism, defined as mass production with flexible automation systems and job enrichment. In Aglietta's ([1976] 2000:128) analysis, "job rotation and job enrichment are simply the ultimate extensions of the principles of Fordism and Taylorism" because they merely allow workers to do more work via multitasking, without any real increase in skills.

For Palloix and Aglietta, then, there was never an alternative between neofordism and postfordism. There was only neofordism, the evolution of fordism into a more flexible model. Following the success of Aglietta's book, the term postfordism was subsequently conceived in two distinct ways. First, regulationist scholars used the term postfordism (e.g. Esser and Hirsch 1994; Jessop 1989, 1992; Lipietz 1992, 1997) or "after fordism" (e.g. Boyer and Durand 1997; Boyer and Saillard 2002; Peck and Tickell 2000) to highlight the period after the crisis of fordism that began in the late 1960s (Glyn et al. 2007; Vidal 2015). The question of whether a progressive model of postfordism would be forged or whether a regressive model would reign was left as an open question, although these scholars tended to highlight regressive tendencies.

A second group of scholars conceived of postfordism as a radical change in society toward a post-taylorist resurgence of industrial democracy and decentralized, flexible organizational forms (e.g. Hall and Jacques 1990; Matthews 1989; Piore and Sabel 1984; Sabel 1982). Sabel (1982: 220) counterposed neofordism, defined as flexible automation within an otherwise fordist model, to postfordism, defined as a post-taylorist model of highly skilled and autonomous workers within decentralized and networked firms. Sabel's vision of postfordism shifted the focus of the fordist framework from its critical emphasis on regressive tendencies to a prescriptive approach celebrating allegedly post-taylorist tendencies. While Sabel (1982: 220) adopted the regulationist terminology of fordism, neofordism and postfordism, Piore and Sabel's *Second Industrial Divide* shed this language, instead discussing mass production versus flexible specialization. Nonetheless, their argument was widely read as a form of postfordist theory (Amin 1994; Smith 1989; Smith and Meiksins 1995).

The neo- versus post-fordism debate has always seemed misguided and fruitless to me. It was not a distinction developed by the originators of the theory (Aglietta [1976] 2000; Palloix 1976). Under the broad influence of Sabel, the conceptual framework was stripped of its critical edge and refashioned into a prescriptive theory. This view of postfordism was always based on a heavy dose of optimistic speculation about some future state seen to be possible according to ostensibly emerging tendencies. Critics of this conceptualization are correct that it presents an untenable notion of a radical break with the past (Smith 1989; Thompson 2003).

With many authors claiming lean to be a new postfordist utopia, it was natural that the critics who paid close attention to the experiences of production workers would conclude that lean is neofordist (e.g. Danford 1999; Delbridge 2003; Dohse et al. 1985). But their focus was on the *neo*taylorist nature of lean: it maintained an emphasis on standardization but included job rotation and the solicitation of ideas from workers. While the distinction between neotaylorism and post-taylorism is sound, the attempt to maintain a distinction between neofordism and postfordism has generated more heat than light. The concept of neofordism helpfully highlights continuity with fordism, but does not acknowledge important discontinuities: demand-driven, just-in-time production based on economies of flexibility. This is more than an extension of fordism.

In my formulation, fordism and lean are not monolithic production models but are institutional logics of best practice, which are widely used as models but not uniformly adopted across the economy or even within a single sector. Postfordism is used here to refer to the period after fordism, as elaborated in Chapter 1.

The central question of this book is precisely to understand and explain variation in the extent to which the logic of best practice is adopted and implemented. Although lean is the dominant model of postfordist production, in practice there are a range of hybrid forms including some that implement work intensification with no empowerment and others that implement individual autonomy.

Diffusion and Hybridization

The Toyota Production System is based on an innovative transformation of the fordist model within the particular set of conditions facing Japan during the 1930s and 1940s. With severe resource constraints and a small market that could not justify huge volumes with dedicated machinery, Toyota developed the just-in-time system, emphasizing low inventories and a shift from an exclusive focus on economies of scale to also emphasizing economies of scope and flexibility (Krafcik 1988; Ohno 1988; Oliver and Wilkinson 1992; Tolliday 1998). Though still a form of mass production based in part on scale economies, the just-in-time system introduced a radical change: demand-driven flow production. In making these changes Toyota incorporated other American ideas beyond those from Ford; Total Quality Management was created by American engineers Joseph M. Juran and W. Edwards Deming, whose ideas were largely ignored in the USA but enthusiastically adopted in Japan, including by Toyota.

When the Toyota Production System began to diffuse to the west, a key question concerned whether it would—and should—be transferred whole-cloth or be hybridized with host-country practices. Strong culturalist accounts suggested that hybridization necessarily dilutes the Japanese model, leading to suboptimal performance (Abo 1994). By contrast, Steven Tolliday and collaborators (1998: 1–2) argued that because of the need for a fit between production models and distinct institutional contexts, "direct transplantation or imitation of productive models is rarely feasible or even desirable.... Hybridization ... is inevitable." Such hybridization is seen as a source of innovation (Boyer et al. 1998; Liker et al. 1999b).

While it is clear that hybridization regularly happens, and that the process of selective adoption and adaptation can lead to new models, as it did in the case of the Toyota Production System, the emphasis on hybridization has overshadowed an important fact: the striking similarity of the *core production practices*—as opposed to peripheral human resource management practices—of leading firms across the industrialized world during the decades before and after the Second World War and again during the most recent two-plus decades. When considering the entire package of organizational practices associated with a particular model, including the full set of human resource management practices, hybridization effectively becomes a foregone conclusion. This makes it rather meaningless unless one holds to an exceptionally crude idea of universal best practice. Of course, adaptation and modification will occur as models travel to different contexts with distinct institutions. The important question is whether such modifications are made to peripheral or core practices.

There is robust evidence that the core production model of the Toyota Production System has been broadly transferred across national institutional contexts, shorn of certain traditional Japanese human resource management practices that are peripheral to that core model, without a negative impact on performance (Liker et al. 1999b; Mishina 1998; Oliver and Wilkinson 1992). Drawing on and reworking Liker and collaborators (1999a), we can distinguish the production system from the broader employment relations system. A *production system* consists of a set of organizational principles, procedures, and applications, including a division of labor, operational models, individual practices, and hard technologies (machines, computers, software). Importantly, some human resource management practices—particularly training and forms of employee involvement—may be central to the operation of the production system and hence part of it. The lean production model that has diffused globally includes principles of and associated practices for just-in-time production (pull production, continuous flow, low inventories), continuous improvement (e.g. value-stream mapping, root cause analysis, setup reduction, standardized work), and employee involvement (teamwork with cross-training for job rotation, problem-solving groups, Total Quality Management).

The *employment relations system*, then, includes human resource management practices that are more peripheral to the production system (practices regarding recruitment, selection, and retention, pay, motivation, and performance appraisal) along with labor-management relations more broadly, including collective bargaining where a union is present. If carefully designed and competently implemented, these practices can positively impact the production system in various ways. But, in an age of mobile capital and rising labor market insecurity (real or perceived), a suite of complementary human resource practices aimed at instilling loyalty and commitment is demonstrably unnecessary to implement a lean system realizing satisfactory performance. Further, as shown in the empirical chapters below, realizing high levels of cognitive labor in problem solving and decision making is incredibly difficult, due to contradictions endemic to the labor process, which peripheral human resource management practices can ameliorate but not eliminate. In any case, the core lean production model has diffused widely, independently of peripheral Japanese employment relation practices such as lifetime employment and seniority-based wage and promotion systems.

For Steven Tolliday (1998: 84), the "inevitable" existence of hybridization undermines the idea of a dominant model of production. In his analysis, hybridization is generally efficiency increasing: "selective and intelligent adaptation in the face of local constraints" and the "creative reworking" of old practices to produce "innovative" new practices. Robert Boyer (1998: 25, 27), a leading advocate of the notion of production models, also sees hybridization in similar, efficiency-increasing terms: models provide templates but local managers must make their local production system "internally coherent and externally relevant" by "adapting strategy and organization to different contexts in time and space." Both Tolliday and Boyer suggest that the need for organizations to establish a fit with their institutional context makes the notion of one best way untenable.

By the end of the 1990s, however, lean production had emerged as a global, dominant model of production, based on a set of concrete practices, and had already diffused across North America and Western Europe (Liker et al. 1999b; Mishina 1998; Oliver and Wilkinson 1992), including Germany (Herrigel and Sabel 1999; Jürgens 2004) and Scandinavia (Sandberg 1995). Two decades later lean continues to be the dominant model of production, having spread from manufacturing to healthcare, banking, insurance, civil service, education, airline services, and restaurants. To be sure, there is no small amount of hybridization in practice. But rather than being driven by strategic adaptation and innovation, it is typically the result of satisficing. Most firms are imitators. Very few are innovators.

One Best Way

It is demonstrably true that organizations can be viable and profitable using a range of production models and human resource configurations. There are many satisfactory ways to make a profit. But whether there are multiple ways to achieve truly world-class performance is another question entirely. It does not seem plausible that there are even a few production model/human resource configurations which can achieve the same levels of performance in terms of dynamic efficiency, that is, achieve comparable outcomes in terms of sustained and increasing levels of productivity, quality and learning over time. To excel at dynamic efficiency requires a delicate balance between discipline and coordination, between standardization and empowerment. In my analysis, only a high-involvement approach to lean achieves this balance at a theoretical level and, as argued below, the empirical evidence supports this.

An early criticism of the notion of one best way to organize production was articulated by Marc Maurice and collaborators (1986) who argued that because national institutions are resilient and the efficiency of a given model of production depends on its fit with the wider institutional context, there cannot be a single best way. Subsequent critics have invoked the same argument (Boyer et al. 1998; Freyssenet et al. 1998). Thus, Boyer (1998: 26) argued that "the superiority of a model exists only in relation to the context in which it operates." Yet we have seen above that the core production model of lean has diffused widely across the globe, being implemented across a range of institutional contexts, independently of wider institutions, including in Germany, which was considered by some leading commentators to be culturally and institutionally incompatible with lean (e.g. Streeck 1996).

It has also been argued that fordism failed in the UK, providing evidence that there is no such thing as a universal best way to organize production (Boyer 1998; Tolliday 1998). Tolliday argued that fordism failed in the UK because it was not suited to the market context there, which was a quasi-luxury market that demanded a wider range of mid-priced cars than fordism was able to produce. As such, Ford struggled during the 1910s and 1920s, only beginning a recovery after it accepted the need for local models and regular design changes after 1932. But this mirrors what happened in the USA: the Model-T system failed because it was based on a single-product strategy. Ford learned the same lesson during the same period in two different countries: it would have to modify its approach to include model changes and hence batch production.

This is not to downplay the problems that Ford had adjusting to a more diversified market with lower volumes through the 1930s and 1940s. But by Tolliday's own explanation this was primarily to do with miscalculations by Ford headquarters in Detroit, which attempted to control design of UK cars and built a megaplant in Dagenham that was too large for the UK market. Although the UK market was smaller, this was still mass production and there were economies of scale to be reaped. Most importantly, the core elements of fordism remained at Ford and were eventually adopted by all of its competitors in the UK: forecast-driven, batch production of standardized products, economies of scale, and process standardization within taylorist division of labor (Gospel 1992; Littler 1982; Vidal 2015).

Finally, in his criticism of one best way, Boyer (1998: 25) suggested that even within a single institutional context, "the firm's environment never stops changing," meaning that managers must continually adjust firm strategy. But this heroic vision of managers strategically adapting to an ever-changing environment is at odds with the organizational sociology literature, which has shown that inertial forces within organizations are powerful (Hannan and Freeman 1984; Levitt and March 1988; Milliken and Lant 1991; Nelson and Winter 1982) and that most firms are imitators (David Strang and W. Macy 2001; DiMaggio and Powell 1983; Fligstein 1985; Haveman 1993; Westphal et al. 1997).

In sum, there may be many ways to profitably organize production, but critics of a single best way provide neither compelling theory nor evidence that distinct models (including human resource configurations) provide comparable performance in terms of dynamic efficiency. Fordism was the dominant model of production from the 1930s through the 1960s, and lean has been the dominant model since the 1990s. During periods of transition, a range of distinct models may be developed, but these converge on a dominant production model, and during periods of institutional settlement most firms are imitators. Hybridization occurs either in distinct employment relations practices varying around a core production model or selective adoption of core practices due to satisficing.

Turning to the organization of production today, in my reading of the evidence—both quantitative and qualitative—the superior performance effects of the core package of technical lean practices is unequivocal. The evidence regarding the performance effects of employee involvement is less consistent; many scholars are convinced that the evidence shows that participation improves organizational performance, but some continue to suggest that the effects are either weak or practically insignificant. I am in the former camp.

Taking employee involvement first, the literature distinguishes between various forms of participation, with the most important being substantive versus consultative. A number of meta-analyses of the research literature have found that although the results are inconsistent across the various types of participation, when considering substantive participation there is a consistent, statistically significant effect on performance (Cotton et al. 1988; Cotton 1993; Levine and Tyson 1990; Miller and Monge 1986). Based on their review of both statistical studies and case studies of leading firms including Hewlett-Packard, NUMMI, and large firms from Japan and Sweden, David Levine and Laura Tyson (1990: 183–4) concluded that "participation is more likely to have a positive long-term effect on productivity when it involves decisions related to shopfloor daily life [and] when it involves substantive decisionmaking rights rather than purely consultative arrangements."

The critics have largely focused on the size of the effect, such as whether a correlation coefficient in a meta-analysis below 0.30 should be interpreted as "small" or "practically insignificant" (Wagner 1994). In my reading, given the multiple factors shaping performance and the problems of measuring participation—many studies collapse different types of participation; the measures are typically subjective—it is remarkable that statistically significant findings are consistently found in meta-analyses at all.

Most importantly, there is the matter of internal fit between elements of a production system. High-involvement practices are most effective when they fit well with other organizational practices, resulting in a comprehensive package of complementary practices (Appelbaum et al. 2000; Cotton 1993; Lawler 1992; Levine and Tyson 1990). Robust empirical evidence on the fit between employee involvement and supportive human resource practices shows that packages of complementary practices have stronger effects than individual practices (Appelbaum et al. 2000; Delery and Doty 1996; Ichniowski et al. 1997; MacDuffie 1995; Pil and MacDuffie 1996).

Beyond the question of fit between employee involvement and human resource practices, lean appears to have developed the most productive configuration based on the internal fit between the devolution of problem-solving responsibility and other organizational practices which will harness that most effectively for continuous improvement.

Leading organizational economists regard the package of lean practices for continuous improvement as constituting a preeminent learning routine—that is, a routine that institutionalizes learning capability within an organization (P. S. Adler et al. 1999; Winter 2000). However, the institutionalization of such learning capability requires adopting the correct configuration of complementary practices. In my analysis, the lean learning-routine package requires the following practices. First, true continuous flow creates a fragile, bufferless system that makes problems easily surface. Second, value-stream mapping must be used proactively and regularly as a basis for continuous improvement. Third, continuous improvement is most effectively driven by substantively empowered workers. Finally, there must be a relentless emphasis on process standardization so that when innovative solutions are found by teams of workers, they are diffused throughout the organization, facilitating organization-wide learning.

I take the foregoing evidence to broadly support the notion that substantive empowerment—participation in problem solving and decision making, with relevant training—generates substantial performance improvements over other forms of participation and non-participatory forms of work organization. Further, substantive participation will contribute to organizational learning most effectively within the context of a highly lean factory regime.

Turning to the empirical evidence on lean, the MIT International Assembly Plant Study, which included responses from seventy plants out of the population of ninety plants in sixteen countries, remains the largest and most comparative study on performance to date. A cluster analysis inductively distinguished three types of factory, which they labeled lean, traditional, and transitional (MacDuffie 1995). The lean plants outperformed the traditional plants in terms of both productivity and quality. The average hour per vehicle was 20.9 for the lean plants, 33.4 for the transitional plants, and 36.6 for the traditional plants, while defects per 100 vehicles was, respectively, 49.5, 73.9, and 94.1. Each of the indices had higher correlations with productivity and quality than any of the individual component variables, providing evidence to support the hypothesis of complementarities (internal fit) among the practices within each package.

Nick Oliver and collaborators (1994) conducted a similar analysis with auto parts suppliers, comparing nine British with nine Japanese factories. They found that the high-performance plants adopted the core technical package of lean practices regarding just-in-time production. A later study by the same team (Lowe et al. 1997) examined seventy-one supplier plants across ten countries, finding thirteen to be high performers on both productivity and quality. The high performers were all leaner than the low performers across all their measures (including inventory levels, delivery frequency, and delivery time).

The Lowe and Oliver team also examined the effects of employee involvement *within* lean, which are the only two quantitative studies I know of that do so. In the 1994 study, they found that the high performers averaged higher worker participation than the low performers across five measures: the number of problem-solving groups, number of meetings per month, percentage of workers participating, suggestions per worker, and suggestions accepted.

Curiously, the 1997 study found more variation in the extent of employee involvement across the high and low performing plants. Of the thirteen high performers, four (all western plants) did not have teams. Based on these findings they concluded that their data "do not support the argument that high manufacturing performance is associated with the devolution of responsibility" (Lowe et al. 1997: 791). In my reading this conclusion is unwarranted given that they did not present data ranking the high performers, which could have been used to show whether those with teams and/or more devolution of quality control were the best performers or not.

High-Involvement Lean: Better than Toyota?

I have argued that efficiency-enhancing hybridization, driven by strategic adaptation of a production model to a new institutional context, is rare. Hybridization often happens, but it is typically an outcome of selective adoption of best practices by satisficing managers. I have also argued that lean with substantive empowerment—what I call high-involvement lean—is the global best practice, at the technological frontier. Yet, the literature indicates teamwork at Toyota is of a more consultative than substantive nature. Specifically, the literature suggests work at Toyota, and in Japan more broadly, is organized to encourage front-line workers to give suggestions for improvement, yet remains extremely hierarchical, with *kaizen* being driven by engineers, supervisors, and sometimes skilled maintenance workers, but with front-line workers largely excluded from decision making (P. S. Adler and Cole 1993; Marsh 1992; Masami 1994). What gives?

I am suggesting that the American model of lean has made an important improvement on the Toyota model via a more substantive orientation toward teamwork and worker participation. As we saw in Chapter 1, there is a long history of experiments in labor-management cooperation and co-management in the USA, dating back to joint labor-management committees during the First World War, co-management experiments in the 1920s in American Federation of Labor shops, and advocacy from the progressive wing of the Taylor Society (Fantasia et al. 1988; Jacoby 1983). Following labor revolts against scientific management—wildcat strikes, absenteeism, sabotage—beginning in the 1970s and through the 1980s there was a resurgence in employee involvement programs and joint labor-management committees, this time with substantial support from business leaders.

While it may have been the case that business support for employee involvement programs was often part and parcel of an attempt to eliminate unions (Fantasia et al. 1988: 470–1, 473), it is an oversimplification to reduce these programs exclusively to attempts to "weaken workers' power" and "prevent workers from expanding the scope of their participation." No doubt this is how some employers used participation programs. But the importance of the widespread rhetoric, and perhaps more limited but still substantive practice of worker participation should not be discounted. Even critics like Fantasia and collaborators conceded that during the 1970s and 1980s, "the language of workers' participation permeate[d] a wider sphere of activity. Participation, then, may not reflect genuine control, but its rhetoric would seem at least to make an ideology of control available to workers."

Even more, I would add, if we accept the evidence that substantive participation improves performance, then managers who did implement participation programs with sincerity, or were forced by unions to adopt joint labor-management committees (which can facilitate substantive participation in online and offline contexts), would have realized that these improved performance. During the 1980s, experiments in self-directed work teams were becoming common (Appelbaum and Batt 1994; Orsburn et al. 1990; Wellins et al. 1991). And it is into this context that lean production was introduced into American manufacturing.

As we have seen, under highly lean systems, self-directed teams are not possible due to the priority of standardization. Workers may be able to engage in some minor forms of individual problem solving and decision making when engaged in Total Productive Maintenance and Total Quality Management at their workstation. But substantive empowerment under lean generally takes the form of problem solving and decision making within teams. This happens online when, after identifying a problem, an ad hoc team is convened to solve the problem on the line or in the cell. It also happens in offline teams, including *kaizen* events (which may extend over several days) focused on standard setting, 5S reorganizations, setup reduction, cell design, etc., and in cross-functional teams (which meet for longer periods) focused on process improvement (e.g. Six Sigma teams), value-stream mapping, production ramp-ups, etc. In many cases, cross-functional teams will generate tasks for *kaizen* events. Finally, substantive participation can happen within labor-management partnerships and joint management committees.

If such design decisions only affect a single operation, then they can be made by an existing production team. If they impact the rest of the plant's operations, then a higher-level team, bringing in workers across production teams, along with engineers, can be to be convened. But the decision still resides with the team, which may include shopfloor workers.

I am thus proposing that, if we take Toyota as a baseline and assume that the dominant form of participation there is consultative, then its performance could be further improved by adopting substantive empowerment in the form of collective autonomy. Or if another firm was able to master the technical core of lean practices while adopting substantive empowerment, that it would outperform Toyota. I present data in Chapters 5 through 9 to support the argument. I do not have systematic performance data to directly test the hypothesis that high-involvement lean outperforms a consultative approach to lean in the Toyota mold, but I believe the data I present will be sufficiently compelling to make the hypothesis plausible and motivate future research.

While high-involvement lean could thus be considered a form of hybridization, I think it's better conceived as a progressive refinement of the production model. In any case, it is not a strategic adaptation in the sense articulated by Boyer or Tolliday, of managers proactively modifying a model to fit a new context. Rather, it is more a case of serendipity, in which there were unintended complementarities between Toyota's consultative approach and the practice of substantive participation within the American political economy.

Conclusion

In this chapter I argued that lean production is a package of practices that can be implemented with or without genuine worker empowerment. It can also be implemented with or without work intensification. My review of the evidence suggests that, in a broad range of manufacturing sectors, the full package of lean practices with substantive empowerment is the one best way to achieve a combination of low costs, high quality and flexibility, and continuous improvement. This high-involvement model of lean is a progressive refinement on the consultative Toyota Production System. The analysis implies that lean with substantive empowerment is the one best way wherever the repeated production of a good or service requires a sequence of steps, including in many service sectors. (This excludes contexts, such as software development and project work, where each output is original, distinctive, or individualized.)

Yet, managers satisfice. In response to the difficulties of genuinely empowering workers to take on managerial responsibilities, to engage in problem solving and decision making, managers often fail to substantively empower their workers. In response to competitive pressures, managers often intensify work, particularly in auto assembly where cost competition is extreme, downtime is exceptionally expensive, and the industry benchmark is to keep workers busy for 55 or 57 seconds of every minute. This emphasis on uptime and physical labor often takes precedence over engaging workers in decision making, both online and offline.

More broadly, hybridization is common, but it is typically not the result of strategic adaptation and innovation. Rather, hybridization is the result of satisficing, as managers settle for good enough. In the next chapter I theorize how the contradictory pressures generated by the capitalist labor-management relation are a primary factor leading managers with low or moderate aspiration levels to satisfice.

PART II
THEORY

3

A Theory of Organizational Political Economy

This chapter develops a theory I call organizational political economy.[1] It is a form of political economy because it builds on a classical marxist foundation; it is organizational because it incorporates key concepts from organization theory. At the macro level, I flesh out a marxist stage theory of socioeconomic development using the concepts of institutional logic and organizational field. At the micro level I develop labor process theory using the concepts of institutional logic, individual satisficing, and organizational routine.

The first section outlines my theory of organizational political economy. The second section reviews the labor process literature on engagements with institutional theory; the critical distinction between the labor process and the valorization process; managerial agency; worker alienation; and the capitalist production of inefficiency. The third section revisits Marx on management and the dialectic between alienation and socialization. The final section elaborates the theory.

Organizational Political Economy: An Outline

Managers must adopt both a labor process strategy and a valorization strategy. The labor process is about the organization of work as such: the division of labor, cooperation, workflow, production control and quality control, etc. The valorization process is about the production and appropriation of surplus labor—output beyond that necessary to cover a worker's wages—within the capitalist employment relation.

[1] In Vidal (2017) I presented an organization theoretic, empirical analysis drawing on some of the data that form the basis of this book, developing a theoretical synthesis of institutional logics theory and the behavioral theory of the firm. In Vidal (2019c) I presented theoretical reformulation of marxist labor process theory, emphasizing the contradictory pressures facing managers and workers. This chapter draws on, integrates, and substantially develops the theories presented in those papers.

Management Divided. Matt Vidal, Oxford University Press. © Matt Vidal (2022).
DOI: 10.1093/oso/9780198795278.003.0003

The valorization question concerns the best way to utilize labor within the overall labor process, including the extent of training and the degree to which workers are used for intellectual or physical labor. Defined as such, the valorization strategy includes aspects of what is normally understood to be human resource management: training and employee involvement. These are central to the operation of the labor process: strategic choices on these dimensions define whether the overall approach is low-skill or high-skill, disempowering or empowering. Managers face contradictory pressures: to substantively empower workers to engage in problem solving and decision making or to limit workers to semiskilled, physical labor to ensure sufficient output (perhaps with some nominal empowerment via asking workers to contribute ideas).

Capitalism develops across stages. Growth stages are based in institutional settlements around cornerstone institutional logics in the domains of production, competition, and the state. The dominant logic of production entails a specific articulation between sectors (manufacturing, finance, and retail) around which a web of organizational fields develops, being more or less influenced by the cornerstone logics specific to each stage. During the fordist period, the cornerstone institutional logic of labor management was fordist-taylorism. In the postfordist period, the cornerstone logics of labor management are lean production and worker empowerment. However, formerly dominant institutional logics of work organization and valorization continue to influence some managers and workers (and may have become taken-for-granted beliefs).

Human beings have limited information-processing capability and variable aspiration levels (March and Simon [1958] 1993). Human cognition is shaped by top-down and bottom-up processes (Ocasio 2011; Thornton et al. 2012). The former is a schema-driven process in which institutional logics shape the focus of attention, goals, and practices of individuals. The latter is a feedback-driven process in which individuals evaluate existing performance for satisfactoriness according to their own aspiration levels.

Within the labor process, the politics of production in postfordist American component supplier factories are what I call *routine politics*, revolving around managerial attempts to change routines and worker defense of existing routines, based on competing visions of efficiency. Selling one's labor is an objective form of alienation—submitting to the authority of another—which may generate subjective feelings of powerlessness due to lack of control over one's labor, and apathy and meaninglessness due to work being directed by another rather than being a self-driven expression of creativity (Marx [1844] 1978, [1867] 1990). Some alienated workers simply disengage. But a desire to creatively express oneself, realize a purpose, or feel pride leads many workers to attempt to mitigate their alienation by embracing their work, becoming committed to doing high-quality, efficient work and the success of their company. Their understandings of efficiency are often fordist, rooted in workplace culture, custom, and practice—which leads to conflict over managerial attempts to implement postfordist routines.

Deviation from widely agreed best practice is possible—and likely—due to the presence of contradictory pressures, competing logics of practice, conflict over routines, and managerial satisficing. Suboptimal practice persists because real-world markets are permissive of widespread inefficiency. There is broad variation in organizational performance, including a majority of organizations in any particular sector being middling performers (Angeriz et al. 2006; Caves and Barton 1990; Frantz 1988; Green and Mayes 1991; Luria 1996). Such variation means that the small number of top performers cannot drive out the large number of mediocre performers (Winter 1964).

Labor Process Theory

Labor Process Theory and Institutional Theory

As far as I am aware, there have been precisely two efforts to systematically engage labor process theory with institutional theory. The more well-known effort is the system-society-dominance theory of Chris Smith and collaborators (Elger and Smith 1994, 2005; C. Smith and Meiksins 1995). This approach engages labor process theory with comparative institutional analysis in the societal effects tradition (à la Maurice et al. 1980; Maurice et al. 1986; Sorge 1991).

The second is an unfortunately little-cited article by Chris Warhurst (1997). He suggested that labor process theory and sociological institutionalism are complementary projects, each of which can help overcome deficiencies of the other. Institutional theory neglects political economy, including accumulation pressures and labor process dynamics. It had also neglected the market as an institution—although this has been partially rectified by institutional logics theory (Friedland and Alford 1991; Lounsbury 2007; Thornton 2004; Thornton et al. 2012). For its part, labor process theory has largely neglected the role of institutions other than the capital-labor relation and the market. And it has been unable to explain the widespread variation in management practice, including variation within the same sector and place.

Yet, as institutional research has demonstrated, firms are embedded in institutional contexts—both formal institutions and cultural meaning systems, including logics of labor management—that vary across time and space. The institutional emphasis on meaning systems and cognition provides theoretical tools for helping to explain such variation. The theory developed in this chapter answers Warhurst's call for synthesis and is kindred with Smith's theory (see C. Smith and Vidal 2021).

The Labor Process and the Valorization Process

For Marx ([1867] 1965: 127), the labor process refers to human cooperation to produce goods or services. In a justly famous analogy, Marx explained that it is a distinctly human labor process that distinguishes humans from animals:

> A spider conducts operations that resemble those of a weaver, and a bee puts to shame many an architect in the construction of her cells. But what distinguishes the worst architect from the best of bees is this, that the architect raises his structure in imagination before he erects it in reality. At the end of every labour-process, we get a result that already existed in the imagination of the labourer at its commencement. He not only effects a change of form in the material on which he works, but he also realises a purpose of his own that gives the law to his modus operandi, and to which he must subordinate his will.

The basis of the labor process is human creativity, purposive action to realize a preconceived idea. And it is this—human ideation, human creativity—that is the basis of the forces of production.

If the labor process is a transhistorical expression of human creativity, the valorization process is a specifically capitalist process of ensuring that sufficient levels of surplus labor are produced by workers and appropriating that surplus.[2]

[2] Valorized labor—i.e. surplus labor transformed into goods and services—must be realized in the market by being sold for profit. I follow Marx ([1867] 1990: 302) in treating this realization of profit as a separate process from "the valorization process, which is entirely confined to the sphere of production."

We can think of these twin processes in terms of questions facing management. The labor process question concerns how to organize the overall production process, including the division of labor, production and inventory control, process control, and quality control. The valorization question concerns the narrower issue of how to best utilize labor within an overall labor process. As argued in Chapter 1, in the postfordist era of flexible organizations and rapid technical change, the valorization question becomes a real dilemma for management: whether to empower workers via multiskilling, problem-solving, and decision-making authority? The broader labor process question regards which set of practices—above and beyond those relating to labor effort—to adopt.

Curiously, with a few noteworthy exceptions (Cohen 1987; Elger 1979; Spencer 2000), Marx's fundamental distinction has not been appreciated by labor process theory. Nearly all existing labor process theory has simply theorized or assumed a *capitalist* labor process, conceived in terms of a problem of control faced by managers regarding the effort of workers (one notable exception is Chris Warhurst's (1998) study of the communal socialist labor process in the Israeli kibbutz).

In short, labor process theory has conflated the valorization process and the labor process. This is unfortunate because distinction is crucial: the problem of securing sufficient labor effort is only part of the problem of management. Managers must also determine issues regarding workflow, batch size, inventory and production control, quality control, and continuous improvement. In fact, as I have shown elsewhere (Vidal 2017) and document in the Chapters 5 and 9, decisions regarding the valorization and labor processes can be made relatively independently from each other; a manager could make a decision on each independently and then combine the two into an overall production regime. However, this independence is only relative, or partial, because certain labor process practices (e.g. true continuous flow production) are difficult without—and greatly facilitated by—specific valorization practices (i.e. substantively empowered labor). As such, a deeper understanding of technical change and a fuller explanation of variation across organizational forms require appreciating this distinction.

Managerial Agency

Labor process research has not systematically investigated the question of how managers decide which practices to adopt, whether for valorization or other organizational practices. The first wave of labor process research theorized managers as omniscient agents of capital, maximizing labor control and hence valorization (Braverman 1974; R. Edwards 1979; Friedman 1977). In response, several key contributions argued that managers face contradictory pressures to both deskill and upskill labor (Cressey and MacInnes 1980; Elger 1979; Littler 1982; Mallet 1975; C. Smith 1987; Storey 1985; Thompson 1983). Further contributions highlighted the role of managerial agency in responding to contradictory pressures—the need to "balance inducements and penalties" to entice effort and ensure compliance, rooted in a "contradictory relationship between dominant and subordinate groups in which elements of antagonism and co-operation are necessarily intertwined" (P. K. Edwards 1986: 70–1). In response to these contradictory pressures, managerial strategy regarding labor is often inconsistent and incoherent (Paul K. Edwards and Scullion 1982; Friedman 1987; Storey 1985).

These fundamental insights regarding contradictory pressures and managerial agency have not been systematically incorporated into what has emerged as the theoretical core common to most labor process theory (Thompson 1990; Thompson and Newsome 2004). Labor process scholars ritually refer to contradictions, but generally the concept has not been used analytically. The few exceptions are scholars who have noted conflicting pressures managers face for standardization versus flexibility (Korczynski 2009; McKay 2006; Taylor and Bain 1999; Vallas 1993) or highlighted tensions workers experience between participating in employee involvement programs under work intensification (Graham 1995; Rinehart et al. 1997; Thompson 2003). These findings have been based on empirical observations and not theorized as rooted in the capital-labor relation as such.

Beyond a handful of important, early interventions (Armstrong 1984; Paul K. Edwards and Scullion 1982; P. K. Edwards 1986; Friedman 1987; Storey 1985), I am not aware of any other labor process contributions that take managerial agency seriously, at least in the sense of trying to explain why managers facing more-or-less identical technical, competitive, institutional contexts adopt different labor management and work organization strategies. To theorize agency I develop a cultural-satisficing model. But first I discuss worker alienation and the capitalist inefficiency thesis, and then return to Marx on management.

Worker Alienation

Most labor process theory has focused on managerial control and the impact of various control regimes on labor. The problem of control for capitalist management stems from the fact that labor power is, in Marx's terms, "variable"—it can be more or less intense and the purchase of labor power does not guarantee a given level of intensity. On the question of worker motivation, this problem has been prominently theorized in crude, economistic terms, in which workers are treated as a homogeneous category, whose interests are imputed based on the alienating nature of the capitalist labor process.

For Marx, alienation has both objective and subjective aspects. Selling one's labor to another is an objective act of alienation in which the worker submits to the authority of capitalist management. Because the product and process of labor are now controlled by another, the worker is subjectively alienated, estranged from her own labor, which is no longer a self-driven expression of creativity and self-actualization (Marx [1844] 1978).

Economistic interpretations begin with the fact of objective alienation and, from this, ascribe to workers an interest in minimizing their effort: "Having been forced to sell their labor power to another, the workers also surrender their interest in the labor process, which has now been 'alienated'" (Braverman 1974: 39). Hence "any exertion beyond the minimum need to avert boredom will not be in the workers' interest" (R. Edwards 1979: 12); workers "have an interest in expending as little effort as possible" (Lazonick 1990: 14).

By contrast, sociological interpretations have emphasized how subjective alienation can generate resistance and proactive attempts to make work less alienating, theorizing worker interests as ideologically conditioned. While not directly engaging the theory of alienation, Michael Burawoy (1982) suggested that workers proactively try to make their work interesting by playing games around output targets. Hugh Willmott (1990) and Randy Hodson (2001) emphasized how workers may respond to subjective alienation by attempting to derive some meaning from their work, to reclaim some degree of control and self-actualization within the alienating capitalist labor process.

I build on the sociological contributions. The drive to express oneself creatively through labor is a fundamental human characteristic that is not extinguished by the alienating nature of the capitalist employment relation. Although individual orientations vary due to personality and cultural-cognitive factors, a desire to creatively express oneself, realize a purpose, or feel pride leads many workers to attempt to mitigate their alienation by embracing their work, becoming committed to doing high-quality, efficient work. Thus, attempts to maintain dignity or establish autonomy may result in commitment as well as a range of forms of resistance or non-compliant behavior—implicit and explicit, individual and collective (Ackroyd and Thompson 1999; Hodson 2001).

Beyond the control-resistance framework, there is another problematic in the broad labor process tradition concerning the relation between technical change, capitalist authority, and efficiency. My research program attempts to move beyond the control optic by returning focus to the capitalist inefficiency thesis.

The Capitalist Production of Inefficiency

A provocative argument from the labor process tradition is that managers design production to ensure labor discipline and the extraction of surplus labor, often at the expense of efficiency (Braverman 1974; R. Edwards 1979; D. M. Gordon 1976; D. Gordon et al. 1982; Noble 1986). While these scholars were correct that capitalist managers often adopt relatively inefficient practices, their formulation of the issue is problematic.

David Gordon (1976) and Richard Edwards (1979: 112) both posed a straightforward choice between valorization *versus* efficiency. In Edwards' formulation, managers consider "transforming labor power into labor" independently of the "possibilities for achieving efficiencies." As I have argued at length elsewhere (Vidal 2020), this distinction is theoretically unsound.

Transforming labor power into labor is identical to labor productivity. It is thus necessarily an efficiency concern. Further, both mainstream economic theory and marxist theory predict that managers will substitute more efficient forms of mechanization and automation for labor; it is implausible that managers and engineers would sacrifice radical productivity improvements of automation in order to keep workers employed (to increase the production of surplus labor).

David Noble (1986) recognized this and flipped the argument: in pursuing automation, engineers and managers were foregoing more efficient practices that utilize skilled labor due to a concern with maintaining control. As I have shown in detail elsewhere (Vidal 2020), however, Noble did not provide any examples of viable practices using skilled labor, which were demonstrably more efficient than automation but rejected in favor of automation. His historical analysis simply did not demonstrate that a preoccupation with labor control overwhelmed the concern of engineers with efficiency. Instead, his examples show the influence of the automation logic within the engineering profession: a deeply held belief that full automation is more efficient than skilled labor.

Now, I do not mean to suggest it is uncommon for decisions inside the firm to prioritize some other goal over efficiency. As Robert Thomas (1994) persuasively demonstrated, decisions on new technologies are often made according to goals defined by powerful groups inside the organization rather than what is most efficient. But the tradeoff here concerned efficiency versus other goals, rather than efficiency versus control. Against Noble's picture of a homogeneous engineering profession, Thomas illustrated how engineers inside firms develop distinct goals concerning their relative statuses, which affect the identification of problems and solutions.

I theorize the managerial production of inefficiency using a satisficing model. But first I revisit Marx to better theorize the structural contradictions inherent to the capitalist labor process.

Rereading Marx on Management

Coordination versus Discipline

A material contradiction exists where a social process consists of two interdependent processes that are potentially in conflict (Callinicos 2009). One of the most fundamental contradictions of human society is between the forces and relations of production. Within the workplace, the contradiction between the forces and relations of production operates via conflicting pressures associated with the labor process and the valorization process. As human *techniques* for producing use-values, labor processes (including intellectual labor) are constituent of the forces of production. As power relations for extracting surplus value from labor, specific to capitalism, valorization processes are a manifestation of the relations of production.

In line with his theory of technical change as a contradictory process, Marx ([1867] 1990: 617–18, emphasis added) envisioned a progressive tendency conflicting with the regressive tendency of deskilling:

> *Large-scale industry, by its very nature, necessitates variation of labor, fluidity of functions, and mobility of the worker in all directions.* But on the other hand, in its capitalist form it reproduces the old division of labor with its ossified particularities. We have seen how this absolute contradiction does away with all repose, all fixity and all security as far as the worker's life-situation is concerned . . . in the ceaseless human sacrifices required from the working class . . .. This is the negative side. But . . . large-scale industry, through its very catastrophes, makes the recognition of variation of labor and hence of the fitness of the worker for the maximum number of different kinds of labor into a question of life and death. *This possibility of varying labor must become a general law of social production, and the existing relations must be adapted to permit its realisation in practice.* That monstrosity, the disposable working population held in reserve, in misery, for the changing requirements of capitalist exploitation, must be replaced by the individual man who is absolutely available for the different kinds of labor required of him; *the partially developed individual, who is merely the bearer of one specialised social function, must be replaced by the totally developed individual, for whom the different social functions are different modes of activity he takes up in turn.*

To be sure, deskilling remains widespread in the twenty-first century. The detail division of labor and standardization continue to generate economies of scale. Marx was theorizing a developmental tendency within large-scale industry—and within the dynamic of technical change—toward the multiskilling of labor, although such a trend would be retarded by capitalist management. Such a development should be understood within the context of Marx's ([1859] 1978: 5) argument that "higher relations of production never appear before the material conditions of their existence have matured in the womb of the old society itself."

The contradictory nature of capitalism is reflected in the dual nature of capitalist management (Marx [1867] 1990: 449). On the one hand, management plays a productive role: "The work of directing, superintending and adjusting becomes one of the functions of capital, from the moment that the labor under capital's control becomes co-operative." On the other hand, management plays an unproductive role: "The control exercised by the capitalist is not only a special function arising from the nature of the social labor process, but it is, at the same time a function of the exploitation of a social labor process, and is consequently conditioned by the unavoidable antagonism between the exploiter and the raw material of his exploitation."

I interpret Marx's distinction between the different roles of management as a manifestation of the contradiction between the forces and relations of production. Managers *coordinate* the division of labor to increase efficiency but they also must *discipline* the workforce to ensure workers follow instructions and exert sufficient levels of effort. While Marx ([1894] 1981: 510) saw the dual functions of management as "inseparably fused," analytically they stem from distinct sources: coordination is about ensuring the efficient organization of the labor process, while the need for worker discipline flows from antagonistic production relations.

On the one hand, managers increase organizational efficiency by coordinating the division and utilization of labor, such as through planning, process design, allocation of labor, and training. On the other hand, managers also must discipline the workforce to ensure labor valorization, for example via direct observation, enforcement of standards, technical control, reducing down time, or increasing workloads. Managers play an unproductive role when enforcing discipline, for instance when engaging in direct observation. While some practices are simultaneously coordinative and disciplinary (such as with time and motion study, which increases efficiency while enforcing discipline via standardization), in general managers experience contradictory pressures regarding which roles to emphasize and which practices to adopt. As I will demonstrate in the empirical chapters of this book, where managers satisfice, a preoccupation with discipline to ensure sufficient (not optimal) levels of output can take priority over concerns with adopting best practice regarding efficiency.

Socialization versus Alienation

Marx vehemently denounced the denial of the needs of workers as humans, in terms of skill development and opportunities for intellectual engagement in work, under the detail division of labor. This, however, this must be seen in the context of his dialectical theory of history as consisting of contradictory forces that develop and mature over distinct stages. In the *Manifesto*, Marx and Friedrich Engels ([1848] 1978: 575–7) wrote eloquently of how the world market brings humanity together, having given:

> immense development to commerce, to navigation, to communication by land. . . . The bourgeoisie has through its exploitation of the world-market given a cosmopolitan character to production and consumption in every country. . . . National one-sidedness and narrow-mindedness become more and more impossible . . . The bourgeoisie, by the rapid improvement of all instruments of

> production, by the immensely facilitated means of communication, draws all, even the most barbarian, nations into civilization. . . . It has created enormous cities . . . and has thus rescued a considerable part of the population from the idiocy of rural life.

Paul Adler (1990, 2007) interprets this and other passages as indicating that alongside shorter-term processes of degradation and immiseration, Marx theorized a longer-term tendency toward a more progressive form of socialization. This notion of socialization (*Vergesellschaftung*) refers to the transformation of people and means of production from individual/private into collective/social. Marx's use of the concept of socialization, what I refer to as productive socialization, is expansive. Building on Adler, I read Marx as theorizing a process of upgrading the capabilities of humans and technology over time based on the progressive accumulation of scientific and technical knowledge.

In the *Grundrisse*, Marx ([1857–8] 1993: 162) discussed how the universality of capitalist production and exchange "produces not only the alienation of the individual from himself and from others, but also the universality and the comprehensiveness of his relations and capacities." In *Capital*, he wrote of how "[w]hen the worker cooperates in a planned way with others, he strips off the fetters of his individuality, and develops the capabilities of his species" (Marx [1867] 1990: 447, 1024). And "it is only socialised labor that is capable of applying the general products of human development, such as mathematics, to the immediate process of production."

Now, Marx often discussed "socialized labor" in the form of the "collective worker," referring to how the basic unit of production in capitalism is not the individual but the collective within an interdependent division of labor. And he did write that "In manufacture, the social productive power of the collective worker, hence of capital, is enriched through the impoverishment of the worker in individual productive power" (Marx [1867] 1990: 483, 617). By manufacture, he referred specifically to the detail division of labor in extreme form, with one worker responsible for a single, simple task. His theory of capitalist dynamism posited a tendency toward the multiskilling of labor: "Modern industry never views or treats the existing form of a production process as the definitive one. Its technical basis is therefore revolutionary . . . . [I]t is continually transforming not only the technical basis of production, but also in the functions of the worker and the social combinations of the labor process."

As technical complexity and interdependence increase under the ever-changing division of labor, productive socialization—both inside and outside the workplace—will generate increasingly sophisticated workers, although this may be limited by contradictory tendencies. In numerous places, Marx ([1867] 1990: 613, 617–18; [1894] 1981: 414–15) wrote of popular education as a fundamental force increasing the technical sophistication and managerial capabilities of workers.

To be sure, Marx clearly argued that workers are "impoverished" due to the loss of individual autonomy and suppression of their creative expression under capitalist management. I agree with Adler (2007), however, that individual autonomy is the wrong yardstick. Workers are—potentially, partially—enriched by working ever more complex technical contexts and gaining skills for collective self-management. In particular, the shift from fordism to teamwork, employee involvement, and lean production is part of the progressive socialization of the forces of production, in which increased interdependency provides the basis for improved flexibility, efficiency, and learning capability.

In sum, Marx theorized a contradictory dynamic between alienation and deskilling, on the one hand, and the productive socialization of labor via increasing its organizational and technical capabilities, on the other. A long-term, progressive trend toward productive socialization is inherent to capitalist development but distorted and retarded by short-term concerns with securing surplus value.

I now turn to develop my theory of organizational political economy. I begin with a brief specification of the management and workforce contradictions, which I argue are inherent to the employment relation. Next, I develop the institutionalist theory of growth stages. Following this, I develop a cultural-satisficing model of agency, a general model applied in my analysis of how managers and workers respond to contradictory pressures. To flesh out the political and cultural context of the organization in terms of labor process dynamics, I develop a theory of routine politics of production. Finally, to close the loop on how widespread satisficing is possible in a competitive market economy, I develop a theory of the permissive institutionalization of competitive fields.

A Theory of Organizational Political Economy

The Management Contradiction

As noted above, the argument that managers face contradictory pressures to both deskill and upskill labor was an important theme in early labor process theory, and some recent work has empirically observed conflicting pressures for standardization versus flexibility. In my analysis, a structural contradiction inherent to the employment relation is that managers face contradictory pressures between increasing efficiency (coordination), including developing and fully harnessing the productivity of labor, versus ensuring sufficient levels of output (discipline). In Chapter 1, I argued that the management contradiction was substantially subdued from the earliest stages of capitalism through the fordist stage. When the goal is to maximize output, using semiskilled workers restricted to a single task is a highly efficient use of labor. In this context, coordination and discipline are achieved via the same practices: direct observation, work simplification, technical control, time and motion study, standardization.

In the era of postfordism, there is a real efficiency advantage to empowering workers, via both multiskilling and employee involvement in problem solving and decision making. Postfordist capitalism has thus initiated an intensification of the contradiction between coordination and discipline, which takes the form of empowerment versus deskilling.

The Workforce Contradiction

A few labor process theorists have alluded to what I call the workforce contradiction, namely, the tension workers experience between managerial attempts to empower them, in necessarily limited ways, and their continued alienation within the capitalist labor process. Andrew Friedman (1977) suggested a contradiction between the independent will of the worker versus her subjugation and alienation within the capitalist labor process. James Rinehart and colleagues (1997) noted a contradiction between workers being asked to give their ideas but withdrawing their participation after seeing these ideas used to speed up their work. Similarly, Randy Hodson (2001) argued that employee involvement programs are contradictory because they have the potential to either increase dignity or intensify abuse and exploitation. Paul Adler (2007: 1324) discussed a contradiction between socialization and valorization, proposing that the productive socialization of labor is variously "stimulated, retarded and distorted" by valorization pressures.

In my interpretation, what all of these authors are circling around is a contradiction workers experience between productive socialization (the upgrading of their productive capabilities) and alienation. Chapters 6 and 7 demonstrate worker resistance to and reticence toward their own partial empowerment, in the form of cross training and increased problem-solving and decision-making opportunities. I argue that this stems from two concrete manifestations of alienation.

First, managers routinely dismiss workers' ideas, either by never considering them in the first place or by asking for input but then rejecting it. Further, workers regularly experience management fads of the month and aborted or failed initiatives. As a result, workers develop a distrust of and skepticism toward management. Second, as discussed above, workers attempt to make work meaningful, realize a purpose, or feel pride in response to their alienation by embracing particular notions of efficiency and the proper ownership of responsibilities, which often conflict with managerial initiatives.

These contradictory experiences of workers—disagreeing with and/or being skeptical of managerial attempts to upskill and empower them—are a primary source of contestation in the postfordist firm. And even if workers are offered some genuine increases in their skills and decision-making authority, they understand that they will be asked to take on managerial responsibilities without any commensurate increase in managerial rights. Indeed, their empowerment will be limited to concerns with process improvement, while traditional management will continue to be the ultimate authority, ready to exercise a veto or remove (partial) worker empowerment at any time (T. Smith 2000). The contradiction between (partial) empowerment and (continued) alienation drives skepticism, reticence, and resistance toward the former.

Institutional Logics and Organizational Fields Within Growth Stages

In another justly famous observation, Marx ([1852] 1994) wrote:

> Men make their own history, but they do not make it just as they please; they do not make it under circumstances chosen by themselves, but under circumstances directly encountered, given and transmitted from the past. The tradition of all the dead generations weighs like a nightmare on the brain of the living.

This aphorism succinctly encapsulates a realist, social constructionist theory of society (Berger and Luckmann 1966; Vidal and Peck 2012). Social interaction, over time, produces widely shared cultural logics and conceptual frameworks that exist independently of individuals and are experienced as external forces that both constrain and enable action. In marxist analysis, the social construction of reality occurs through the ideological constitution of individual consciousness and subjectivity (Althusser 2001; Nicolaus 1968; Therborn [1980] 1999), where ideologies are understood to reflect material conditions, and hegemonic ideologies present the interests of the ruling class as the interests of all, with some degree of concrete coordination of interests of the dominant and subordinate classes (Gramsci [1929–35] 1999; Hall 1986). Institutionalist sociology can be developed within, and enriched by, a historical materialist framework.

Of course, the marxist thesis that class structure constitutes the base of society is contested. The basic claim is that human history has been patterned according to a distinctive set of modes of production based in a class structure, and that cultural and political institutions are co-produced as part of human economic activity. Most institutional sociology does not see class structure as playing a foundational role in capitalist society.

However, the founders of institutional logics theory, Roger Friedland and Robert Alford (1991: 248, 259), acknowledged capitalism as a central institutional order of western society, arguing that "the institutional logic of capitalism is accumulation and the commodification of human activity." Explicitly attempting to move beyond functionalist theories of institutions, they made the concept of institutional contradiction central, noting that "the premise of institutional contradiction derives from class theory," particularly Gramscian theories of "class conflict as simultaneously culturally and materially generated through institutional contradiction." In addition to contradictions internal to the capitalist order, they suggested emergent contradictions between and within other foundational social orders of the west: democracy, the state, the family, and religion.

The emphasis on capitalism and class was dropped when logics theory was developed by Patricia Thornton and collaborators (Lounsbury 2001, 2007; Thornton and Ocasio 1999; 2012) into a leading approach within organization studies; in place of the logic of capitalism they refer to the logic of the market. Nonetheless, logics theory provides a complementary and fruitful basis for developing a mid-range, historical-materialist institutional, and organizational analysis. Logics can be seen as elements of ideology, hegemony, and counterhegemony, and the microfoundations of institutional logics as microfoundations of ideology, rooted in material practice.

In Chapter 1, I combined regulation theory (Aglietta [1976] 2000; Boyer 1988; Lipietz 1987; Vidal 2012, 2013, 2015, 2019) and sociological institutionalism (Friedland and Alford 1991; Scott 2008; Thornton et al. 2012) to sketch a theory of growth stages as being based in institutional settlements across three domains: (i) the dominant model of production, understood in broad terms to include employment relations, interfirm relations, and the articulation between sectors; (ii) the form of competition; and (iii) the form of state. Growth stages are based in an institutional settlement around a dominant, cornerstone logic for each domain, along with a web of settled organizational fields based in various organizational populations, typically sectors. Cornerstone logics exert influence across many, though not all, organizational fields.

Organizational fields may be characterized by two or more institutional logics that each articulate and legitimate competing goals or practices (Greenwood et al. 2011; Kraatz and Block 2008; Lounsbury 2007; Purdy and Gray 2009; Schneiberg and Soule 2005; Thornton and Ocasio 1999; Thornton 2004). Or fields may be characterized by a dominant institutional logic, widely seen as best practice, which is particularly likely in the for-profit sector. For example, the manufacturing field typically becomes settled around overarching logics of best practice for an extend period until it is destabilized by some force, such as an economic crisis or a new, competing practice (Fligstein 1990: 123).

Even if they have lost legitimacy in favor of a newly dominant logic, however, formerly dominant logics may continue to be influential, providing alternative visions, goals, templates, or understandings, often embedded in organizational practice even if not widely articulated as legitimate practice within field-level discourse. Formerly dominant logics may continue to influence action either as a result of deliberative cognition (DiMaggio 1997), via conscious and strategic appeal to the historical legacy of prior institutional orders (Schneiberg 2007) or, more automatically, if a conceptual schema associated with a formerly dominant logic continues to exert a powerful influence on the cognition of an individual (Thornton et al. 2012). Rather than simply adopt a formerly dominant logic as such, a more common approach would be for a manager to blend elements of the formerly dominant and the newly dominant logic into hybrid practice (Adler 1999; Binder 2007; Boyer 1998; Greenwood et al. 2011; Pache and Santos 2010).

In Chapter 4, I show that in the fordist era there was a single dominant logic of production that covered both the labor process and the valorization process: mass production with scientific management (aka fordist taylorism). In the postfordist era, the labor process question and the valorization question have become partially detached. The dominant labor process logic is lean management and the dominant logic of valorization substantive worker empowerment.

Chapters 5, 7, and 8 show that managers either adopt the dominant logic of substantive empowerment or a hybrid logic that I call consultative neo-taylorism. I define these two logics precisely in Chapter 5. Chapters 5 and 9 show that managers either adopt the dominant logic lean-as-system or a hybrid logic, lean-as-toolbox, which blends elements of lean and fordist mass production.

Finally, organizations typically embody multiple logics from their fields, which become instantiated through the interaction of individuals and coalitions in the organization (Besharov and Smith 2014; Binder 2007). At the level of the company as a whole, there may be an explicit attempt by executives to develop a company culture through mission statements or corporate philosophies such as the Toyota Way (Jürgens and Krzywdzinski 2016). Whether explicitly articulated as a company culture or not, all organizations have a management culture that will typically include a complementary combination of various logics (including hybrid logics) for organizational goals, production strategy (including for service organizations), and human resource management. But management culture generally does not become hegemonic within an organization; departments or subunits often have distinctive cultures, including production departments, which also are based in institutional logics. In Chapter 7 I examine shopfloor culture, and in Chapter 8 I note how company culture can be a hybrid which differs from dominant field-level logics, hence being a source of variation in operational strategy.

A Cultural-Satisficing Model of Agency

Human cognition is shaped by two processes: a top-down process in which institutional logics provide culture frames and conceptual schemas, and a bottom-up process in which the environment provides stimuli and feedback. This top-down/bottom-up model was developed by William Ocasio and collaborators (Ocasio 2011; Thornton et al. 2012), who developed the model by drawing on institutional theory plus Simon and March's behavioral theory.

In their brief discussions of bottom-up information processing, Ocasio (2011) and Thornton et al. (2012) suggested selective attention to environmental stimuli. Individuals vary in executive attention (ability to process multiple goals) and attentional vigilance (ability to sustain concentration) (Ocasio 2011). I propose that aspiration levels are central to how environmental feedback is processed (Vidal 2017). Although Ocasio and collaborators did not incorporate aspiration levels into their theory, the model can easily accommodate them, being based in part on the work of Simon and March. Having developed the theory of institutional logics in the previous section, the current section focuses on aspiration levels.

Following the lead of Braverman, Richard Edwards, and others, labor process theory has, in general, explicitly or implicitly adopted a maximizing model of agency, proposing that managers maximize labor control. However, organization theory and sociology have long noted that the maximizing model is an unrealistic and inaccurate theory of human behavior (Cyert and March [1963] 1992; March and Simon [1958] 1993; Nelson and Winter 1982; Vidal 2017; Winter 2000). Within the labor process tradition, references to satisficing, implicit or explicit, have been rare; the only exceptions I am aware of are Delbridge (2003) and Elger and Smith (2005).

I use the concept of satisficing to explain variation in managerial approaches. Managers with low or moderate aspiration levels settle for good enough. This argument is partially inspired by but contrasts with that of Gordon and Edwards, who suggested management maximizes labor valorization at the expense of efficiency. Managers settle for limited forms of worker empowerment that produce satisfactory increases in efficiency, while stopping short of substantive worker empowerment, which would yield larger increases in efficiency, flexibility, and learning capability, but is exceptionally difficult to implement, due, as elaborated below, to routine politics of production.

The theory of satisficing—or bounded rationality—was developed by the great polymath political scientist, Herbert Simon (March and Simon [1958] 1993; Simon 1955). It has been interpreted—incorrectly—by leading economists a model of maximizing under information and cognitive constraints (Jensen and Meckling 1976; Williamson 1985). Consider Michael Jensen and William Meckling's "Theory of the Firm" (1976: 211, emphasis added), a journal article with over 85,000 citations (according to Google Scholar as of April 2020):

> Simon (1955) developed a model of human choice incorporating information (search) and computational costs which has important implications for the behavior of managers. Unfortunately, *Simon's work has been misinterpreted as a denial of maximizing behavior*, and misused, especially in the marketing and behavioral science literature. His later use of the term "satisficing" (Simon 1959) has undoubtedly contributed to this confusion because it suggests rejection of maximizing behavior rather than maximization subject to costs of information and of decision making.

Quite the contrary, Simon explicitly intended his theory of satisficing to be a rejection of maximizing behavior. Indeed, responding to the attempt of new institutional economists to make bounded rationality a theory of maximizing subject to computational constraints, referring explicitly to the work of Oliver Williamson, Simon (1991: 26) was acerbic, noting that they "introduce a sort of bounded rationality into the behavior, with the exogeneity of the limits of rationality allowing the theory to remain within the magical domains of utility and profit maximization." Simon's core concepts of aspiration level and sequential (rather than global) search fundamentally dispense with any notion of maximizing or optimization.

The satisficing model has two elements: a person's "definition of the situation" and her aspiration level. On the former, March and Simon ([1958] 1993: 160) argued that, due to incomplete information and limited cognitive capability, individuals adopt a "limited, approximate, simplified" model of the situation. Sociological institutionalists have developed a rich theoretical and empirical body of literature on how individuals define their situation according to institutional logics that provide goals, principles, and practices for action. Curiously, however, they have largely ignored Simon and March on aspiration levels.

The concepts of aspiration level and sequential search are of fundamental importance. As March and Simon ([1958] 1993: 161) wrote, "finding an optimal alternative is a radically different problem from finding a satisfactory alternative." In the maximizing model, *all* alternatives *and* their anticipated outcomes must be considered and judged according to the same set of criteria. By contrast, in the satisficing model, an individual has an aspiration level for a given alternative or outcome, which is either satisfactory or not, according to a given criterion or set of criteria. Search is thus sequential, typically starting with the most accessible and local alternatives. If an alternative satisfies the aspiration level, the search ceases and that alternative is adopted.

March and Simon suggested that aspiration levels tend to adjust over time to the level of achievement (Cyert and March [1963] 1992; March and Simon [1958] 1993). The working hypothesis in the literature has been that if performance exceeds aspirations, they will adjust upward, and if performance is below aspirations, they will adjust downward (Levinthal and March 1981). Although a few studies provide some limited support for the hypothesis of aspirational adjustment (Baum and Dahlin 2007; Greve 1998; Lant and Montgomery 1987; Lant 1992; Mezias et al. 2002), the literature has also noted powerful inertial forces that stabilize aspirations "in spite of discrepancies with realized outcomes" (Winter 2000: 998).

I theorize aspirations as generally being stable, for three reasons. First, cognitive factors can function to stabilize aspiration levels. Belief systems and interpretive frames "are generally resistant to experience" (Levitt and March 1988: 324) and, indeed, may be used to interpret "performance feedback in ways that allow the organization to stay inert" (Greve 1998: 58). Commitment to existing interpretive frames engenders resistance to change (Grinyer and McKiernan 1990; Milliken and Lant 1991) and hence can stabilize aspirations.

Second, experience-based factors can generate resistance to change and thus stabilize aspiration levels. Extended experience with a given practice can lead to psychological investment and strong commitment to previously made decisions (Greve 1998; Milliken and Lant 1991). Similarly, accumulated experience with a practice generates competencies specific to that practice, which can result in perceived high costs of switching, even to an ostensibly superior practice (Levitt and March 1988). Further, in real-world practice managers have competing priorities and multiple demands on their time; in a context of immediate demands for output it is difficult to find time to dedicate to upgrading and learning (Winter 2000).

Finally, informal learning based on incremental adaptation to experience typically leads to the stabilization of routines and hence habitual behavior (Cyert and March [1963] 1992; Levitt and March 1988; Nelson and Winter 1982; Winter 2000). Sustained and overt organizational learning requires the establishment of what have variously been called learning routines (Levitt and March 1988), metaroutines (Adler et al. 1999), dynamic capabilities (Gavetti 2005), or routines for change (Nigam et al. 2016). In the absence of well-established learning routines, short periods of upgrading spurred by a problem with production (or by institutional pressures) will be followed by a period of routinized production (Winter 2000). Whether a period of overt learning is subsequently activated is a function of the interaction between performance, aspirations, and institutional pressures.

In sum, several reinforcing inertial forces operate to stabilize aspiration levels. A deeper source of such stability is likely variation in individual personality traits, in particular conscientiousness (achievement striving, competence, self-discipline) and openness (to new ideas, flexibility of thought, imagination) (Digman 1990; John and Srivastava 2001). Individuals with lower conscientiousness and openness will likely have lower aspiration levels.

Aspiration levels can shape how an outcome or situation is framed. The social psychology literature has shown that individuals often rationalize poor performance in order to maintain the appearance of competence and to avoid cognitive dissonance (Milliken and Lant 1991; Staw et al. 1983). Thus managers may rationalize poor performance by appealing to external factors, such as the industry or environment, rather than to internal factors under their own control. But poor performance, or a discrepancy between local practice and widely perceived best practice, may also be rationalized along the lines of "Our situation is different" (Winter 2000: 988). Taking a cue from Winter and drawing on the literature on the internal fit of practices (Ansari et al. 2010), an additional way for managers to rationalize deviation from best practice is to frame that practice as a poor fit with their organizational context (Vidal 2017).

Given that failure to adopt what is widely considered best practice may be a dereliction of duty, and in any case would violate deeply held norms and beliefs regarding managerial duties and performance, we should not expect managers to attribute their strategy or practice to a low aspiration level. Indeed, they may not even be consciously aware of this. Thus, my expectation is that, in a bottom-up process, if managers with moderate aspiration levels are satisfied with existing practice (and do not face severe external pressures for change), they will frame practices that are expected to improve performance but difficult to implement as a misfit—technical, cultural, political, or otherwise—with their context. In Chapters 8 and 9, I present cases of factories matched on technical, market, and organizational factors to provide evidence of this rationalization process in the context of unacknowledged aspiration levels.

Routine Politics of Production

I argued above the distinction between the labor process and the valorization process is critical because labor management includes organizational concerns that go beyond labor valorization. In addition to the valorization concern of ensuring sufficient labor effort, managers in postfordist firms are concerned with the qualitative transformation of work to improve efficiency, quality, flexibility, and learning capability. When they seek to implement new workplace strategies and practices—both for labor process organization and valorization—their initiatives must be operationalized as specific organizational routines and enacted by workers.

Here I develop the theory of routine politics of production, in which the notion of organizational routine plays a dual role. On the one hand, as organization theory teaches, routines are the basis of organizational capability (Becker 2004; Cyert and March [1963] 1992; Hodgson 1997; Levitt and March 1988; Nelson and Winter 1982; Winter 2000). If we intend to explain variations in organizational performance, it is important to theorize organizational capability as based in operational routines.

On the other hand, routines are the focus of conflict between workers and managers. Labor process theory suggests that managerial attempts to establish control often lead to resistance and noncompliance motivated by concerns with autonomy and dignity. A few labor process scholars have noted that workers develop stakes in, and attachments to particular routines (Burawoy 1987; Minssen 2006; Willmott 1990), but routines have not been theorized explicitly as a locus of contention. Empirical studies have found conflict in response to managerial attempts to implement new practices, but not theorized it in terms of routines (Delbridge 2003; Elger and Smith 2005; Friedman 1977; Rinehart et al. 1997).

The findings presented in this book suggest that in postfordist America, workplace politics largely revolve around managerial attempts to change routines and workers' defense of their existing routines, based on competing visions of efficiency, concerns for product quality, and understandings of the proper division of labor between management and workers.

While organization theory emphasizes the difficulty of implementing new routines due to the role of tacit knowledge (Langlois and Foss 1999: 208; Nelson and Winter 1982) routines may become a source of conflict. Such conflict over routines, however, has not been appreciated within organization theory or labor process theory. While the latter sees conflict as central, it has generally been theorized in terms of the "effort bargain," including informal negotiation over workplace norms and standards regarding sufficient effort levels (Ackroyd and Thompson 1999; P. K. Edwards 1986; Thompson and Smith 2009a, 2009b).

The most sophisticated and sustained analyses of control and resistance in the labor process have been developed Paul Edwards, Stephen

Ackroyd, Paul Thompson, and Randy Hodson. Edwards (1986)—building on the work of Littler (1982)—theorized the labor process as relatively autonomous in the sense that conflict is not necessarily determined by broader class relations and in many times and places operates largely independently from these. Ackroyd and Thompson (1999) theorized the basis of worker resistance as the pursuit of autonomy in response to managerial control regimes. Hodson (2001) theorized the basis of worker resistance as the pursuit of dignity in response to mismanagement, abuse, overwork, and limits on autonomy. Ackroyd and Thompson and Hodson usefully extend beyond the effort bargain, although all see it as a fundamental axis of workplace resistance and conflict.

The concept of the effort bargain fails to capture the fact that workers often contest management over work organization for reasons beyond (quantitative) effort levels. Organized labor has often sought to increase worker participation in decision making and strategic planning. Chapter 1 discussed the US history, including efforts of the American Federation of Labor (AFL) in the early twentieth century to engage in joint management, of the Congress of Industrial Organizations (CIO) to do the same during the Second World War, and of efforts by the AFL-CIO that have continued, from the joint training program initiatives of the 1980s (Marschall and Scully-Russ 2010) to the labor management partnerships of the present.[3] And of course there are various forms of codetermination across Western Europe, including establishment-level works councils, which have statutory status in many countries, as a result of powerful unions (Kluge 2005).

These longstanding initiatives of workers and their unions to engage in co-management are broader than establishing a fair effort bargain and driven by more than worker identification with employer goals. Alienation engenders skepticism toward management, which is amplified and reinforced by the experience many workers have with management fads of the month, failed initiatives, bad management, or vindictive managers. However, the data presented in Chapters 6 and 7 show that while some workers disengage or remain reticent, most become committed to particular routines because they want to do high-quality, efficient work in order to make their work meaningful, to realize a purpose, and feel pride. While they certainly wanted to be treated with dignity, in general the workers I interviewed did not articulate concerns about establishing autonomy. Rather,

[3] https://aflcio.org/what-unions-do/labor-management-partnerships. Last visited on June 30, 2021.

they contested managerial attempts to change routines, even to upskill and empower them, due to skepticism and competing visions of efficiency.

In line with the cultural-satisficing model of agency, workers' understandings are also shaped by institutional logics of practice. Managers have responsibilities, and experience pressures, that make them more attuned to global logics of best practice, while workers' orientations are more likely to be shaped by local workplace culture, custom, and practice, where former logics of best practice are more likely to be resilient. The traditional, fordist-taylorist logic of best practice, which emphasizes excelling at a specialized task, following instructions and maximizing physical effort, may be highly resonant with workers seeking to do high-quality work. Indeed, this very logic of a highly specialized division of labor, with clearly defined work roles and responsibilities, has been enshrined in union contracts for decades, as an attempt to safeguard against arbitrary and capricious management.

In addition to experience with fads of the month, managerial incompetence or satisficing often means that managers cut corners, leaving workers to defend a pure version of fordist rationality against managerial practices that, wittingly or otherwise, undermine it (Forrant 2000). Skepticism toward management and commitment to a fordist logic reinforce each other, encouraging resistance and reticence toward postfordist managerial initiatives.

Finally, it is critical to remember that workers are often internally divided due to contradictions in their experiences and in the ideologies which shape their consciousness, both within broader society, before they come to work, and within the workplace (Nichols and Armstrong 1976). To the extent that there is ideological variation within the workforce (perhaps driven by more basic variation in personality traits and emotional temperament), we should expect variations and how workers respond to management initiatives and practices. Chapters 6 and 7 examine the role of competing factions within the workplace and the union.

Permissively Institutionalized Competitive Fields

The institutional literature has focused mainly on heavily regulated fields such as education, healthcare, and banking, in which there is an authority to enforce a given institutional logic (centralized fields) or those in which competing authorities present conflicting demands or prescriptions for other organizations (fragmented centralization) (Greenwood et al. 2011; Pache and Santos 2010). This focus, however, has led to a neglect of fields that are decentralized—with no authority to enforce any institutional logic—such as lightly regulated, for-profit sectors like most manufacturing and many service fields. The manufacturing field is decentralized in the following sense: a large number of small- and mid-sized establishments depend on small number of industrial customers (prime contractors), giant retailers, parent firms, industry associations, and consultants for business, resources, and technical information. Yet, the powerful actors in this field do not possess regulatory authority.

In thinking through the question of authority within fields, Royston Greenwood and colleagues (2011: 338) emphasized different enforcement mechanisms, ranging from the coercive powers of the state and regulatory powers of accreditation agencies to "the more normative authority of professional associations." While normative authority may powerfully influence some organizations, however, it should be analytically distinguished from forms of authority, such as state laws or regulations, which are backed by the power to exclude organizations from operating in a given field or otherwise penalize them for failure to conform. Because norms cannot, by definition, be enforced, I distinguish mechanisms of *enforcement* (compulsion) associated with regulatory authorities or powerful resource providers from mechanisms of *influence* associated with normative prescriptions.

A field structured by normative logics without enforcement mechanisms permits deviation from institutional prescriptions based on satisficing. I now turn to theorize how even *competitive* fields may be permissively institutionalized to allow relatively inefficient organizations to survive.

Harvey Leibenstein (1966: 392) famously presented a heretical argument in *The American Economic Review* that economics has been unjustifiably focused on the allocative efficiency, which is in fact a "trivial" problem, while neglecting technical (organizational) inefficiency, which he hypothesized to be widespread throughout market economies. While this argument was largely dismissed by the mainstream, in particular by theoretically driven economists, the applied economics literature documents widespread technical inefficiency (Angeriz et al. 2006; Caves and Barton 1990; Frantz 1988; Green and Mayes 1991; Luria 1996).

In mainstream economic theory, technical inefficiency results from incentive problems or incomplete information (Martin 1993;

Kalirajan and Shand 1999; Frantz 1988). But market competition is widely seen as a selection mechanism that drives inefficient producers out of business. In the classic statement, Armen Alchian (1950: 213) argued that the primary selection criterion is "positive profits," which (consistent with my argument) require only "relative efficiency" (hence permitting relative inefficiency). But the association of market selection (and profit maximization) with efficiency maximization remains widespread: "competitive challenges represent a surprisingly strong force for efficiency" (Sjöström and Weitzman 1996: 27).

In theorizing a permissively institutionalized competitive field, we can set aside incentive problems because our focus is specifically on market selection (and because we have rejected maximizing models in favor of a cultural-satisficing model). Necessary conditions for a permissively institutionalized competitive field are that it is structured by normative logics without enforcement mechanisms and that market competition is too blunt a selection mechanism to drive middling (modal) performers to either upgrade or go out of business.

On the latter, Sydney Winter (1964: 243) noted that the theory of market selection is based on several untenable assumptions. Dropping these assumptions, he formally demonstrated that under conditions characteristic of real markets, "maximizers and non-maximizers may coexist indefinitely." A scale advantage may allow a non-maximizer to have higher profits and growth rates than a maximizer with an identical production function. Similarly, maximizers and non-maximizers may coexist if they sell different products, have different expansion policies (e.g. paying dividends versus reinvestment), different technologies, or if the non-maximizer has superior access to funding (and is thus able to weather large losses).

Most importantly, mainstream theory assumes that all firms are maximizers. If we adopt the more realistic assumption that most managers are satisficers, then we would expect the majority of any particular sector to consist of middling performers—especially in a context of uncertainty. In such a context, while the worst performers will eventually drive themselves out of business, the small number of top performers cannot drive out the large number of middling performers (Winter 1964). This constitutes a second necessary condition of permissive institutionalization: to the extent that markets contain widespread variation across technologies (including management systems), inputs, outputs, and strategies, world-class firms will not be able to drive out satisficing competitors.

In addition to these two conditions which allow organization inefficiency in markets, an additional factor within postfordist fields—relational contracting—both attenuates competitive pressures and facilitates reproduction of inefficient practices. Long-term relations between customers and suppliers of complex parts have become increasingly common since the 1980s, when corporate America vertically disintegrated via outsourcing and subcontracting (Helper and Kiehl 2004; Herrigel 2004; Whitford 2005). But establishing highly functional and mutually beneficial network ties, such as those among Japanese manufacturers (Helper and Kiehl 2004), is difficult.

While manufacturing suppliers are dependent on industrial customers for business, neither relational contracting nor arms-length contracting allows customers to dictate how their suppliers operate. As Josh Whitford (2005: 87) has shown, suppliers often "buy business by lowering margins to win contracts with a hope of getting a foot in the door," and often stock inventory to be responsive rather than getting lean to achieve low cost and high flexibility. Even where customers and suppliers enter into collaborative, long-term relations, the former are characterized by factional and departmental conflicts; in particular purchasing departments often work at cross-purposes with supplier development departments. Supplier development efforts inside partner suppliers are often short-lived, and these suppliers get mixed messages, often being subject to hard-nosed bargaining and whipsawing by the purchasing department (Herrigel 2004; Whitford 2005).

On the one hand, then, supply chain contracting can facilitate inefficiencies due to suppliers gaming the metrics and to conflicting signals from their industrial customers. On the other hand, the existence of technical and relational embeddedness may attenuate competitive pressures. Even if a supplier gamed the metrics to get in, once a long-term contract is granted and so long as the targets are being met, ongoing relations between purchasing managers and supplier factories, along with possible asset specificities associated with making complex parts, further attenuate competitive pressures. At the end of the contract, unless the supplier has failed in some major way, due to the ongoing relationships or to the costs of changing suppliers under asset-specific contracting, purchasing agents will have incentives to maintain rather than change suppliers.

In sum, two conditions are necessary and sufficient for permissive competition: a competitive field is structured by normative logics without enforcement mechanisms; and the sector contains substantial variation across organizations in terms of strategy and performance. Further, organizational inefficiencies are produced by factional and departmental conflict in multinational corporations, which leads to contradictory initiatives, suboptimal compromises, or inefficient practices, particularly within supply chain management. The existence of technical and relational embeddedness and complexity in supply networks further attenuates competitive pressures and facilitate satisficing.

Summary: Capitalist Management, Worker Alienation, and Routine Inefficiency

I have presented a theory to explain variation in organizational form and performance. Institutional logics of work organization and labor management specify widely agreed best practice in detail. Managers may deviate from best practice because the logic of former best practice resonates with them, so they reject (consciously or unconsciously) parts of the current logic of best practice. Managers also may deviate from best practice because they satisfice in response to the management contradiction, settling for manual labor and standardization over substantive empowerment. Or managers may satisfice in response to routine politics of production, as workers defend their existing routines, making the establishment of new routines too difficult for managers with moderate aspiration levels.

For any of these reasons—individually or in combination—organizations may adopt suboptimal routines. If an organization has not established learning routines, so long as it is satisfying existing customers, it is subject to multiple forces for inertia and as such suboptimal routines are likely to be durable. Organizational inefficiency is doubly routine: in the sense that it is based in organizational routines and in the sense of it being regular and commonplace.

Deviation from best practice is possible because real-world markets are in fact permissive of widespread (relative) inefficiency. Market discipline does not penetrate organizations to select on routines and capabilities because competitive fields contain substantial variation in terms of operational strategy and performance. Although competition may drive out laggard organizations that do not meet a certain baseline of efficiency, the range of variation in performance is vast, with the performance and capabilities of the median establishment being far below that of the top establishments. Competitive pressure is further attenuated within supply chains due to the existence of technical and relational embeddedness in customer-supplier relations.

PART III
ANALYSIS

4

The Postfordist Field in American Manufacturing

We saw in Chapter 1 that the American manufacturing field was fordist from roughly the late 1920s, when Ford's River Rouge complex was completed, until the long crisis of the 1970s. In the fordist field, competition was low and profits were high. The fordist logic of the firm included vertical integration and standardized mass production with a taylorist division of labor (Aglietta [1976] 2000; Boyer 1997; Littler 1982; Vidal 2015). Competition was oligopolistic within domestically oriented markets (Fligstein 1990; Vidal 2015).

In this chapter I sketch the transition from a single logic of production under fordism (mass production with scientific management) to two complementary but distinct logics under postfordism (lean production and worker empowerment).[1] I then present an overview of my study. The analysis of the field begins with a description of its organizational ecology and a demonstration that a highly specified model of lean production has been institutionalized, along with a substantive model of worker empowerment, as best practice. Then, based on my qualitative data—fortified by statistical data from a sample of the same field—I explain how the postfordist field has been institutionalized in a way that permits substantial variation in organizational performance, including a small number of highly efficient firms and a large number of relatively inefficient firms. This chapter sets the scene for the analysis in the following chapters of variation in lean production regimes, labor process contradictions, and routine politics of production.

[1] This chapter draws on previously published material (Vidal 2017) and also includes a substantial amount of unpublished, new empirical material.

Management Divided. Matt Vidal, Oxford University Press. © Matt Vidal (2022).
DOI: 10.1093/oso/9780198795278.003.0004

Dominant Logics of Production: From Fordism to Postfordism

As we saw in Chapter 1, Marx ([1867] 1990) distinguished the labor process from the valorization process. The former refers to the social organization of work as such, in any mode of production, the latter to the extraction of surplus value from workers within capitalism. For management, the labor process question concerns how to best organize the production process, while the valorization question concerns how to secure sufficient output from workers, including whether workers should be primarily used a sources of manual labor or also for cognitive labor.

We saw in Chapter 3 that fields often become settled around an overarching logic of best practice for an extend period until destabilized by some force, such as an economic crisis or a new, competing practice (Fligstein 1990: 123). After a dominant logic is challenged by a new logic, the former may lose legitimacy in favor of the newly dominant logic, yet it may continue to influence action either as a result of deliberate cognition (DiMaggio 1997; Schneiberg 2007) or more automatically, if a conceptual schema associated with a formerly dominant logic continues to exert a powerful influence on the cognition of an individual (DiMaggio 1997; Thornton et al. 2012).

My proposition here is that in the postfordist era, where there is a premium on multiskilling and worker participation, the question of how to organize work and how to valorize labor have become partially detached, meaning that managers now must make a distinct choice regarding each, as opposed to the fordist era in which taylorism provided a single model for work organization and labor valorization. This proposition is diagramed in Figure 4.1.

In the fordist era there was a single institutional logic of production providing a template for work organization and human resource management: mass production with scientific management (aka fordist taylorism). Taylorism simultaneously addressed the valorization problem and the organization of the labor process: the combination of process standardization, task fragmentation, and task specialization provided a model of work organization and labor valorization. This taylorist logic of labor specialization and standardization is highly complementary with the fordist logic of forecast-driven (push) production, large production runs, and functional organization focused on scale economies and output maximization. The result was a single, tightly integrated logic of fordist-taylorist production, which was institutionalized and widely implemented as such.

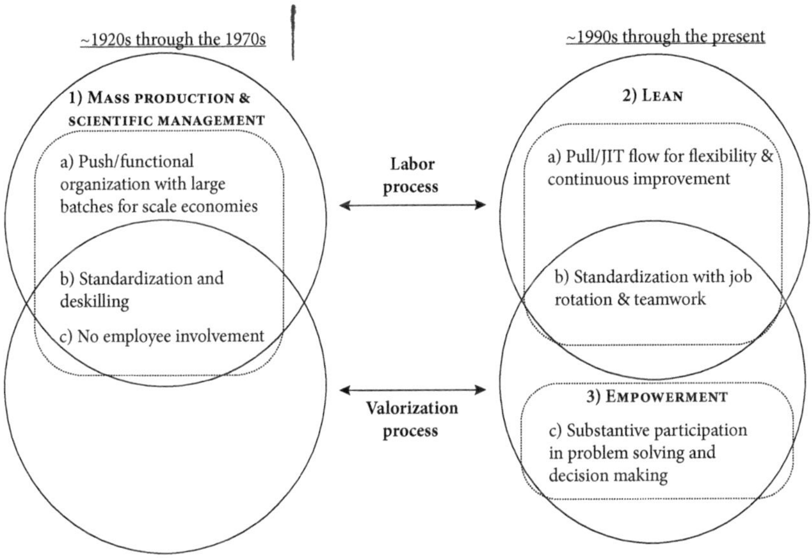

Fig. 4.1 Core principles of three institutional logics of production in the US manufacturing field

Source: Author

Note: Numbers indicate institutional logics, which are enclosed in dashed lines. Letters indicate core principles, which were tightly integrated into a single logic in the fordist period but have become separated into two relatively independent logics in the postfordist period. Circles indicate whether a core principle addresses a labor process question, valorization question, or both. Deskilling refers to task fragmentation and specialization.

It is unclear whether there is any efficiency benefit of worker participation in such a model, in which each worker is responsible for a single operation, with no view or understanding of the larger production process. Insofar as the efficiency basis of the model is output maximization and scale economies within a push system, efficiency is primarily about unit cost reduction and, as such, the best practice is to have workers doing simple, fragmented tasks. Rotation among fragmented, low-skill tasks will ease boredom and ergonomic risk, but any provision of skills beyond multitasking will mainly add training costs.

But this consideration was not even on the table: scientific management was not just the dominant institutional logic of labor management; it was the only logic of labor management, taylorism being the first coherent theory of labor management. The idea that worker empowerment could provide a direct means to improve efficiency and organizational learning, by tapping the knowledge and intellectual capabilities of workers, had not even been articulated. To the extent that employee involvement was considered, it was seen as a basis for improving motivation and commitment, not as "useful for its own sake" in terms of increased efficiency, flexibility or organizational learning (Miles 1965: 153). This remained true of the concepts of job enlargement, developed at IBM in the 1940s (Walker 1950) and job enrichment, developed at AT&T others in the late 1960s (Herzberg 1968). Job enrichment guru Frederick Herzberg's hugely influential 1968 article – which by 1987 had sold over 1.2 million reprints, more than any other *Harvard Business Review* article – is exclusively focused on the problem of motivating workers.

The roots of the new, high-involvement human resource model, in which worker participation in problem solving and decision making are explicitly conceived as improving "the decision making and total performance efficiency of the organization" (Miles 1965: 153), were planted in the 1950s. In Britain, experiments with autonomous teams in British coal mining gave rise to sociotechnical systems theory, developed by Eric Trist and colleagues at the Tavistock Institute of Human Relations in London (Trist 1981). In Japan, the quality control movement, including the contributions of the Union of Japanese Scientists and Engineers (Tsutsui, 1996), W. Edwards Deming (1982) and Joseph M. Juran ([1970] 1993), produced the concepts of Total Quality Management, statistical process control, and quality circles.

Whereas job enrichment theory tinkered with traditional taylorism, remaining a job-level analysis and merely seeking to increase motivation, sociotechnical systems and the quality movement (in Japan alongside the Toyota Production System) articulated a more fundamental rethinking of the work process and role of labor within it, developing a systems-level analysis focused on work system redesign and harnessing the knowledge and abstract cognitive capabilities of workers.

It was only in the 1980s that the high-involvement model took off in the United States. In 1980, NBC aired a documentary called "If Japan Can, Why Can't We?," inaugurating the deification of Deming (Tsutsui, 1996). By the early 1990s, the high-involvement model was widely advocated within the field, with many influential scholars and consultants advocating self-directed teams (but not the Toyota Production System) (e.g. Lawler 1992; Orsburn et al. 1990; Pfeffer 1998; Wellins et al. 1991). I stylistically date the institutionalization of the empowerment model (and the lean model) from the 1990s, when these models were adopted by leading firms and widely championed as best practice in management discourse (New United Motor Manufacturing, Inc. (NUMMI), the GM-Toyota joint venture in Fremont, CA, opened in 1984, John Krafcik published the paper that christened the Toyota Production System "lean production" in 1988, and James

Womack and collaborators published their hugely influential book on lean in 1990).

These developments and others in Germany and Sweden led to several competing postfordist production models rather than a single model. The various models for self-directed teams, Total Quality Management, and high-involvement human resource management resulted in the institutionalization of a logic of worker empowerment. At the same time, lean and other models of work organization and process control emphasized new efficiencies from economies of flexibility and continuous improvement, while being vague on the form of teamwork and participation. Lean became institutionalized as the dominant logic of work organization, based in demand-driven flow production, and widely adopted across the global manufacturing landscape and beyond. But managers still have to make a separate choice on whether they do job rotation among narrow tasks (multitasking) or some form of real cross training across enlarged and enriched tasks (multiskilling). And they need to decide whether to adopt consultative or substantive employee involvement.

Again, two factors are in play here. When there is a premium on flexibility and learning, there is a clear efficiency advantage to multiskilling and empowerment. Within process-flow organization and job rotation, the potential performance benefits of participation are high. And in the USA, the institutionalization of employee involvement has taken on a substantive cast. In practice, in the postfordist context of competition on flexibility and continuous improvement, managers are faced with a choice between substantive empowerment (multiskilling + inclusion in problem solving and decision making) and nominal empowerment (multitasking + consultation).

While substantive worker empowerment is highly complementary with lean production, the empowerment model of labor valorization is partially detached from the lean model of work organization. The latter includes standardization with job rotation (see Figure 4.1), but managers must make an additional decision regarding whether to empower their workers and, if so, to what degree. To complicate things further, the logic of fordist-taylorism continues to exert a powerful influence on actors in the field, providing alternative logics that guide action.

I provide evidence supporting these arguments in Chapters 5 through 9, which focus in depth on the management of the labor process within organizations. In Chapters 5, 7, and 8, I demonstrate the detachment between work organization and valorization strategies. In Chapters 7 through 9,

I show that many managers continue to think partially in terms of fordist-taylorist logics. In the present chapter, I focus on the institutionalization of the postfordist field.

Overview of the Case Study

My case study is the durable goods sector of American manufacturing, with a particular focus on the components subsector in the US Midwest. Component suppliers form a subsector because they share a common position: supplying industrial customers across a range of industrial sectors (Dan Luria et al. 2005). And this sector is where many of the manufacturing jobs are; as large brand-name firms began outsourcing and vertically designating in the 1980s, there was growth in the supplier sector. The percentage of all manufacturing workers employed in the components subsector rose from 16.3 in 1970 to 19.8 in 2002, despite a 13.7% decline in overall manufacturing employment during the same period. In the early 2000s, at the time of my study, for a John Deere lawn tractor that cost $3,000, around $1,800 of that cost was in purchased components. For a Ford truck that cost $25,000, purchased components accounted for around $14,500.

According to my fieldwork log, I interacted with 486 individuals from fifty-nine organizations over a total of 332 hours. I conducted qualitative interviews with 109 individuals in thirty-one firms across Wisconsin, Michigan, and Illinois (totaling 163 hours). Seven of the thirty-one firms are brand-name multinational prime contractors that each do over one billion in sales per year, twenty-one are small- or mid-sized component suppliers (less than 500 employees), one is a large component supplier (650 employees), one is a large component supplier that also produces a line of brand-name products (640 employees), and one a painter. The primes sell air conditioners, engines, trucks, agricultural, lawn, recreational, and industrial equipment. The suppliers sell a variety of metal forgings and fabrications, plastics, and subassemblies to industrial customers across a wide range of durable goods industries, from cars to computers. Three of the suppliers are primarily in auto, and two others do some business in auto.

My interviews included forty-seven managers and engineers, fifty-nine workers, and three union business agents. The management/engineer/business agent interviews were typically around two hours each, with some lasting over five hours in multiple sessions, and the worker interviews were typically half an hour, with some extending to an hour. I received plant tours in almost all cases.

I also conducted 169 hours of direct observation on fifty-nine occasions. For a period of fifteen months I followed two union suppliers—Second Tier Specialist and Mini OE—including interviews with four managers across seven occasions, interviews with twelve workers and two union presidents, observation of a local union meeting, and participation in nineteen Labor-Management Partnership Committee meetings and one Worker Education Committee meeting. At one of these factories I engaged in a shop-floor training exercise to develop standard work instructions. I also followed a nonunion supplier, Metalfab Plus, over a twenty-month period, including interviews with four managers across three visits, six workers, participation in a half-day "Lean 101" training for workers, and observation of a supplier development project, run by a large industrial customer, over eight sessions totaling nineteen hours.

I observed two half-day meetings of the Wisconsin Manufacturers' Development Consortium (WMDC), including seven multinational prime contractors, one supplier representative, and the Wisconsin Manufacturing Extension Partnership (WMEP); fifteen two-hour Supplier Networking meetings associated with the WMDC; seven meetings of prime contractor unions and the Wisconsin Regional Training Partnership (WRTP); and six other meetings involving the WMEP and WRTP.

My prolonged engagement in the field facilitated extensive triangulation and "member checking" (Lofland et al. 2005), allowing me to increasingly adopt the role of an expert and talk shop with managers, engineers, and workers, providing a built-in validity check on my emerging interpretations. All of this gives me considerable confidence that my findings are not presentational accounts but accurate reflections of actual practice, in Becker's (2001) sense that extended observation of people in their operational contexts allows the qualitative researcher to gain deep familiarity with the people being studied, their understandings, concerns, and behaviors.

The thirty-one firms were *not* picked on the basis of their operational strategy—that is, whether they adopted lean production—but were picked on the basis of industry and location in the supply chain, using cold calling and snowballing techniques. My goal in picking the cases was to get a reasonably broad cross section of factories in the components subsector. My interviews in the twenty-three component suppliers and one painter focused on work organization and labor management. My interviews with the large prime contractors focused largely on supply chain management. All thirty-one companies are referred to here by pseudonyms.

The Institutionalization of a Permissively Competitive Field

We saw in Chapter 3 that the US manufacturing field is decentralized: a large number of small- and mid-sized establishments depend on small number of industrial customers (prime contractors), giant retailers, parent firms, industry associations, and consultants for business, resources, and technical information. Here I paint a fuller picture of the field. I begin with a more detailed description of the organizational ecology of the field. I then specify the institutional logics of best practice and present data to demonstrate their normative nature: Managers understand these as best practices that they *should* adopt to improve performance and appear legitimate. I then provide statistics showing widespread variation in organizational performance, followed by qualitative data to demonstrate permissive competition due to network embeddedness and satisficing in the customer-supplier relation.

Organizational Ecology and Institutional Logics

For the typical small- to mid-sized manufacturer, operational strategy is not based on a hyper-rational information search and systematic evaluation of alternatives. Even where managers attempt a rational information search, they immediately confront an environment where lean is everywhere: adopted by leading customers and competitors, advocated by customers, business associations, trade magazines, management books, and consultants. Table 4.1 lists high-profile prime contractors that have publicly embraced lean and are key customers of the suppliers that I observed. It also lists a range of industry associations that have explicitly adopted lean as best practice for modern manufacturing, along with a cottage industry of consultants.

Of the twenty-four supplier plants I observed, twenty-two had been doing lean for years. Of the two who had not adopted lean, one was a painter that had a continuous-process technology in which unpainted parts were

Table 4.1 Field-level diffusion of lean

Adopted by:

- Toyota, Chrysler, Ford, GM, Volvo
- Case New Holland, Caterpillar, John Deere
- Harley-Davidson, Oshkosh Truck
- Dell, Hewlett Packard, IBM, Samsung
- Boeing, Lockheed Martin, General Electric
- Numerous others

Endorsed by:

- National Association of Manufacturers
- Society of Manufacturing Engineers
- National Association for Job Shops and Small Manufacturers
- Institute of Industrial Engineers
- Association for Manufacturing Excellence

Technical assistance provide by:

- Industrial customers
- 60 local centers of the Manufacturing Extension Partnership, National Institute of Standards and Technology
- Cottage industry of private sector lean consultants

fed in and fully painted parts churned out. Lean was not applicable to this core process (although it could have been implemented in the office). The other was a metal stamping and fabrication job shop that recently enlisted WMEP to help improve workflow and reduce inventory but had "been a pretty traditional company over the last 95 years." Its main process was high-volume progressive stamping, in which coil metal is fed into a single machine and run through several stations to produce a complete part from a single machine.

For the remainder of the book, I focus on the twenty-two supplier factories that adopted lean. However, I do bring in relevant material from the seven multinational prime contractors.

The major sources leading these twenty-two suppliers to lean are listed in Table 4.2. Nineteen were pushed to get lean either by a major industrial customer (thirteen of the nineteen), a parent company (three of the nineteen) or both (three of the nineteen). Of the three suppliers who were *not* pushed by a customer or a parent to get lean, all received outside help: two received lean training from a technical college and/or Manufacturing Extension Partnership (MEP) center and one received lean training from an industry association.

Table 4.2 Institutional sources of competitive strategy

Plants	Industrial customer	Parent company	Tech college and/or MEP	Industry assoc.	Hired a lean expert	Consultant	Rational info search + innovative strategy
1. Custom Seats	X					X	
2. Designer Railings	X		X	X			
3. Industrial Pumps			X				
4. Inspired Castings	X		X				X
5. Mini Metalfab	X		X				
6. Mini OE		X			X	X	
7. Performance Brakes	X					X	
8. Second Tier Specialist		X			X		
9. Custom Blinds		X				X	
10. Deep Stampings	X	X					
11. Lost-Foam Castings	X			X		X	
12. Hydraulic Systems	X		X				
13. LV Gaskets	X	X	X				
14. Complex Iron Castings	X		X				
15. Major Castings	X	X	X				
16. Metalfab Plus	X		X		X		
17. Plastic Containers				X			
18. Precision Metalfab	X		X				
19. Spindles & Machining			X				
20. Tiny Plastic Parts	X		X				
21. Tubefab	X					X	
22. Zinc Castings	X					X	

Note: An X indicates a source that was highlighted by managers in my interviews; lack of an X does not necessarily mean that a plant did not also use or get pressure from a given source. MEP is the Manufacturing Extension Partnership, a publicly subsidized program providing technical assistance to small- and mid-sized organizations. For ease of comparison, plants are ordered identically to Table 5.1 in the following chapter, which presents a typology of leanness. All plant names are pseudonyms.

Of the twenty-two lean suppliers, only in one did management conduct something that approximated a rational information search that ended in a truly innovative production strategy. The executive Vice President (VP) of Inspired Castings, a precision metal casting operation, explained how they developed a continuous-flow system in 1993. He claimed that "continuous flow manufacturing concepts" were "really not even invented when we started . . . we finally saw a magazine article that said, 'Continuous flow manufacturing is this and this,' and it was all of the different criteria that we had actually come up with. We're not saying we invented it, it doesn't matter to us about that."

I say they approximated a rational information search because, unlike the other suppliers in my sample, who adopted lean after it had been institutionalized as best practice in the US manufacturing field, Inspired was ahead of the curve, particularly for their subsector. But even they were inspired by others: "We'd had like the Toyota just-in-time type of thing. We had read the book, *The Goal*, and it was along those lines that we were thinking, and that got us thinking along those things." *The Goal* is a management novel by Eliyahu Goldratt and Jeff Cox, which outlines a continuous flow approach focused on removing bottlenecks and continuous improvement.

Their innovation was being able to implement continuous-flow principles in a process (investment casting) where such practices were previously thought inapplicable, radically driving down lead time and uniting disparate processes through highly creative reconceptualization and substantial technical investment. They reduced total throughput time from six weeks to three days, and their lead times for customers were one week versus nine weeks for their competitors. They claimed that other investment casters could not even understand how continuous flow would be implemented in investment casting.

The VP at Inspired preferred to call their approach continuous flow rather than lean, because "It's never that it's been, 'Let's develop lean here,' you know, we've always been I think on that path, it's just been called different things all the time." Without minimizing their creativity, it is noteworthy that they did receive substantial technical assistance, not only from the local technical college for things like leadership, problem solving, communication, and teamwork, but also from "a lot of customers who've helped us along the way."

Companies, consultants, associations, and state agencies have converged around a well-specified model of lean. The core principles (as listed in

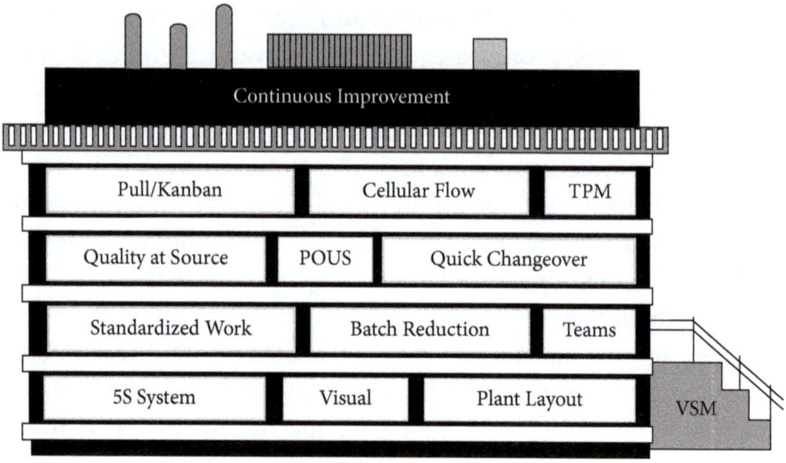

Fig. 4.2 The postfordist template of work organization
Source: Wisconsin Manufacturing Extension Partnership, *Manufacturing Matters!* Newsletter, 2005.

Figure 4.1) are just-in-time production, standardization, and continuous improvement.[2] The core principles and practices are illustrated with a graphic called the House of Lean.

Figure 4.2 presents the House of Lean developed by the Wisconsin Manufacturing Extension Partnership. The WMEP is part of the US Manufacturing Extension Partnership, a public-private partnership that is part of the National Institute of Standards and Technology, an agency of the US Commerce Department. The MEP serves small- and mid-sized manufacturers, delivering services—including lean as its model for production operations—via a network of state-level centers, covering all fifty states.

A Google search for "House of Lean" generated fifteen identical versions of this figure produced by other consulting organizations, and no fewer than seventy versions that were nearly identical to it.[3] In the WMEP

[2] According to the founder of the Toyota Production System, Taiichi Ohno (1988: 4), its two pillars are just-in-time (JIT) production and "autonomation, or automation with a human touch." JIT refers to a customer-driven, flow production process in which parts are produced only when there is an order for them, with minimal inventory and a focus on eliminating waste through the analysis of work flows and processes. Autonomation, also known as *jidoka*, refers to equipping all machines with an automatic stopping mechanism so that when an error is detected workers can stop the line to solve the problem. Ohno was deeply influenced by Ford, seeing standardized work as fundamental and conceiving the problem-solving process as the progressive revision of work standards. As the Toyota Production System was rebranded to lean production, Ohno's two pillars became articulated as three core principles: JIT, standardization, and continuous improvement.

[3] Search conducted on 16 July 2015.

House the principle of just-in-time production includes the practices of pull/*kanban*, cellular flow, batch reduction, plant layout, quick changeover, and value-stream mapping (VSM); the principle of standardization includes the practices of standardized work, 5S, and value-stream mapping; and the principle of continuous improvement via worker empowerment includes the practices of total productive maintenance (TPM), quality at source, teams, visual, and value-stream mapping.

The principles and practices in the WMEP House of Lean are included in nearly every House of Lean and constitute the basic package of lean principles and practices applicable to a broad range of industries and organizations. Beyond what is listed in the WMEP House, other Houses of Lean include *jidoka* (stopping work to solve problems when they arise) and its key practices: *poka-yoke* (mistake proofing that automatically stops production if there is an error), and *andon* (a visual display of the status of operations, including problems). In the WMEP House the principle of *jidoka* is subsumed under "Continuous improvement," "Quality at source," and "Visual [management]." Some Houses of Lean also include the principle of *heijunka* (production leveling or smoothing to reduce batch size and work-in-progress inventory) and the associated practice of *takt* time (production time divided by customer demand). In the WMEP House the principle of *heijunka* is subsumed under "pull/kanban," "cellular flow," and "VSM." There are several additional concrete practices associated with lean, but all fall under one of the core principles of (i) JIT/flow, (ii) standardization, and (iii) continuous improvement/worker empowerment.

Finally, lean is often bundled together with "Six Sigma." The latter is a quality control methodology developed by Motorola, which focuses on statistical process control and the DMAIC approach (define, measure, analyze, improve, control). "Lean Six Sigma" is a common model in the field.

Managers discuss modern manufacturing practice in terms of lean production. As the plant manager at Mini Metalfab stated, "Everybody's going to a just-in-time lean situation." Similarly, the plant manager at Industrial Pumps declared that "If we had not been into lean manufacturing in the last two to three years with the economy the way it was, we'd have been a real hurting company. I really honestly believe that."

Of the practices in Figure 4.2, perhaps the most basic is *batch size reduction*. One of the central ways of reducing batch sizes is with *quick changeover* (also known as setup reduction or single-minute exchange of dies (SMED)). If a factory wants to reduce its batch sizes it has to reduce the time it takes to change over its tooling: the longer a setup takes, the larger the minimum batch size required to justify it economically; the smaller the batch size, the wider variety of batches that can be run in a given shift. All of the suppliers I visited were doing batch size reduction and quick changeover. As the plant manager at Tubefab stated, they were focused on "Setup reduction type stuff and cycle time reduction and, you know, just general lean manufacturing type things."

Another practice adopted at all of the factories was the *5S system* of standardization, which roughly translates from Japanese into sort, set in order, shine, standardize, and sustain. The owner-manager of Spindles & Machining indicated that they were doing "5S and some lean, quick setup projects." The managers at Industrial Pumps explain how effective 5S can be:

> Manager A: We pulled seven Craftsman toolboxes out of just that assembly department down below the steps.
>
> Manager B: Three guys working the area, seven toolboxes!
>
> Manager A: If you'd go up and you'd ask a guy for a torque wrench, he'd go through three drawers, or four drawers.
>
> Manager B: Unlock the drawer, look, no. Unlock the drawer, 'There's the case. There's no torque wrench.' That was the area we did our first 5S . . . There was a complete set of metric wrenches and a complete set of English wrenches. And out of all of that, we found out you don't even need a wrench to build the pumps they built. So seven sets of wrenches went on the auction block.

Other lean practices that were adopted by all the suppliers I visited included a suite of practices to encourage workers to engage in quality control and continuous improvement. The general principle is *Quality at Source*, in which workers are responsible for quality control of each piece of work (rather than having inspectors check quality at the end of the line). Lean practices for quality at the source include *standardized work*, *point of use storage* (POUS), *visual management*, and *total productive maintenance* (TPM), in which machine operators do simple maintenance to avoid unplanned downtime. The plant manager of Integrated Blinds stated that they do "Quality at the source teaming with best practice work instructions for every work center."

Beyond the foregoing basic lean practices, adopted by all of the twenty-two lean factories I observed, the other lean practices get significantly more complicated and were variably implemented across factories. These are practices for improving *plant layout* and process control, including *pull/kanban* and *cells* or *cellular flow*. The idea is to move from the push system of fordist mass production, with long production runs based on forecasts and functional organization with distinct departments for machining, stamping, etc., to a pull system of short runs driven by customer demand with product-focused organization.

Supplier factories, which typically do not run long assembly lines, tend to organize continuous flow production through work cells, which are groups of machines and processes needed to produce a product family organized in close physical proximity to each other, normally in a U-shape. However, to establish true continuous flow across an entire value stream requires a *kanban* system of production control. A *kanban* is a low-tech indicator system developed at Toyota, either a card or a container that is a signal to build for an upstream operation. In the leanest systems, a continuous flow process is scheduled at a single point (the pacemaker) based on customer demand, and then the entire sequence of operations is controlled via *kanban* signals.

The plant manager at Integrated Blinds noted that they had "come up with a new way of scheduling, which is basically just-in-time . . . it doesn't push things through, it pulls them through." The plant manager of Lost-Foam castings indicated they were "going through lean efforts right now. . .. We do the cellular, yep, you bet," and the plant manager of Hydraulic Systems stated they've "got a lot of cells set up. And we do have a pull system." At Deep Stampings the manager indicated they are focusing on "inventory reduction, *kanban*, visual management . . . lean manufacturing." And the plant manager at Mini OE described how their "number one goal is to eliminate non-value added activities. . .. We're looking at *kanban* tickets, we're looking at more of a pull system."

As suggested in Figure 4.2, *VSM* provides the steps to realize a truly lean operation, in particular, to realize continuous flow driven by customer demand and to guide continuous improvement efforts. It is a form of process mapping, which in some factories was highly sophisticated, based on detailed statistical analysis of processes, and in others much cruder, based on gut feelings. *Continuous improvement* often goes by the Japanese term, *kaizen*. The plant manager of LV Gaskets noted how they will "put a team together, we'll decide what the *kaizen* is going to be on, okay? We do basically two types of *kaizen*: we do a 5S *kaizen* and we do a production *kaizen*."

In a truly lean organization, value-stream mapping is the core of lean continuous improvement. A team maps out the flow of a product family from order to delivery, dividing the process into three categories: value added, necessary non-value added, and unnecessary non-value added. This allows organizations to eliminate unnecessary non-value added time, uncover bottlenecks, and reduce lot sizes, as the following two examples show.

Metalfab Plus was picked by an industrial customer for a supplier development project. I observed the team meetings, which included Metalfab employees but were run by a team of outside engineers from the industrial customer and the WMEP. The project focused on a new laser the supplier had recently purchased and was struggling with in terms of process flow. The mapping project produced the following statistics. Fully 3000 different part numbers were produced by seventy-three operation codes. These were combined into 393 process flows for product families. Focusing on a foot pedal for a lawn tractor sold by the prime contractor, they found that sixteen of the 393 process flows accounted for 51% of the laser run hours. Further, the exercise revealed that the operations for the foot pedal consisted of 0.01% value added time, 0.22% necessary non-value added time, and 99.77% unnecessary non-value added time. The material handling to make the part amounted to parts traveling 6041 feet over several weeks. In the series of disconnected operations needed to make the foot pedal, batches of parts were made and put into inventory, independent of the other batches. The project team set the goal of getting this down to less than 100 feet over a number of hours.

In another example, the plant manager at Second Tier Specialist provides a good illustration of using value-stream mapping to reduce setup/changeover times in order to reduce batch sizes:

> What we do is we focus in from value-stream mappings on where we need to target to get the biggest bang for the buck for the *kaizen* activities. . . . My approach is you keep halving [batch sizes]. We were running as high on some of these end caps as several hundred. We're now down into the eight to 24 quantities when we run them. The goal eventually is to get it down to six or four. So we just keep reducing down, and then you find the new bottle neck, and then work on that through setup reductions, and then you keep bringing it down.

Together, the entire set of practices just discussed—understood explicitly as a complementary package—constitute the dominant logic of the lean labor process.

The final lean practice is teamwork. Because it concerns employee involvement—hence the balance between manual and cognitive labor output—it is a question of valorization. Inspired Castings provides a good illustration of a management team that has implemented substantive empowerment on a widespread scale. The VP, who had a very hands-on approach, explained that the initiative for continuous improvement is "better coming up from the shop floor . . . because then they can fix it and all that. And a lot of times we'll put the problems back and challenges back to them: 'Here, solve this problem.'" He continued: "The president and myself get up in front of all the employees on a team-by-team basis, and we say, 'Here's where we felt short last quarter. Here's what needs to be improved. Go back and work on it.'"

Inspired sought to involve as much of its production workforce as possible in substantive participation, which may take a range of forms: "On a small scale, [a team] can start something up [in] the cell and they can work on something themselves, or . . . the whole plant can work on it, or set up a team that's separate on that."

My discussions with the personnel manager confirmed that worker-driven continuous improvement is the norm at this foundry. As she stated:

> Well, you can have many going on at one time, and I wouldn't even be aware of them. Some of the employees in Module 1 at one point in time had a real interest in the grind area and knew how they could streamline it and make it better. They talked to the plant manager. "Fine, go ahead. Start working on it." They'd come in and work on things here and there.
>
> *They'd just come in and do it on their own?*
>
> Um-hmm. And then they came up with some programs to really help the process, implement it, reduced times drastically, you know, in setups and things like that to standardize stuff.

The final comment here is key: Continuous improvement can only happen organization-wide if there is a procedure for standardizing best practice. This means that within a lean-as-system approach worker empowerment must be limited to collective autonomy, that is, involving workers in group decisions, thus precluding high levels of individual autonomy.

By contrast, as I will show in Chapters 5 through 9, a common approach in my sample was consultative participation: Asking workers for their input but without giving them real decision-making or problem-solving authority. And a few companies opted for substantive individual empowerment within a lean-as-toolbox approach.

I will demonstrate in Chapters 5, 7, and 8 that a manager can make a decision on each logic independently and then combine the two into an overall production regime. However—as I will demonstrate in Chapter 9—this independence is only relative because there are two distinct situations in which a decision to deviate from the logic of substantive empowerment will make the adoption of lean-as-system much more difficult: with consultative participation it is difficult to drive continuous improvement; with individual autonomy, it is impossible to standardize best practice.

Nearly every manager I spoke with agreed that, in theory, the package of practices specified in the House of Lean constitute—as a complete package—best practice. And many also agreed that substantive empowerment is best practice. However, as I show in Chapters 8 and 9, many claimed that this complete package was not fully applicable to their specific factory context. I will provide evidence that this claim is in fact a rationalization of a satisficing approach; specifically, I match pairs of effectively identical factory contexts in which one manager claimed that best practice is not a good fit, while another manager implemented best practice thoroughly. Some managers continued to think partially in terms of the fordist-taylorist logic, thus deviating from best practice. For the remainder of the present chapter, I focus on how the competitive field permits variation in organizational performance, including relatively unlean, inefficient, and inflexible organizations.

Permissive Competition

In Chapter 3 I developed a theory of permissive competition, based on two characteristics of real-world manufacturing markets. First, within competitive fields, institutional logics of best practice do not have enforcement mechanisms, while formerly dominant logics associated with inefficient practices continue to influence some individuals. Second, due to widespread satisficing and variations in strategy, substantial variation exists across organizations in performance, meaning that the majority of firms are middling performers and the small number of world-class firms cannot drive these satisficers out of business. Further, there are factors that facilitate inefficiency and satisficing within organizations: The existence of factional and departmental conflict leads to contradictory initiatives, sub-optimal compromises, or inefficient practices. And there are additional factors that further attenuate competitive pressures and facilitate satisficing: technical and relational embeddedness and complexity in supply networks.

Statistical data demonstrate wide variation in productivity levels and other performance metrics. The Performance Benchmarking Service of the Industrial Technology Institute, an MEP center in Ann Arbor, MI, began surveying small- and mid-sized manufacturers in 1992. By 1996 it had data on over 3000 firms with fewer than 500 employees. This sample is from the same population of firms as my case study. The Benchmarking study found:

> Metal-formers making the same products for the same customers have value added per employee anywhere between $40,000 and $140,000. Indeed, in every industry the productivity level achieved by the most productive 10 percent of shops is at least 160 percent of the industry median. The seventy-fifth percentile is invariably twice the twenty-fifth percentile value. While less pronounced than for value added per employee, the huge dispersion in performance applies to nearly every metric the database supports, from on-time delivery to scrap rate to inventory turnover.
>
> (Luria 1996: 13)

The majority of factories are clustered in the middle of the distribution, and the difference between the median performers and top performers is vast.

I now turn to demonstrate, based on my qualitative data, the institutional factors that facilitate relative inefficiency and satisficing within organizations and make competition permissive of wide variation in supplier performance. I begin first with some illustrations of satisficing on both sides of the customer-supplier relation, and then turn to factional conflict, departmental conflict, and embeddedness and complexity in supply networks.

Satisficing on Both Sides of the Customer-Supplier Relation

Both managers in prime contractors and in subcontractors described how purchasing agents are often concerned only with getting parts of sufficient cost, quality, and delivery, without regard for how these targets are achieved. A plant manager at Mini Metalfab explained how—being a key supplier for a particular customer—his plant makes so many parts it would be very hard for them to drop him as a supplier. For that customer they "do probably at least 800 different parts for them. So I mean . . . if you were the purchasing guy at [the customer] and your boss said, 'Pull all the stuff out of [the supplier]' if you have 800 parts to try to source somewhere, it's just a huge task. A huge task."

This manager explained further that, in his experience, purchasing managers generally are not concerned with suppliers' internal processes: "You've got purchasing people doing the buying, they're not really looking at processes and what can they do to shave 50 cents off here or 50 cents off this part. They're just ordering parts." A supplier development engineer in a multinational prime contractor agreed:

> If you're a buyer or whatever you're getting measured on the performance of your suppliers. Why would you care [how they hit their targets]? As long as they're meeting their cost, delivery and quality goals, you're looking good, your suppliers are looking good, why would you care?

Because purchasing managers are generally only concerned with output, it is possible for suppliers to game the metrics to get the business. Indeed, as another supplier development engineer in a multinational prime contractor explained, the standard metrics (cost, quality, and delivery time) not only allow but even encourage gaming, hence satisficing:

> Let's look at quality. Well, if you start beating up suppliers for quality, what do they do? They put inspectors on the end of the line. So they start rejecting everything everywhere and then there's rework all through their system. Their as-delivered quality, the quality you see may improve, but it drastically increases their cost, reduced their flexibility, makes a mess of their systems. Delivery. Okay, everybody wants to get stuff on time. But what happens if you start beating up suppliers for delivery? Well, they build you a big warehouse and put your name on it. And who ends up paying for that? You do. . .. Price. Okay, you can think, well, price is the one that makes sense. No. Price is terrible. We have suppliers that, one of two things: They'll either try to buy our business . . .. Or, we have suppliers–even more dangerous–who don't understand their costs.

As he went on to explain, small suppliers often don't have the knowledge or resources to meet customer targets in the most efficient manner. They typically do "not have the ability to hire specialists, i.e. most of their managerial personnel are generalists expected to 'wear many hats.' ... So, when a customer sets performance standards in front of them, they usually address them in general rather than specialized ways."

The first supplier development engineer quoted above agreed with this point:

> We've dealt with some suppliers... And they basically don't have the resources to work on that [upgrading project], and some of that's legitimate, and I can understand that. But there also can be an element of passive resistance.... I have no doubt that when you're moving your factory around you're going to use a lot of resources. That's completely understandable. But ... it's very easy to say that that's going to take up all your resources [focusing on one problem so they cannot address another problem], and that's kind of a form of passive resistance.

What he refers to as passive resistance is what I have theorized as satisficing: settling for good enough. Aspiration levels vary across managers, and the lower the aspiration level, the more likely it is that a manager will passively resist further upgrading and continuous improvement in the face of multiple, competing demands and the pressure to get products out the door. The lower the aspiration level, the more likely they are to meet customer targets through non-lean, inefficient methods such as intensive sorting (for quality), pre-building stocks (for delivery), and even sacrificing their own margins (for costs).

Once a supplier has gotten into a customer, which can be done by gaming the metrics, they may be given some slack on particular performance metrics. The president of Metalfab Plus explained his experience in terms of lead-time performance:

> It's really first time in is where it becomes an issue. It's getting in the door. You know with [our two longest-term customers] we don't necessarily lose any business. I mean I can't tell you they don't pick up the phone and harangue us for it. But if we come back and say, this, you know they want it in two weeks, we tell them, 'I'm sorry, the best you're going to get is five,' we don't lose that work; they just get upset with us on the front end.... [Even with other customers] for the

> most part it's, once you've won, once you're qualified as a supplier with somebody, they generally, as I said, they'll give you enough room to work with the lead times.

Similarly, as a manager at Mini Metalfab put it, "Once a part is being made and there's no problems with it, and it's going through, you know, they're getting their parts on time and it's working fine, I think there's little incentive for them to say, 'How can we improve the process?'" Purchasing managers may be satisfied with getting good parts from a reliable supplier, without regard for the internal processes of the supplier.

As a VP of purchasing at a multinational prime contractor suggested, suppliers can keep business by being keyed into a key customer's needs rather than more efficient/lean. Some of "the most competitive [suppliers] are the ones that are, have gotten to know [our company's] buying habits" really well. Thus, for instance, they are given a "five piece release" and are supposed to make these parts just in time. But they have learned that the company will order "50, 60 of those a year." So the customer decides "'I'll make 60 of them. . . . I'll put 60 of them on my shelf and release them to him.' And they're the smart guys that know us better than we know ourselves and are competitive that way. So, I don't encourage them to carry inventory, but some of the fabricators do it where they've got big setups, absolutely." This may be a form of short-term optimizing, given the situation in which they can predict demand for this particular customer. But it is suboptimal, hence satisficing in the mid and long term insofar as these timescales are inherently uncertain (market conditions change, etc.) and they have not built in the capability to do true just-in-time delivery.

But things are even more complex than simply gaming metrics. In fact, suppliers get conflicting signals in terms of how customers want them to reach their targets. Many suppliers reported hearing, implicitly or explicitly, that customers *want* them to hold inventory to be responsive. Suppliers did report feeling pressure from customers to be responsive by getting lean, but they are receiving mixed signals. The executive VP from Inspired Castings explained how they resisted those pressures and ultimately come up with a way to minimize inventory throughout their process:

> I think we've had conflicting pressures throughout. . . . And we responded to that and we listened to them. And then we saw what [customers] did right and we saw what they did wrong, and we came up with the concept overall of just the best way to do it is to eliminate all inventory. And we have had tremendous

> pressure to put in inventory, and we have fought that pressure, to get the customers to understand that this is the best way and the lowest cost overall.

Now, there are industrial customers with high organizational expectations across the board, and purchasing managers with high aspiration levels in terms of supplier performance. For example, a supply chain manager in a multinational prime contractor explained that his organization does not sacrifice price for quality and delivery:

> It is certainly true that we have some suppliers that do an exceptional job on quality and on-time delivery, but whose pricing is invariably higher than everybody else's. Long term, we don't think it's necessary to have higher prices to give good quality and delivery. So we don't see that as a conflict, and eventually, if they can't get their price down, we're going to move them out.... we believe that out there somewhere there is a global benchmark for somebody who is capable of delivering quality and delivering it on time and doing that at the lowest possible cost. And our goal is to find that supplier and use them.

At the same time, however, this manager indicated that having all of their suppliers be lean and able to do just-in-time delivery is not a priority. They are happy to have suppliers warehousing and relatively unconcerned with how suppliers meet their performance targets:

> *Are you guys doing just-in-time with your suppliers?*
>
> It depends. If we have, if a supplier has the ability to provide parts to us on a just-in-time basis, we do that. We have some material that we keep in our warehouse on consignment; we don't get charged for it until we use it. We have material that comes in, just scheduled in within a day or two of when we need it, pretty close to just-in-time.
>
> *Okay. So you have some suppliers that can do just-in-time and some that can't, and are you attempting to get the ones that can't into a just-in-time position?*
>
> It is not a major effort for us.

To be sure, there is always a threat of losing the business, and of course suppliers do loose business when new bids are put out. But as shown above, relatively inefficient suppliers can get and keep business. And as I now turn to show, factional conflict and departmental conflict contribute to organizational satisficing on both sides of the customer-supplier relation, while embeddedness and complexity in supply networks further attenuate competitive pressures. Suppliers I observed maintained key customers for decades, supplying parts and meeting customer targets, but without using the leanest/most efficient practices to do so.

Factional conflict, contradictory strategies, and destructive competition. Conflict between competing factions is a fact of organizational life. The larger and more complex the organization, the more likely that factional conflict will be intense. Multinational prime contracting manufacturers are riven by a deep-seated conflict between long-termist and short-termist factions in supply chain management. A supplier development engineer explained this factional conflict within his company, a household-name American firm:

> So there's this great battle within [the company] between people who want the long term, you know, "Let's get the good suppliers; they're going to be with us for the long term," and the people who just want short-term performance or a stock [price that] looks good in the next year so they get their options and bonuses maxed out. And it's this great short-term versus long-term [battle].
>
> Right now the short-term people are winning big. You know we are doing now foreign sourcing, which I sound negative toward and I am just because I think it reflects greater long-term cost than we're actually quantifying, but we have now, it's not just you have to take the one with the lower piece price, you've got to go with the one in China for $9.50 or $9.99 over the domestic one for $10. We are now having foreign sourcing as a metric, meaning even if they're $10 in China, it's now foreign sourcing for foreign sourcing's sake.

The engineer explained that he thinks such short-term behavior is being driven in his organization because they have gone to an outside Board of Directors, "business professors and stuff like that [and] they've taken a very short-term focus, they've given our CEO very short-term performance metrics, and this is driving the short-term behaviors throughout the company." A primary source of short-term pressures is quarterly stock reporting: "Nobody thinks core competency anymore. Everybody just thinks global—what's going to work for our stock's performance next quarter? That is the only motivation."

The same engineer elaborated on how, in his company, these factions have been institutionalized into different teams at different levels. Within Strategic Sourcing, there is a centralized team that makes decisions on which suppliers to use, while teams at local factories work with their suppliers to help upgrade their capabilities:

> [T]here's a greater disconnect between the people making the sourcing decision and the people who have to make sure that the suppliers are working out. And when you have a greater disconnect, what you'll see is that the strategic people [who decide which suppliers to use] will be more likely to go with a lower quality, lower cost, lower performing supplier because then they can save a few bucks. . .. we're getting more cost savings but we're also, I think the trend will be toward decreasing performance or at least in supplier performance that isn't improving as quickly.

In addition, suppliers also have to deal with a cost management group, which tries to "break the cost down and nickel dime the suppliers." In the vivid terms of this engineer, "The strategic sourcing managers are like lions going to devour suppliers. And the cost management people . . . they're kind of like the hyenas . . .." In this complex arrangement—at an industry leading, household-name, multibillion dollar American corporation—strategic sourcing is responsible for picking, firing, and consolidating suppliers; cost management attempts to reduce cost with existing suppliers; and supplier development is responsible for upgrading supplier capabilities.

A senior supplier development manager in the same company, with decades of experience in supply chain management, elaborated on this battle. He described how the short-termist faction focuses only on immediate costs, while the long-termist faction focuses also on overall capability, including the flexibility to quickly respond to changes in market demand, which is only possible with flexible domestic suppliers:

> Two years ago McKinsey came in to do this study and said, "Why are you buying anything in the U.S.? Why do you even have supplier development in the U.S., because you'll never make them competitive enough to compete with the Indian and Chinese suppliers." And in the end, we were right, because they weren't taking into account "satisfy market demand," they were taking into account strictly cost of production. They weren't taking into account potential lost sales. There's always going to be factions like that, and for a while they were beating us down. Now they're there, they know who they are, we know who we are, but we're getting heard more, and we're getting our things institutionalized.

Such factional conflict is clear to, and often problematic for, suppliers. The president of Precision Metalfab indicated that his business strategy is to provide extra capabilities and services for customers, but this only works where he can get business with longer-term customers oriented toward collaboration. Otherwise, he will simply be underbid by cost competitors. He thinks it's fine for prime contractors to use:

> as the denominator to get a unit of measure, piece price. But you shouldn't look at just the fact that, "let's get on the books a nickel less." I mean what, how is [the supplier] providing material for, how is he handling the logistics and the delivery and so forth. Let's give it value, because it's shortsighted. . .. We had, and this happened on another product probably a year ago. We helped [a customer] prototype the development of about a 600-pound weldment, it's a nice product. And so we knew what it was going to take. And then the company goes out and bids it on an auction. Which, we pretty much stopped participating.
>
> We wanted some business on that one, but we pretty much stopped. And that company came in and, less than, in round numbers, I think, you know, we might sell the item for about $600. It was a pretty decent size weldment, and I want to say material was around $300. And so we bid it and we came down a little bit, and then this other company comes in at $425. Well, there's no way. We know, we built the product; you can't do it. . .. So a couple months go by and we get a call from the [customer] saying, "These guys were supposed to deliver to us in a couple days. We went out there, it's all messed up. They can't, there's no way in the world; they got in over their heads. Can you take it on?" We went back and said, "You know, we've got to go back to the price we gave you." And they did and it's been here since . . .

This supplier would like to provide many design, logistical, and other services for customers. But this strategy is only viable if collaborationist factions are winning in prime contractors—and such longer-term strategies are constantly under threat by short-termist factions within and across organizations.

I did speak with one group of managers in a multinational prime contractor in which the collaborationist faction appeared to be winning—at that particular moment. Now, it should be noted that this company—a different household-name corporation from the one just discussed—has an intensely loyal customer base, so it is in a relatively uncommon position that contributes to its ability to fend off short-term pressures. Nonetheless, the case is instructive. One of the purchasing managers noted how there is an impulse to manage their explosive growth through outsourcing and offshoring. But the company has "looked at it from just the opposite way . . . we are growing, there are opportunities to grow your relationship with our workforce" and supply base. The manager continued:

> I just thought for a minute of the benefit of the three people you're talking to right now? We, all three of us in some way, shape or form worked for General Electric in some past life. And we saw the other end . . . the pressure to outsource, the pressure for, you know, lower the piece price and get it out of here. Where "manufacturing," quote/unquote, is now reduced to nothing more than bringing in huge, huge subassemblies, sticking a cable between them and putting them on test for a minute and then ship them out the door to a customer.

One of the other managers in this interview noted that an advantage of their domestic sourcing strategy—which is managed in close partnership with their local union—is that "our quality has improved greatly. I've seen that a lot." But any triumph by the long-termist faction is always precarious: Since I left the field, this corporation has gone on record as increasing the content of its products that is sourced from overseas.

In contrast to this firm, in the multinational prime contractor discussed above where the short-termist faction is more dominant, the senior purchasing manager related a story about a domestic strategic supplier with whom the purchasing manager has worked closely:

> My boss sat down with me late last week and said, "You know, [this supplier you are advocating] will be lucky to have any business with [our company] in five years." And I said, "Well, I understand they'll probably be losing some because we're going to do more foreign sourcing." He says, "Well we're going to be sourcing exactly that commodity." I said, "Well, we just had them recognized for outstanding performance. They are a unique supplier and you're telling me . . ." I said, "I don't accept that. I think we can keep business with them." He says, "Well, I'd like to . . . but I'm just telling you that's probably what's going to happen."

As the foregoing examples show, the short-termist approach to supply chain management within industrial customers increases competitive pressure on suppliers, but in a way that sacrifices dynamic efficiency for immediate costs savings. This supports suppliers of mediocre capability at the expense of the overall capability and flexibility of the supply chain. There are possibilities for great gains from collaboration, but the more that short-termist factions win in multinational prime contractors, the more difficult it becomes to pursue collaborationist strategies.

A short-termist focus on piece price exclusively is a false economy. Union members at a multinational prime contract explained to me how a new short-termist management team was brought in and imposed increased outsourcing, based solely on piece price. Some suppliers regularly shipped defective tools or parts. This resulted in substantial amounts of rework having to be done in-house, but management refused to properly account for these costs by adding them into the price of the parts. Remarkably, according to these two union members, management would add the cost of rework to their own internal operational costs rather than to the cost of the outsourced parts. Below I provide an extended discussion I had with these union members on this situation:

Union member A: The three guys that were in charge of manufacturing, you know they all, all three of them came from Briggs and Stratton. And basically they brought those Briggs and Stratton philosophies with them and decided that, you know, we're going to impose them now . . . they had a game plan to do a lot of outsourcing.

Union member B: Like the tool grinding for instance, they had a place sharpening our tools that couldn't do it right for anything. I mean everything that was coming back in, an operator would get their tooling and it would burn up in a matter of a couple of holes, and I mean it was costing them a lot of money before we got a stop put to it . . . not only are you getting tooling, you know, two and three times, or bad tooling, and you're possibly scrapping out parts, or a lot of time, tool trouble and that for the operators because this stuff is just junk.

You know and all it was was we went to the cheapest place that would sharpen the tools for us, and without really an accurate [quote on total costs]. What they did was there's five guys in a tool-grinding department, and the reality of it was there was only one guy on the day shift that dedicated his time mostly to sharpening tools. But we took all five guys, took their time, 40-hour week, and overtime, and said, "They all were tool sharpeners so . . ."

That's how management calculated the costs?

Union member B: Right. So they said, "Everybody's wages and that, and benefits and that, we tally that up and this is our cost for tool sharpening, and so this place can do it for this. So we're saving $200,000 a year," or whatever the actual figure was.

Now were you guys able to, did you present them with these costs and say, "This is . . ."

Union member B: Oh, yeah, that's . . .

Union member A: Initially the old management that they had in there, they didn't want to hear it. They had a game plan and, you know . . .

That was that.

Union member A: That was that.

Did they even hear your, I mean did they even hear your plea that, "Hey, you guys, you're not really getting the true costs here."

Union member B: They did but . . .

They just weren't going to hear it anyway.

Union member B: No, I mean our insource/outsource was, when we got back, it was run basically like an auction.

Union member A: Yeah.

Union member B: Normally we all have input and say.

So you guys have a committee, right?

Right.

And so, is it, in the contract do you have language that you have a committee?

Yes.

And so you guys are supposed to have some say and actually . . .

Union member B: Right. Three bargaining unit and three from the company. . . . Well, when we got back, no matter what we said negative for the outsourcing—and a lot of it had to do with costs and proving to them that their numbers were not reality—it would just go around, they'd listen to us, and then it would come back . . . and they'd be, "Well, that's it. The decision is, it goes out."

Union member A: They would come up with cost savings no matter what.
Right. If they keep looking for it they're going to find it, type of thing?

Union member A: Yeah. Yep. Well, we couldn't actually get true numbers. They would figure out some type of costing on the part that made it more expensive inside, so it would justify sending it out. Now when we would, you know, if there were parts that we'd have problems with every now and then in the shop, and you know our, we have a Q-Track system for defective parts. You know, when you make a bad part, you put a Q-Track on it. Well, they would add in, you know, all of the Q-Tracks and everything into our cost saying, you know, "Well, if we have an outside supplier make them they're going to make them right before they get in the building and that cost will go away." So, but you know, they would add that cost into our costing for internal.

Um-hmm.

Union member A: And then, you know, the parts would go out and these parts would be machined on the outside, they'd come in, and we'd find problems with them. And you know, when we'd address that, saying, "Well, there's also quality issues when you're having them made on the outside, you know, what's going to go on?" You know, how can that not affect their cost if we're throwing them away and starting over from scratch, you know, sending them more castings, or if we're doing the rework ourselves on the parts, you know . . .

Union member B: That should be added to their cost.

Union member A: Yeah, we'd tell them, yeah, it should be, that should be added onto their cost and the cost of waiting, you know, engines waiting on the line for those parts like they were adding into ours. And, you know, nothing was ever done about that. They would say, "Well, we'll send one of our quality guys over there to make sure that next time they send us good ones." You know and sometimes we'd get good parts and sometimes you'd get bad. But like I said, you know, they would go out of their way to figure out ways of getting parts sent out.

While I was not able to get independent verification, I have no reason to doubt the veracity of this story. And it is consistent with stories relayed above in which a company metric to increase outsourcing drives short-term thinking and behavior (which may reap rewards in short-term stock price) even against evidence that the behavior is inefficient under more dynamic and longer-term considerations. Beyond the metric, consistent with the theory of satisficing developed in Chapter 3, this management team had a strategy and they were committed to that strategy no matter what.

In sum, on supply chain management strategy, management is divided between conflicting strategies pursued by warring factions. And while the short-termist strategy increases competitive pressure on suppliers, this increased competition focuses only on piece price, which can both increase overall costs to the prime contractor and crowd out suppliers who are more dynamically efficient in terms of internal capabilities regarding quality and flexibility. The short-termist approach favors suppliers that offer the cheapest piece prices (however that low cost was achieved) over more dynamically efficient ones—not only permitting but actively facilitating inefficiency in the market. At the same time, as we now turn to see, managerial satisficing, embeddedness, and complexity attenuate competitive pressures, contributing to the permissive institutionalization of the field.

Embeddedness and complexity in supply networks. The nature of supply chain management often results in stable, embedded relations between customers and suppliers. To begin, although the cost reduction pressures that suppliers face are often intense, sometimes suppliers can push back because it is hard for customers to resource these products. As the plant manager at Deep Stampings explains, their parts are so hard to produce that they have some leverage. The price pressures are:

> never-ending, I mean there's no such thing as a price increase. . . . actually maybe a year ago it seemed like we were getting some ridiculous demands with 10 percent [annual price reduction], it was like, you know, for three years. It's like, wait a minute, you know, we can't do that. And we pushed back. You know again, the beauty of where we sit is we do tough [components, so] they can't just go down the street and say, "Hey, can you do this?" . . . So we have some leverage, we do have some leverage. Yeah, we usually end up having to give something. So that's, the important thing is that we continue to keep the pipeline full and get the new work and, you know, usually you can command the higher margin on the front end.

In many other cases it's hard for customers to easily switch suppliers. For example, the plant manager at Complex Iron Castings explains how it is hard for customers to switch suppliers because it takes so long to qualify casters for the parts they supply, their tooling is expensive, and their volumes are low:

If you're a machine shop, you either machine it to the spec or to the print, and it's easy to measure it. You put it in a layout machine and you measure it. There are so many variables in our process that getting someone up to speed could take time, and that should be your cost of process. I will tell you that a lot of our complex parts may take, before we're fully qualified, eight months, nine months, okay? Now will that stop them? No. I mean they'll go out and they'll shop and they'll do all those things. . .. if the incentive is great enough, obviously they'll go. But there is a balancing thing.

We have a little less sensitivity to it because the volumes that we produce are lower volume jobs. So if it takes $40-, $50-, $60-, $70,000 to qualify guys to supply them, okay? And you're making 300 parts a year. Are you going to go through that exercise? And if you go through that exercise—and then the other part is building the tooling. And because of the price, the complexity of our parts, you know. Tooling for a block, an automotive style block, can run somewhere between $150- to $200,000. Now most of them don't have the capability of taking the tooling out of here and taking it to somebody else that they don't have qualified and spending five, six months bringing them up to speed. So that means you've got to build another set of tooling.

A manager at another casting plant, Zinc Castings, explains that for similar reasons it is so expensive to change casters that his plant has been able to flatly resist demands for price reductions:

When you go ahead and quote a die-casting die, you usually, you've got your best rates on there, I mean otherwise you don't get the job. So unless they go and actually physically change the design of their parts to reduce mass or something like that, there's no way of cost reducing it. So we end up going back to our customers and saying that we'd love to participate in the design review with their engineering departments and that we're available five days a week to do that, and you just name the time and we'll come and see you. And then it dies right there.

If the price is right, of course, customers will move the business. But, as the plant manager at LV Gaskets explained, supplying a highly-engineered product makes it unlikely that a customer will switch suppliers so long as the supplier continues to perform:

If you are truly making a commodity, I mean the price pressure has got to be absolutely huge. If you're making an engineered product of one sort of another,

> you know, I think there is less of it because—you know, if we were in the vacuum cleaner business, that's very highly price driven at this point in time.... That's not true obviously in diesel engines and things like that, they are high-ticket items. So obviously, when you work on that, you have a limited number of applications with a limited number of units to be produced, you can't have everybody chasing everything. So, in some ways, once you've won the business, unless you just absolutely falter because of quality or delivery or whatever, you're married to that particular design or that particular engine, because it's a huge investment.

Similarly, a purchasing manager at a multinational prime contractor explained how their hood supplier has design capability that makes them very difficult to change. Thus the supplier is:

> going to continue making the hoods because they have basically taken over our design function. It would be pretty difficult to change horses in midstream. We have a cost management function—that happens to report to me—that's telling [supplier] right now that their overhead costs and some of their costs are out of line and they need to get them in line. But because they're a long-term supplier we're going to give them several years to do this.

Further, the supplier is at the cutting edge of technology, and if the customer tried to ship their injection molding tools to another supplier, they would "probably would tell us they couldn't use them to make products, because there's so much difference that they wouldn't be able to figure out how to retrofit them into their machines." So this supplier is locked in to the customer.

Industrial customers may be more concerned with the flow of their production processes than with saving a few bucks. The manager at Mini Metalfab reasons that the sheet metal suppliers are relatively safe from hyper-cost competition, in this case losing business by being underbid, because the real opportunities for cost reduction are in the high-ticket parts:

> It depends I think a lot on the critical nature of the part. There may be some parts that we're making that we wouldn't want to interrupt that flow to take a chance on saving a few dollars. I think if you look at building a truck, that the sheet metal probably is the low end of the cost. When you're looking at engines and tires and transmissions and electrical, when you get down to cutting, forming and welding metal, that's not something that you normally look at and say,

"I can take a lot of cost out of this," because there's usually not a lot of cost, a lot of extra built into it. Nobody comes in with huge margins.

Although the foregoing examples all refer to embeddedness around complex parts, I spoke with suppliers of more basic products that maintain long-term relations with customers and experience relatively muted competitive pressures. For example, Tubefab supplies relatively simple mufflers yet does not face a hypercompetitive environment. The plant manager indicated that they "been doing business" with one key customer "for 60 years." In both cases there are reasons why suppliers may be shielded from being underbid by a cost competitor. For complex products, there are asset specificities and sunk engineering costs. For simpler parts, achieving ball-park costs with superior quality and delivery may be sufficient.

On the latter point, customer-supplier relations are often multiplex, even within individual relationships between two firms, being assessed simultaneously on different levels such that at any one level pressures are not exacting. A good relationship with the right people at a key customer, for example, perhaps gained through bending over backwards to offer service to that customer, can shield suppliers from pure cost competition. The president at Precision Metalfab explains how he has forged good relationships with senior management at a key customer based on particular logistical services his firm can offer that may simply be overlooked by lower-level purchasing agents looking strictly at cost. With their strategic alliance at a key customer:

I can call them up, I can call their VP of Procurement, and he will almost, unless he's not around, will call back within an hour or two. And, you know I mean, we're having discussions about important things, I think, relating to how we're working together. . . . [In contrast,] some won't listen, some are buyers that frankly are lower level purchasing people that are paid to get parts in the door, and they're valued in their jobs based on the absolute, you know, hard cost dollar, what we pay. And if that happens and they can get it for a nickel less, they're going to get it for a nickel less . . .

Levels of expectation and aspiration thus vary across individuals and organizations, opening up some wiggle room for variation in supplier performance. Even where managers have high aspiration levels, however, the sheer complexity of supply management can lead to satisficing behavior. For example, a purchasing manager at another multinational prime contractor explains how the organization's attempts at tiering their supply base, supposed to simplify the process, have increased complexity and problems.

> The issue that we run into is that we find a supplier that's acceptable to us and then we try to, we work with that supplier and they work with our other suppliers, and it gets, it becomes a, in some cases it becomes pretty much a mess. But it's because, in a lot of cases I mean for us, for instance a good example is like with our chroming suppliers, you know where we've got very high specifications for our chrome. So when we do find a chrome supplier that can meet our standards, you know, any supplier that we have that, you know, needs parts that are chromed, want to glob onto that supplier because they know that they're acceptable to [our organization]. So then that becomes a big tiering nightmare.

Such complexity abounds in supply chain management, and manufacturing management more generally, often leading all-too-human managers to satisfice, particularly when, as shortcuts have to be taken, short-term profit considerations trump longer-term efficiency and capability considerations.

Conclusion

In this chapter I presented an overview of the American manufacturing field in the 2000s. I began with a historical sketch of the transition from a fordist field to a postfordist field. Whereas the fordist logic of production was unitary—scientific management was universally seen by managers as a core element of mass production—in the postfordist era where there is a premium on employee involvement, managers having discrete choices regarding their core production model and their approach to training and worker participation.

After providing an overview of my study, I demonstrated that lean has been deeply institutionalized in the field. Companies, consultants, associations, and state agencies have all converged on a well-specified model of lean production—the House of Lean—which specifies a set of complementary practices in detail and is widely reproduced throughout the field.

I then argued that the postfordist field has been institutionalized in a way that permits substantial variation in organizational performance. Consistent with the theory of permissive competition developed in Chapter 3, I presented statistics showing that the field consists of a small number of highly efficient firms and a large number of relatively inefficient firms. This was followed by a qualitative analysis of how the field is structured by networked supply chains. I demonstrated that within these supply networks there is satisficing on both sides of the relation.

Within multinational prime contractors, management is divided regarding short-term versus long-term strategies in supply chain management. I presented evidence on how factional conflict and departmental conflict within large prime contractors contribute to organizational satisficing on both sides of the customer-supplier relation. A short-termist approach in supply chain management increases competitive pressure on suppliers but such competition is destructive insofar as it harms the overall capability and flexibility of the supply chain. And I presented further data on how, within this contradictory context, embeddedness and complexity in supply networks attenuate competitive pressures on suppliers.

5

A Typology of Approaches to Lean Production

As we saw in Chapter 4, in the American manufacturing field companies, consultants, associations, and state agencies have converged around a well-specified model of best practice, called the House of Lean (Figure 4.2). The House of Lean is widely understood as a package of complementary practices, which only produces world-class performance when implemented as a package, and is applicable across a range of sectoral, organizational, and technological contexts. Best practice for teamwork and worker empowerment is widely understood to include substantive participation in problem solving and decision making. However, we also saw that the field is institutionalized in such a way as to permit substantial variation in organizational performance. Of the twenty-three component suppliers I observed, only one had not adopted lean in any meaningful way. The other twenty-two suppliers had all implemented lean with serious technical intent, though with varying degrees of thoroughness and commitment to the dominant logics of best practice.

In this chapter I present descriptive findings showing that while some factories fully adopted one or both of the dominant logics (the full House of Lean and substantive worker empowerment), others adopted them partially, implementing the most basic elements but not the more advanced, difficult practices.[1] The result is four different approaches to lean, which I suggest are stable types. After developing and presenting the typology of four lean regimes, I present an exemplar case of each type, along with some indication of their performance on key metrics.

Comparing organizational performance is far from straightforward, for three reasons. First, as we saw in Chapter 4, factories can achieve good quality and delivery performance by adding inspectors and holding inventory but not being very lean in terms of quality-at-the-source, low

[1] This chapter draws on Vidal (2017) but also includes a substantial amount of new, unpublished empirical material.

Management Divided. Matt Vidal, Oxford University Press. © Matt Vidal (2022).
DOI: 10.1093/oso/9780198795278.003.0005

inventory, or workflow. Likewise, workers are generally interested in producing high-quality output and often engage in quality control efforts against management practices that harm quality, such as emphasizing output maximization and throughput (Forrant 2000). Quality may thus be high due to worker initiative, while managers can realize cost reductions and static efficiency with a combination of lean tools and traditional approaches, such as maximizing output to gain economies of scale. Yet leaner companies are more dynamically efficient, capable of continuous improvement and organization learning.

Second, there were variations on how long each company had been doing lean and how far along they were in restructuring to realize the lean transformation management had envisioned. This was particularly the case with some of the eight organizations whose management had particularly high aspiration levels and was working toward a thorough transformation to adopt the full House of Lean with widespread, substantive empowerment of their workforce. In these eight companies there was variation on the extent to which this had been realized, with some having realized thorough transformations and others who were working methodically and systematically toward this goal but in relatively early stages.

In the other fourteen cases, as I will demonstrate in this and the following chapters, many managers had ruled out such thorough transformations, opting instead for more limited and selective adoption of lean practices. The managers in these organizations had lower aspiration levels and, as such, are more susceptible to the powerful inertial forces that stabilize routines and engender resistance to change. As discussed in Chapter 3, learning is typically informal and based on incremental adaptation to experience, which generally leads to the stabilization of routines and hence habitual behavior. Commitment to existing interpretive frames tends to stabilize aspirations and engender resistance to change. And managers have competing priorities and multiple demands on their time, making it difficult to find time for upgrading.

Finally, more prosaically, it was difficult for me to get hard data from my informants. I asked for and was typically promised that quantitative performance metrics would be sent to me after the interview, but only one manager followed through. This is entirely understandable because these managers were busy and preoccupied with running their businesses. I was lucky to get any time from them. In most cases, I only received managers' narrative accounts of their performance metrics. However, I have no reason to doubt their veracity. While one or two managers appeared to be giving me the public-relations version of their experience, in the vast majority of cases the managers freely disclosed to me various problems and shortcomings in their organizations, and by all appearances were candid in their discussions.

What I intend to do in this chapter is provide some evidence that the least lean type—lean enough—generates significant performance improvements over traditional fordism, while the leanest and most complementary type—learning lean—achieves better performance on key metrics. But my core argument is that the learning lean regime is far more dynamically efficient than the other three types, based on superior capabilities that institutionalize learning routines so that continuous improvement is truly continuous (Adler et al. 1999; Winter 2000). As will be elaborated in more detail below and in the following chapters, however, institutionalizing routines for true continuous improvement requires a specific configuration of practices that are exceptionally difficult to implement and maintain. I present qualitative evidence to support this argument in this and the next four chapters. Subsequent chapters make this case while explaining the variation I present in this chapter.

Dominant Logics and Deviant Approaches

Chapter 3 discussed two ways in which managers may deviate from the dominant institutional logic of best practice. First, it may be blended with a former dominant logic of best practice to produce hybrid practice. This is a top-down process emanating from conflicting institutional logics in the field, where managers continue to be influenced by old logics of best practice. Second, managers with moderate aspiration levels will settle for good enough, opting for partial rather than full adoption of best practice. This is a bottom-up process in which partial adoption of best practice produces relative performance improvements that satisfy the manger's aspirations.

I call the dominant institutional logic of work organization in the postfordist field *lean-as-system*, which consists of the entire package of principles and practices from the House of Lean (Figure 4.2). The factories that adopted the lean-as-system approach adopted all or nearly all of the practices from the House of Lean, including the most advanced practices regarding continuous improvement in plant layout. There are two distinguishing features of this approach. First, management engages in frequent and sophisticated use of value-stream mapping (VSM) throughout the factory. Second, management implements true continuous flow: a pull system in which production is organized in a product-focused layout (typically a cell), driven by customer demand via a *kanban* signal that authorizes single-piece or small-batch flow production through a complete sequence of processing steps, with parts also supplied via *kanban* (again throughout the factory). These are the most advanced and difficult practices to implement and institutionalize within an organization, but they provide the foundation for distinct, robust capabilities that are necessary for continuous improvement and organizational learning. Eleven of the twenty-two factories adopted a lean-as-system approach.

The remaining eleven factories adopted what I call the *lean-as-toolbox* approach. This approach may result from management satisficing or from blending the fordist logic with the lean logic, for example by adhering to fordist principles of output maximization (versus the lean principle of just-in-time). While all eleven of these factories did some sort of value-stream mapping to reorganize at least some of their production from a traditional, functional basis into a product-focused basis, this was typically a single, major reorganization based on a one-off mapping exercise. In no case was value-stream mapping used regularly, on an ongoing basis, as in the lean-as-system approach. Further, factories doing lean-as-toolbox typically used a rather crude approach to process mapping and did so only for a portion of their overall production process.

These 11 factories adopted most or all of the basic practices. Nine of them adopted batch reduction, quick changeover, 5S system, quality at source (self-checking, error proofing), visual management, point of use storage (POUS), total productive maintenance (TPM), and standardized work. As explained in more detail below, two factories, Hydraulic Systems and LV Gaskets, did not implement standard work instructions but did implement the other basic lean practices just listed. The distinguishing feature of the lean-as-toolbox approach is that value-stream mapping is *not* used on a regular basis and—although there may be improved flow and cellular-type structures—there is no true continuous flow controlled via *kanban*. As I will show in detail in Chapters 6 and 7, implementing true continuous flow with *kanban* is very difficult and requires high management aspirations.

The manager from Tubefab expresses the lean-as-toolbox logic, arguing that he would rather add additional lead time into the system—a cardinal sin among lean gurus—than attempt to work on quick changeovers and value-stream mapping to get a true pull system working with *kanban* control and minimal inventory: "In the seminars and things I've sat in on where they talk about *kanbans*, it is a true pull system but their inventory levels at every stage in the system are so high that . . . I mean when we looked at pull systems for different things, and unless your reaction time is so low, you end up with more things sitting in the system than you would if you just added a week into lead time." I return to the Tubefab case in Chapter 9 compare their approach in depth with the approach of Second Tier Specialist, who adopted a lean-as-system approach: "Do what needs to be done to get the orders out, don't make extra inventory unless you absolutely need it, because you can't replenish those particular parts within the lead times you need to get your product to your customer."

I call the dominant logic of labor valorization in the postfordist field *substantive empowerment.* It entails cross training in broad skillsets (multiskilling) and devolution of problem-solving and decision-making responsibility. Multiskilling includes cross training in enlarged (horizontally expanded) tasksets and enriched (vertically expanded) responsibilities. Substantive empowerment can be post-taylorist, allowing individual or team autonomy (e.g. self-directed teams) or neotaylorist, with high levels of process and task standardization (hence limited individual autonomy) but worker participation in group problem solving and decision making. The latter is the form necessarily adopted under the lean-as-system approach, which emphasizes standardization as a basis for process control and organizational learning. While self-directed teams are allowed discretion over work methods and task execution, under lean the "collective autonomy" of group decision making is limited to task and process design, with methods and task execution prescribed by work standards and process design decisions subordinated to organization-level process standardization (Klein 1991: 333).

The alternative approach is a logic I call *nominal empowerment*, a form of *consultative neotaylorism*, which blends elements of classical taylorism (standardized work and using workers primarily for manual labor) with elements of substantive empowerment (job rotation and asking workers to contribute ideas but without participation in problem solving or decision making) (Vidal 2007: 234). Consultative neotaylorism may take the form of true multiskilling but the main form it takes in my sample is multitasking: rotation among narrow, simple tasks.

Throughout this book, I generally use the term *substantive empowerment* as a shorthand for substantive neotaylorist empowerment, which is the main form of empowerment found in my qualitative sample. In two cases (Hydraulic Systems and LV Gaskets), managers prioritized individual autonomy over neotaylorist standardization. In these cases, the regime is one of substantive post-taylorist empowerment. But for simplicity I generally use the term substantive empowerment for both neo- and post-taylorist regimes, explicitly noting when it involves individual autonomy. I generally use the term *nominal empowerment* to refer to consultative neotaylorism (i.e. multiskilling with consultative participation). Management in ten of the factories had implemented or were systematically working on implementing substantive empowerment throughout their workforce, including wide engagement in problem solving and decision making. Eight adopted the neotaylorist form of collective autonomy and two (Hydraulic Systems and LV Gaskets) adopted high levels of individual autonomy. In the other twelve factories, management adopted nominal empowerment for all or the vast majority of their production workforce.

My data show that although there are complementarities to be gained by fully adopting both best practices, the decision about whether to fully adopt one can be made independently of the decision about whether to fully adopt the other. As reflected in Figure 5.1, all four combinations are viable: a manager could decide first to adopt either lean-as-system or lean-as-toolbox, and, in either case, adopt substantive or consultative participation. Likewise, a manager could decide first to adopt either substantive or consultative participation and, in either case, adopt lean-as-system or lean-as-toolbox.

Although the decision regarding each logic can be made independently, there are three situations in which an interaction effect is produced. First, a regime of substantive empowerment with collective worker autonomy greatly facilities lean-as-system because empowered workers can drive continuous improvement. This is illustrated clearly in the cases of Industrial Pumps (discussed in depth in Chapter 8) and Second Tier Specialist (discussed in depth in Chapter 9). In both cases, the managers explicitly discuss how they realized from experience that implementing true continuous flow is exceptionally difficult without substantively empowered workers. It also illustrated negatively in the case of Metalfab Plus (discussed in depth in Chapter 8), where the plant manager expresses a taylorist approach to valorization, which reinforces satisficing with a lean-as-toolbox approach.

Second, a regime of consultative participation means the fragility of lean-as-system must be diligently managed by management rather than empowered workers. This configuration is the lean-standardization type, which

I argue below, is neither complementary nor coherent—a proposition consistent with my (admittedly non-representative) sample containing only three such regimes out of twenty-two factories. The cases of Custom Blinds and Deep Stampings are discussed in depth in Chapter 8. Finally, a regime of individual autonomy will conflict with standardization requirements of lean-as-system, which occurs in the autonomous lean type. Again, below I argue this type is neither complementary nor coherent, which is consistent with my sample including only two such types. Both cases (LV Gaskets and Hydraulic Systems) are discussed in depth in Chapter 9.

A Typology of Lean Production Approaches

The four approaches along the two dimensions combine to produce a typology of four lean production regimes. Figure 5.1 presents this typology. Table 5.1 provides basic details on the plants within each type.

The most complementary regime is what I call the *high-involvement lean* regime: lean-as-system with substantive participation. This regime is what advocates have in mind when they promote lean; it is both fragile and difficult to institutionalize inside an organization, but when done correctly should generate truly world class performance. In this approach, a system of true continuous flow is controlled by *kanban* and managed by workers; if there is a problem at one point in the system, the entire cell or line shuts down, and production workers are empowered to engage in problem solving and decision making to find and fix the root cause. Continuous flow and frequent value-stream mapping provide the technical basis for systematic continuous improvement, while substantive participation provides the most propitious basis for organizational learning because workers gain critical information from their everyday experience on the shopfloor and because a culture of substantive participation leads to worker-driven continuous improvement. The combination of continuous flow, substantive empowerment, and regular value-stream mapping constitutes a learning

	LEAN-AS-SYSTEM	LEAN-AS-TOOLBOX
SUBSTANTIVE EMPOWERMENT	High-involvement lean	Autonomous lean
NOMINAL EMPOWERMENT	Lean standardization	Lean enough

Fig. 5.1 A typology of lean production regimes

Table 5.1 Plant characteristics and approaches to production

Plants	Plant characteristics					Approach to production	
	Main products	Processes	Ownership	Prod. Empl.	Union	Labor control	Work organization
High-Involvement lean							
1. Custom Seats	Leather and vinyl seats	Sewing, upholstery, assembly	Public, branch plant	220	Yes	Substantive participation	Lean-as-system
2. Designer Railings	Handrail systems and parts	Fabrication, assembly	Private, branch	90	No	Substantive participation	Lean-as-system
3. Industrial Pumps	Industrial pumps	Machining, assembly	German parent	35	No	Substantive participation	Lean-as-system
4. Inspired Castings	Steel castings	Investment casting	Private, branch plant	500	No	Substantive participation	Lean-as-system
5. Mini Metalfab	Metal fabrications	Fabrication, assembly	Private, independent	27	No	Substantive participation	Lean-as-system
6. Mini OE	Wire wheels/ Brushes	Assembly	German parent	105	Yes	Substantive participation	Lean-as-system
7. Performance Brakes	Hydraulic disc brakes	Machining, assembly	Private, branch plant	250	Yes	Substantive participation	Lean-as-system
8. Second Tier Specialist	Industrial cylinders	Machining, assembly	Public, branch plant	80	Yes	Substantive participation	Lean-as-system
Lean standardization							
1. Custom Blinds	Blinds, components	Plastics molding & extrusion, stamping, assembly	Private, branch	640	No	Consultative participation	Lean-as-system

Table 5.1 *Continued*

Plants	Plant characteristics					Approach to production	
	Main products	Processes	Ownership	Prod. Empl.	Union	Labor control	Work organization
2. Deep Stampings	Deep draw stampings	Stamping, secondary ops, assembly	Public, branch plant	300	No	Consultative participation	Lean-as-system
3. Lost-Foam Castings	Aluminum castings	Die and investment casting	Public, branch plant	180	Yes	Consultative participation	Lean-as-system
Autonomous Lean							
1. Hydraulic Systems	Hydraulic systems	Machining, fabrication, assembly	Private, branch plant	90	Yes	Substantive participation	Lean-as-toolbox
2. LV Gaskets	Engine gaskets	Fabrication, assembly	Public, branch plant	300	No	Substantive participation	Lean-as-toolbox
Lean enough							
1. Complex Iron Castings	Iron castings	Sand casting	Private, independent	120	Yes	Consultative participation	Lean-as-toolbox
2. Major Castings	Aluminum castings	Die casting	Public, branch plant	650	No	Consultative participation	Lean-as-toolbox
3. Metalfab Plus	Metal fabrications	Fabrication, stamping, assembly, machining	ESOP, independent	450	No	Consultative participation	Lean-as-toolbox
4. Plastic Containers	Plastic containers	Thermoforming	Private, independent	220	No	Consultative participation	Lean-as-toolbox
5. Precision Metalfab	Metal fabrications	Fabrication, assembly	Private, independent	110	No	Consultative participation	Lean-as-toolbox

Table 5.1 *Continued*

Plants	Plant characteristics					Approach to production	
	Main products	Processes	Ownership	Prod. Empl.	Union	Labor control	Work organization
6. Spindles & Machining	Spindles, hubs	Machining, assembly	Private, independent	30	No	Consultative participation	Lean-as-toolbox
7. Tiny Plastic Parts	Plastic parts	Injection Molding	Private, branch plant	400	No	Consultative participation	Lean-as-toolbox
8. Tubefab	Mufflers, air filters	Stamping, assembly	Public, branch plant	150	No	Consultative participation	Lean-as-toolbox
9. Zinc Castings	Zinc castings	Die casting	Private, branch plant	32	Yes	Consultative participation	Lean-as-toolbox

Note: Factories coded "lean-as-toolbox" adopted or were working on implementing some combination of the following practices: batch reduction, quick changeover, 5S and standardization, quality at the source and TPM, point-of-use storage, and visual management, with infrequent use of value-stream mapping. Factories coded "lean-as-system" adopted or were working on implementing all of the foregoing practices along with demand-driven continuous flow (pull/*kanban*) and frequent use of value-stream mapping.

routine package. Eight of the twenty-two factories I observed adopted a high-involvement lean regime (Table 5.1).

At the opposite end of the spectrum is the *lean-enough* regime, which results where management adopts lean-as-toolbox with consultative participation. I characterize this regime as lean enough because the plants I observed adopting this regime experienced substantial performance improvements that satisfied both their own management and their industrial customers. While lean-enough regimes are not complementary in the sense that consultative participation does not improve the performance of lean-as-toolbox or vice versa, this regime does have some degree of coherence insofar as there are no incompatibilities between the two logics. Nine factories I observed adopted lean-enough regimes (Table 5.1).

The remaining two regimes are neither complimentary nor coherent. A *lean-standardization* regime obtains where managers adopt lean-as-system with consultative participation. These plants focus on using lean tools to standardize processes throughout the plant, going beyond inventory and batch size reduction to engage more systematically in value-stream mapping to realize some degree of ongoing improvement in workflow and process standards. But because managers have adopted consultative participation, continuous improvement is entirely management-driven. Three factories I observed implemented lean-standardization regimes.

In the interests of transparency, I note that it was difficult for me to decide whether to code Deep Stampings as a lean-standardization (lean-as-system) or lean-enough (lean-as-toolbox) approach based on my one interview there, which was one of my first interviews, in which I was focused on worker participation and didn't have a sufficiently deep understanding of lean that would have motivated me to probe more deeply about their use of value-stream mapping, *kanban*, and pull production. I opted to code it as lean standardization. I discuss Stampings in depth in Chapter 8, where I note that further probing may reveal it to be a lean-enough approach, given that there are open questions about the frequency with which they use value-stream mapping and the extent to which they have implemented or plan to implement demand-driven continuous flow. I am surer about the other two lean-standardization cases. And I am confident that the primary criteria for differentiating a lean-as-system approach from a lean-as-toolbox approach—whether an organization uses value-stream mapping frequently or infrequently and whether they have adopted or are attempting to implement demand-driven, continuous-flow production—is theoretically sound.

As discussed below in the case of Custom Blinds, in a lean-standardization approach management takes a systematic and frequent approach to value-stream mapping, with a goal of implementing continuous flow production. This differentiates them from lean-enough approaches. However, all three of the cases I coded as lean standardization do not use value-stream mapping to the extent that the high-involvement lean factories did, suggesting that a systematic culture of substantive participation greatly facilitates the implementation of a highly interdependent and fragile lean system.

However, because it is based on a logic of lean-as-system, lean standardization is the nearest of the other types to high-involvement lean in terms of learning capability. Indeed, if management is determined enough, it can implement true continuous flow and maintain systematic continuous improvement with nominal empowerment. My understanding of the Toyota Production System suggests it is a lean-standardization regime that achieves the capabilities of a learning lean regime: Workers are not substantively empowered, but management is sufficiently skilled and determined, and shopfloor workers are sufficiently motivated to regularly contribute ideas and solve problems, that true continuous flow and continuous improvement are achieved. With sufficient skill and determination by management plus a culture of continuous improvement among a nominally empowered workforce, a lean-standardization approach thus approximates a learning lean approach. The three lean-standardization regimes I observed did not report engaging in routinized continuous improvement. I discuss these regimes more in Chapter 8.

An *autonomous lean* regime obtains where management adopts lean-as-toolbox and a form of substantive participation that is at the high end of individual worker autonomy. High levels of individual autonomy limit the ability to implement high levels of process standardization necessary for lean-as-system, again as discussed further in Chapters 8 and 9. Two factories I observed adopted an *autonomous lean* regime.

Lean-standardization and autonomous lean regimes are neither complementary nor coherent configurations because there is not a good fit between the two approaches. The lean-standardization approach includes an attempt to implement lean-as-system, but under consultative participation it is difficult to maintain true continuous improvement because it must be driven by managers. With the autonomous lean approach it is difficult to standardize process improvements across the factory, which is a core source of lean efficiency.

Learning Lean

An exemplar of the learning lean type is Second Tier Specialist, a low-volume producer that did $15 million in sales in 2001, supplying cylinders to first tiers such as Tower Automotive and prime contractors outside auto, heavily in the food processing and machine press industries. About 50% of their products are custom make-to-order and about 50% come from previously made designs. They began implementing lean when a new plant manager was brought in. Within three years they converted the entire factory to three cells and are now mostly working on "cultural change." The plant manager has brought in national reps from the International Association of Machinists union, along with a pro-labor workforce intermediary called the Wisconsin Regional Training Partnership to help implement a labor-management partnership as one mechanism for substantively empowering the workforce. Foremen have been replaced with "cell leaders." They also created an hourly "cell lead" person position for each cell. The cell lead will do scheduling:

> [This frees up the] cell leader's time, to be looking at how do we do training for the employees, how do we do brainstorming, problem-solving analysis, root-cause analysis, those sorts of things, team building, having team meetings that just involve the people out there on the factory floor. Instead of chasing all the jobs, like the cell leaders currently do, there's other people in the cell that will be doing that.

Cylinder management is noteworthy for its relatively systematic and long-term approach to restructuring: "It's going to be a long time to actually get into peer pressure types of issues with the factory floor employees exerting that pressure on each other. That's a real long-term challenge. We won't get there for 3 or 4 years. However, within the next year you'll really see the scheduling of jobs done by shop floor employees."[2]

[2] It has been widely noted in the literature that such peer pressure can lead to forms of workforce discipline that are highly effective and more difficult to resist than bureaucratic control (Barker 1993, 1999; Dassbach 1996; Delbridge 2003; Graham 1995; Kenney and Florida 1993) Tony Smith (2000)

The cells are highly lean, with all of the product routing and production control via *kanban*. To get their cellular flow and *kanban* systems set up and work out the many kinks, they had to go through several rounds of *kaizen* events, using expertise the plant manager gained from his previous employer along with additional help from their parent company. Although there is still resistance and reticence within the workforce, they continue working on having direct workers take on new responsibilities—fixturing adjustments, setup reduction, resizing *kanbans*, TPM, problem solving, root-cause analysis—through *kaizen* events, which are often multiple-day events and still used on a regular basis. The manufacturing engineer, who used to be involved in supervision but now resides on the shop floor, is now engaged in "coaching the cell members to provide their own input on what we need to do from a fixturing standpoint. And what that cell needs to spend money on. He will work with each cell so the people in the cell start making some of those decisions." Cell leaders are being trained to run *kaizen* events. On-time delivery improved from 27% to the 80-plus% in the first two years. Lead time (purchase order to ship) has been reduced on two common cylinders from eighteen days to eight and five, respectively.

Here I briefly provide a few more examples of the stated performance in factories I have coded as learning lean. Industrial Pumps has gone "from about 15 pumps a day to about 22 now. And with the same 35 guys working on our shop floor doing that same work, but going from 40% on-time to almost 90%." On lead time, Industrial Pumps was "more of a two to four-week company, and now we're more of a three to four-day company to ship a pump, and we can respond in a day without really throwing our company upside down." At Designer Railings, the plant manager said they have gotten their lead times down from months to under five days for a key customer. He went on to explain that:

> That's been in a phenomenally successful lean manufacturing operation. I have less successful ones, but still successful. I've got one that's coming up that has been very successful initially, and I think has the opportunity to double our productivity, if we execute on it, which we will. So we've made a lot of little islands of: this works better, this works better, this works better.

noted that within lean systems, the burden of slow or absent workers is felt by fellow workers, which may lead to coworkers exerting peer pressure to discipline each other, with intra-worker conflict displacing labor-management conflict. However, this was not a theme that emerged in my interviews with workers.

In the same cell "we're down at six [defect] parts per million, which I think is a six sigma number that anybody would be really happy with over a 13-month period."

Another key lean metric is inventory turns, which measures how quickly a company goes through its inventory, that is, how efficiently a plant manages its inventory (higher being better). At Custom Seats, the plant manager said that "We've taken inventory turns up every year. When I started here in '98, they were around six. They're up to about 18 to 21 right now." He went on to explain that "it's gone up about three to five turns a year every year, since the cellularization effort." On delivery for a major customer, he noted that "prior to the going into a cellular process back in the mid-'90s . . . our best performance on delivery . . . was 92%. . . . And since making those changes . . . we've been, you know, 99.7 plus percent on-time delivery for them for years."

Lean Enough

An exemplar of the lean-enough type is Metalfab Plus, a metal fabricator making parts such as cabinets and chasses, linkages, and shifters for customers including John Deere, Mercury Marine, and Siemens. After losing a major customer to Chinese suppliers in the 1990s, they eventually settled at $40 million annual sales and 450 employees, and are now essentially a job shop doing mostly make-to-order work. Workers are organized into nominal teams based around "departments or areas," but they only meet quarterly at most. Management wants to eventually have the teams meet at least once per week, but they do not have any vision of more extensive employee involvement. They currently do informal job rotation and have plans to set up a formal cross training program.

The plant management did a one-time, major reorganization of the factory to improve workflow, which they now consider "90 percent done." The plant manager had some background in lean, which was their basis for the relayout, and they did not bring in any other help, neither customers nor consultants, as he proudly stated: "No consultants. We have not brought consultants into this business at all." They have some quasi-cells, with lasers feeding work to press brakes and then welding, but there are also remain functional areas for stamping, machining, and welding. Only 5–10% of their products are on a *kanban* system, and there are no plans to expand this. They are not prioritizing batch reduction:

> Once you get the setup right, you know, we'll try to run based on forecasts, and willing to invest in the inventory rather than reset the press. . . . Well, I'm not going to make two at a time. I may make three months' worth of parts and get the setup right and then make them, and then I know I've got the parts right. And then wait until the next three months and set it up and run it again.

The managers at Metalfab Plus claimed their performance metrics have been systematically improving across the board—cost, quality, delivery—but I was not able to get any hard numbers. They have been getting increased business from key customers and gaining new customers. However, I did have the opportunity to talk with some engineers from the Wisconsin Manufacturing Extension Partnership, who went into Metalfab Plus after a major industrial customer picked them for a supplier development project setting up a cell for a product family. The lead engineer confirmed my own observations. As discussed in depth in Chapter 9, Metalfab had recently purchased a large laser cutter to add capacity. According to my field notes from that meeting I observed, the engineer's assessment was:

> They don't have any analysis of what the best flow is going to be, what is a good balance between this [the new laser] and other machines. They're going to set up some [press] brakes and CNC turret presses behind it, but they're just doing it on hunches. They're shooting from the hip. They said they can move them later, but this is doing things twice when they don't need to be.

At Metalfab Plus plant management stated that inventory "turns have been in the range of 10 to 12," up from around five a few years ago (compared with 18–21 turns for the learning lean Custom Seats). Their lean-enough changes such as product-focused layout, standardization, and batch reduction are combined with holding extra inventory to respond quickly and running larger production runs than demanded by the market. With this regime, they achieved significant performance improvements and were gaining new business:

> We've recently landed Siemens Medical, for their oncology and ultrasound equipment, all their work. We've landed . . . Federal Signal, to do a mechanism for some of their utility vehicles. We've landed work with a company called Zantrax that makes the control cabinets for the GE Windpower Systems.

The manager Tubefab, another lean-enough regime, was among the few managers that did provide me with data from his factory, which confirmed what he told me. Again, they were heavily focused on maintaining business with key customers:

> But for the most part we get, with John Deere for example, their highest quality rating, or level of quality expectation is about 400 parts per million on our class of part. We generally run on Deere about 200 parts per million. So we're well within their quality limits. On quality we are, on a parts per million basis, we are always at the high end of vendor expectations.

According to the internal metrics he provided me, parts per million (PPM) rejects went from 1666 three years ago and 4410 two years ago to just 112 last year. On-time delivery, another key metric for customers, has gone from 89% three years ago and 94% two years ago to 98% last year. Finally, inventory turns improved appreciably from 4.35 three years ago and 4.06 two years ago to 7.73 (but still less than half of what Custom Seats achieved).

Lean Standardization

The lean-standardization type is exemplified by Custom Blinds, which sells both brand-name products and supplies components to other assembly plants owned by its parent and to other prime contractors. They do very high-volume plastic parts and mid- to low-volume in assembly of custom blinds, making every part that goes into the final assembly of various types of blinds, including plastic and fabric blinds. Being such a vertically integrated factory, they have over a dozen departments, including metal stamping, injection molding, extrusion, assembly, maintenance, and then a number of product-focused cells. The parent company has annual sales of $2.3 billion and 18,000 employees, with about 640 production workers at this plant.

With the help of their parent company they have been working on cells, continuous-flow and pull systems via value-stream mapping for two full years. But they are doing this in a very management-driven manner: "We have our own systems group here too. . . . We have some very creative people up there . . . they look at something and they'll say, 'Well, how can we make it better.'" The plant manager told me, during a plant tour which was not recorded, that they had done a lot of value-stream mapping, but basically once they get a new process working well, they stick to it and don't further alter it. Because they only do consultative participation, they are not engaging in high levels of continuous improvement and are not able to push in that direction.

Blinds has an elaborate team system and consistently attempts to get input from workers, but it is all consultative. There is a "TQM Leadership Steering Committee," and "Quality Leadership Teams" for manufacturing, safety, quality, and 5S/Visual workplace. Below these higher-level teams are eleven Quality Assurance Teams that are assigned to departments. There are opportunities for front-line workers to contribute ideas through these various offline team activities although these are organized hierarchically, with many layers of management. Within departments they have managers, engineers, supervisors, lead people (management), and workers. While high-involvement lean regimes have online teams based in cells, Blinds does not have this type of online team.

Autonomous Lean

The autonomous lean type is exemplified by Hydraulic Systems, which, like Second Tier Specialist, is a low-volume union job shop that primarily does machining and assembly, making hydraulic presses for customers like Deere, Volvo, and GM. Sales at this plant were around $35 million in 2003, with around ninety production employees. The workforce consists of highly skilled workers with a lot of craft pride. The plant manager has allowed and encouraged a high level of individual and group autonomy. While they don't do any formal, scheduled job rotation, the workers are all multiskilled and generally work outside their job classifications whenever necessary. The workers take a lot of ownership of the factory, doing whatever work needs to be done. Indeed, it has been such a non-issue that management has not even had to consider collapsing the job classifications (in contrast to others, such as Second Tier Specialist, who went from over fifty job classifications to a small number of flexible classifications). In the plant manager's words, "about everybody wears three hats." There are a lot of ad hoc offline teams but no formal online teams, although the workers informally consider themselves to be in teams.

Hydraulic Systems has cellular-type organization for product families, and they do schedule production based on customer demand, but continue to schedule all the work centers based on forecasts. As the plant manager explains:

> It will be a customer order will trigger. We don't have a *kanban*, per se. It's just the customer order . . . You know when we've got an MRP [material requirements planning system] and that, when they sell that pump or that valve or whatever, that gets loaded, they explode the bill of material, that will have a ship date. So then it goes from there and it goes back: these are parts I need and when I need them, and it schedules every work center they need.

Thus, while customer orders trigger production, they still effectively have "a push system, but we'll order materials and even release a certain number of the orders based on a forecast." This is largely because he wants to allow the operators significant levels of individual and group autonomy. Indeed, because they have been very successful with this system, the plant manager sees no reason to increase standardization.

Toward an Explanation of Variation in Lean Production Regimes

As we saw in Chapter 2, a common explanation for variation in organizational form is that managers are maximizing fit with their organizational context—and that there is no one best way. However, in Chapter 4 I showed that both advocates and practitioners see the House of Lean as best practice, being widely applicable across organizational and technical contexts. I now examine whether the technical or structural characteristics of organizations in my sample provide any leverage on explaining the variation I found.

Table 5.1 presents the plants, ordered by type of lean, along with key characteristics. Within my qualitative sample, there is wide variation in *firm size* within each of the polar types—high-involvement lean and lean enough—each having small and large firms. *Plant technology* also varies broadly within the polar types, with each including assembly, expandable mold (investment and sand) casting; machining; and metal fabrication. This suggests these characteristics provide little explanatory leverage on variations in lean regimes. There are three technologies that are only represented in the lean-enough type: thermoforming, plastic injection molding, and die (non-expandable mold) casting. However, the reason the factories using these technologies are in the lean-enough category concerns the simplicity of their products, not the technology as such.

Plants with simple products that can be produced in a single operation have less need for a comprehensive package of complementary lean practices, in particular, for lean workflow. For example, Plastic Containers makes simple containers using a single thermoforming press: plastic roll is fed in, heated up, formed in a mold, and trimmed, pumping out products ready for packing and shipping. Contrast this with the manufacture of an automotive body panel: the core process is thermoforming, but making a panel can require up to 12 steps or more: Mixing and blending the composite material; making the film; cutting and preparing the film for the press; thermoforming the part; cooling; deflashing; dry guiding; punching; drilling; water jet; bonding; and painting. In the latter case, cellular flow, pull, just-in-time, and continuous improvement are all applicable. In the former case, these lean practices have less applicability.

Ownership structure appears to have some relationship to leanness. Among the learning lean plants all combinations of ownership type are represented (see Table 5.1). However, privately-held, independent plants appear to be overrepresented in the category of lean enough. This is consistent with a broader theme that emerges from my analysis: outside resources, such as that of a parent company or customer or consultant, play an important role in disseminating knowledge and capability.

The most important aspects of the organizational environment seem to be *location in the supply chain* and the *competitiveness of the product market*, which, not coincidentally, are related to each other and to product complexity. Thus, the simplest products to make—"commodity products"—are also in the most competitive markets and at the top of the supply chain. For these products, such as screws or simple plastic parts, there is intense competition and little need to engage in collaborative relations with suppliers. Looking at Table 5.1, these are the same plants as those noted above for product simplicity—the thermoformers, injection molders, and stamping outfits that do little assembly—are among the least lean plants on my typology.

Location in the supply chain, in turn, seems to affect supplier leanness primarily as a function of the influence of large prime contractors, who demand that their upper tier (downstream) suppliers get lean, and in a similar mechanism to that of ownership type, may offer technical knowledge. Thus, many of the subsystems producers are overrepresented in the leanest plants in part because of the more intense pressure, and better knowledge, they receive from the prime contractors. Those further upstream appear to receive less direct pressure, presumably as a function of their distance from the primes.

Ultimately, however, the sources of variation that appear to be most important have to do with the strategic orientation and aspiration levels of management. Although far from having the capabilities of a learning lean plant, in particular with regard to continuous improvement capability, the lean-enough factories are profitable and growing. At the level of specific practices and routines, managers in these plants do not feel intense pressures to adopt world-class lean practices. If my argument is correct that the differences are primarily due to the distinct orientations and aspiration levels of management, that the competitive environment for component suppliers is permissive with regard to internal performance, and that lean-enough regimes are producing output that is satisfactory for their industrial customers, then lean-enough and the other intermediate types are likely to be relatively stable organizational forms.

My argument is that managers use different logics of action, different rationalities, to understand and interpret their situation. Some of the managers embrace the logics of lean-as-system with substantive employee involvement, interpreting their situation through these logics. But other managers continue to be influenced by old logics of best practice. They satisfice, looking for satisfactory solutions to problems as they understand them. Using blended logics, they interpret some existing practices in a positive light, seeing partial modifications to the existing system as good enough.

Conclusion

In this chapter I developed and presented a typology of four approaches to lean production. The most complementary regime is the *high-involvement lean* regime: lean-as-system with substantive participation. This combination of practices provides the foundation for institutionalizing learning routines in the organization, resulting in true continuous improvement. At the opposite end of the spectrum is the *lean-enough* regime: lean-as-toolbox with consultative participation. A lean-enough regime can generate substantial performance improvements, but does not provide the capabilities for dynamic efficiency and organizational learning.

A *lean-standardization* regime results from a combination of lean-as-system with consultative participation. By adopting lean-as-system, this approach may be able to achieve dynamic efficiency and true continuous improvement, but because managers have adopted consultative participation, continuous improvement is entirely management-driven. An *autonomous lean* regime results where management adopts lean-as-toolbox and substantive participation in the form of individual autonomy. The emphasis on individual autonomy limits the process standardization necessary for lean-as-system, again as discussed further in Chapters 8 and 9.

I presented evidence suggesting that the source of the variation is not technical or structural factors associated with different organizational contexts. Firm size and plant technology are all represented within each type of lean, suggesting these characteristics provide little explanatory leverage on variations in lean regimes. The most important aspects of the organizational environment seem to be location in the supply chain, product complexity, and competitiveness of the product market, all of which are related. Factories that make simple products are in highly competitive markets at the top of the supply chain; where the product and process are simple (and hence competition is high), there is less opportunity or need for continuous flow production.

In my analysis, the primary explanation for the variation is the strategic orientation and aspiration levels of management. The theory of satisficing suggests that these types are stable and not transitional. Individuals are typically committed to their existing interpretative frameworks and aspiration levels are generally stable. Chapters 6 and 7 begin the analysis of routine politics of production, focusing on worker views and experiences. Chapters 8 and 9 focus on managers, including their strategic orientations and aspiration levels.

6
Routine Politics of Production: Quality Not Quantity

As we saw in Chapters 1 and 2, a common criticism of lean management is that its performance benefits come not from harnessing the skill and knowledge of workers but from work intensification, particularly in the form of speedup and reduction of downtime (Carter et al. 2011, 2013a; Carter et al. 2013b; Danford 1999; Graham 1995; Parker and Slaughter 1995; Rinehart et al. 1997; Stewart et al. 2009). I suggested that while lean includes practices and tools that can be used to quantitatively intensify work, how it is implemented depends on the orientation of management (and the power of labor); lean can be implemented in a way that prioritizes qualitative improvement in routines over quantitative increases in effort. I also argued it is important to differentiate quantitative from qualitative work intensification, and to consider the subjective experience of intensification, noting that some workers may experience moderate forms of either type of intensification as an improvement in their work situation by reducing boredom and monotony.

Combining the two types of intensification with the two impacts produces four potential outcomes, in addition to the possibility of no intensification. *Negative quantitative intensification* occurs when the work pace has become so fast, or the reduction of downtime so extreme, it makes the work more dangerous or otherwise negatively impacts worker well-being. *Positive quantitative intensification* happens where reductions in downtime are perceived to make the work less boring and the day go faster. *Negative qualitative intensification* occurs when increased intellectual demands make the work more dangerous or otherwise negatively impact worker well-being. *Positive qualitative intensification* is when work has become more intellectually demanding, but the worker perceives this as a welcome challenge, something that relieves boredom and makes the work more interesting.

Management Divided. Matt Vidal, Oxford University Press.
 DOI: 10.1093/oso/9780198795278.003.0006

In this chapter I present the voice of every single worker I interviewed in a supplier factory: fifty-two workers in total, across twelve companies.[1] I found only one worker who complained of negative quantitative intensification and thirty-nine workers who did not experience any work intensification. Among the twelve who experienced intensification that they deemed to have improved their work experience, eight mentioned qualitative intensification, two mentioned quantitative, and two mentioned both. To be sure, my interviews reveal all manner of frustrations among the workers, including some who said more intellectually demanding work would create unwanted stress rather than a welcome challenge. And some workers I interviewed reported complaints by their colleagues about qualitative intensification. But among the qualitative (non-representative) sample of workers I interviewed, workers who preferred positions that did not demand cognitive labor were able to work in such contexts—either because lean practices did not qualitatively intensify their particular job or, in one case, the worker was able to transfer to a position that was not qualitatively intensified under lean.

The point of the present chapter is twofold. First, I present thick description to demonstrate that lean production can be implemented without quantitative or qualitative work intensification, and that some workers experience qualitative intensification as an improvement.

Second, the chapter lays the groundwork for making a more analytical argument, which is developed across this and the following two chapters, hinted at in the title for this chapter: Under routine politics of production, management is not primarily concerned with increasing effort levels (quantity) but with making qualitative changes to routines and operational systems that improve performance (quality). I begin making this point by presenting the views of workers on effort under lean in this chapter, and then develop the argument in the following two chapters. Chapter 7 shows that workers are primarily concerned with defending their existing routines, which they embrace in attempt to make their work meaningful. Chapter 8 presents views from managers to demonstrate that they are concerned with improving routines and systems, not with quantitative intensification.

[1] I interviewed fifty-nine workers, including fifty-two workers from twelve supplier factories, and seven workers from multinational prime contractors. The interviews in the prime contractors focused on supply chain management issues, while the interviews in the suppliers focused on work organization. In this chapter I focus on the workers in the supplier factories.

The present chapter reveals that some workplaces are characterized by overt conflict and struggle, while others are not. Of the twelve factories discussed in this chapter, Second Tier Specialist, Custom Seats, and Hydraulic Systems (all union shops) had intense labor-management conflict. But this was not struggle over effort levels, work intensification, or attempts to establish autonomy. Rather, workplace politics centered around managerial attempts to change routines and worker defense of existing routines, based on competing visions of efficiency. At Designer Railings, the manager said the most problematic source of resistance was first-line supervisors, who were older workers whom he was not able to fire because the firm was family-run and paternalistic, along with a relatively small faction of resistant workers. At the other eight factories, neither management nor labor discussed any overt conflict or struggle.

Methodological and Expositional Considerations

In my early interviews I asked the effort question multiple ways in each interview. After hearing one worker after another say she had not experienced work intensification, and given the limited amount of time I had with each worker, in later interviews I often did not ask directly about effort, instead digging into what *was* on their mind.[2] Effort was simply not a salient issue for the overwhelming majority of workers I spoke with. They expressed other concerns: defending routines to which they had become committed, perceived threats to quality and efficiency by management initiatives, being treated with dignity, pay and incentive systems, and job security.

My interviews are supplemented by direct observation in three of the firms below. At Second Tier Specialist, a union shop, I engaged in direct observation for a total of thirty-eight hours over fifteen months, including 30.5 hours in fifteen Labor-Management Partnership Committee meetings, one hour in a Worker Education Committee Meeting, ninety minutes in a local union membership meeting, and five hours attending a High Performance Work Organization Presentation by the International Association of Machinists. The labor-management partnership was facilitated by the Wisconsin Regional Training Partnership (WRTP), a union-backed workforce intermediary. The plant manager had also formally

[2] I interviewed workers on company time and therefore only asked for thirty minutes per worker, although in some cases worker interviews extended to forty-five minutes or up to an hour.

signed on to the International Association of Machinists (IAM) High Performance Work Organization (HPWO) program, including "Shared decision-making around the vital functions that are critical to the business, its costs, and the processes," "Shared technical and financial information," "Ongoing joint determination of the cost of the design, prototype development, production, and administrative overhead," and "A jointly developed Strategic Business Plan."[3]

At Metalfab Plus, a nonunion shop, I engaged in direct observation for a total of twenty-four hours over sixteen months, including nineteen hours observing a supplier development project, in which a major multinational prime contractor trained them in a value-stream mapping process on a product family, and five hours in a Lean 101 training session along with shopfloor workers.

At Mini OE, a union shop (United Steelworkers), I engaged in direct observation for a total of nine hours over seven months, including eight hours in four Labor-Management Committee meetings (also facilitated by the WRTP) and one hour of participant observation doing a shopfloor training exercise to develop standard work instructions.

In the following I present discussions I had with workers around effort, empowerment, and their main concerns about their work situation. The chapter is organized according to lean type: Five high-involvement lean factories, two autonomous-lean factories, one lean-standardization factory, and four lean-enough factories. Within each type, I start with the earlier interviews, where I directly asked the effort question, and then turn to the later interviews, where I had stopped asking the question directly, instead asking broad questions and following the lead of the interviewees. In most cases there were one or two main issues in each factory that were salient across the individual interviews.

In many cases I present extended, unedited discussions. This provides some transparency on the nature of the data, and helps demonstrate that many workers have complex and sometimes ambivalent attitudes toward their work, managers, and organizations, and that their assessments of their work experience often have little to do with the question of effort or intensity as such.

I summarize the findings in Table 6.1, which is presented at the beginning of the chapter to help guide the reader. Each worker is coded

[3] For a summary of the full program, now apparently defunct, see https://www.goiam.org/uncategorized/hpwo-components/. Last visited on June 30, 2021.

Table 6.1 Work intensification under lean according to 52 workers

	No intensification	Positive intensification		Negative intensification	
		Qualitative—Like the challenge	Quantitative—Makes day go faster	Qualitative—Increases stress	Quantitative—Working too fast or insufficient downtime
Second Tier Specialist					
Machinist (34 years)			X		
Machinist (8 years)		X			
Parts coordinator	X				
Machinist (15 years)	X				
Sweeper & parts washer	X				
Industrial Pumps					
Assembler		X	X		
Assembly supervisor		X			
Machinist	X				
Polisher			X		
Shipping and receiving		X			
Mini OE					
Brush maker (23 years)	X				
Brush maker (25 years)	X				
Machine tech	X				
Lead person	X				
Designer Railings					
Setup press operator	X				
Bender		X			
Gripper	X				

Continued

Table 6.1 *Continued*

	No intensification	Positive intensification		Negative intensification	
		Qualitative—Like the challenge	Quantitative—Makes day go faster	Qualitative—Increases stress	Quantitative—Working too fast or insufficient downtime
Lead person	X				
Maintenance worker	X				
Custom Seats					
Welder	X				
Stapler	X				
Sewer	X				
Forklift driver					X
Hydraulic Systems					
Machinist, union Shop Chair	X				
Machinist, union President	X				
Machinist	X				
General foreman, former machinist	X				
LV Gaskets					
Electrician	X				
Trainer, blanking area		X	X		
Tool and die maker	X				
Shipping worker	X				
Press operator	X				
Gasket tech	X				
Custom Blinds					
Training coordinator	X				

Continued

Table 6.1 *Continued*

	No intensification	Positive intensification		Negative intensification	
		Qualitative—Like the challenge	Quantitative—Makes day go faster	Qualitative—Increases stress	Quantitative—Working too fast or insufficient downtime
Machine builder	X				
Master mechanic	X				
Assembler		X			
Tubefab					
QA technician	X				
Welder (10 years)	X				
Welder (5 years)	X				
Press operator	X				
Assistant supervisor	X				
Metalfab Plus					
Team coordinator	X				
Utility technician		X			
Drill press operator	X				
Assembler	X				
Plastic Containers					
Process technician		X			
Machine operator		X			
Zinc Castings					
Die caster	X				
Machine operator	X				
Maintenance worker	X				
Shop lead foreman	X				

according to my judgement based on several readings of the whole interview, along with my direct observations in the case of the three firms mentioned above. But in each case I try to provide some quotation that supports my coding, while still offering a narrative about each factory and keeping the chapter to a reasonable length. In each case I indicate in the text how I code the worker.

Five High-Involvement Lean Factories

Second Tier Specialist

In 36.5 hours of direct observation in Labor-Management Committee meetings, observation of a local union meeting, and an informal chat over a beer at the pub after the union meeting, concerns about work intensification were never brought up. I developed good rapport with the union leadership and the plant manager at Specialist. In my reading of their case, the plant manager was genuinely committed to substantive empowerment and developing a truly high-involvement lean factory.

I interviewed five workers at Second Tier Specialist, a union shop. The first worker was a machinist with thirty-four years' tenure, whom I code as *positive quantitative intensification*. He said that cross training made the work less boring, made the day go by faster, and improved flexibility:

> I think the effort level is going to be the same. Some guys, some will get hepped up and some will get let down, depending upon the cycle. If we're busy, we maintain a plodding along busy, busy status where everybody's moving right along and all of that. When we're slow, you turn your level down. You're barely, you can hardly justify taking your check home sometimes because you're that doggone slow. And it's tough. We always would rather be busy, either working ahead a little bit. . . .
>
> *Okay. So you think that the workers in general will, the people out on the shop floor will feel like it makes them less bored, or gives them . . .*
>
> Definitely. *Definitely less bored* because there's more flexibility, and you're able to stay busy longer. And as long as you stay—if you don't have to look at a time clock, or the clock, it moves faster. As soon as you look at that clock, it moves

> slower. So if we're busy, to any reasonable speed, reasonable amount of effort, a steady pace, then it would be better because then we can move.[4]
>
> Say you're down one man in that particular cell. Knowing how to do the job, one man could conceivably—or two people—could do the job of three, or just picking up the slack of one. . . . But having the ability to perform all of those jobs gives that, at least most of the customers are going to get their product.

He expected effort levels to go down due to a combination of cellular production and automatic machines:

> *Okay, so in one sense this reorganization combined with some automation has led to a decrease in some parts of worker effort, and it's led to an increase in other parts. Is that a fair . . . ?*
>
> Probably a decrease in worker effort and an increase in production, if those don't offset each other.

This machinist also noted that the workers played a central role in the design of the cells: "I think for the overall input as far as how the machines go together in the particular cell to produce the product, that was basically our input."

The second worker was a machinist and cell lead person and union president with eight years' tenure, whom I code as *positive qualitative intensification*. He was the leader of a collaborative faction in the workforce who were supporting the lean transformation and the labor-management HPWO partnership. He described qualitative intensification in positive terms of learning more about product knowledge and customer names, and those resisting lean and empowerment as a separate faction giving them "trouble":

> *Now, do you think that the cells have increased the level of effort that's expected of people at all?*
>
> I think that the effort is not greater, but more intense. They're more concerned with what comes across the table, as opposed to just making a rod or an endcap. They're familiarizing themselves with customer names. And that tells me that they're more involved with their psyche as to what goes across that machine, whereas they've just got a block or a tube or anything like that.
>
> *Now do you think that this is, there's two ways that I think people could respond to this. They could either enjoy it because it reduces some boredom and makes their*

[4] All emphasis within the interview quotations is mine.

job more exciting somehow, or they could say, you know, "fuck that, man, I just want to come in and run my machine and that's it."

There's a certain amount of that and you're not going to get away from that. I think that we're going to go down, over the next four or five years, survive this business, the survival business, with those people who are near retirement, *those are ones that are giving us the trouble*. They're going to go out the door with the same attitude they have right now.

Do you think there's a group of people that have, that like the challenge, if that's the way you want to put it?

Yeah, I definitely think there are.

A third worker was a parts coordinator and Shop Committee Chair with thirty years' tenure, whom I code as *no intensification*. He said the main concern was too little work due to a recession. His comments suggest that he perceives of effort in terms of how many hours one gets per week—the more the better—rather than having to work harder:

Have the cells in this type of reorganization, has it led to a change in the effort levels that workers have to do out there?

Yeah. The first thought that popped into my mind is that people are more open to doing more tasks, but we're not real busy right now. You know I think a real true test of all this is going to be, you know, historically we were always a 45 to 50, maybe even sometimes a 55-hour a week. . . . We were always an overtime shop. We haven't worked any overtime in about a year now. And people, you know, I don't mind working nine hours a day and a couple on Saturday. *The work gets done* and I make a little money, whatever, you know.

A fourth was another machinist, with fifteen years' tenure, whom I code as *no intensification*. He saw the effort question primarily in terms of variations in worker orientations (some work hard, some don't) and wished the factory would get busier:

Now do you think then that this new form of organization, has it changed the effort levels that workers are expected to perform?

No, they haven't.

So they haven't, it hasn't made people have to work harder or anything like that?

No. Especially being slow right now.

Yeah, it's hard to tell.

Right, you still have people standing around and you still have people that are busting their butt.

The fifth worker was a sweeper and parts washer with four years' tenure, whom I code as *no intensification*. She stated that in her understanding the main concerns of the workers had to do with lean organization reducing the number of jobs. She was not aware of any complaints about intensification:

Do people think that in a sense it's making them have to work harder and they don't like it, or do you think it maybe relieves some boredom sometimes because they get to do different things?

I haven't heard any of the guys talk about either one of those things. The main thing I've heard them complain about is the lack of job opportunities.

Oh, for training. So like if they're in one of those groups where . . .

Not so much for training purposes, but it's going to make us ultimately lose positions. Now we've got, you know, everybody who can do this job, we don't need to fill this position, because when they're slow over here, we'll just pull them over there. So we don't need to hire anybody anymore. That's the biggest complaint I've heard from the union.

Okay. So that there hasn't been—a very legitimate complaint too—but there hasn't been any complaints about specifically an increase in work effort or anything like that.

No, I have not heard that.

Industrial Pumps

I interviewed five workers at Industrial Pumps, a nonunion shop. The first was a senior assembler with four years' tenure, whom I code as *positive qualitative and quantitative intensification* because he described participation in problem solving, and being busier at work, both in positive terms. When I asked him a general question about what has changed, he gave an example of how lean tools have helped them improve processes to save time:

Can you talk about maybe what some of the big differences you've seen are in your job since after lean production?

Well, I think what it's done is it's made the company take a look at how we manufacture. We were using old methods of putting bearings on shafts. . . . So that saved us a lot of time.

> *So just taking a step out of the process and improving the process.*
>
> Right. Correct. And then what we've now gone to is a different type of bearing, in which it resembles what we were using before, but we can shorten up the lead times by creating different length spacers in the bearings. . . .
>
> *Um-hmm. And how did you find these changes?*
>
> Through the mapping of the processes, and through the lean manufacturing that we had done. We found out where our time, we did a lot of time studies. We did some videotaping of some of the activities to find out where the wastes were.

After much more discussion, I circled back again and asked if the new system has led to changes in his daily routine. He responded that he feels like he has more control over his work processes and a better understanding of the overall process:

> I feel like I've got a better hands-on my job, I have a little bit more control of saying . . .
>
> *Um-hmm, so you do feel like you have more control?*
>
> Yeah. Yeah, I do.
>
> *Do you, with all these changes, do you also feel like you get a, have a better picture of the overall production process now, and your role in it?*
>
> Yeah, I've seen that through the value stream, you know, that you're finding out where the processes start out, you know, in doing the maps and finding out what is an outside vendor issue and what isn't.

On the question of effort, he described being less stressed out, being less bored, and feeling more effective. The improved flow means that:

> I know that I can get more work done. . . . Where now, we know that something's coming, coming our direction, and we don't have to worry about waiting too long.
>
> *Right. So it makes you feel like your job is more effective.*
>
> Yeah.
>
> *Does it also make you, do you feel like you're working harder now, doing more responsibilities?*
>
> No. . . . I know that, I know for me physically, at the end of the day, I've worked an eight-hour day, physically I've worked an eight-hour day. *I've gotten a lot more*

> *accomplished than I did before, and a lot less stressed out as far as*, you know, feeling like I went to work and I actually accomplished something, whether it be building two pumps or three pumps and a gearbox or whatever, every day. But constantly keeping busy. I know that the day goes by very fast when you're busy.
>
> *So, you're keeping busier which is helping the time pass.*
>
> Um-hmm.
>
> *And you're also, while you're working hard you're also getting more accomplished.*
>
> Um-hmm.
>
> *So it's not that you're working harder, I mean it's not stressing you out more?*
>
> No.
>
> *So it actually makes you feel like you're working smarter than harder?*
>
> Right.

The second worker was an assembly supervisor with four years' tenure, whom I code as *positive qualitative intensification*. He described how continuous improvement activities demand more intellectual labor, but overall this is a positive development:

> *Has it led to any sort of like increased workload for people at the plant? Did they, I mean . . .*
>
> Sometimes, yeah. Sometimes it has, yeah. But like I said, we're just trying to set, we're always moving our area to try to improve it, you know, "Well, this should be closer, and this doesn't need to be here." I guess I'm not still, you know, I mean you've got to figure out yourself too with programming; Lean isn't going to fix it all for you, you've still got to use your head a little bit and make it work.
>
> *Right. And so this continually moving things around, how did this work on a, I mean is it, do you get together in a team meeting and discuss it, or how does it . . . ?*
>
> Yeah. We'll get together and brainstorm, you know, "What do you feel about this, or what's your idea on it?" And I guess you've got to look at the cause and effect of it too. If we move this, who is it going to affect or what's it going to affect too, you know. And that's sometimes the hardest part, you know?

Workers are allowed to experiment with changes "which is nice, they'll give us the option to be able to do that, you know."

This assembler expressed support for the continuous-flow system and agreement with the principle of only making what there is an order for:

> They've cut down orders to being one-piece flow for us to build, instead of an order of ten pumps on one order. . . . But I do like the one-piece better. . . . they're working on things we need. I mean that's the best part about it. You know, you're not making 20 of one thing just so we'll have it here.

This assembler saw job enlargement as a positive change:

> When I first started it was just building, just building pumps. I mean now it's went to pulling your own parts, refilling up bins, which we went to *kanban*. I mean, we've eliminated other jobs that people have done for us, but yet we're building just as fast. So that's a plus that you've seen to the lean.

The third worker was a machinist with fifteen years' tenure, whom I code as *no intensification*. In contrast with the previous assembler, the main concern of the machinist was that he didn't fully agree with the move to smaller batches because he thought it made him spend too much time on setups, and not enough time actually running parts. In his view, this was inefficient. Nonetheless, he said he was adapting to the new system and that in general it didn't change his overall job satisfaction:

> *Do you like your job better now with these new lean initiatives, or worse, or the same?*
>
> I guess *about the same, now that I'm used to it*. You know, the change thing is always difficult to get used to doing it that way, you know what I mean? One day you're running 10 to 20 parts, and it's down to one and three or four. . . . It's just the thing of getting used to it. *You adapt.*

He went on to say that the new system "made more work" for him. On further probing, this was not about having to work at a faster pace, or having less downtime, but about having to do so many setups and not being able to "get anything done":

> It actually made more work for me, but you know, still the thing is, you know, I get paid by the hour, so.
>
> *Right. So it has made a little bit more work? It's not too, it's not extreme?*
>
> It ain't like it's extremely difficult work to get it done. I mean it's just the pain of having to do it two or three different times a day, you know. . . .

Personally, I guess I feel that you don't really get anything done, because you're setting up jobs all the time. But they don't want you working on stuff that ain't needed today, you know.

And he acknowledged that it made his work less boring, which made the day go by faster, although given his ambivalent language ("might … probably") I did not code him as positive intensification:

I guess as far as running the small batches [between one and four parts], it is, you know, you might not get as bored as if you're running 10 or 20 of the same parts at, you know, 10 minutes a piece. . . . So, all in all, I mean it ain't all bad as far as *it probably makes the day move a little* faster I guess.

The fourth was a polisher with six years' tenure, whom I code as *positive quantitative intensification*. He explained how he is gaining more skills and how job rotation breaks up the monotony and makes the day go by faster:

So how has your job changed over the time, and especially with this new lean production?

When I first started I was just a raw impeller polisher, and that was pretty much it. And I wanted to try housings. And then I got moved to housings and I wanted to keep moving and advancing, so I tried up the high grit now, inside, outsides.

Okay. So, and then in terms of the, this, with this job rotation, or the rotation that you're talking about, is that something new?

Yeah, they're starting to cross train everybody, so everybody gets a break and gets to jump back, and other people get a feel of knowing more pumps and doing . . .

Right, and how do you like that?

I like it. It's good.

It breaks up the monotony a bit?

Yeah. You bet. Everything ain't so tight then.

For this polisher, the main change was having a wider variety of skills and being able to use them to help make sure products get out on time. Job rotation reduces boredom and makes the day go faster:

> *Has that increased, does it actually increase your workload and your stress at all?*
>
> Oh, I wouldn't say that.
>
> *Or does it maybe save monotony, make the day go faster?*
>
> Oh, yeah. The days fly, because you're just steady busy, you know.

The fifth was a worker in shipping and receiving with seventeen years' tenure, whom I code as *positive qualitative intensification*. He said he has to pay more attention and contribute intellectual labor under just-in-time inventory control, but overall he thinks that lean has improved his job:

> *And can you talk a bit then about how this just-in-time stuff has changed your job, if at all?*
>
> Just-in-time has affected our job a lot, because *it has bettered our job*, but also made it more, you have to keep under it all the time. You have to make sure you know all the inventory that you have, almost all the time. . . . It works when everything flows: we get our parts in, we don't have people on vacation, someone off sick or something. So, when you're that lean, you really have to be on top of everything.

For this worker, "At first it was very, very stressful because we had to, you know, really watch because we all were in the learning process also." But now that they have worked out some kinks:

> Actually it's gotten easier. . . . I think the 5S program has worked to a point now. Now I feel there has to be some fine-tuning and some, I feel, changes that fit our people. You know, not just because 5S says it needs to be done. We have to fine-tune it to fit us. And the just-in-time, that's gotten better. I think *it has made my job more satisfying*. I mean, it's been, *it's a challenge*. Every day is a challenge. It's not a hard job, but it's a job that I, like I say, you have to be real attentive, you know, too.

Mini OE

Management at Mini OE brought in Wisconsin Regional Training Partnership (WRTP) to facilitate the development of a labor-management partnership. The WRTP also helped them do extensive training in literacy and numeracy, including blueprint reading and measurement, which management understands explicitly as a first step toward empowering their workforce. Direct employee classifications had been reduced from four to a single job classification and all employees moved up to a single pay rate.

In the four Labor-Management Committee meetings I observed, the problem of work intensification was never mentioned. The entire operation had been transformed into sixteen assembly cells, and every indication I had was that management was genuinely attempting to develop self-managed teams to run the cells, pursuing a strategy of qualitative transformation in capability, focused on flexibility, quality, and continuous improvement, rather than speedup.

I interviewed four workers at Mini OE, a union shop. The first was a brush maker with thirty-three years' tenure, whom I code as *no intensification*. He liked working in cells because they improve quality:

> I like them. Because instead of making a brush, we used to put them in barrels, and then later they would get shipped out, you know, where they had to get assembled, send them back. A lot of times there'd be a whole lot of bad brushes in there. This way, you're completing your brushes, you can tell if it's good or bad.
>
> *Now in terms of, you know, either being worked too hard or not having enough work and being bored, has that changed at all since you've gone to cells? Has it increased your workload or has it made you enjoy your work more or less at all?*
>
> I like it. I wish we could have our radios back, but that ain't the point I guess.
>
> *Do you think that under the cells, that people are expected to work harder, to take on more tasks?*
>
> No, *they're just doing the same job now*, but instead of just sitting there and putting them in the barrel, they've got to keep moving around and completing everything.

The second was a brush maker with twenty-five years' tenure, whom I code as *no intensification*. He was particularly reticent, offering short answers to all of my questions and not elaborating when probed:

> *Has there been any change in the level of effort that workers are expected to exert now that the cells—you know either maybe the effort's increased for some reason or decreased? Or is it about the same?*
>
> I would say about the same.

Another thing with cells is sometimes the people end up having to work harder because now they're running two machines at once or something like that. You haven't noticed any of that?

Unh-unh.

The third worker was a machine tech with twenty-four years' tenure, whom I code as *no intensification*. As a tech who did repair and troubleshooting, he didn't work in the cells. He had heard "some comments" about workers having to run multiple machines but said it was not "a major problem":

Now, with these cells, do you think that this has led to a change in the effort level that's expected of workers?

There have been some comments about that. But I don't see that to be a major problem.

What were the comments about?

Having to work harder by running more pieces of equipment.

But it hasn't been a big deal, just some comments?

No.

Nothing that anybody brought to the union or anything like that.

Nope. It hasn't been a major issue where they would have brought the union in and say, "Let's go and talk to management about me being treated unfair because I've got to run various pieces of equipment within this here cell." No, none of that.

The fourth was a lead person with thirty years' tenure, whom I code as *no intensification*. He said some complained about having more work, but in his view there wasn't "much difference." For him the main problem was mistakes were happening because the workers didn't get a raise with the move to cells. And a big complaint was that management took away their chairs:

Now considering that the change to cells out there and all the kind of restructuring that's been going on, how do you think that the workforce has reacted in terms of their job satisfaction and this kind of stuff?

They don't mind cells, some workers be saying, but they're not getting any more money, but they added more work to them. You know.

Um-hmm. So you do think that the cells have increased the amount of effort that workers are expected to . . . ?

They—it's really hard to say, because they won't get them in the cells, and I don't feel they agree with those cells yet, because it too many mistakes out there. Too many mistakes.

Why do you think they make mistakes?

Because they don't change and they don't care because they just, maybe they go and do what they've got to do and get on out of there, because they don't get no more money.

Now you mentioned a minute ago that you think that people are expected to work harder in some senses. Do you think that, is that, has the cellular organization just increased the pace of work, or is that now you have, you're supposed to run more than one machine at the same time? I mean what kind of things is it that makes people have to work harder?

I don't see too much difference because they're still in the cells and they're still going to be the same thing.

Still doing the same things.

Uh-huh, but a lot of them's getting mad about because they can't have no chairs. . . . management thinks we shouldn't have chairs, depending on what job you're on. You know and some jobs you've got to have a chair, and the workers don't like that.

Designer Railings

I interviewed five workers at Designer Railings, a nonunion shop. Four said their main source of frustration was an ongoing problem with being short of steel stock, leading to late orders. I interviewed the workers after I interviewed the manager, which made it difficult to discern the nature of this problem. The manager said they had been making improvements in inventory management over the last few years. He did mention that "steel has risen in price quite a bit in the last six months," but otherwise didn't mention any problems with stock. The workers only discussed steel but not aluminum or brass, which they also use extensively, suggesting there could have been a specific problem with the steel supply market.

The first worker was a setup press operator with nine years' tenure, whom I coded as *no intensification*. He was very frustrated with lean, but his primary concerns were having to run so many setups for short production runs along with low inventories, both of which he saw as inefficient, and lack of communication over all the changes being made. On inventory, this press operator gave an example of how running out of stock leads to late orders, which has a cumulative negative impact on the system: "Okay, I had put in a job last week, we only had half the steel we need. . . . And then we're sitting there and the customer is going to be late; it's a snowballing effect."

A second worker was a pipe bender with eleven years' tenure, whom I code as *positive qualitative intensification*. Her main complaint was also the lack of inventory leading to late orders. But she said lean has been an improvement for her, providing her with more understanding of the overall process and improving product quality. Her job satisfaction is:

> Very high. You know, I'm satisfied with what I do.
>
> *And has that changed as a result of these changes over the last couple years, or not, it hasn't affected it much.*
>
> Yeah.
>
> *It has affected it?*
>
> Yeah.
>
> *And has it made it better or worse?*
>
> *It made it better*. You know, it keeps you focused on what's coming in and what you have to work with and it keeps you focused on knowing that you're sending out something that's going to be accepted by people that are buying it, you know.
>
> *Right. And how exactly do you think it has increased your focus? Is it just more emphasis on quality or how exactly is it?*
>
> It is more emphasis on quality.

The third worker was a gripper (who boxes parts) with five years' tenure, whom I code as *no intensification*. He too had the same complaint regarding lack of stock. The other negative change this worker mentioned was having to spend so much time scanning in and out of jobs under the new system:

> You've got to scan in and out on jobs, you know, and just—it's something that I'm not used to. . . . I do, I like to come in and do my work for eight hours. That's all they pay me is for eight hours, and I don't understand why we have to scan in and out for every minute of our day so they can split it up between the jobs. I mean if I do a job one time and I have given them a scanned time on it, for the whole job, there's no reason that I should have to do it every time I do it. They know how long it takes of my time.

He went on to explain that he thinks it is a form of unnecessary oversight that is an affront to his integrity:

> They say it's to find out how long you're doing, it's to find out how long you are spending time on each job. But I think that I myself can say that I take it as more of, you're going to account for working eight hours because I'm paying you eight hours. And it's kind of a shame that integrity and the person's honesty and their integrity counts for nothing anymore. You know, if I come in here and I say I worked eight hours, then I worked eight hours, that means nothing if I haven't done a little laser beam on a card.

The focus of this worker's complaint is on increased surveillance. In our discussion of negative changes, he did not mention an increased pace of work, reduced downtime, or intellectually demanding work.

The fourth was a lead person with seven years' tenure, whom I code as *no intensification*. He reported being happy with his job, making good money and getting good training:

> Yeah, I'm pleased. If I was not pleased here, I could leave a long time ago. But, like I say, I am pleased, these last two years, things have been going well. . . . *I love it*. I know it back and forth. I know that it, you know, *I learned here* too. I got trained here. And I am happy here.

The fifth was a maintenance worker with ten years' tenure, whom I code as *no intensification*. He was the only one that didn't lead with the stock complaint. Rather, he described how lean has improved his job by reducing clutter:

Now, I've been talking with other people, a lot about the lean manufacturing initiative here and how these changes have affected their job. Has it affected your job in maintenance much?

I see less clutter. I mean as far as for me to get around, to get to a machine, to work on stuff, it seems like—I don't know if clutter is a good word or not, but I mean, you know, you usually get a pile of, "What is that?" laying there. And it seems like that has cleaned it up quite a bit.

Right. That's probably a result of this 5S training and that type of stuff.

Yeah, we had that, that was actually pretty interesting . . . with such a variety of difference between fuses and parts and, it's just a lot better. It helps, considerably helps, you know. So that part I suppose is, identify it, you know, and get rid of junk that you're never going to use.

Custom Seats

I interviewed four workers at Custom Seats, a union shop. The main concerns of these workers had to do with new payment and incentive systems, not with lean production as such. One issue was a recent switch from piece rates to an hourly wage. A second issue was an associated, new gainsharing system.

The first worker was a former assembler with thirty-three years' tenure who moved to welding after the switch from piece rates, whom I code as *no intensification*. He was averaging $27 per hour under piece rates and was concerned about a negative impact on productivity under the new hourly rate: "Our production is way down because of this. Because who's going to work for $17.55 an hour and be as productive as they were making piecework." His other main grievance was that the new management was not as open and responsive as the old management team was:

This used to be a great place to work. Terrific. Everybody was friendly. Like I say, the vice president of the company would come out and talk to you, the president. Now it's, it's their way or no way. . . . Before . . . I wouldn't have to go through a chain of command; I mean inspectors, QEs, MEs. And this guy drops the ball and nothing gets done. I'd go to the vice-president, president, say, "Guys, this has got to be fixed. It's got to be fixed." And it was fixed, you know, in a couple days, not six months, not three months.

The second worker was a stapler (and former assembler) with six years' tenure, whom I code as *no intensification*. His main complaint concerned the gainsharing program, which was based on teams spanning two shifts, and which he thought was unfair:

> It's a first and second shift in one cell; they have to, they share the gainsharing. So it's like, how am I supposed to know what these guys are doing at night? You know, am I working harder during the day and then they're not at night? So I worked hard to put money in their pockets. It's just things like that.

The third worker was a sewer with three years' tenure, whom I code as *no intensification*. She said that her main complaint was where there is a lack of communication or a dispute over the division of labor within a cell:

> *Now are there things about the cells, I mean it's a pretty different way of doing manufacturing. Are there things about it that you particularly . . . like or dislike?*
>
> There's—half and half. There's some things I like, some things I don't like.
>
> *Which things do you like?*
>
> Like the way we divide up jobs and the way we do our work. And, I guess that's it.
>
> *So is it like, so just the way that the work is divided up between the group of people in the cells?*
>
> Yes. Instead of doing all in one order by myself, we split up the work.
>
> *And what things do you dislike?*
>
> Dislike is when we mis . . . mis-dividing up the work and miscommunicating with a teammate. We both, we're all kind of like thinking instead of talking and asking. I'm thinking that, oh, she does that one, and then the other one did this many, and the other one did that many of them.
>
> *So that causes problems?*
>
> Yes.
>
> *What kind of problems does it cause?*
>
> Like sometimes we have a hard time where a person refuses to do the extra piece. Like some jobs divide up odd numbers, and then that one person kind of like, "Oh, I did this already. I don't want to do it today." And then that, you know, stuff like that.

Regarding effort, she said, "Sometimes, one day it's a lot of work, sometimes it's not, even if the same amount of people show up." She explained that she doesn't understand why there is variation in work levels, and she asked her supervisor but hasn't gotten an answer: "We don't know how that works, but we asked him a couple times . . . We don't get no answer out from that."

The fourth was a forklift driver with twenty-five years' tenure, whom I code as *negative quantitative intensification.* He explained that with four people in the cells, they are producing more output than one person, making him busier delivering parts to the cell and finished products from the cell:

> *Has your work at all changed from the way, because with the cells and stuff now they've changed the way that they schedule and run jobs and hold inventory and stuff pretty dramatically, has that affected your work?*
>
> It's changed as far as I have a lot more work to do, you know. Which, they usually act like, they wanted the cells to be self-sufficient; I actually have more work than I ever had. . . .
>
> *You said more work. Can you talk about that a little bit?*
>
> Well, for one thing there's more people. I used to have less people. And now they're working as a group.
>
> *More people you have to deal with, is that . . . ?*
>
> Yes, more people that I have to deal with. And now I've got a group of people. This job, that's mainly a big cell in my department, it used to be done by one person, and he was on piecework then. Well now, I have four people doing this same job. And so it's going out quicker. You know, there's four people, you know.

Despite saying that four people are producing faster output, the main complaint of the forklift driver—the point he spent the most time talking about—was that the overall impact on productivity has been negative:

> I've got to be honest with you, I'm not, I think things were generally better before the cells. I think that, we were told we'd have to go cellularized, but nobody told us how to do it. And it's, the flow [i.e. productivity] is going much worse because production has gone way down, attitudes have gotten very bad. A lot of people lost a lot of money, that's one of the reasons, you know. It's taking four people now to do what one used to do, and I don't know how this is beneficial, but that's what's happening.

Two Autonomous-Lean Factories

Hydraulic Systems

I interviewed four workers at Hydraulic Systems, a union shop. A machinist with twenty-three years' tenure who was the union Shop Chair, and whom I coded as *no intensification*, said his main concern was that the workers are not embracing the increased opportunities for employee involvement. He explained that management is trying to give the workers real opportunities to contribute to problem solving and decision making, but that the workers still have a traditional view of the responsibilities of management and labor, which is making them reluctant to take on new responsibilities they see as managerial:

> Well, for me, I mean I have awesome power on the floor, you know.
>
> *Because you're the Shop Chair, or because you've been here for so long?*
>
> I've been here for a while. You know, I mean I think I've earned the respect of top management, middle management, low management. They come out, they talk to me, they give me my data, so on and so forth. As far as the guys on the floor, this is a different kind of place. You know, they still have this, "I'm the worker, you're management; you tell me what to do" mentality. . . . But, [Hydraulic Systems] tries to give you the decision-making power.

This factory had a labor-management partnership, facilitated by the WRTP. While the plant manager had brought the WRTP to help establish a partnership, according to the Shop Chair the plant manager was resisting bringing in the International Association of Machinists' HPWO department:

> Now see we've talked about HPWO, you know, High Performance Work Organization. We wanted to bring in Jim Reid from Washington. And see now, [the plant manager] seems to have a problem with that. [The plant manager is] an alright guy. Alright, I mean let's get that straight right now. . . . But when [he] starts to lose a little bit of his power, [he] gets real goofy. You know? [He] likes having absolute power.

As the following discussion I had with the manager illustrates, he did express some hesitation toward giving the union a role in decisions like "hiring and outsourcing and costing," but said he was considering it, that he found the union very helpful in general, and that they are allowing union participation in decision making, just not in a structured a way as a formal HPWO partnership as designed by the Machinists Union:

> We're very fortunate that we have the Machinists here and they work very closely with us to keep the work here.
>
> *Did you work with their High Performance Work Organization Department?*
>
> That's come up recently. We're not big enough, we don't really need, that requires a certain amount of resources [chuckles] for what they want. It worked very good for the Harleys and the bigger people, but for us to take the time because there's some education for the high performance work organization. We've been knocking it around; we'd like to do it, we see the benefits of it.
>
> *Well it sounds like you are doing it in . . .*
>
> We're doing it informally, yeah.
>
> *Right.*
>
> But like when they were in and we saw the presentation where you get them involved in hiring and outsourcing and costing and, you know, we do it more on a, we get the guys together and we talk to them, but it's not done as formally as the actual high performance work organization and structure. . . . We have a leadership team that includes, you know, myself, there's four of us from management, and then there were four from the union. And we meet, we were meeting once a week, now we're meeting every other week. And we do run a lot of these decisions, like we'll set up committees, we're doing the 5Ss, we're doing setup reduction. This is a, you'd call it a steering committee, a leadership team. And we try to get consensus on that.

The union president was also a machinist, whom I code as *no intensification*. He said the three main changes under lean were: operators now do quality inspection, rather than having an inspector do it; operators do more material handling for themselves; and "Problem solving. We do a lot of the problem solving ourselves." He saw increased responsibilities for quality control and opportunities for participation on problem solving and decision making as improvements. But because he did not explicitly discuss reduced boredom or a welcome increase in challenging work, I code him as no intensification. They have Standard Operating Procedures and:

> [a]nything that deviates from that, we make note of that on our inspection card. Or if it's something that we feel—and again, *we're making our own decisions*—we feel would interfere with the process as the part goes through the shop, then we get Inspection involved. We have somebody who's an inspector and machine operator. So we can call them over, make a judgment, write a ticket on it if need be, to have it corrected.

When I asked directly about working harder, he saw steady work with limited downtime in a positive light and referred to lean setup reduction as "work smarter, not to work harder":

> I mean you know, to me it's a steady, you work steady throughout your whole shift. There's just not a lot of lag time this whole time. And it's, *there's a sense of accomplishment* and you know you're getting it done. I don't have a problem with it. And I don't think anybody at [Hydraulic Systems] is under a whip. You know they're not out there whipping you saying you've got to work twice as fast. As a matter of fact, these setup reduction programs in working with WRTP are to *work smarter, not to work harder*.

He elaborated on how workers are given real input into decisions made within *kaizen* problem-solving groups:

> It really helps for people to sit down, especially to view a video, because it focuses you. You know everybody's looking at this video, everybody's looking at this problem, everybody's looking at this job. We share our ideas that we already know, with the idea—and I'm a facilitator for some of these—with the idea that no ideas are wrong, they're just different. Some of them might work and some of them might not because of the cost or whatever, and those all have to be taken into consideration. So let's throw all of the ideas out there and then we'll look over each one of them and see if they'll work. . . . people are not afraid to say, you know, "If we only use this fixture on this machine for this job, why do we put it back in the rack every time?"

Another machinist, with twenty-three years' tenure, whom I code as *no intensification*, explained how having to do setups while another machine is running has several benefits: he gets to do his own scheduling, which improves the process, and it allows work to be done simultaneously with changeovers. Because he did not explicitly discuss reduced boredom or a welcome increase in challenging work, I code him as no intensification. They redesigned the work during a *kaizen* event:

> *It actually did a lot of good* . . . it wasn't as much the workers out on my machine doing it faster as much as it was that we needed get a scheduling program set up that they would let us do our own scheduling for the most part so we could, I have a two-pallet machine, and if they let me do the scheduling and skip to the scheduling, we could make a higher percent. Otherwise, if they just, if they scheduled as the jobs come in, we're running one pallet and we're tearing it down and we're doing setup after setup after setup and just dragging our feet. . . .
>
> *It makes it easier*. . . . still have to show some productivity. And *in the old way you were always behind*, always behind on your time. You'd get to the end of the day, it's just like, "I worked all day and I didn't get anything done," because you're doing changeovers all the time and . . . But now . . . you can build up more time because you can keep the machine running while you're setting up.

Finally, one of the employees I interviewed was a general foreman, a machinist with forty-three years' tenure, whom I code as *no intensification*. In the interview he focused on providing examples of all the opportunities the workers had participation in problem solving and decision making through the "manifold teams here, that's all of the floor." In one example:

> We picked two machines, we picked all of the operators, first, second, and third shift. We sat them down, we said, "What can we do?" And I don't have numbers on that. That was about four or five years ago. We cut the cost like in half. And we do a hell of a job right now. We dedicate a bunch of tooling for the manifolds, and everybody's trained on it, they know what they're doing. You know, so it's just, *it's working out well*. The people on the floor help, they really do. And they know it's . . .
>
> *And you get enthusiastic support now from the . . .*
>
> Oh, absolutely, yeah. There's guys that just, they can't do enough, really, and there are . . . everybody gets right in there. They do their thing, you know. And it's off the line. And they know, the way the economic things are right now in the world, that if we don't compete, if we don't get these costs down, we're screwed and we're going to be closing our doors here. I'm not saying that that's the way it is, but that's the way it could be.

LV Gaskets

I interviewed six workers at LV Gaskets, a nonunion shop. One is an electrician in the maintenance department, with five years' tenure, whom I code as *no intensification*. While the shift to a lean organization didn't affect the maintenance department too much, the maintenance workers are involved in *kaizen* events. The main change was substantially more involvement of workers in problem solving and decision making:

> They do seem to involve more people as far as getting together and making changes out on the floor. They'll get together what they call a *kaizen* group and they're decide—they'll look at a product or a machine or a small area, and they'll come up with some ideas on how to improve. They'll usually get a list of maybe 10 or 12 people depending on what the problem is or what they're looking to correct, and then they'll ask for volunteers. They try to get people from each area, to get some diversity in there, and they usually get one person from maintenance.

This electrician said that these *kaizen* events can last up to a week, depending on the nature of the problem, noting that they try to make decisions by consensus:

> Yeah, they'll come to a consensus and then they . . . they list the different items they want to make improvements on, and then prioritize them, and then find solutions on a way to implement them. And sometimes stuff gets implemented right away, sometimes it's something that has to wait further down. And then there's some that just don't get implemented because of importance or need.

A second worker was a trainer in the blanking area with twelve years' tenure, whom I code as *positive qualitative and quantitative intensification*. She thought the *kaizen* events were very effective in improving processes but that it was difficult to get some people to accept or embrace lean:

> Yes. Um-hmm. *It's improvement. It's great.* I mean, you sometimes get in a rut, you know, and it's just not flowing right. And you'd be surprised, with all the ideas. I mean I was amazed, you know, all the ideas come up. And try it, you know, and pretty soon it's working. Like I said, the change, to get the people to buy in to change, that's half your battle.

She said they attempt to try out all the ideas workers propose:

> Yes. Everybody's idea, we try it. And improve it here, improve it there, add on a little bit. Yeah, there's . . . we go with everybody's idea, yep. And we work together as a group. We all, you know, talk it over and hash it out, and go up and see what would be the best for everybody involved.

She experienced qualitative intensification under lean as a positive change: it kept her busy, made her work more challenging, and helped to ensure she has a job, by making her company competitive:

> *Now, in terms of these changes we were talking about with the lean production initiatives, how have they changed your job?*
>
> Well, that's a hard one to answer. It's changed dramatically for me. I mean everything's faster now. It's faster—like I said, you've got to buy in to understand why.
>
> *Is it more work?*
>
> Yeah.
>
> *Yeah. And more intense work?*
>
> Yes. Yep.
>
> *Okay.*
>
> You're busy. And that's what I need to be. I mean I can't not be.
>
> *Right. And is that the main way that it's changed your job is just to kind of make it more intense and busier?*
>
> Yeah. Yeah, I'd say yes.
>
> *Has it, on the whole . . . and you experience that as a good change because it . . .*
>
> Um-hmm, I do. I feel it is.
>
> *Uh-huh. And I guess I don't want to put words in your mouth, so if you can talk about why you think it's . . .*
>
> Good?
>
> *Yeah.*
>
> Well, the way this day and age is now, this is happening out there. And I know about the inventory, they want to reduce inventory. I understand all that, you

know. And we can only go up with this. If we stay in the rut we were in, I can't see it working. They're constantly trying to improve. *And it's good for me because I like that kind of stuff.* I need a job. I like my job, you know. But I like, I need to stay busy. And the people I work with are the same way, they need to stay busy also.

I guess *I like the challenge* is that part out there. There's, every day there are new ones, every single day. And I've got to use my brain, I've got to think past this second. You've got to think about the next ten minutes, to tomorrow, and with the scheduling, and will this work in this press? and figure out, you know, ergonomically, is this correct for everybody? I'm always doing that, and I like that.

And those are the things you like most about your job, the challenge and the change in doing the things and so forth.

Um-hmm.

Are there things that you dislike about your job?

I guess I'm not too thrilled about seven days a week. You know, I'd like to have a life too. . . . But that's the only thing about—I wish, I'd get more money for one, and two, I wouldn't have to work seven days a week. [Laughs.] Other than that, I'm not too upset about anything else.

The third was a tool and die maker with nine years' tenure, whom I code as *no intensification.* On the *kaizen* events, he said, "Most of them, we are the ones that come up with the ideas." Beyond this, he has not experienced any significant changes in his work routines: "Since I've been here, there's nothing that I dislike at all. *I pretty much enjoy what I'm doing.* I enjoy the people, so."

The fourth was a shipping worker with one year's tenure, whom I code as *no intensification.* He described how a *kaizen* event in his area at first seemed "odd" to him but ended up being "pretty cool":

Recently we just had one over in the shipping department. And it was kind of odd to me, you know, I wasn't really against it, but it was odd because production wise, a lot of the things that we were seeing that could have went production wise to help us out wasn't necessarily focused on. It was a lot of house arrangements, you know, this moved here, this moved here. So, me on the outside looking in, I was kind of, you know, reluctant towards it. [But] actually, a lot of it has been working out. Like we got new desks, you know, new work area.

> When you got a nicer place to work, your production level is a lot different, you know, whether you notice it or not. So that was pretty cool.

The fifth worker was a press operator with two years' tenure, whom I code as *no intensification*. He had not participated in any *kaizen* events yet, but said he "might in the future, yeah. I wasn't really sure about what they were all about until they got going or whatever." He thought that overall lean had been an improvement:

> I mean after they do a *kaizen*, we have our plant meetings every month, any *kaizen* that they do, once it's complete and things that they're working on, they show you all the stuff that was implemented from all the employees came up with ideas, and they show you all the ones they can do, what they can't do, ones that are being worked on. . . . So, from what I've seen, most of them have been good.

The sixth was a gasket tech with ten years' tenure, whom I code as *no intensification*. She had not experienced any work intensification or substantial change to her routine:

> *Now are there changes that have affected your work in any significant ways?*
>
> Not really. The only place that it was kind of hectic was like, oh, my gosh, when they did a *kaizen* in the shipping area.

When I asked about things she dislikes, the only thing she said was that her job is boring: "The job is pretty much the same thing, and it's boring." But, she added, "It's easy. It's not a hard job, you know, like you go home, 'Oh, my body aches!' And it's good pay."

One Lean-Standardization Factory

Custom Blinds

I interviewed four workers at Custom Blinds, a nonunion shop. The first worker was a training coordinator in the extrusion department, who had worked there for twenty-four years, having been a former assembler, machine operator, and group leader, whom I code as *no intensification*. The extrusion department runs large batches and, according to the training coordinator, had not really begun to implement much just-in-time production. She said "*I love the job I have right now.* I really do. I have kind of flexible work hours and I'm able to move around a lot, you know, I'm not tied to a machine. So I like that."

The second worker was machine builder with twenty years' tenure, whom I code as *no intensification.* He spent most of his time "in the office," working "with the computerized maintenance system, which like I say, supports both the tool room and the maintenance." I asked if any of the new lean practices had increased his work effort, or that of the workforce, and he said what he thought really matters is individual skill; if one has enough skill, then the work isn't too hard:

> Well, I mean that's really hard for me to judge if a person's working harder now than then, because if a person is doing his job in a good fashion, you don't have to really work hard to get a lot done. You know I see people out there, some conjunction job, sweating like a son-of-a-gun, and you never see anything they get done. But yet the other guy, you'd think he's really isn't working but the guy's produced, or the guy or gal is producing.

The third was a master mechanic with twenty-seven years' tenure, whom I code as *no intensification.* For him the main issue was that the maintenance department had been restructured from having maintenance workers assigned to either scheduled work or emergency work, to one in which they were assigned to departments, with each mechanism responsible for both scheduled and emergency work. He noted that it "didn't work out all that bad," but he found one thing frustrating:

> They want scheduled work done on a certain basis, but you're always having to drop what you're doing to go out on [an emergency] job, you know, do something. A lot of times you'd have to pick up all your stuff you had laid out, you were working on, put it away, whatever, go out, take the call, and then come back and get all set up to start doing your stuff again, and maybe you'd have to drop it again and run out.

This mechanic did not complain about the work being more physically or intellectually demanding. Rather, his frustration was about what he saw as an inefficient use of labor; it would be better to have dedicated workers for emergency and scheduled maintenance.

The fourth was an assembler with nineteen years' tenure, whom I code as *positive qualitative intensification.* He had direct experience with just-in-time and flow production. He described a form of qualitative intensification that he perceived as a welcome challenge. His work is:

> pretty much the same, but the pressure to make sure that things go on date is always there. But that's the business, you know, and that's the number one thing is, it's competitive. And if we're not making our dates, you know, so we all . . . But *we tend to take it as a challenge*, I think, the group does. They really do. We work really well together. You know like I say, if there's a cart gets pushed out, well, we've got to go, we've got two hours left of go, go, you know. We work really well on that, I think. *I consider it a challenge*. I think most people do. You know, so that's really good.

Four Lean-Enough Cases

Tubefab

I interviewed four workers and one assistant supervisor at Tubefab, a nonunion shop. The first was a QA Tech with ten years' tenure, whom I code as *no intensification.* He thought job rotation provided workers with more knowledge but, if anything, made them work less hard:

> *Do you think that, with these new forms of work organization do you think that the level of effort expected of workers, or the actual level of effort, do you think that that's increased or decreased at all?*
>
> Well, you're expected to know more. Every time you cross train to a different job, you have to, there's other things you've got to know. There's more safety—everything from safety to quality things you have to know for that particular job.
>
> *Do you think that the workers actually end up working harder when they come in and they have to, you know, rotate around in a day rather than just working the same machine all day long?*
>
> I don't think really, you know, depending on what you have, you're on, it's probably easier on the body to move around to different jobs instead of doing the same thing all the time. As far as your tendons and whatnot, you know, connective tissue, it's easier on that. But I would say in general *you're probably not working as hard* as if you were on one, if you're put on one hard job all day long and you have to do that all day, as opposed to like in a work cell where you may

have the hard job for an hour and then you go to the easy jobs, and people would be back into that hard job. On them ones, you're probably not working as hard.

The second was a welder with ten years' tenure, whom I code as *no intensification.* He agreed that cellular production does not require people to worker harder. He described how the biggest change was that teamwork made the work less stressful, because team members can help each other out:

Has the stuff, the cells and job rotation led to changes in the effort levels that are expected of workers? Maybe they have to work harder, or maybe they don't have to work as hard?

I think they don't have to work that hard.

You think they have to work less hard now?

Well, if they've got extra people, more, you know, you're not really working hard, you're . . . you know, you're going around, you're doing your job, you know.

Right. [Discussion about lunch.] So you were saying, maybe there's more people to do, in terms of the work effort?

Well, like on our line, they're more, you know like if you've got another backup to help you out with your parts, you don't have to stop and get your parts or stuff like that there, you'll see, you know, *there'll be less stress on you*. And then you've got little tickets you've got to fill out and stuff like that, and so that be if somebody's done that, have that taken care of, that is more stress off of you. With that, I mean, you can keep running, you know. . . .

Okay. So in general then you don't see that it's necessarily changed too much.

No.

The third was also a welder, with five years' tenure, whom I code as *no intensification.* He lauded the benefits of teamwork and job rotation, including relieving boredom and providing more product knowledge for the workers:

Considering these transitions, these changes, such as the cells and the job rotation and stuff, have there been, how has the workforce adjusted to this do you think?

It's hard to speak for everybody, but *I like it*. I think it's really brought on a lot. Because I remember the way it used to be. You'd come in and you'd sit and you'd do the same job for three or four days and it would just be ugly. And with the cells, it breaks things up some and you can kind of—you know now at least you can watch the part and you know—you've got five guys that normally run it and they know what to look for.

So you kind of know what else happens to it and where it's going and stuff.

Yeah.

So you feel like you know a little more about the product and position.

Yeah.

Do you think that these changes have led to changes in the effort levels that are expected of workers?

That's a hard one to say. And there's people out there that really work hard and there's people that just kind of, you know, they just kind of flow along.

The fourth was a press operator with seven years' tenure, whom I code as *no intensification.* He described how he likes his job because he never gets bored:

So basically, all these changes over the last few years, the job rotation in cells haven't really affected your job that much?

Not really. You know, like in a line or something, then I'd probably ask for rotation because doing the same thing—see, I'm doing several different things. Even though I'm running on the press, you know, I'm filling baskets, I'm changing dies. . . .

Okay. So you haven't had, again, since you haven't been affected much, you haven't had much new responsibilities with the new cellular manufacturing stuff?

No. The only time we'd have something different is like if we do get a new job or a new design of muffler and have to put a different die in. That would be about it. You know trying to get it to work, where you can run it down the line.

The fifth was an assistant supervisor with fourteen years' tenure, whom I code as *no intensification.* He suggested that continuous flow improved quality and, if anything, made the pace easier:

In terms of this change to cells and the sort of breaking down the work roles and giving people more tasks, do you think that this has led to an increase in the amount of effort that's expected of employees?

The amount of effort?

Yeah.

I don't know about amount of effort. *I think it's raised the quality level*, you know, by going to one-piece flow. Because now the operator sees, "Okay, this job was a little bit more difficult than I thought, so maybe I shouldn't have been burying Joe behind me," or whatever. So it's just, you know, where one person is doing it all, they see, "Okay, there's something that I have to look at a little bit more in this station." So he just goes ahead and does it and he's running more an equal pace. *It's just easier*, it's easier to pace out two people compared to ten people, you know. . . .

I mean the biggest thing that we can see is quality. Now you might have one or two scrap parts, where before you might have a thousand before it got caught. But with the one-piece flow, it's a completed part, a completed component part, and so you know the quality sooner.

Metalfab Plus

I interviewed four workers at Metalfab Plus, a nonunion shop. The first was a team coordinator for the punch press department, with nine years' tenure, whom I code as *no intensification.* He found the new lean practices an improvement to his work experience. The main thing he mentioned was a lean visual management board:

Now, I'm wondering what your sort of general reaction is to, you know, these new types of things that we've been discussing: the cells, and maybe the kanbans, *that kind of stuff?*

At first I didn't believe in the *kanbans*, but once I got to know it, I really like it.

Okay. And how has it like affected your work or your experience out there?

It's just easier to just look at the board. I think it's easier, just look at the board, "Okay, I know I have to run this within the next day or so." It was a lot easier I think.

The second was a utility tech with thirteen years' tenure, whom I code as *positive qualitative intensification.* He noted that running three manual machines in a cell does require more mental effort, having to be concerned with three quality issues instead of one. But he said he didn't have any complaints about this and thinks "change is good":

> Well, I guess it's easier running [only the press] brake because you have more things to watch for when you're running all of it [in a cell]. Once you get trained on it or used to it, I guess, it's more stuff to watch, but it works out alright.
>
> *Working in the cell and being responsible for the multiple processes?*
>
> Yeah. Correct. That's the hardest part is to keep an eye on everything instead of just one thing. . . . to make sure your pems are straight and then when you're bending it, make sure you bend it right; when you're punching it, make sure that there's no slug marks.
>
> *Uh-huh. But you didn't find any one particularly more arduous than the other or . . .*
>
> No. . . . I don't really have that many complaints. Kind of go with the flow. . . . Change is good. Try to make it the best you can.

The third was a drill press operator with eight years' tenure, whom I code as *no intensification.* The main changes she experienced were that raw materials (coil steel) and tools are now located within the department rather than outside of it. When I asked her about any major changes, she noted that a new tool crib means she doesn't have to run all over the place:

> *Have there been any changes—I mean so there's been some reorganization out there, not drastic transformation—but has there been things that, you know, have made your job particularly easier, harder, more interesting, more boring? Any of the above?*
>
> [Laughs] Yeah. It's nice that they have, they put a tool crib out in our area to keep the tooling that we use more out there right by us so we aren't running back and forth across the shop to get it. But, they just have to keep all the right stuff in there. But other than that, not that I've really—unh-unh.

The fourth worker was an assembler with five years' tenure, whom I code as *no intensification.* Her main concern was that the business had been "slowing down." After a long conversation about her work, I asked her a broad question about job satisfaction, and she indicated that she liked her work:

> *So if I could kind of ask a pretty general question here, are there particular aspects of your job that you like, any particular ones that you dislike? Anything that just pops into your head?*

I like the line. I like the whole line.

You do?

Yep. That's what I'm doing.

That's good. Are there particular aspects about it that you like, I mean that . . .

More than others?

Yeah, I mean is it just that it's kind of, you know, interesting work or it keeps you busy, that kind of stuff, or . . . ?

I know what I'm doing, you know. It goes day by day, you know, which job you like better, and some days you don't get on that job because the person's staying caught up. But I think most of all the whole line, you know, I like about the same.

Plastic Containers

I interviewed two workers at Plastic Containers, a nonunion shop. The first worker was a process technician with fourteen years' tenure, whom I code as *positive qualitative intensification*. He explained how management explicitly opted for speedup *instead* of getting leaner: rather than reducing batch sizes and running a larger number of smaller batches, they opted to focus on maximizing machine uptime and having workers run two machines. While he noted that many workers did complain about speedup, from his perspective running one machine is so boring—these are automatic machines—that having to run two is an improvement and having to pay more attention makes the work less boring:

Have there been any other changes in the layout or the organization out there, the way that the work is done?

Oh, a little bit. They've tried to get it into a cell type deal, where you'd have four people working, one to a pair of machines. But . . . we don't even really do that . . . because our fourth machine is just basically sitting idle right now because they decided they'd rather load up three machines and run them 24 hours, seven days a week, than bounce between machinery. . . .

And so we've basically become more efficient and the people that are picking parts can't just stand there and pick. Unless it's a really fast job, you have to pick the parts, watch the tub that the regrind is falling in, and go out and stack parts, stack boxes after you're done. And if it's a really slow job you get to run the recycling out to the grinding area and bring it back here and do tubs on your own too.

Okay, so in some sense it's increased the responsibilities out there.

Yeah. And forced more cooperation basically.

How have people reacted to that? To taking on new responsibilities and having to work together more?

Working together more isn't the problem. When they told them they'd have to, one person would have to run two machines they, "Oh, oh, oh!" Screech, screech, you know. *But it's no more work if you pay attention to what you're doing.* The only time it's really any more work is the first thing when you come in. Then you have to get everything straightened out and you've got two machines to worry about instead of one (emphasis added). Well, when you've got to actually move a lot faster, you don't have as much time to get bored.

The second was a machine operator with two years' tenure, whom I code as *positive qualitative intensification*. He also described a reduction in downtime, but saw this—along with job rotation—in largely positive light, having reduced boredom:

And then can you just tell me what you do on an average day, your routine?

Well, it varies between picking the parts and putting them in a box and actually running machines. One machine is actually three simultaneously, so you have to coordinate those together. It's governed by a touch-screen computer, and it goes through an oven, you know, so you have to coordinate all those. And then when the job's done you have to tear it apart and set up a new, you know, all three tools for the new job.

And how often do you do a changeover or a setup?

In any given week, probably three or four times. It depends on how long a job runs. A job could run 24 hours, you know, or three, depending on what the order is.

Okay. So, and those changeovers then, do you usually do—I mean the setup, you do that, can you do setups on your own?

You can, yeah. I can set all three machines up, but you know, time is money really. They want two or three people doing it at the same time. Our average setups take about two hours and ten minutes, two hours, fifteen minutes.

And, but you set the final tolerances and all that stuff?

Yeah, you have to get it just right. It's like solving a Rubik's Cube, you know, because you have guide bars to guide the parts down; you have to get the tension just right on that or they'll crack it or break or whatever. . . .

Okay. How long does it take to get proficient at that?

Well, when I got hired I was primarily packing, you know, and they kind of eased me into it. But, oh, it probably took me a couple months, two or three months to get it just right. You know they have so many different parts, you know, you have to get familiar with every one of them. You want to get it right, you know. So that takes a while.

Okay. And how about the job rotation out there then? Do you sometimes, like do you do operating more often than picking, or . . . ?

Yeah, my boss is pretty good about shuffling us around, because picking parts gets pretty tedious. You know, you do that all week you're not looking forward to your job. So he's pretty good about, you know, one day I'll operate, the next day I'll pick. . . .

Right.So that that's one of the advantages then, or one of the good things is . . .

Yeah, *one of the good things is you're not doing the same thing every day*, all week. You know, the parts are different. You might have, changeovers are actually good because you don't look at the clock all day, you know. I usually look up, all of a sudden two hours went by, you know, instead of watching it every minute while you're packing parts. No, you never know what you're going to get every day you walk in.

Okay. Now sort of a general question. Are there any specific aspects of the job here that you either particularly like or particularly dislike?

Well, I don't like . . . it gets boring packing parts for eight hours. That gets, that's pretty much . . . What I like about it is it's like being a mechanic; you work with your hands. . . . And if you do it just right you don't have to tweak it up after it's running, you know. You start it up and everything comes out perfect, you know, that's what I like doing. Like I don't have to do anything, you know, just sit there all day and watch it go by, and maybe sweep up the floor.

Zinc Castings

I interviewed four workers at Zinc Castings, a union shop. They used to have separate departments for casting, trimming, machining, and vibrating. Now all the operations are connected in a cell, which has a caster and machine operator, the latter doing trimming, drilling, tapping, sanding, and coating. The first worker was a die caster with seven years' tenure, whom I code as *no intensification.* His main concern was that the shop had been losing work due to defective parts. In the following discussion, he described a general problem with quality control, which in his view resulted from use of temporary workers—"the problem now is we have a lot of temps"—and bad management:

> Part of the QA Department should actually be the one that's actually in charge of whether or not it's a good part, because they have to deal with the customer when a customer calls and says, "You just shipped us a bunch of junk." Because management stepped on his foot and said, "It's a good part, ship it anyway." And I've seen that a lot.
>
> *Oh, so the QA would maybe not be happy with the part, but management will say, "Ship it anyway."*
>
> Yep.
>
> *How often does that happen?*
>
> Quite a bit. That happens quite a bit. I've actually watched our plant manager—not plant manager—our shop supervisor . . . they had a bunch of parts, I think they were bent, and he was out there beating them with a hammer trying to straighten them out and ship them. And he did. He got away with it, but the customer sent them all right back. And that's the kind of stupid crap they do around here. . . .
>
> And that, you know, the economy the way it is today, everything's just disappearing out of here, and then you're going to take, we're still making these parts and you're going to beat them with a hammer and then ship them to our customer? It's senseless.

A second was a machine operator with four years' tenure, whom I code as *no intensification.* She didn't have any complaints and said she liked her job:

> *Are there other things that we have not talked about in terms of your job, things that you either particularly like or dislike?*
>
> No. I'm pretty happy here.

A third was a maintenance person with three years' tenure, whom I code as *no intensification.* He was very happy with his job: "Oh, I really enjoy it." He did not mention any form of work intensification.

The fourth was a shop lead foreman who had four years' tenure and whom I code as *no intensification.* The plant had moved to cellular production before he was there, so he didn't experience much change: "Nothing has really changed that much. We've gotten rid of one old machine, moved a couple around a little bit, but that's about it. It's pretty much the same as it was." His only complaint was that management was keeping too much distance from the workers and not expressing appreciation for their hard work:

> I mean you need to have more, you know, to know that management is backing, you know, all of management is backing us out there. There's been times that I've gone, I've pulled some 12s [12-hour shifts] and that stuff and never even got a thanks. You know, but it's something that slips by. It's the little things like that. You know it's like, "Hey, you guys did a great job," or whatever.

Conclusion

My convenience sample is not representative. Indeed, it may be skewed toward factories whose management has strategically chosen to focus on making qualitative changes to routines and operational systems that improve performance (quality) rather than focus primarily on increasing effort levels (quantity). Managers adopting an intensification strategy may be less likely to agree to participate in a research study.

In any case, the findings are striking in light of the literature, in which critics charge that lean is first and foremost a system of work intensification (Carter et al. 2011, 2013a; Carter et al. 2013b; Danford 1999; Graham 1995; Parker and Slaughter 1995; Rinehart et al. 1997; Stewart et al. 2009). These critics see work intensification primarily in quantitative terms, focusing on speedup and the removal of buffers. I do not question their findings but believe they have too hastily generalized from case studies of auto assembly plants. As discussed more in Chapter 10, the context of auto assembly—a combination of razor-thin margins, astronomical downtime costs, and high volumes—focuses managerial attention on throughput as a key metric and work intensification as a priority.

My findings—in this and the following three chapters, based on evidence from managers *and* workers—document a cross-section of American mangers using lean to pursue qualitative transformation of the labor process rather than quantitative work intensification. Paul Thompson (2003) highlighted the qualitative intensification of labor across sectors in the postfordist era: increasing demands for intellectual labor (and for emotional labor in service contexts). Lean is one of a broader set of management systems and practices that can be used to increase intensification in search of flexibility and organizational learning. But the story here is not one of (i) uniform intensification or of (ii) uniformly negative experiences with intensification.

First, within any of the four approaches to lean I have identified, organizations are internally heterogeneous: some positions and jobs are more impacted than others by lean practices, and not every worker is subject to these demands. Many workers described little impact to their daily routines under lean, other than job rotation and working with lower inventories and shorter, more frequent production runs.

Second, all but one of the workers who reported work intensification experienced it as a positive change that made their work less boring or more challenging. That being noted, some workers I interviewed did not desire more intellectually demanding work. For these workers, qualitative intensification is a negative, stress-inducing situation. In my sample all workers of this orientation worked in or were able to transfer to non-intellectually demanding positions. But I heard reports of colleagues stressed out by intellectually demanding work.

While some of this variation in worker orientations is surely rooted in personality traits, my findings are suggestive of adaptation and changing preferences regarding work. They are also suggestive of the critical role of local culture and ideology within each workplace. The findings document divergent reactions to identical practices, including variation within and across workplaces. This is clearest in the case of cross training, which was welcome in most workplaces, but was met with serious resistance among much of the workforce at Second Tier Specialist. Similarly, teamwork and gainsharing are often welcome but were met with serious resistance at Custom Seats. Without meaning to cast any judgement, it seems in both cases an oppositional narrative was fueling resistance on the shopfloor.

The standard labor process interpretation would be to see this opposition as a righteous form of resistance to managerial attempts to maximize exploitation and control. While such resistance may be well-justified based on a lifetime of working for bad, incompetent, or vindictive managers, the standard labor process interpretation is too crude. The managers I interviewed were interested in qualitatively improving their labor processes, not in maximizing quantitative intensification or control. And the workers varied in their orientations. In short, labor process theory should not impute homogeneous interests to labor or management.

7

The Workforce Contradiction

As we saw in Chapter 3, one vein of labor process theory postulates that because workers have "been forced to sell their labor power to another" (Braverman 1974: 39), they "have an interest in expending as little effort as possible" (see also Edwards 1979: 12; Lazonick 1990: 14). In this rational choice analysis—a crude model with no textual basis in Marx—workers are a homogeneous category with uniform interests in minimizing effort due to the fact that they have alienated their labor to the authority of capitalist management.

In contrast, my position builds on the sociological contributions of Michael Burawoy (1982), Hugh Willmott (1990), and Randy Hodson (2001). Burawoy argued that workers proactively try to make their work interesting by playing games around output targets. Willmott suggested that workers embrace deskilled work routines *because* of their alienation, in an attempt to establish a stable identity. Hodson argued that workers try to make their work meaningful, taking pride in their work and seeking to be efficient, productive workers.

This chapter begins with thick description to make two points. First, I document variation in individual orientations toward work, including preferences toward lean practices in particular and intellectually demanding work more generally. Many of the factories I observed had oppositional factions within the workforce, putting up concerted resistance to lean, often in battle with collaborationist factions. Other factories had little overt resistance, but in all cases where management adopted strategy of substantive empowerment, managers complained of worker reticence. Second, I provide some evidence that orientations and preferences are adaptable.

Turning from description to analysis, I examine the workforce contradiction and offer an explanation for why some workers resist or are reticent toward their own empowerment. On the one hand, workers experience productive socialization via education and skill acquisition, both outside and inside the workplace. Within the workplace, training in new skills and

Management Divided. Matt Vidal, Oxford University Press. © Matt Vidal (2022).
DOI: 10.1093/oso/9780198795278.003.0007

inclusion in problem solving and decision making are objective (though limited and precarious) forms of empowerment. On the other hand, workers objectively alienate their labor to capitalist management, which may produce subjective alienation, feelings of powerlessness due to lack of control over one's labor, and apathy and meaninglessness due to work being directed by another rather than being a self-driven expression of creativity. This leads some workers to be skeptical of management. They have experience with management rejection of their ideas, broken promises, and, in many cases, incompetent or bad management. And in the context of weak unions and no institutionalized mechanisms for worker voice (such as statutory works councils), they know that their contributions to decision making will be limited to specific issues and that management can override their decisions or revoke their empowerment at any time. This contradictory situation produces a contradictory consciousness for workers, making managerial attempts to get knowledge and ideas from workers, or train them in new skills, deeply contested.

The findings in this chapter highlight a specific aspect of managerial authority: the rejection of worker ideas. This often happens even when there are channels for workers to give input or be involved in group problem solving and decision making, due to the assertion of managerial prerogative. Further, while most workers are interested in doing high-quality, efficient work and in the success of their company, many conceive of quality and efficiency, and of the proper division of labor between managers and workers, through a fordist lens. The logic of fordism continues to have a strong influence on workplace culture, custom, and practice, often having been enshrined in union contracts for decades. Such fordist views remain prevalent among the workforce, conflicting with the postfordist practice of management.

Two caveats are in order. First, I don't mean to suggest that some workers are simply being nostalgic for fordism. Rather, the theory is that (i) some workers are skeptical of management and (ii) some workers continue to think through fordist conceptual frameworks (most likely through unconscious or automatic cognition).

Second, in addition to skepticism toward management, workers and union leaders may also be skeptical toward lean over fear of job loss due to efficiency increases and to workers being easily replaceable due to cross training and the collapse of job classifications. For example, in Chapter 6, the sweeper and parts washer at Second Tier Specialist noted that some union members were worried that multiskilling would lead to reduced employment because workers can cover multiple jobs. I highlight skepticism due to rejection of worker ideas and the influence of fordist logics efficiency and the division of labor because they were the most prominent themes in my interviews. My data suggest that skepticism toward management and fordist conceptual schemas are both critical factors. Understanding the weight of their influence versus generalized skepticism toward management or concerns about job loss and replaceability must await future research.

Variation in Individual Orientations Toward Work

As noted in Chapter 6, of the twelve factories in which I interviewed managers and workers, my informants reported overt and substantial resistance to managerial attempts to implement lean practices in three (Second Tier Specialist, Custom Seats, and Hydraulic Systems, all union shops), a moderate amount of resistance at one (Designer Railings, nonunion), and no overt resistance in eight. In this chapter I primarily focus on the four factories just named, along with Industrial Pumps, another nonunion shop in which workers expressed frustration and disagreement with management. These more sustained analyses are supplemented with assorted quotes from other establishments.

A common theme in the factories where there was substantial resistance to lean is that there are three factions on the shop floor: those who embrace the change and see it as a welcome challenge; those who actively resist it; and those in the middle who are ambivalent and reticent. The latter category includes workers who quietly cooperate with new practices, but generally do not expend discretionary effort to proactively engage in problem solving or even offer ideas for improvement. This middle group of ambivalent workers—according to both managers and workers—includes many who are susceptible to the influence of shopfloor leaders from one of the more vocal camps.

The plant manager at Designer Railings summed up the three groups:

> You know, there's really three, there's a group of three: there's the violently opposed, there are the ones that are very willing to change and try and move on, and then there's the great unwashed in the middle that will move back and forth until they finally choose a side.

He noted that the situation on the shopfloor is fluid and potentially volatile because of the role leaders on the shopfloor can play in swaying opinion. If there is a detractor, "to the extent that that person is a leader on the shop floor or vocal or critical or respected, that becomes an issue to be overcome."

The plant manager at Second Tier Specialist made the same point about the influence of leaders on the floor:

> And it just, it takes, you're never going to get 100 percent, and I wouldn't expect to, but you need to get a significant quantity of the informal leaders converted over. And if you don't, they're going to fight you. You know, they might even smile and shake their heads yes in meetings, but boy, out on that shop floor they're talking it down.

In his shop, "I think initially it was more fighting it. There's less fighting in now. I'd say instead of 70% fighting it now we're down to 30 or 40% fighting the change."

The machinist with thirty-four years' tenure at Specialist expressed the same point about three groups:

> Because some guys will run to the challenge, and some guys choose to run away from the challenge. Some guys want to stay locked in and do this [battle management]. And there again, those numbers are few. Some guys want to keep things as status quo as possible, and will learn new things as they're presented to them, and that's the main body. And then there's some, the leadership guys want to go forward and pick up and learn as much as we can and move the system forward. So I think we've still got those three separate entities still working.

A different machinist from Specialist, the union president, was an advocate of the high-performance work organization partnership. He described the fierce debates they have on the shopfloor, including serious resistance to lean by one faction within the workforce. Much of the resistance is to cross training and job rotation, a flashpoint issue in ongoing union negotiations in which management was attempting to reduce job classifications from over fifty to seven flexible jobs. He noted that a history of acrimonious relations with past management has contributed to dissatisfaction and resistance to management initiatives. As he explained:

> Yeah, the management leadership team, you know, it's comprised of our shop floor committee, there's a couple of guys in there had gone around with me more than once in the last eight months over this whole thing. And they continue to go around with me. . . . And boy, I had fights out there on the floor where, I mean, people were just screaming at the top of their lungs. . . .
>
> The backlash that I receive is intense, in that the guys that are for it don't have a gripe and they go along with it, but the guys that aren't really for it aren't accustomed to change, really seem to get on me and I would expect a few of the other people on the executive board. I've had a few clashes with the committee . . . we've bumped heads in the past as far as how we're going to proceed with some of the training issues. . . .
>
> I do think it's going to blow over. I think the initial shock of the whole thing, a lot of things were coming down at once here with the new job positions, people being laid off, there was some animosity on the floor over past management. Just a lot of things involved in the pie that people were concerned with and there was a high stress situation out there. I think they're starting to tone down a little bit.

Other managers didn't experience much overt or organized resistance but were concerned with worker reticence. At Mini OE, a union shop, the VP of Operations explained:

> It wasn't as much resistance, but [problems with] active participation, I want to say apathy, it might not be the right word, but, just kind of standing around to see what happens. With another program, is it going to go away in a couple of weeks? You know, "I'm happy doing what I want to do, I don't want to do any more than that." So, you know, we work around them. They're starting to come over but it's not very active.
>
> It's normally the senior employees. Most of the new hires, it's just their job, it's just the way we do things. The culture change that we've been able to achieve has been greater than if we had 100 twenty-year employees, versus ten 15-year employees and 90 new ones.

The plant manager at Industrial Pumps also discussed this middle group, suggesting that much of this reticence stems from workers have a traditional view of the responsibilities of labor and management.

[They] will basically do what you tell them to do. You know they don't want to, they're not what you would call, you know, they're not going to go stick their necks out and give you a bunch of good ideas. And, you know, that's unfortunate, it's the nature of manufacturing sometimes; you've got people that just want to be told what to do. . . . you get an occasional idea from them . . . But not, you know, they're not going to come out and offer you five or six different ways to improve.

An engineer from Pumps seconded this sentiment:

They're not going to come out and say, "Can we tear my work area up and move stuff around because I think it would be better this way." They'll just be like, "When are they going to come fix my area?" And wait, and wait, and wait.

While worker orientations can change and leaders can play a role in swaying opinion, oppositional factions have two deeper sources, both of which are concrete manifestations of alienation. First, workers develop a distrust of and skepticism toward management due to experience with management fads of the month, previously aborted, or failed initiatives. In the words of the union president at Specialist, a machinist with eight years' tenure: "We had some people come in here and said they were going to do wonderful things for us. . . . And things didn't transpire the way they said they would." The perceptive plant manager at Specialist was aware of this problem, acknowledging that "in the past it was just management's fad of the month, just a program to exert on the workforce."

In the local union meeting I attended, such sentiment was common. This meeting was attended by a facilitator from the IAM HPWO department, who was in town to give a presentation at Specialist to the whole workforce, on company time, along with the Business Agent for the union district, and two facilitators from the WRTP. In their discussion of the IAM HPWO Partnership, I recorded the following quotes from an extended conversation:

We've been hit the face with the mallet so many times before, it's hard to know what to believe.

We've done *kaizen* before and they were all gung-ho about it . . . for about 4 days.

We're all skeptical—what they say one day can change the next day, one hour to the next hour.

Both sides are looking at each other and asking if they can trust each other.

Business Agent: Management is giving up some rights here and we have some power. We have to change the culture [of the workplace].

HPWO facilitator: HPWO is more than a self-directed workforce.

Business Agent: If it ever gets to the point where they give us lip service, we're out of there. But we have to adapt to changing markets and technologies.

We see the boss in the morning and then in the evening. We already run this shop—we need to get equal say in the decisions.

They are really giving us some say here in structure and strategy.

We have 68 members and only 14 here. You can see what they think about it.

More broadly, workers' experience with management initiatives implemented in a top-down fashion, without consultation or negotiation, leads to frustration and skepticism. Further, as demonstrated below, when management does encourage workers to give ideas, a common outcome is that workers see their ideas being rejected, again generating skepticism and distrust. In sum, for very good reasons—aborted management initiatives, failed initiatives, top-down management, bad management—these workers developed a "definition of the situation" (March and Simon [1958] 1993: 160) in which there is a clear demarcation between their interests and that of management.

The second source contributing to the formation of oppositional factions in the workplace is that worker orientations often derive from and are rooted in custom and practice, which conflicts with new management ideas and practices. For example, the cases of Second Tier Specialist and Custom Seats illustrate how workers who have mastered one particular skillset/machine/process become accustomed to coming in every day and working only on *their* machine or process. These workers had a deep craft pride in their work and expressed keen interest in the performance of the plant as a whole, seeing practices such as job rotation and just-in-time production as inefficient.

Such workers' understanding of *their* work was very much based in and around the routine they had developed by working on a single machine or process. They were not interested in cross training and job rotation; their work values were based in doing one thing and doing it well, producing high levels of high-quality output. And in union shops, new routines and responsibilities required a substantial reorganization of work arrangements that the workforce had appropriated as their own and solidified in a union contract. The plant manager at Systems was sensitive to this problem:

> Again, the company here has over 50 job descriptions . . . we came from a very traditional manufacturing environment where, let's say, Henry ran his lathe, he trained on it, didn't even necessarily go through an apprenticeship, learned it and is on it until he retires. Again, we're moving away from that now to cross training, moving people to where the work is, not looking at the efficiency of the machine as far as the machine producing as many parts as it can to capacity . . . Instead, the whole goal in the future, as we go forward here, is move the people to where the work is, have them as highly trained and able to run different machines, perform different operations as possible.

Pride in one's work and preferences for doing one thing and doing it well are not limited to union shops. For example, a press operator from Tubefab explained that he preferred working on the same machine to having to rotate and learn about new routines:

> Actually I like running the same machine. I mean, just walking into the job and start running. Where you, some of the other jobs, if you're not used to running them you've got to figure out the ins and outs in a lot of them . . . Most of the jobs I've got on that big press I can usually jump right on and get it going right away.

To be sure, this worker saw benefits to variety, but he was able to get sufficient variety from working his machine: "I'm doing several different things. Even though I'm running on the press . . . I'm filling baskets, I'm changing dies. Where for a person on the line that's just welding all day long, then you probably want [job] rotation." Running his press involved a complex array of activities that involved careful attention and detailed, precise work that he considered challenging and rewarding. Yet this worker expressed little interest in learning new tasks and skills, gaining a greater understanding of the overall production process. He made his work meaningful by becoming an expert in a particular operation, embracing it as something he can excel at and derive satisfaction from, but not wanting to learn other machines or develop new skills.

As the foregoing quote suggests, job rotation relieves boredom when the job consists of simple, discrete tasks. But even many semiskilled jobs are sufficiently complex to make the job interesting enough for some workers. Other workers I spoke with expressed preferences for running a single machine, noting that being a press operator can be more interesting than it might appear. A tube bender at Designer Railings, who was not involved in job rotation, said "it's an interesting job, you know, something that you know that you're going to be bending, but you bend different degrees and you have different tangents every day, which makes the job interesting." Similarly, a trainer at LV Gaskets explained that being a press operator, a semiskilled job, requires a high level of attention. He described the blanking machine:

> And there's things to watch out for, it's not just push some buttons. It sounds easy, but you've got to make sure your tool's alright, about making scrap, you've got to be fully aware of what's going on around you. And the safety issue is major here, and I really applaud that. Safety's first. We had like electric eye light curtains and stuff, and thank goodness, we haven't had a problem.

By way of contrast, the machinist with thirty-four years' tenure at Specialist saw cross training as a welcome challenge and an opportunity to become a more highly skilled worker:

> I like the challenge and I want to learn something different. So I'm perfectly willing to move forward . . . It makes us more overall machinists rather than machine operators. And for the longest time it used to be the other way around, where you were an apprentice, the old apprenticeship system where you learned in a work circle, and you learned how to be a machinist on a drill press, on a lathe, and a grinder and other stuff. I think we're moving back toward that now where we're training everybody that they can go on a situation and perform the job.

Beyond the specific practices associated with lean, there is variation in worker orientations toward engagement in problem solving and decision making. A machinist at Hydraulic Systems again described three distinct groups:

> Now you've got about 10 percent of the people that will get involved, okay? You've got 80 percent that will just sit and wait, and you've got 10 percent that it doesn't make any difference what you did, they won't do anything.

Like the managers from Industrial Pumps quoted above, this machinist thinks that reticence toward providing ideas and cognitive labor is due to workers having a traditional view of the responsibilities of labor and management. Such people prefer not to have what they see as managerial responsibilities:

> They don't seem to want to be involved. They're real content being told what to do.
>
> *Um-hmm.*
>
> I mean I don't know what else to tell you on that one. They're just content being told what to do.
>
> *Sure. I mean I think that makes sense for some people, you know. If they, you know, that they want to come into work and just do their job and be told what to do and not have to deal with all the stress and other stuff.*
>
> Well, yeah. That goes back to that old philosophy of, you know, we hired you for your back not your mind, you know.
>
> *Right.*
>
> I mean there's some people that still believe in that philosophy. . . . They just believe that's the way it is, because it's been that way for a bazillion years.

A sweeper and parts washer at Second Tier Specialist expressed such a traditional view with regard to committees. Specialist had several committees, which are ways for workers to get involved in decision making, including through the Labor-Management Committee and the Training Committee. However, in her view:

> it seems like they have too many committees. I don't know why they need to have all these committees. I don't think that's necessary. I think they should just deal with the union committee, period. I don't think there should be all this training committee . . .

I return to workers who do not want to have managerial responsibilities below, arguing that in some cases this is due to a fordist view of the proper division of labor. But in other cases, the issue is that such intellectually demanding work is stress-inducing. When I interviewed the forklift driver at Custom Seats, we were physically located on the side of the building where they are doing the most continuous improvement, which this worker avoided: "They're always changing things around here. I don't get on this side that often. It's a jungle, I don't like it on that side."

Similarly, an assembler at Integrated Blinds explained how she doesn't want decision making responsibility because it would be too much stress:

> I've always told myself that if I can come in and do my job and like what I'm doing, and not take it home, that's the kind of person I am. I wouldn't be probably good at an office or anything, because I don't want a higher-level job where I'd have stress that I would have to take home. For me it's, what's outside of work, you know. You've got to love your job too, but I mean I'm happy to leave it here and then just be able to go home and, you know, I have three kids, so, enjoyment. But I'm real happy with it.

By contrast, other workers appreciate being involved in continuous improvement activities. At Hydraulic Systems, the Wisconsin Regional Training Partnership (WRTP), the union-backed workforce intermediary, facilitated the development of a 5S committee and taught them how run *kaizen* events. A machinist explained how helpful he found a setup reduction *kaizen* event:

> They came in here and they actually showed us how to do these, run these meetings. We went out there and we did a job and we videotaped it while I did the job, and we came back upstairs and then we put it on the monitor and we—you actually could see how many steps we were taking that were way too many, you know. We had to, you know, we made shadow boards and we made a, we moved stuff and we organized. And it helped. Helped a lot. But that was the 20 percent; the 80 percent was the scheduling.

I return to this example and this machinist below. Similarly, an assembler at Industrial Pumps, who had just been promoted to supervisor and had been involved in 5S and value-stream mapping *kaizen* events, explained how they were beneficial:

> It flows, the flow is so much better than what it used to be. I mean introducing lean, you know the 5S program, I mean I like those programs. They really help take out things that are a waste of time, you know.

To conclude this section, I present some brief evidence that such orientations and preferences are adaptable, that workers can learn to appreciate a practice they initially were skeptical of or resistant toward once they have some experience with it. For the team coordinator for the punch press department at Metalfab Plus, "At first I didn't believe in the *kanbans*, but once I got to know it, I really like it." Similarly, for a machinist at Industrial Pumps, "I've gotten used to the change, I guess . . . I've gotten used to just kind going with the flow, and if that's what they want, you know, and not—I don't make too many waves." And a trainer at LG Gaskets described his initial reaction to a Lean 101 training, and then his changed position after seeing it work on is shopfloor: "I'll tell you, it floored all of us at first, you know. It's just like, 'What?' But when you, you know, see it in action and you—it makes sense. It does."

In sum, workers vary in their orientations toward specific lean practices and more generally toward taking on managerial responsibilities. Workplaces are often split into factions regarding change: resistant, supportive, and reticent. Worker resistance often results due to well-motivated skepticism and distrust from past experience or an orientation based in custom and practice. But workers also vary in their orientations toward intellectually demanding work, some welcoming the challenge, others finding it stressful. At the same time, workers can be adaptable in their orientations, both based on the influence of leaders and gaining experience with a new practice.

Having demonstrated worker resistance to and reticence toward their own partial empowerment, and previewed the reasons why, I now present a more sustained analysis of these reasons. In addition to skepticism toward management based on experience, my data highlight how worker resistance or reticence toward empowerment stems from two concrete manifestations of alienation. First, managers routinely reject workers' ideas. Second, to make work meaningful, realize a purpose, or feel pride in response to their alienation, workers embrace particular notions of efficiency and the proper ownership of responsibilities. These worker orientations are often based in local workplace culture, custom, and practice, in which fordist logics of efficiency and the proper division of labor continue to exert a strong influence.

The Rejection of Workers' Ideas and Assertion of Managerial Prerogative

One common experience of factory workers is that in the past management would not even consider their suggestions. In more recent years, managers have encouraged workers to give their ideas and often give them serious consideration, but sometimes reject their suggestions. Both situations—refusal to consider worker suggestions or rejection of them after consideration—can drive frustration and resentment.

In Chapter 6 I quoted a machinist from Hydraulic Systems (a union shop) with twenty-five years' tenure who preferred doing setups while another machine is running because it improves efficiency and reduces downtime, but this would only be possible if the workers were allowed to do their own scheduling. I also quoted him above explaining that he found setup reduction to be very helpful. As he went on to explain, he almost did not participate in the 5S Committee due to a history of management refusing to consider his suggestions. However, in response to competitive pressures, "now that things got so bad, it was either listen or we're going under, one of the—I mean we just were really struggling." Hence management allowed the WRTP to come in and develop a labor-management partnership to modernize the workplace and empower the workforce. In this context, the worker was able to make his participation conditional on management empowering him to do his own scheduling:

That's the 5S Committee?

Yes. That, it actually did a lot of good. I actually, I could have told them the answers ten years ago, but nobody wanted to listen. . . .

Did you tell them this ten years ago?

Oh, absolutely. I said, absolutely, becuase when they first came in with this whole, with this whole thing, I told them, I said, "The only way I'm going to get involved in this committee is," I says, "Number one, if you don't change scheduling, then we're banging our heads against the wall and it's not going to work. I mean you're going, you know, you're talking 10, 15 minutes time you're saving, instead of hours."

And when you, you said this ten years ago, they just didn't listen then with that?

Yeah. No, they wouldn't listen.

Yeah. Now are there other, are you also able to offer other ideas for changing things and making things better in your routine? Like if you're doing something and you see that, oh, maybe if we, you know, move this machine here, or did this, or changed this . . .

They're pretty good that way.

They're pretty good?

Yeah, especially after this committee, they really kind of woke up and found out that everybody's on the same page and we're not just trying to, you know, get out of doing some work, it's making our jobs easier. We're producing more and making our jobs easier.

The Shop Chair from Hydraulic Systems, also a machinist, with twenty-three years' tenure, elaborated on how management may consider and then reject worker suggestions. In his view, management genuinely was listening to workers and considering their ideas, but nonetheless he noted that when their ideas get rejected, some workers take it very badly:

You get an idea that you think is great, okay? You take it to management, they do their little study, they look at it, and after they digest it, so to speak, okay, it wasn't that great of an idea. Well then these guys get crushed. Instead of looking at it and saying, "Oh, I never looked at it that way or that way. Yeah, maybe this isn't as big a cost savings as I thought it would be," or something like that, you know. They just look at it like, "Well! Management didn't want to listen to me." That's not true. You know, because when we had our suggestion program, I mean they took every suggestion. We used like 80 percent of them.

Well, then you've got the other problem where, "Hey, I didn't get any money for this." You know, everything's money, money, money. You know, well, you've got a job. You get $33 in benefits, you know? How many places can still say that today? You've got to keep [Hydraulic Systems] functioning, so that you have a job for the next 30 years.

The workers at Second Tier Specialist told a similar story. The union president, a machinist with eight years' tenure and part of the collaborationist faction, noted that those resisting empowerment were the same people who in the past regularly complained about management not listening to workers:

I see more people getting on the bandwagon. It isn't happening as quickly as I'd like to see it happen, but it is happening. I think most of the . . . the feeling that I get is most of the older employees who have been here a long time, I get the feeling that we're trying to tell them what they need to do in their job and that's a tough row to hoe.

I don't, I've been out there speaking positively about the whole management issue and the union working together, but these people are unmoving. But I had said to the union membership, "Look, how many times in the past have you said, 'Management doesn't know what the hell they're doing. Why don't they listen to us?"' And now we have an atmosphere where management has come in and the union has been here with management and they won't work with us. And we've got teams now. We've got cell lead people that are involved, that has just taken off. We've got more committees than we had before. We have union involvement, more so than we had before.

It is noteworthy that he suggested this group consists mainly of workers with a long tenure. The longer management refuses to listen, it seems, the more likely workers are to be skeptical of management and become entrenched in a confrontational position.

The Shop Committee Chair at Specialist, the parts coordinator, noted that workers have "always had a really good input, it's just a matter of having people listen to that input." As he went on to explain, even when managers ask for input they don't always accept or implement workers' ideas:

They'll always say, you know, "We need your input. We want your input. Tell us where there's problems." And there's times when you tell them and nothing gets done though, either. You know? That's my opinion, and I believe a lot of other people's opinion. And you sit there and you just kind of shake your head and you go, "You know, they say they want your input; come and talk to me, come and talk to us." You know, it could be anybody from management saying this. And when you go and talk to them, and you think you really suggested a good idea, and you know there's other people that have that same idea as you, but then nothing gets done, you just shake your head and you wonder. You know, you want input, I gave you some solid input here, but you haven't gone that way. Now, why, you know? So that's . . . I think sometimes it's frustrating.

At Industrial Pumps, a shipping and receiving worker similarly noted such frustration with management rejecting worker suggestions. He noted that he understood that management has a better view of the overall process, but added that it is vexing nonetheless, for him and his fellow workers:

They take our opinions. They weigh them. Sometimes they weigh against us. [Laughs] But, so that's all in—and they see the whole picture, where I only see my area that I deal with. And I think that, you know, to me it's terrible to be out of a nickel part. And because the levels went down so low, it also took that level of nickel part down. But the nickel part can make that $12,000 pump not go out the door.

Because lean has not stopped moving, I mean we—I mean lean means you're always striving for improvement. And in the last several years since lean has come in, we haven't stopped moving. Which I feel—and now again, I was on the planning committee, and everything that we talked about in the planning committee didn't come around.

What was the planning committee?

We, the floor planning committee, where different machines or assemblies or stations should be set up; the flow of the pump, or parts, through the shop.

Was this part of the value-stream mapping?

Yes, the value-stream mapping.

Okay. And so you're actually on the, in the value-stream mapping. . .

Yes.

Were there just two shop floor workers, was it just you and someone else?

I think there was actually one from each department.

One from each department?

Um-hmm, yeah. And, you know, we had a lot of great ideas, we took our ideas—of course there's only just Roger and I, and Kim in the storage area, so you know, whatever I brought down, I relayed on to them. Which didn't really necessarily involve our area that much. Where, you know, where it involved was, the biggest involvement was either polishing or the machine shop. Because you can't move polishing and you can't move the machines. So we had, we have to work around that.

And now, you said that the planning committee, they came up with some ideas and they didn't get implemented.

Unh-unh.

Was the planning committee the whole value-stream mapping committee or was it just . . . ?

No, it was, people from it, we were the planning, the floor planning committee.

The floor, okay, so it was the shop floor workers, was the planning committee.
Yeah.

And they had their suggestions and they just didn't take them.

No.

And they did something else.

Yes.

How did that go over with the . . .

Like a lead balloon! [Laughs] Very frustrating. And we're in the process of dealing with that right now. I think that the 5S program has failed in that aspect. They do things before—I don't think in sequence. You know, you see it, you see something being moved where, if they'd have done something differently it would have been able to . . .

You know, so I mean I see the process of one, two, three not happening. They maybe took two, or three, and didn't move one. So, but, and that's not my decision. I only see in this, they don't come over and ask. You know, they just did it. So there was a lot of frustration at that point.

At Designer Railings, the plant manager reported that every single employee had been to a Lean 101 training, that he had been working on systematically communicating with the workforce about their lean restructuring, and attempting to devolve problem-solving and decision-making responsibility. But he did note a serious problem of resistance from his supervisors. Regarding shopfloor workers, he said, "If I could empower them all, I would. But that's the chain of command issues and all that, you know. The empire builders are still out there, you know." As a result, his factory consists of "islands of excellence surrounded by a sea of mediocrity."

The plant manager described how, with their first cell, they got a product that used to take weeks to complete under fordist organization down to "less than a minute a piece" (the full quote is presented in the discussion of Railings in Chapter 8). The cell was designed by a team that included "a quality guy, the two guys that run the cell, one of the tooling guys, the guy in shipping and receiving in that group that works, that does the shipping and receiving for them, and a guy from the customer." The shopfloor workers "sat through every meeting" and were "involved very much."

The plant manager described their broader use of *kaizen* events:

> We have had *kaizen* events where we spent a day a week doing something for like three or four weeks because what needed to take place in between those days would occupy one of the maintenance guys or somebody, some significant amount of time. We couldn't get it all done in a . . . you know, most people think of a *kaizen* as two or three days' intense effort. And we can't, I don't have enough support staff to create something completely new in two or three days. So sometimes we spread those a little bit.

But as the plant manager noted, he has been struggling to diffuse lean and employee involvement throughout his factory. Thus, when I asked a setup press operator with nine years' tenure about continuous improvement, he complained that this appeared to be just another fad of the month:

> *Now you said they were doing more of it. I mean do you do, do you have official, do they call them* kaizen *events? Do they do that here or not?*
>
> No. No. We had, I think, one meeting about that about a year and a half ago, and that was dropped too, pretty much.
>
> *Do you have any idea why it was dropped? Do you think they're going to pick it up in the future, or you don't know?*
>
> I don't think so. They have a, there's a lot of projects here that they just don't actually get done, or changed, or just walk around [laughs].

He noted that "they have more meetings there than you can shake a stick at," but didn't think workers were sufficiently involved:

> *Have there been any other new ways for workers to contribute their ideas in terms of either problem solving-committees or suggestion programs?*
>
> Yeah, they have that. It's the supervisors mainly that are in the meetings. They have the tool and die meetings and things, setup meetings, things like that. But actually the employees, I think the employees on the floor aren't really involved with it. They say if you've got any suggestions bring it in.

And he expressed frustration at a top-down decision-making process in which there were too many supervisors but they would not consider workers' suggestions:

> Well, okay, we have people up here to tell the people downstairs, downstairs people [to] tell that certain department, and there's never an input. We're told what to do, *and a lot of times we can have better ideas on how it's done*, but there's . . . okay, we have office, then we have a Safety Director, then we have Tool and Die supervisors. And they're all trying to improve our job, so everybody's down there. And so I'm listening to a safety guy who, we should be doing this. Tool and Die comes in and says, "You should be doing this." Okay, I'm told to do something else by my supervisor. Okay, where are you? I've got three different supervisors here now. Well, okay. So I'm just going to have to do what my supervisor says. . . . With my supervisors, everybody, it's just, it's frustrating.[1]

I return to this worker in the section below, where he articulates his view that reducing batch sizes is inefficient.

In Chapter 6 I quoted a welder (former assembler) with thirty-three years' experience at Custom Seats, who lost around $10 per hour in the move from piece rates to hourly rates with gainsharing. This worker was terribly frustrated with the new system, which he disagreed with based on his understanding of what is most efficient. I return to this worker in the following section. For now, I simply note that, given his disagreement with lean, his experience of working in problem-solving groups only reinforces his frustration, because he feels like his input is always ignored:

> Yeah, like, I'll go to a meeting and I'll say, "Well, this won't work, that won't work." And then they'll, a couple days later, a week later, I'll hear, "Well, they're doing it." And then I'll hear from somebody else, "Well, [worker's name] was at the meeting." Yeah, I was at the meeting but I didn't agree with what a gall-darn thing you guys did!

Finally, a stapler (former assembler) at Custom Seats, with six years' tenure, illustrates the case that even where workers do not want to be involved in decision making, they still want management to listen to their suggestions. As this stapler explained:

> It's very tough when people don't want to listen to you. You know it's like you're talking to the wall. And you know that it could work out if, but you can only do so much; it's management's job to take care of the rest.

[1] All emphasis in the quotations is mine, unless otherwise noted.

His last comment about "management's job" suggests he has a traditional view of the proper division of labor between management and workers. I now turn to examine such views in more depth.

Commitment to a Vision of Efficiency or of Proper Ownership of Responsibilities

In my interviews with managers, many complained of "cultural" obstacles or of workers having a particular "mindset" that makes it difficult to establish new practices. At Designer Railings, the plant manager described batch size reduction and quick changeover as "one of the cultural issues we are impaling ourselves on right now." He elaborated:

> Our setup issues are real important to us, because if we're going to even get at this demand-driven production we've got to get very good at setups. We've got to have a lot of different dies and, and there are some, *a lot of cultural barriers to overcome*, you know, the idea that it's more important to put a die in a press today than it is to put the die in the right press, operating in the right conditions tomorrow, okay? . . . it's a huge issue.
>
> You know, "Well, we've got to get these out tomorrow!" Well, then put them in the right press tomorrow and do it tomorrow. Because putting it in the wrong press today almost guarantees that we're going to either fail or we're going to do it very unproductively. So we won't fail, but the cost will be very high; which means we will fail. And there's this cultural, "Oh, we've got to get it out today." No, we don't. Not if it's going to be the wrong die going in the wrong press, creating safety issues, quality issues, productivity issues, and . . . and that's, it's a tough thing.

At Industrial Pumps, the plant manager referred to "mental hurdles," by which he meant conventional understandings through which the workforce interprets new practices:

> We do want to get to the one-part flow in time. Something that makes it more difficult for us is the shared equipment, shared resources. *We still struggle with the mental aspect of it too, that we could pull things through the shop*. Everybody still gets really stuck on the fact that we don't make maybe more than two of the exact same part number in any one day. And people just feel that, because we're not making 50 identical lawnmowers all day . . . there's a little bit of difference to

> everything that we do and a lot of shared resources. *We have that mental hurdle to get over.*

And at LV Gaskets, when I asked about continuous flow, the plant manager referred to a "batch shop mentality" and "mindset":

> Well, yes, we are working towards that. We're not very good at it at this point in time. There's always a, you know, *a batch shop mentality* in an operation like this that's been around this long, and people don't feel secure when they don't see inventory. *So some of it simply becomes a mindset change as much as anything else*. You know, and you walk through it and everything goes well for a few weeks, and then everything goes well for a few months, and then you have a hiccup and people will all come back and say, "See, I told you we should have more inventory." And then they want to fall back to the way they were doing it in the past. So, it becomes somewhat of a battle to implement that and get people thinking along that line.

This manager suggested the primary issue is one of security. What I want to show in this section is that it's more than that. The mindset these managers refer to is a specific mindset, namely, a fordist one. And, as I now turn to demonstrate, the concerns of these workers have to do with what they perceive as best practice—in terms of efficiency for the organization. Many workers are committed to a fordist version of efficiency—something that has become part of local workplace culture, custom, and practice—and they defend this against what they see as managerial initiatives that harm efficiency or quality.

I begin with Custom Seats. Both of the managers I spoke with referred to a "mindset" behind resistance to teamwork and job rotation within cells. According to one, on the experience of the individual piece-rate work:

> What this has done culturally however, is *it's created that same mindset* . . . that there's something uniquely complicated or difficult about that, and that I'm the only one who can do it, and this is our expert on this product, and this is our expert on that product. When in fact [the process] actually lends itself more to what I described earlier where, if we could divide the work, and we are as we create cells, you can get to the point where there isn't as much dependence on the skill of the operator. It's something that anybody can learn to do fairly quickly.

> And following the work instructions and the procedures, can learn and will be rotating within an environment very fast.
>
> And they resent efforts that we're making to, I'll say commoditize it, but to break it up so that anybody can do it. Because, "Wait a minute. That's my job. That's where I'm uniquely skilled and . . ." "No, [name], you've got a lot of product knowledge and we respect that, but every one of these guys around you can do it too." And we're going to teach them. You're going to work together in a cell environment doing it together.

He described a form of taylorist work simplification, but seeing this pure deskilling is too reductive. In my reading of the Custom Seats case, management was genuinely offering real opportunities for substantive empowerment, including multiskilling, problem solving, and decision making.

Two of the workers I interviewed were former assemblers who lost income due to the shift from piecework to hourly wages with gainsharing, and had subsequently transferred out of that position. These workers were extremely resentful and rightfully so, given their income loss. However, I want to show here that the source of their resentment was deeper, including their conviction that the new system was inefficient and would be harmful for the company. The sample that management at Seats picked included several disaffected workers, whereas at others, notably Second Tier Specialist, management seems to have included mainly workers from the collaborative faction, so I don't have quotes from these workers expressing conflicting views of efficiency. However, I am able to include quotes here from workers at the remaining plants with overt resistance (Hydraulic Systems and Designer Railings), along with quotes from workers at Industrial Pumps, Tubefab, and Plastic Containers.

I concluded the previous section with the stapler (former assembler) at Custom Seats, who invoked a traditional, fordist view of the proper division of labor between management and workers. In the following extended discussion he expressed a series of complaints, but a common thread among them is a fordist viewpoint, including that the old system, based on individuals maximizing output, was better functioning and more efficient than lean:

> Well, right now I'm a stapler. And then, the cell that I'm in right now, it was one of the original cells that [Custom Seats] started. So I've been in this cell right now for like five months, but before that I was a pieceworker on the hard goods

side . . . And while I was in there it was an incentive job and then the reason why I kind of left was because they took like my job that I did by myself and another, you know, one shift and two shifts. And the reason why I kind of got out of there was because it was so hard for me to do what I do and then put four people in there, three other people, I mean *I had a routine* that I did every day and it was so hard for me to, if I wanted to do something.

So right now I'm stapling in a cell, and the cell that I'm working in, if you've got a bunch of people that work good with each other, it's fine. But if you get one or two people that don't want to work, then it just, it causes a lot of chaos. I mean, you know, it's all who you work with to tell you the truth.

Is that a problem you experience in the new cell?

No.

Or was it something you were experiencing in the old?

Well, it's just something that I see all around. In one cell there, people aren't getting along with each other, so they fight all the time with each other. You know, it's tough. It's like working with your brother or sister too, you know, sometimes you get on each other's nerves. I mean you've got to work with each other every day, 10, 12 hours a day sometimes and it gets tough. Some people handle things differently, you know.

But as far as I'm concerned, going from incentive work to cellular manufacturing, I thought things ran just as good incentive wise than it does for cellular manufacturing. Like going back to the old job that I used to do, I mean they've got four people over there doing what I used to do by myself, you know. And it's like, *I just don't see how that's benefiting anybody or anything*.

When I asked whether thinks these problems have to do with teamwork in general, or with cellular production in particular, he affirmed it was the latter. Here, he said part of the problem was an unclear division of labor, too many people have responsibility having responsibility:

The process involves all four people, and I think a lot of it has to do with there's *too many chiefs and not enough Indians*. That's the way I see it in some other cells, you know. I mean, the cell that I'm in right now, we just do it because, you know, we're on this, all on the same, you know we're all on for the gainsharing that the company's got set up. We all want it, so we do it but, with this company I think that they didn't learn enough about it before they put it into effect. I mean they

> saw what it looked like on paper but it's a lot harder. Like other companies that, this goes here, then it goes there and then it goes there. But with [Custom Seats] there's also a lot of parts that have to go into one particular thing and if you run out of the part, it screws a lot of things up. . . .
>
> But I think everything could work here if there was just better communication between management and the workers on the floor, you know. We know what we're doing. We deal with this stuff every day. We know what the problems are. You know, it's just, there's *too many little committees set up to fix a problem*. You know, and this person will blame it on that person and that person will blame it on the other person. It's just too much like that now.
>
> It seems like for a lot of companies nowadays, you know, I think that they worry about having meetings, they spend more time in meetings than they do doing anything else. So that's the way I see manufacturing nowadays. And my dad, he's been in manufacturing all his life, and just even from when he used to work and how it is now, it's just like, it doesn't seem like it's working as good as it used to.

Again noting a preference for a clear division of labor between management and workers, he explained how he felt that management got them started on a continuous improvement activity but then expected them to finish it:

> They have these brainstorms, where everything looks good on paper. And then they'll set it up that way and then they'll just leave. And then they'll expect the people that are in that cell to make it work, but it's like, *you just give us half the stuff, you're not there to see it all the way through to the end*.
>
> You know they'll say, "Okay, we'll move this bench here, then we'll move it there," you know, and then they'll leave. And it's like, you know, *someone's got to be out there all the time to make sure that it works*. I mean, you need something, you know. But they just like get you going and then they'll stop and then they'll start another one. And it's like, you've got to see it through to the end, you know. And it's total chaos. Everybody's bumping everybody, people are moving, they're not happy.

Management's goal was to devolve responsibility for completing continuous improvement activities to the workforce, and they reported extensive training and communication on this and other issues. But this worker expressed a fordist view that such problem solving and decision making was not the responsibility of workers.

A welder, also a former assembler who lost income due to the switch from piecework, had a similar view. Again, while the loss of income surely shaped his overall view, it is noteworthy that he articulated a position seeing an overall negative impact on company performance—and this is despite the company having been working on lean for eight years and, according to both managers I interviewed, having done extensive communication about the reasons for the new approach. Management brought in the WRTP, the union-backed intermediary that helps union companies develop co-management policies and practices and transition to lean. Yet he continued to see lean as less efficient than traditional fordist production:

> Well, it was batch manufacturing basically. So they would look out maybe two months and see what kind of orders we'd have, and then we'd run that for two months out. And even though we had a basket of parts, which we do now even worse, but they says, we can't have that, we have to have a one-piece flow. *But one-piece flow, it just doesn't make any sense to me.* Like I said, we've got a guy standing over here, he does his little bit, and he'll walk over and give it to this guy, and he does his little bit, and he'll walk over to this guy, and he'll walk around that table and give him the part. . . .
>
> Okay, so a customer calls up, they want eight pieces. Okay, sets up that molder. The molder takes an hour and a half to set up. Now, sales knows, I'm sure, six weeks in advance how many parts are coming out. Okay, so we set up that molder. It takes an hour and a half to set up a molder. They'll run eight pieces. Two days later they come back, "We need eight more pieces." See that, the job he was on at this time two days later, he's got to pull that out and put this eight pieces again. Then maybe next week Monday or Tuesday he's got an order for 16. *And yes, this is considered one-piece flow. I mean it's . . . doesn't make sense to me*. . . . I don't know how they can say you cut out waste. There's more waste. . . .

He went on to criticize the continuous improvement process and said that cellular production was "forced" on them, arguing from the perspective of individual productivity and not overall organizational efficiency and flexibility:

> And as far as the company, so they changed to cells. *It was very productive, you know, people were on piecework.* So we had a couple areas that we have two people, *had* two people on piecework. Now, so they're going through [company acronym for *kaizen*] events and setting up these areas where they put four people in. They have a piece walkover, gave it to this guy, and this guy assembled it and you walk over to this guy. *It's a joke.*
>
> They come in and change the area. We're having a [company acronym for *kaizen*] event. Whatever, I don't even know what a [company acronym for *kaizen*] event means. They need to get five or six people from, four people from the office, four people from the floor, and [the manager] says, "Well, we want your ideas for, to have this guy stand here and carry this part to this guy, and we'll grab this part and we'll grab it to this guy." So that one guy, all the parts right here, he puts it together, it's done. It just doesn't make sense to me. So they wrecked the areas, and then they expect all this walking, all this, to get out the same production that they got before. It's, it doesn't work. *It just doesn't . . . everything is non-productive as far as I'm concerned. . . .*
>
> I'm not closed-minded to cellularization. But when they just forced it on everyone and didn't even look, you know, how production [productivity] would be so destroyed.

This welder clearly articulated a fordist view, including a preference for just-in-case production, which he sees as more efficient overall:

> And now with all the outsourcing—I don't know if you know we have outsourcing now—they just, they took away the whole pressroom. So all our parts come in from other companies, pressrooms and now stamping outfits. So they come in, *you run out of one part, you shut down a whole area.* The parts come in, they use their part number, not our part number. Baskets, so they have a nice big label on, and a little label, it's up on the rack, you can't even see it. You're wasting time pulling baskets down, putting baskets up. *Material handling is a waste of time; you're just wasting your time.*

He feared that continuing to do lean may put the company out of business, again taking the fordist perspective of individual productivity, and not accepting the lean perspective that management had been pushing, focusing on overall system efficiency and flexibility:

> Well, anyway, *these two guys, they're on piecework, probably did a time-and-a-half more than what these four guys are doing. It's sad.* I see a good company,

> [Custom Seats] was in business for 85 years, something like that. It was a productive company, prosperous company. And I don't see it.

Finally, the forklift driver at Seats also expressed disagreement with management's shift from piece work to team-based gainsharing, which he thought had a negative impact on productivity.

> And the people still are not doing what they're supposed to, the quota. And in a lot of cases it's very legitimate that they can't make the quota. Because what they did was they took an average of the whole department to come up with these new rates, and for some it's so easy and for some it's unreachable. *I don't understand the point of what they did.*

I also interviewed the Business Agent for the union at Custom Seats. When I asked if the workers understand a need to adapt to keep up with their competition in order to save jobs, he stated "I actually don't think they have a clue. I mean they, the average person on the floor, I think thinks, 'This is my job. It's going to be here forever. All I've got to do is come in when I feel like it, and that's it.'"

Turning to Hydraulic Systems, in Chapter 6 I quoted the Shop Chair machinist with twenty-three years' tenure who lamented that most of his fellow workers still have a traditional "mentality" regarding the responsibilities of management and labor: "They still have this, 'I'm the worker, you're management; you tell me what to do, mentality' . . . But, [Hydraulic Systems] tries to give you the decision-making power." While he was enthusiastic about opportunities for workers to contribute to problem solving and decision making, he too expressed a fordist view regarding one-piece flow and too little inventory:

> We've complained that we wanted inventory because you do one piece, then three weeks we do another one piece, and then in two weeks we do another one piece. And we say, well, why don't you give us four pieces and then stick three of them on the shelf. But they say taxes or something like this or whatever, they don't do that.
>
> *Okay. And so they've actually—you used to do that and actually now they don't do that, you are making one piece when they need it.*
>
> No, we haven't done inventory. We haven't put anything on the shelf in a lot of years. We just don't do that. But we used to make a lot more pumps, so we used

> to get larger quantities. But now everything is down on—I mean ten would be a large quantity.

The setup press operator from Designer Railings expressed a similar concern. Like many workers, he continued to see small batch production as inefficient given the long setups required. He also said that the low inventories were causing everything to get backed up and run late:

> There's some pros and cons to this. I am putting the lean, this lean manufacturing, we have no . . . they're reducing the inventory. But I'm seeing jobs now where I'm putting in a two-hour setup to run parts for 15 minutes.
> Right.
>
> *I can't see it. And, you know, and I'm putting this same die in every other week. It doesn't make sense*. Get a stockpile of stuff, I'm thinking. There's got to be some reason for it, but I don't see it. And the same with the pipe, talked to them, because we're putting in the same setups. It takes longer to do the setup than it does to do the run.
>
> *Now, if there's a type of, either you see from your work that this doesn't seem to make sense, if it's taking so long to do the changeover and then you're running such small amounts. Have you been able to express this concern to management? Or are there other people out there, is it a common complaint?*
>
> Well, yeah. Oh, no, the supervisors, I explain it all to the supervisors. *And it's not just me; I mean it's everybody else in the plant is just* . . . the inventory—you know, from what I understand, I don't get involved with that too much—is way down. I know they don't, with this lean manufacturing, I know that the press department right now, we are so far behind. I mean weeks and weeks and weeks. But we're working. It was last Friday, I believe we changed 40 due dates. We pushed them to the next day, and we couldn't get them out on time. We didn't even have the orders.
>
> I can see that it would be good for the companies not stockpiling, because that's money, you know, that's money. They don't have, before the steel prices and everything where we're getting it in, they don't have to be ordering and stockpiling it and it's saving that money too, until they actually do need it. That would be good for the company, *but for the manufacturing part of it, not having inventory is—now I know we're sitting on a rush, we've got to get this done, we've got to get this done, rushing. And we're just running in circles now*. But as far as the company,

> I can see where the inventory they'd want to reduce. That's all money just sitting there.

Finally, a machinist at Industrial Pumps expressed the same concern. In the following discussion, he noted that he has come to see some benefits of setup reduction, but he's still not fully convinced. He continues to think that small batch production has too many setups and is inefficient:

> Yeah. Yeah. I mean at first it was like, "This is bullshit," you know, "What the hell are we doing this for?" I guess it's all about money, so.
>
> *Um-hmm. But once you, I mean, do you think it's a little less bullshit now after you've seen it, or . . . ?*
>
> A little less, but not a whole less [laughs], but not all that much less.
> *Yeah. Okay.*
>
> No, it's just, like I said, trying to keep, you know, it's fine if you're just doing one part, you know, and that's all you need to do. But when you're running the same part you run at 8:00 and you could run another one at 2:00, it's just, I don't think it's productive and not cost efficient, you know? . . .
>
> You've got just as much changeover as you're running the machine.

The Pumps machinist described his experience with setup reduction events. A team is assembled including a plant manager, lean engineer, supervisor, and all of the machinists on the shift. They video record the process and then analyze it. When I asked if it was useful, he acknowledged that it might be helpful for the machinists to be involved in setup reductions on machines that were not theirs, in order to improve the knowledge. "I suppose you have to kind of keep them keyed on what maybe they could do."

He also said "I think it helped, I guess, as far as seeing what you can do to . . . ." After a pause, however, he explained how he thought the managers, who did not have detailed knowledge of the process, made suggestions to shave seconds off the process which would have a determinantal impact on the maintenance of these expensive machines:

> A lot of times though, the people doing it have never been on the manufacturing floor and, you know, it's like, "Why are you blowing that off. You already blew it off once," or, "You blew it off, now you're wiping it off," you know. So, you know, I like to take care of my equipment because if you don't take, you know, that's the thing, I won't just hurry up and throw it on there, well you know, you ruin your

threads and then what are you going to do with that $200,000 machine when the threads are shot, you know?

Well, like yeah, they come in here and, "Why are you doing this? Why are you doing that?" And it's like, you shouldn't have to do that twice, you know, even if it took five seconds to take the rag and wipe that off after you had blown it off, because it's sticky coolant, you know, and the chips get gathered down there and if you don't wipe it, a lot of times they're still stuck there.

Right. And so they'll basically say, "Here's a thing that you've done twice. You don't need to do it. And here's something you can cut out to save 30 seconds here," and so forth?

Yeah. Every second counts.

In sum, management was too focused on seeing "things that should be done faster," to the exclusion of other concerns. But he also noted that the managers were open to ideas from the workers: "Yeah, it's not cut and dried with them. You know, usually what, you know they usually, they try to work with us I guess."

At Plastic Containers, a process tech expressed the same concern about small batches and too many changeovers:

They've been trying to reduce inventories, *unfortunately*, which means we do more changeovers on our stock jobs . . . When you run long runs, you set it up once, you get it going good, and it stays in there for 48, 50 hours, you know. You get it fine-tuned; everything gets smooth. If . . . you're running for six hours, that's not so bad when it's a six-hour total and there's three hours of setup and three hours of run. You get really frustrated when it's a five-hour setup and there's only one hour to run.

Finally, a welder at Tubefab noted that job rotation within shifts may relieve boredom, but he was concerned that it was too inefficient. He thought workers should stay on the same job all day, but would do different jobs in different shifts:

Oh, well I think *if they kept the welders just doing the welding, I think it would be better.* I think the ones that runs the machines knows how to run the machines and stuff. I think it would run a lot smoother that way. Yeah, it would, you know. But the rotation, then you've got this guy here trying to figure out which way this and that there, so you just lost about five, you know, and then he gets all mad at you. If they stay at their own station . . .

So you think it is more efficient to keep people at their own station.

Yeah. If they stay, yeah, if they won't stay, yeah. Yeah.

But it's . . . what do you think the advantages are of the way that they're doing it now?

I think they lose a lot.

Really.

Yeah. Yeah, you know, I just ran this job today and these guys here, you know, they're Manpower and they've been here for a while and one guy is not fast and one guy is. And that's normal, but that's where you're going to lose your spot. So that means, well, when he gets off there, then he's got to go up there, I've got to really pound them to try to get up to amount, you know. And that's not right for me either, but you know. *Yeah, if they stay in their own area and stay there for the day, I think it would work out fine*. And then every day you should change, rotate. Every day. You know, you stay there for the whole day . . .

For a day, rotate. Okay, I got you.

Yeah. And then you, I think it will work out 100 percent better. You know why, when you come back from lunch you know what you've got to do, you know how much you're got to get done.

Conclusion

This chapter has two main goals. First, to provide empirical substantiation (along with Chapters 6 and 8) of the theory of routine politics of production, that in many postfordist workplaces, production politics revolve around attempts to change and defend existing routines. Second, to present evidence that routine politics of production are driven by the workforce contradiction, in the form of worker reticence and resistance toward their own empowerment, with skepticism toward management based in worker commitments to quality and visions of efficiency.

This chapter documented substantial variation in individual orientations to work, lean, and problem-solving and decision-making responsibility, alongside worker resistance to and reticence toward empowerment. I argued that this outcome is a result of two concreate manifestations of alienation: managerial rejection of workers' ideas, which is possible because they alienated their labor, and which drives frustration and resentment; and worker views of efficiency and the proper division of labor. I showed that many workers articulate consistently fordist views of the proper ownership of responsibilities. As discussed in Chapter 3, organizational departments often develop their own distinctive cultures. Across the workplaces I studied, the logic of fordism continues to have a powerful influence on shopfloor culture.

Both managers and workers reported that the workforce is often split into three factions: collaborationist, resistant, and reticent. They also noted the role of leaders in shaping opinion, particularly among the reticent. These observations suggest that local culture and ideology play a key role in shaping worker orientations. More speculatively, the cases of Seats and Railings—where there seemed to be irreconcilable differences of interpretation between managers and workers of the same context—suggest that a culture of frustration and resentment may shape how workers interpret their context. While I cannot adjudicate these competing claims of managers and workers based exclusively on interview data, I want to suggest that part of the difference, at least, may be due to impact of local workplace culture on the interpretative frames of some workers.

With regard to managers, my empirical findings lead me to conclude that in postfordist American manufacturing many managers are interested in qualitative improvement rather than quantitative intensification. To be clear: managers are concerned with effort levels and the quantity of output, and they do require a certain minimum level of effort. My point is that their strategic focus is not on quantitative work intensification but on qualitive process improvement. Such an orientation is encouraged by postfordist demands for flexibility and continuous improvement, and is facilitated by the fact that the vast majority of their workers generally work hard, whether due to fear of losing one's job, to having accepted the legitimacy of capitalism and the ideology of "a fair day's work for a fair day's pay," to self-motivation driven by a desire to feel pride in one's work, or, most likely, some combination thereof.

More fundamentally, my findings suggest that the strategic orientation of management is more likely to be shaped by institutional logics of best practice in the field, due to the demands of their role as managers. By contrast, the strategic orientations of workers are more often—though by no means universally—rooted in local culture, custom, and practice, where formerly dominant logics of best practice are resilient.

To be sure, many workers are acutely aware of global competition, attuned to institutional logics of best practice, and able to make innovative contributions strategic decision making at all levels of the organization, based in part on their shopfloor experience. But many workers derive their orientation from local culture, custom, and practice, which often serves as a basis of conflict over management initiatives, even where the latter objectively seek to empower workers. Culture plays a key role here, but within a structural context: the class relation as such, in particular the power that owners and managers have over labor. So long as ownership and power remain concentrated, and managers remain agents of capitalist principals, managers will continue to face factions of resistance and reticence from their workers.

8

The Management Contradiction

The previous two chapters focused on worker experiences with lean production. Chapter 6 showed that some workplaces were characterized by overt conflict, but this was over worker defense of existing routines rather than over effort levels and work intensification. In the postfordist context of strong competitive demands for flexibility and continuous improvement, manufacturing managers are encouraged to focus on upgrading routines and operational systems to improve organizational capability. My findings show that indeed many managers are strategically focused on qualitative process improvement and not on effort levels as such. To be sure, they are concerned with individual and team productivity, but they largely and correctly assume that most of their workforce is willing to put in a sufficient level of effort, and thus management can focus on improving overall performance through process improvement.

Chapter 7 demonstrated the workforce contradiction: worker resistance and reticence toward their own substantive (though partial) empowerment. This is driven by concrete manifestations of alienation: worker visions of efficiency conflict with those of management, and management often rejects suggestions from workers.

The present chapter continues the analysis of routine politics of production, focusing on the management contradiction: managers face conflicting pressures to manage their workers in a taylorist manner, using them for manual labor and emphasizing standardization and task specialization, versus substantively empowering them via cross training and participation in problem solving and decision making.[1] This chapter turns from the thematic analysis of the previous two chapters to an analytical strategy of comparing workplaces matched on key factors.

[1] This chapter draws on Vidal (2017) but adds a substantial amount of new, unpublished material. That article presented an organization theoretic analysis. This chapter develops that analysis within the organizational political economy framework developed this book.

Management Divided. Matt Vidal, Oxford University Press. © Matt Vidal (2022).
DOI: 10.1093/oso/9780198795278.003.0008

Chapter 5 presented a typology of four regimes of lean production. The most complementary regime is the *high-involvement lean* regime: a lean-as-system approach with substantive empowerment. At the opposite end of the spectrum is the *lean-enough* regime: a lean-as-toolbox approach with nominal empowerment.[2] Then there are two intermediate types: the *lean standardization* regime that combines of lean-as-system with nominal empowerment; and the *autonomous lean* regime that combines lean-as-toolbox and substantive participation in the form of individual worker autonomy.

Lean enough, lean standardization, and autonomous lean are not way stations on the road to high-involvement lean. They are stable—though suboptimal—configurations that have been adopted by satisficing managers. Chapter 3 discussed managerial satisficing and the strong forces for organizational inertia: Established routines encourage habitual behavior; managers become committed to existing interpretive frames; and they face competing demands and priorities. In the absence of learning routines, which are exceptionally difficult to establish, overt learning is rare and typically occurs only in response to some sort of shock—an internal crisis or external demand.

Chapter 5 presented evidence suggesting that the main source of variation is not technical or structural variations across organizations. The primary explanation is a combination of the cognitive orientations and aspiration levels of management, which are the focus of this and the following two chapters.

Although work intensification was not a prominent concern of the workers or managers I interviewed, the issue of labor effort remains central. In the postfordist context, the effort question revolves around the problem of intellectual effort, including problem solving and decision making, but more generally around the adoption of new routines. The issue of intellectual effort is particularly problematic because it cannot be coerced; it requires getting workers to voluntarily accept increased responsibilities and new ways of working, which in turn requires disciplined, methodical, patient management.

In Chapter 3, I theorized the effort question as the problem of valorization. As shown in Chapters 4, 5, and 7, the institutional logic of best practice

[2] As defined in Chapter 5, nominal empowerment refers to consultative neotaylorism: job rotation among standardized tasks in the form of multitasking (narrow tasks) or multiskilling (enlarged tasks and enriched responsibilities) with consultative participation (i.e. asking workers to contribute ideas but without participation in problem solving or decision making).

regarding valorization strategy is substantive empowerment. But managers face severe tensions regarding valorization strategy, including resistance and reticence from alienated workers along with pressures that pull in the opposite direction from empowerment. The management contradiction is illustrated by the following comment from a production worker at Tubefab, who notes that managers are often hesitant to give workers time away from production work in order to engage in group problem solving:

> A new job comes into the plant where a lot of times we'll have a meeting . . . to get everybody's ideas. We'll bring welders in and people from press department in, see if they have any ideas on any issues with the new product. A lot of times that will help . . . somebody will bring something up ahead of time that we might not know, we can solve that problem before it becomes a problem. I think we need more of that. . . .
>
> But . . . *the foreman and the production people [the continuous improvement coordinator and manufacturing engineers] don't want to pull these guys off the line, because that's our moneymaker* . . . they don't want to pull them off the line for a half hour to come into a meeting, or for an hour and sit in a meeting, they kind of shy away from that.

In this chapter I illustrate two main processes by which the management contradiction operates to drive deviation from widely agreed best practice. First, the management contradiction is expressed in two competing logics of valorization: substantive empowerment versus traditional taylorism. In a top-down process, some managers continue to be influenced by the fordist-taylorist logic of valorization, thus prioritizing the use of workers for physical labor and failing to engage them in intellectual labor. Second, in a bottom-up process, some managers respond to their local situation by satisficing: settling for good enough performance produced by implementing a package of basic lean practices but failing to devolve responsibility and train workers for engaging in problem solving and decision making. In order to provide some evidence that deviation from the institutional logic of best practice is a form of satisficing—driven by moderate aspiration levels, cognitive orientation shaped by an old logic of best practice, or a combination of the two—I analyze the factories in matched pairs, as I now turn to discuss.

Analytical Considerations

My analytical strategy is to present matched cases, in which factories are matched as closely as possible on relevant technical, market, and organizational factors. This allows me to control for such factors in order to highlight the role of cognitive orientation (logic of practice) and managerial aspiration level in producing variation. Controlling for these factors is critical given that managers are unlikely or unable to articulate a moderate aspiration level as a factor in their decision making. Settling for good enough violates norms regarding managerial duties and performance. In some cases managers may have high aspiration levels but a cognitive orientation based partly in the logic of fordist-taylorism, which results in satisficing decisions and strategies despite high aspiration levels.

As discussed in Chapter 3, managers with moderate aspiration levels are likely to rationalize their deviation from widely agreed best practice by framing that practice as a poor fit with their local organizational context. On substantive empowerment, the focus of this chapter, some managers say that implementing it broadly across a large workforce would be too difficult. However, I match factories on key characteristics, including employment size, showing that some managers adopt a strategy of substantive empowerment—across a workforce of 500 employees (Inspired Castings) and 300 employees (LV Gaskets)—while others do not. In Chapter 9, on lean organizational practices, a misfit is generally invoked along the lines that a practice simply will not work given the circumstances of a particular factory.

By matching cases in which one manager said an institutionally prescribed practice was a poor fit (or too difficult to implement) as a reason for not adopting best practice, while another manager in an effectively identical context fully adopted the same practice, I am able to provide some systematic evidence suggesting the invocation of a poor fit (including being too difficult) reflects a moderate aspiration level. The evidence on aspiration levels and satisficing is necessarily indirect, but the fact that a manager in an effectively identical context has adopted the practice is direct evidence that the issue is not one of fit.

In practice, all the managers who did not adopt substantive participation adopted nominal empowerment. A worker from Tubefab described this approach, in which workers are asked to give input but have no decision-making authority and are not involved in problem solving: "You know they've got meetings where you can put your input in. *I mean if something gets done or not is another story, but they do let you put your input in.*" The methodological goal is to match establishments on factors that bear on the objective fit or difficulty of the practice with the factory context: Is substantive empowerment possible in a given context and does is generate performance improvements?

As just suggested, the main factor bearing on the empowerment question is the size of the workforce; pursuing a strategy of systematic substantive participation across a workforce will be more difficult in a factory of 500 workers than one with fifty workers, given the training required and the problems—documented in Chapter 7 and below—of getting workers to embrace changed routines and new responsibilities. In addition to workforce size, I am able to match cases on technology, production strategy (make-to-order or make-to-stock), and production volume.

Table 8.1 provides details in the matched cases. The top panel lists factories that illustrate a top-down process in which the logic adopted by management shapes interpretation of the local situation. The bottom panel lists those that illustrate a bottom-up process in which managers with moderate aspiration levels satisfice in response to feedback from the local situation.

The table shows variation across the two valorization strategies—substantive versus nominal empowerment—within the following matched factors:

- Inspired Castings (substantive empowerment) versus Custom Blinds (nominal empowerment) matched on employment levels (500 and 650, respectively) and production volumes;[3]
- LV Gaskets (substantive empowerment) versus Deep Stampings (nominal empowerment) matched on employment levels (300 workers each) and technology;[4]
- LV Gaskets (substantive empowerment) versus Metalfab Plus (nominal empowerment) on employment levels (300 and 200, respectively);
- Second Tier Specialist (substantive empowerment) versus Metalfab Plus (nominal empowerment) on technology, strategy, and volume;

[3] Employment size classifications are always arbitrary. I consider size classes of 500–700 and 200–300 to be roughly similar in terms of the problems and issues regarding substantive empowerment.

[4] Both have metalworking technology. As noted in the text below, Deep Stampings uses deep draw forming, in which most of their parts are made in a single operation using presses with multiple stations. While this technology offers less opportunity for continuous improvement via value-stream mapping—versus a fab & assembly shop like LV Gaskets—as discussed in the text the manager noted persistent issues with changeovers and production, suggesting opportunities for operator participation in problem solving and decision making.

- Inspired Castings (substantive empowerment) versus Complex Iron Castings (nominal empowerment) matched on technology, strategy, and volume;
- Industrial Pumps, LV Gaskets, and Second Tier Specialist (substantive empowerment) versus Metalfab Plus and Deep Stampings (nominal empowerment) matched on technology;
- Inspired Castings and Second Tier Specialist (substantive empowerment) versus Complex Iron Castings, Metalfab Plus, and Deep Stampings (nominal empowerment) matched on strategy;
- Industrial Pumps and LV Gaskets (substantive empowerment) versus Custom Blinds (nominal empowerment) matched on strategy.

Most importantly, the analysis reveals:

- Substantive empowerment occurring on a systematic, companywide basis across a range of workforce sizes (35, 300, and 500 production workers);
- Variation on valorization strategy, with each valorization approach being adopted in factories that:
    - Use the same technologies;
    - Have the same production strategy (make-to-order and make-to-stock factories);
    - Are low- to mid-volume producers.

I begin the analysis with the factories in the top panel of Table 8.1, focusing on matched cases that demonstrate competing logics of valorization. I then turn to the bottom panel, focusing on matched cases that show variation in aspiration levels.

The Management Contradiction Expressed in Competing Logics of Valorization

Chapter 3 discussed how managers may blend the currently dominant institutional logic of best practice with the formerly dominant logic to produce hybrid practice. Chapter 5 showed that the practice of nominal empowerment is such a hybrid: based on the logic of scientific management insofar as labor is seen as a source of manual labor that should not be involved in problem solving and decision making, but adding elements of

Table 8.1 Valorization logics with factory cases matched on key characteristics

Factory	Characteristics	Factory	Characteristics
Top-down process: Adopt the logic of substantive empowerment		**Top-down process: Adopt logic of nominal empowerment**	
Inspired Castings	Employment: 500 Technology: Expandable mold casting, assembly Strategy: Make-to-order Volume: Low to mid	Complex Iron Castings	Employment: 120 Technology: Expandable mold casting, assembly Strategy: Make-to-order Volume: Low to mid
		Custom Blinds	Employment: 650 Technology: Plastic injection molding, metal forming, assembly Strategy: Make-to-stock Volume: Mid
Bottom-up process: High aspiration level		**Bottom-up process: Moderate aspiration level**	
Industrial Pumps	Employment: 35 Technology: Machining, assembly Strategy: Make-to-stock Volume: Mid	Metalfab Plus	Employment: 200 Technology: Metal fabrication, machining, assembly Strategy: Make-to-order Volume: Low
LV Gaskets	Employment: 300 Technology: Metal fabrication, assembly Strategy: Make-to-stock Volume: Mid	Deep Stampings	Employment: 300 Technology: Metal forming Strategy: Engineer-to-order Volume: High
Second Tier Specialist	Employment: 80 Technology: Machining, assembly Strategy: Make-to-order Volume: Low		

Note: "Employment" refers to the number of production workers. Substantive and nominal empowerment are defined in Chapter 5.

substantive empowerment, mainly job rotation (perhaps with actual cross training) and asking workers for their input.

In this section I compare the three factories from the top panel of Table 8.1. *Inspired Castings* is a high-involvement lean (substantive empowerment) foundry, a nonunion shop with 500 production workers who make carbon and stainless steel castings for a range of industries, from heavy equipment to motorcycles to hand tools. They are an investment casting operation which involves wax mold making, dipping/coating with ceramic slurry, melting/cleaning, pouring, and finishing.

Complex Iron Castings is a lean-enough (nominal empowerment) foundry, a union shop with 120 production workers who make highly alloyed iron cylinder blocks (which may have "13 or 14 different cores") and other engine components for diesel trains and industrial uses. They are a sand casting operation which involves sand mold making, sand core making, pouring, shaking out, finishing, and assembly. These two factories are highly similar insofar as they are both foundries using expandable mold casting processes (as opposed to permanent mold processes such as die casting) to make complex castings, working on a make-to-order basis at low to mid volumes.

Custom Blinds is a lean standardization (nominal empowerment) factory, a nonunion shop with 650 production workers who make plastic and fabric blinds for the retail consumer market. They are a vertically integrated operation who make all the parts for their blinds in-house, including plastic injection molding and extrusion, metal roll forming and stamping, and assembly. It is similar to Inspired Castings in terms of employment size, use of molding technology and assembly work. It also shares the following characteristics with two substantive empowerment factories (Industrial Pumps and LV Gaskets) discussed in the following section on aspiration levels: metalworking technology with assembly work, make-to-stock strategy, and mid-volume production. It is analyzed in this section because it is a case of logic blending that provides a stark contrast with Inspired Castings regarding labor management and worker participation.

Inspired Castings is a truly impressive organization. I was introduced to Inspired after I asked my contacts at the Wisconsin Manufacturing Extension Partnership (WMEP) if they could put me in contact with one of their leanest and most sophisticated clients. Inspired did not disappoint. The owners built a new facility in the early 2000s based on ideas they developed in the 1990s, after reading two books: *The Machine that Changed the World*, the popular management book by MIT scholars on the Toyota Production

System, and *The Goal*, a book on flow production and continuous improvement by Eliyahu M. Goldratt and Jeff Cox. As the owner/vice president explained: "The Toyota just-in-time type of thing. . . . It was along those lines that we were thinking."

The new facility was designed based entirely on continuous flow concepts to remove buffers and reduce lead time. At the time of my visit, they had gotten their throughput time down from six weeks at their older factory to three days at the new one. Overall lead time, which includes throughput plus order processing, was at one week while their competitors were at six weeks when slow and twelve weeks when busy.

Job titles at Inspired used to include wax press operator, injector, dipper, assembler, and finisher. They have now implemented a new system of extensive cross training in which "All hourly employees are called technicians. And they can move from one job to another throughout the day . . . the technicians can move from one cell to another also, throughout the day."

Remarkably, they have systematically implemented a regime of substantive empowerment across a 500-strong workforce, establishing a culture of employee involvement that is driven by the workforce rather than by management. The owner/vice president, who had a very-hands approach, explained that the initiative for continuous improvement is "better coming up from the shop floor . . . because then they can fix it and all that. And a lot of times we'll put the problems back and challenges back to them: 'Here, solve this problem.'" Inspired sought to involve as much of its production workforce as possible in substantive participation, which may take a range of forms: "On a small scale, [a team] can start something up [in] the cell and they can work on something themselves, or . . . the whole plant can work on it, or set up a team that's separate on that."

My discussions with the personnel manager further revealed the worker-driven, self-directed forms of participation occurring at this foundry. When I asked her about employee involvement in problem-solving teams, she replied:

> Well, you can have many going on at one time, and I wouldn't even be aware of them. Some of the employees in Module 1 at one point in time had a real interest in the grind area and knew how they could streamline it and make it better. They talked to the plant manager. "Fine, go ahead. Start working on it." They'd come in and work on things here and there.
>
> *They'd just come in and do it on their own?*

> Um-hmm. And then they came up with some programs to really help the process, implement it, reduced times drastically, you know, in setups and things like that to standardize stuff.

The emphasis on substantive participation in this foundry contrasts greatly with the situation at Complex Iron Castings, where there were there was relatively narrow cross training and no efforts to involve workers in any form of participation other than suggesting ideas. The job titles are: "core makers, core finishers, mold operators, molding machine operators, assemblers, and pourers. There is not a skill hierarchy in which individuals go from one position up to a higher skilled, better paid position."

In contrast to Inspired, which has moved to a single job category (technician) with broad training across the range of skills, Complex Iron retains job classifications and functional production lines, with cross training on a limited scale, mainly "on the individual lines we try and have multiple people cross-trained on the machines." They worked with WMEP to implement lean production, including inventory and batch-size reduction, along with cellular-type layouts, but these did not involve continuous flow, which would eliminate buffers between processes and hence provide an opportunity for productively engaging workers in substantive participation. The cellular-type layouts are within, rather than across, broad functions: core making, casting, and finishing. They are also not doing formal continuous improvement (*kaizen*):

> I won't necessarily add a cell that's a, you know, a group doing from core-make through cast and clean. But, with the oval operation, it is a cell, you know, the different molding lines and, you know. So, from that standpoint, yes.
>
> *Okay. And so have you found that, have you been able to apply some of those lean principles then?*
>
> Oh, we're, it's been a constant effort.
>
> *Are you doing things like* kaizen *events?*
>
> No, not formally.

Most of Complex Iron's training efforts were focused on remedial math and English, along with limited cross training for job rotation within lines. They were not planning to train workers in problem solving or engage them in decision making. Instead of allowing and encouraging teams of workers to convene offline problem-solving groups, as at Inspired Castings, or having formal *kaizen* events convened on a regular basis by management, continuous improvement efforts were initiated on an ad hoc basis by managers and engineers. They have consultative work teams but these are not used as a basis for employee involvement or continuous improvement:

> The molding lines are teams . . . I guess, the best way to describe it, so for example, one of the molding lines has a ten-man crew. And they all do different things. They all have their spot on it, on the crew. And I, quite honestly, I pay per mold, so they share equally. The meeting might be, you know, "We're starting this job," and they go over the process so that everybody knows what they're supposed to be doing and have at it, you know. I mean, I don't know that there are other, much of, not formal other types of meetings, I guess.

Why did the plant manager of Complex Iron Castings not adopt broader cross training, reduction of job classifications, and employee involvement in problem solving and decision making, as prescribed by the dominant logic of substantive empowerment? His comments suggest that he conceived of work organization and labor management partially in terms of a fordist-taylorist logic. For example, when I asked about setup reductions, he replied that:

> Setup time reduction is important, okay? The hard part is that when you're not running—I guess I'm not sure I want to say this—when you're not running as high a volumes, you know, the equipment we have is pretty basic, okay? So, it's hard to generate enough return to spend a lot of money on setup time reduction. You know, I guess that's probably the easiest way to say that.

He said their setups take around twenty minutes, which *is* simple, with limited opportunities for cost savings (compared with eight-hour setups for some stamping presses). However, the contrast with Inspired is instructive: They moved to a continuous flow process across all operations, focusing on overall throughput and lead time. The emphasis on reducing lead times is central to the lean logic, and it contrasts with the fordist logic of emphasizing capacity utilization—keeping machines busy based on forecasts rather than only building to demand—within departments.

While the plant manager did not emphasize capacity utilization as such, he still thought in terms of functional departments and individual machines, rather than the overall process flow (the value stream). Inspired realized large reductions in lead time due to thinking about overall process flow, rather than individual machines within functional departments. Complex Iron adopted some elements of lean, including cellular-type structures with limited cross training, but the manager was heavily influenced by non-lean, fordist principles, resulting in a hybrid logic.

On the role of labor, the manager at Complex Iron also displayed a taylorist orientation, emphasizing brawn over brain, the overriding need for physical, disciplined, semiskilled labor. What he wants from his workers is:

> Okay, so number one you need to be able to hang in there. Number two is that once you get that started you've got to keep going. So you've got to pace it. You want to fill the, there's a channel or a rudder system, a gating system. You want to bring the gating system up so that it's up, you know, up basically to the top, and you want to bleed it there, and you want to keep it running that way. You don't want to stop; if you stop then you'll have a defective casting. And you don't want to pour any faster than that because then you'll run over. So there is a bunch of skill to that.

> The hardest work probably in our place is in the area where we finish the castings. And a lot of that has to do with the size of the castings we produce. We produce castings that run somewhere between 30 pounds and 500, with the majority of them between 60 and 150. So there is a lot of bull work, you know, repositioning these castings. A lot of that stuff is, I mean it's a guy just repositioning. So that's hard work. Or, the grinders themselves, you know, you've got a 30-pound grinder that you're swinging around all day. So that's really kind of the hardest.

Again, the contrast with Inspired Castings is sharp. In the latter, management embraced the logic of substantive empowerment, implementing broad cross training and encouraging regular substantive worker participation in offline continuous improvement teams. The manager at Complex Iron castings had a partially fordist-taylorist orientation, seeing workers as sources of manual but not cognitive labor. This manager's position was reinforced by the fact they were doing strong and steady business, maintaining key customers, meeting their cost, quality, and delivery targets, and gaining new business. As such, the manager did not experience bottom-up stimuli for a more thorough lean conversion, even if this would improve their performance.

Custom Blinds offers a contrast with previous two cases. It is a lean standardization regime, meaning it shares with Complex Iron Castings a consultative approach to worker participation, but shares with Inspired Castings a lean-as-system approach. Blinds had realized a systematic approach to value-stream mapping and some degree of ongoing improvement in workflow and process standards. But because managers have adopted a nominal empowerment approach, continuous improvement is entirely management-driven, in contrast to Inspired, which has established a culture of worker-driven continuous improvement.

Blinds began their lean conversion two years before I visited them, drawing on consultants and their own internal expertise, including input from shopfloor workers:

> We've had consultants in here in the past, which actually gives us ideas on how to do this. And then we actually now are doing some of this on our own. And we can do this to a degree because we have our own systems group here too. . . . We have some very creative people up there. We have some very creative people on the floor, and our supervisors . . . they look at something and they'll say, "Well, how can we make it better." And all of a sudden, that between that and how we generate our work orders on the floor, they've come up with a new way of scheduling, which is basically just-in-time. But it doesn't push things through, it pulls them through. And that goes all the way back to purchasing where we're ordering the raw materials and it all flows through here.

Their approach is highly systematic, based in value-stream mapping and including basic training for all shopfloor workers:

> Value stream mapping . . . is part two of a seven step process that we're going to go through here . . . And that's taking all your different processes and measuring that out. And we're going to go through—we figure it's going to take two full years to go through [this location. It has also been started in the three other locations]. All of these people, every associate on the floor is going to go through training, at least 12 hours of training this year, with this.

The twelve hours of training, however, was on remedial learning (e.g. English as a second language), firm-specific skills ("How to read those work orders. . . . How the channels are supposed to be packed in the box so things don't get broken. . . . Training all of the functional areas of the organization that the customer is right") and a few transferable skills (e.g. "plastics processing all through very high definition types of processing, getting right down to certain types of plastics and their processing characteristics"). In contrast, learning lean firms including Inspired Castings (discussed above) and Industrial Pumps, Mini Metalfab, and Second Tier Specialist (discussed below) provided their entire workforces with training in lean (typically a Lean 101 class) and some or all of their shopfloor workers with training in problem solving and leadership, which is cascaded down to other workers involved in problem-solving activities.

Value-stream mapping was conceived as part of a major restructuring initiative that would take two years but would then be completed. This contrasts with lean-as-system factories in which value-stream mapping is used on an ongoing, regular basis. Rather than focusing on reducing lead times and moving to entirely product-focused, cellular organization, the value-stream mapping efforts at Blinds focused largely on improving workflow (but without an explicit focus on lead-time reduction) within fordist-style functional departments, with some product-focused cellular layouts.

Blinds had a complex, bureaucratic system of dedicated teams for quality assurance and continuous improvement: a Total Quality Management (TQM) leadership steering committee and several Quality Leadership Teams. Each department had a Quality Assurance Teams (QAT) and between three and six Manufacturing Process Improvement Teams. But they retained a fordist division of labor, including ten shopfloor job classifications, in which "the majority of the shop people are two's, because they are the assemblers and they go all the way up to ten's, which are the very skilled people in maintenance and tooling."

In this approach, the dedicated Process Improvement teams are the driving force for continuous improvement. Teamwork for most of the workforce consists of standardization with opportunities for cross training: "Quality at the Source Teaming with best practice work instructions for every work center," with encouragement to train across many operations. Regular shopfloor workers could feed ideas to the Process Improvement teams, but beyond that there was no attempt to engage the majority of the shopfloor workforce in any type of problem solving or decision making.

The overall system is organized as a hybrid of lean practices (customer focus and just-in-time orientation, value-stream mapping, continuous improvement systems), fordist-style functional organization, and a taylorist approach toward labor. The plant manager's description of their continuous improvement approach suggests that he sees workers and labor management through a traditional taylorist lens, in which workers are for physical labor, while problem solving and decision making is the responsibility of engineers and managers:

> We have manufacturing engineers . . . they are to be out here on the floor, working with the supervisors, talking to the associates on the floor, looking at a piece of equipment, how can they make that more efficient? Obviously you have to look at the costs of doing this, but there are things that these two guys have in their head that just amazes me. . . . If nothing else, if you can make it more ergonomically friendly for the associate, you still have a best experience because the associate's happier, okay?

When I asked the plant manager if there are ways for shopfloor workers to give input, he responded:

> Can they? Yes, absolutely. But it's not designated that they have to go to a specific person. It's really going through their elite person on the floor, going through their supervisor, or stopping an engineer as they're walking down the aisle and saying, "Well, Jim or Daryl, what do you think about this?" Because everybody seems to know everybody here. So, and my people are instructed that you will listen to the associates, alright, because that's where a lot of these ideas are generated, because they work with it every day.

A worker with nineteen years' tenure described her experience with continuous improvement, indicating that for most workers it is largely a process of downward communication:

> Basically it would kind of seem like in years past that we would hear something through the grapevine kind of thing, and then it would happen. And now, when it's going to happen, they'll tell us what's going to happen, and what to expect, and get our input on it now, ahead of time. . . . A lot more communication, a lot more—like the newsletter that comes out, memos. I bet we get at least ten memos a week . . . they've always tried to make the employees—now they call them associates, just I mean like because we feel more like it too—but they really, really communicate, just totally tell us what's going on.
>
> *And then do you think that they're actually, when they're telling you ahead of time, that they actually do consult you and honestly try and get your opinion on the changes and whatnot?*
>
> Yeah. Something like that, you know, there really isn't much for us to say except for the fact that we understand. They're explaining why the business is doing this.

The main opportunity for input, as the plant manager explained, is the informal process of workers suggesting ideas to superiors.

In many respects, Blinds has a systematic and reasonably effective approach to continuous improvement. But it contrasts with the substantive empowerment of Inspired Castings, where workers can and do convene their own offline problem-solving teams, on their own initiative. Management at Inspired had embraced the logic of substantive empowerment, while management at both Complex Iron Castings and Custom Blinds conceived of labor and labor management in terms of the logic of traditional taylorism.

Divergent Responses to the Management Contradiction Based on Aspiration Levels

In this section I compare the three factories from the bottom panel of Table 8.1. Management at Industrial Pumps, Second Tier Specialist, and LV Gaskets adopted substantive empowerment, while management at Metalfab Plus and Deep Stampings adopted nominal empowerment. The five companies are all similar in terms of making complex metal subassemblies using a mix of skilled and semiskilled workers. To simplify the comparisons, I discuss the five companies in two sets, first comparing Pumps, Metalfab, and Second Tier Specialist, then comparing Gaskets with Stampings. Specialist and Metalfab are similar in terms of technology, strategy, and volume; Pumps and Metalfab are similar in terms of technology. (I also note that Pumps and Gaskets, which adopted substantive empowerment, match with Custom Blinds, which adopted nominal empowerment, in terms of being mid-volume, make-to-stock operations.)

Industrial Pumps is a high-involvement lean factory, a nonunion shop with thirty-five production workers who make high-end pumps for the food and beverage industry. They are a make-to-stock, mid-volume company that sells to distributors and directly to industrial customers. Their primary operations are machining and assembly, with secondary operations in welding and polishing. This case illustrates a situation where a manager sees substantive empowerment as necessary for implementing lean-as-system.

Metalfab Plus is a lean-enough factory, a nonunion shop with 200 production workers who make fabricated assemblies (e.g. cabinets, chassis, linkages, and shifters) for the heavy equipment and electronics industries.

They are a make-to-order, low-volume company that sells directly to industrial customers. Their primary operations are metal fabrication (including skilled press brake operators) and assembly, with secondary operations in machining, welding, and painting. This case illustrates a situation where a nominal empowerment approach precludes a lean-as-system approach or, more precisely, a taylorist approach to valorization reinforces satisficing with a lean-as-toolbox approach.

Second Tier Specialist is a high-involvement lean factory, a union shop with eighty production workers who make industrial cylinders for first-tier suppliers, such as Tower International (a Tier 1 auto supplier), multinational prime contractors, and customers in the food processing and stamping press businesses. They are a make-to-order, low-volume company that sells directly to industrial customers and also to non-stocking distributors. Their primary operations are machining and assembly.

Before moving to lean, the system at Industrial Pumps was classically fordist: functionally organized, producing on a just-in-case basis. Each operation was scheduled independently of the others; they worked from forecasts, making dozens of parts for each final assembly with pallets of parts scattered "everywhere." The engineer described how, when he was hired, the plant routinely pumped out identical size batches of all the potential components, without regard for whether they would actually be needed:

> There's probably 27 different models in our centrifugal line, and so for, that means 27 completely different housings, covers, impellers, and then a whole stack of shafts-the shafts kind of cross models ... So we would, at one time, probably have 20 to 27 different skids of 20 housings somewhere randomly out on our shop floor.... So you'd have the polishing area [for example] and they might have six or seven skids of 20 parts sitting around them, picking off and doing whatever they wanted to do for the day.

They had two full-time expeditors who would spend "all day, every day, walking three or four different parts through the plant to just get a couple orders off." This company ran with such a system for twenty-five years before upper management hired a lean engineer—only after its delivery times had dropped and remained below 40%.

The initial move to lean at Industrial Pumps was very top-down: value-stream mapping efforts included only vice presidents, plant manager, and engineers. The result was disastrous: "the people that worked in the area, they just felt violated. Like we rolled in and took half their stuff and threw it away and got in fights about the other half. And, 'This is how we think you should do your job,' kind of thing. It was painful."

Following the failure to implement lean in a top-down, management-driven fashion, they attempted to implement substantively empowered teams with a dedicated team leader. As the following discussion shows, they tried to implement teams "on paper," without sufficient training needed to substantively empower workers to engage in forms of self-management:

> Plant manager: It blew up in our faces.
>
> Engineer: We did it, and what we really struggled with was the leaders in the middle kind of. We ended up throwing people in and saying, "Here is your team. Go nuts." And didn't provide any support or training for the three people that were thrown into the leader positions. . . .
>
> Threw them in and, yeah, like [the plant manager] said, set them up to battle, and they did. And that really, while it was happening was also destroying any of the departmental chemistry that was sitting there before that because then you had people against other people and—we see it really bad in our polishing area right now. Took completely the wrong approach at doing it by just throwing it down on paper and saying, "Let's split the place up into four teams and that's that."
>
> Plant manager: And the hardest part about the teams is people weren't cross trained enough to make that successful. . . .
>
> Engineer: For the size of our company we, it really started to hurt us to try and divide up into teams based on a product, when we really needed some of the people to be able to work on anything based on who was here and who wasn't. . . . So we've taken it a step, I wouldn't even say back, we just, we took a different step now. We're trying to get, first, let's get some strong leaders and get them the support and training and let them learn what they need, and then we'll look at taking another step later. But I'd rather let it happen naturally than force it.
>
> Plant manager: Get some cross training done before you try to do that.
>
> Engineer: Right. So what we really want to do right now, we've got two supervisors in place, we want to get the third person in place, and we're pretty confident

> about the two that are in there right now, that they are good leaders, that they are smart, that they do, they have an idea of where the company wants to go and what we would like to develop into and try to get a third person in that same area, and now provide them with more leadership training, with more manufacturing training. We'd help them learn things about the other departments, so that they can support each other and not just fight against each other the whole time.

The experience of Pumps illustrates how substantively empowering a workforce is a challenging process that requires a systematic approach to training and support. It also shows how high aspiration levels are needed for managers to persevere in the face of such difficulties. Despite such setbacks, management continued to methodically work on cultivating a culture of continuous improvement based on substantively empowered workers. The managers espoused a new approach of trying to bring the workers on board. They:

> not only spent a lot of time on pre-training, but explaining what we expected to get out of it. And even if I knew what I would really like to see them try and do, I wouldn't say it, but I'd try to get them to say it . . . we spent a lot of time just having them discover . . . what a benefit of this could be. . . . We want it to be safe, we want it to be organized, we want it to be something that a lot of people can step up and do the same job at the same bench and get the same results.

As discussed in Chapter 4, the managers told a story of how a 5S exercise resulted in the removal of seven Craftsman toolboxes from an assembly area that had three people. Having worked together in this problem-solving exercise to improve their workspace, making it cleaner and more orderly, the workers become more engaged with participation in lean practices.

They explained how they want workers to drive experimentation for process improvement, without having to go through the plant manager or the engineers. As the plant manager explained:

> There was a lot of micromanaging here for a long time, and it was really hard for a lot of people on the floor to feel comfortable sticking their neck out to do something when they knew, all the way up the chain, everybody was sitting there staring at that one little detail today. You know, you couldn't make a little mistake because you would stand out. And it's going to take a while, but I

would love to see us get that comfort level . . . so [the value stream leader] can feel comfortable saying, "Hey, I think we want to try this." And we can say, "Well, if you've got to have a day to do it, do it." And get the guys together and do it. And not worry about, "Should we let X know that two weeks from now we're going to take two hours to teach these guys this."

At the time of my visit, Pumps had achieved functional flexibility through cross training and job rotation, substantive participation from a few key employees in *kaizen* events on setup reduction and 5S standardization. They were working on improving flow and had developed "value stream leader" positions, filled by production workers, with plans to reduce their ten job classifications. They were providing the value stream leaders with "more leadership training, with more manufacturing training" and helping "them learn things about the other departments, so that they can support each other and not just fight against each other the whole time."

They explicitly discussed how, in order to get to fully cellularized continuous-flow production, they are moving slowly and methodically toward substantively empowered teams, in which the full workforce would engage in self-driven continuous improvement:

What about going towards eliminating the departments and going totally with a product-focused cell?

Plant manager: We've got to do it slowly, correctly, and involve them better.
Engineer: We need to get to the point where our new supervisors along with the people they're working with think to themselves, "It would be a lot easier for me to do this job if that guy was right there." And if they can think that, if we can do the right things to get them to understand that that's a plus, and let them figure it out, we can do it. But if we don't get that part done first, they're forced to do it, and they'll either fight it or not quite grasp why they're doing it, but just kind of go through the motions . . . the goal I'd set for them is, "Try to find a way so you can see everybody making the parts, no matter where you are in the process. So you guys can talk, communicate right while you're making it."

Their efforts at moving to just-in-time production (setup reduction, smaller batches, improved flow) had already yielded significant performance improvements. Setup on their CNC machining centers had improved from an hour and fifteen minutes to ten minutes or less. Five years ago they were quoting lead times at two weeks and typically shipping in about four weeks. Now they're quoting one to two weeks and shipping in about four days. On-time delivery has gone from 30% to about 90%. Inventory turns have gone from below two to a rolling average of six and are currently up around eight. According to the plant manager:

> If we had not been into lean manufacturing in the last two to three years with the economy the way it was, we'd have been a real hurting company. I really honestly believe that. You look at all of our competitors: Every one of our competitors has either laid off, moved to a different area, or are no longer in business. And we never laid anybody off in that time, in fact we hired people.
>
> Engineer: We turned a profit every single year through that.

One worker noted how he really felt that the new system was making his routine better and giving him more power:

> If we find that . . . something doesn't work in this area . . . I feel like I've got a better handle on my job, I have a little bit more control. . . . I've seen that through the value stream [mapping] . . . that you're finding out where the processes start out, you know, in doing the maps and finding out what is an outside vendor issue and what isn't. I've been able to approach . . . purchasing and again be able to ask them about when something's going to come in and not feel like, oh, I'm stepping out of my bounds.

This is one of the workers that management indicated has really enthusiastically taken to worker participation and whom management has focused much of their training and cultivation efforts on, hoping he will be a leader to bring other workers around.

In contrast to Pumps, management at Metalfab Plus had not attempted and did not plan to develop a culture of worker-driven continuous improvement based on substantive empowerment. They had a management-driven approach to lean, which is relatively straightforward insofar as they had adopted a lean-as-toolbox approach. Traditionally their business had grown in phases and they simply added physical capacity to their plant in functional chunks, with no regard for flow throughout the shop.

Like Custom Blinds, Metalfab's lean conversion was conceived as a major, discrete restructuring initiative, using value-stream mapping to implement a re-layout of their organization along more flow-oriented principles. But they did not see value-stream mapping, like lean-as-system managers do, as a tool for ongoing, incremental continuous improvement. Thus, management at Metalfab saw their restructuring as about "90% complete." After I probed him on this point, the plant manager proudly noted they had not brought in consultants:

> *Now, on this reorganization you mentioned last time, you said you're about 90 percent done. Who helped you with that?*
>
> I did that on my own. I mean all the strategy.
>
> *Okay. And no consultants brought in?*
>
> No consultants. We have not brought consultants into this business at all.
>
> *Okay. So you guys did your own value-stream mapping and all that kind of stuff?*
>
> Yes, we did. Yes, we did, yep.

This type of skepticism of outsiders—both consultants and industrial customers—is common among small and mid-sized business managers. And their homegrown approach to lean has generated substantial improvements in performance. Nonetheless, not bringing in consultants is a form of satisficing; all of the lean-as-system factories in my sample brought in outside help, usually both industrial customers and consultants.

A supplier development engineer at a major industrial customer of this company agreed with my analysis, noting that owners or managers in suppliers come up with various reasons for not fully embracing lean as a system. As he told me, "You know, skepticism is a part of a business owner's life. You have to be skeptical." Suppliers often say "they basically don't have the resources to work on that, and some of that's legitimate, and I can understand that. But there also can be an element of passive resistance." He went on to elaborate the problem with not using value-stream mapping as an ongoing tool: "You can't use these tools once and expect . . . that's the whole Toyota mindset, continuous improvement. . . . if you're not constantly checking and remapping out your processes every year or whatever, how do you know you're where you should be?"

A vice president of purchasing in another major multinational prime contractor made a similar point. He explained his frustration with suppliers that would not take the opportunity to use a subsidized training program:

> I'm having a real hard time with [suppliers] when they come in and say, "We can't figure out ways to help us reduce our costs, or reduce your costs in any fashion." And I look at the log of how many classes they've taken in lean manufacturing or anything else and they don't bother to even do it. . . . when I ask them, "What in their curriculum don't you like, why haven't you used them?" very, very seldom is it that, "They don't have what we need." They just say, "We're too busy to do it. . . ."

The managers at Mini Metalfab, a lean-as-system factory, emphasized how important outside information was for their lean implementation. After sending every single employee to a Lean 101 class, they quickly moved on to a value-stream mapping class:

> Manager A: From there we went, after we went through that [Lean 101 class], there was a couple of weeks in between that we went to a value stream—we put a team of people together and we did a value streaming class, and then came back and did a value stream: current state, and a future state of our current manufacturing system and process. And that really kind of opened our eyes up on those things that we were doing internally. We kind of knew it, but this really kind of, really enlightened us a little bit.
>
> Manager B: Yeah, it really validated what we knew we had to do, and also gave us kind of a direction on how to proceed with it. One of the things that you, you see a lot of things that can be fixed, but you don't want to put a band-aid here and a band-aid there, you want to go through the process and make sure you . . . if you're going to change this, what effect does it have on everything else? So that's what we wanted to do is try to take some of the, take some of the noise out of it.

By contrast, management at Metalfab Plus moved to quasi-cells, with lasers feeding work to press brakes and then welding. But they retained functional departments for stamping, machining, and welding, including a lot of relatively large batch processing. While they have been reducing inventory, rather than working on quick changeover in order to facilitate true just-in-time production, they continued to hold inventory to do just-in-time delivery for their customers. The president of Metalfab saw this primarily in financial terms: "at the cost of money today, I can afford to carry some inventory." The plant manager articulated a fordist orientation focusing on economies of scale; rather than working on setup reduction so they can reduce batch sizes to increase economies of scope and flexibility, they were still running long batches to amortize long setups:

> Once you get the setup right, you know, we'll try to run based on forecasts, and willing to invest in the inventory rather than reset the press. We might make, you know . . . Well, I'm not going to make two at a time. I may make three months' worth of parts and get the setup right and then make them, and then I know I've got the parts right. And then wait until the next three months and set it up and run it again.

Again, this strategy does make economic sense in terms of scale economies. And the correct balance between economies of scope and scale, which varies by sector, is not always clear. But this manager was not even working on achieving the capability to increase economies of scope and flexibility through setup reductions and shorter runs. A competitor job shop with such capabilities would have lower costs and greater flexibility.

Workers were organized into consultative teams based around "departments or areas." As the following exchange with the production manager indicates, their approach to worker participation—for the vast majority of their workforce—is consultative, bringing in employees for their input on specific problem issues, but not using teams as a mechanism to encourage substantive worker participation:

> *You guys haven't gone to any teamwork or anything like that?*
>
> Well, we've had different forms of it, in terms of what, again communications is ongoing. We have monthly meetings with departments. When we have problem situations it's not unusual to bring the employee in, or the employees that do well, and do that.
>
> *Now do you have regular team meetings with them?*
>
> We haven't. And when we have, used to have them quarterly, and we're going to work towards having the managers meet with the employees every week for 15 or so minutes.

Metalfab did have some informal job rotation, but "formal job rotation, we do not have anything at this time. We will have a form of cross training program here." He discussed having formal rotation of operators across different machines, like Complex Iron Castings. He was aware of the benefits of substantive empowerment: In a separate building with around ten workers they had broadly cross trained workers given a high degree of decision-making authority. But these workers were selected from their larger group of workers as the cream of the crop. The manager framed substantive empowerment as simply too difficult to maintain with the larger workforce at the main factory:

> It's easy to handle in [our small factory] because it's not that large right now. You're talking eight to ten people. When you get 150, 180 people over here [on one shift], how do you maintain that? That's where you come into the difficulty with cross training. You have to almost—you know, I hate doing it—document things to make sure . . . "Now this week you've got to do this." Because otherwise it's six months and then they forgot about what they got trained on, you know, so you've got to have that discipline to build out there.

Yet, other companies with larger workforces systematically attempted to develop a culture of worker-driven continuous improvement throughout their workforces, including Inspired Castings (500 production workers, discussed above), LV Gaskets (300 workers, discussed below), and Custom Seats (220 production workers, discussed in Chapters 7 and 9). This suggests that the issue with Metalfab Plus management is one of aspiration level, in which the manager confronted the difficulty of institutionalizing widespread cultural change throughout his workforce and framed his context as one in which broad substantive empowerment across the workforce would be too difficult—and unnecessary given that current performance was good enough.

He went on to explain that, again due to lack of discipline among the workforce, it's difficult for them to implement *kanban*-based inventory and production control:

> There has been *kanbans* used over here for the last number of years, some successfully, some unsuccessfully. Again, there's a discipline behind that. When that container returns, if it's a container or if it's an open space or if it's a tag, the employees have to know and have to be disciplined enough to say, "Okay, I've got to build this. I have two or three days to . . ."
> [End of tape side A: begin side B:]
> But then again, along with the forecast, if it, you know, fluctuates where it goes, decreases or increases, somebody's got to be there either to resize your kanbans, make them larger or smaller, however it should be, if it's going to be something over a longer period of time. . . .
>
> *Right, and for the tape, we might have missed that first bit of that conversation. You were saying that there were some problems basically with the employee discipline.*
>
> Well, yeah, the discipline is going to be there from everybody involved, not just for resizing but also when you get that signal; a *kanban* is a signal to build. If we don't build within that timeframe, we're going to be shutting down that next operation. But I think for the most part people are starting to understand that and we've probably got it going a lot better than what it had been.
>
> *Um-hmm. Now if a container comes back empty and the employee, the operator wasn't building based on that, what would the operator be doing?*
>
> They could be doing some other production work.

Something from a forecast or . . .

Sure. It's, see it's, we have, I would say, I think not even five percent of our products, five to ten maybe, we set up on kanbans. The rest is discreet orders so it's a launch from the planners and driven that way. . . .

Okay. And what kinds of training investments are you making with the workers to . . .

Well, they have received some training already. There is no formal plan for those folks to receive any more training on that at this time, but what we do is when we implement a new *kanban* over a new line of products, they'll go through the training, receive the training on how that all is supposed to work: when their signal is, how much time they have to build and replenish and things like that.

In explaining why he didn't adopt substantive empowerment in the main workforce, this manager referred to his experience in which workers "forgot about what they got trained on." And he emphasized an underlying lack of discipline. In other words, in his experience workers were failing to embrace new routines. Compared with the Inspired Castings (500 workers), LV Gaskets (300 workers), and Specialist (eighty workers), whose management provided extensive training to and a long-term approach to empowering their workforces and institutionalizing new routines, the Metalfab Plus manager was satisficing in response to the difficulties of implementing substantive worker empowerment.

The case, however, appears to be more complex than mere satisficing, suggesting a combination of moderate aspiration level and thinking, partially, according to a taylorist logic. The manager did not consider training workers in problem solving and decision making to facilitate responsible autonomy (self-discipline), but was concerned with discipline in the sense of ensuring managerial control via documenting workers' efforts. He explained that he's only sending key managers to lean training, having "sent four or six of our managers to WMEP for the Lean Manufacturing thing and I want to get the rest of them there." For workers, "We do the one-day seminars if it's an appropriate one, you know, for the job content. We have resources that we bring inside for like blueprint training, things of this nature, which all of our people have to go through." This suggests a clear taylorist logic: workers need to be told what to do and not trained in lean principles or problem solving and decision making.

By contrast, high-involvement lean factories sent their entire workforce to lean training. For example, at Mini Metalfab, a metal fabrication job shop like Metalfab Plus, according to the plant manager: "we scheduled our shop so we could shut down on a Friday and have everybody in the entire building go take a Lean 101 class. We felt it was important enough that everybody get the concept and not rely on us managers to try to explain it and probably do a poor job of doing that." And similarly at Designer Railings, producer of handrails whose main processes are also fabrication and assembly, for Lean 101 training they sent:

> every employee. Not [just] every front line [employee]; the owner, the owner's sister, everybody went through it. As a matter of fact, we just are in the process of going through another round of it, because since then we've had people that have left, we have more people that arrived.

The Metalfab Plus case also shows a situation in which the adoption of a consultative model of participation-led management to take a satisficing position the broader work organization question. Managers at Industrial Pumps, LV Gaskets, and Second Tier Specialist all experienced similar problems with lack of discipline and engagement, but they pushed forward with broad substantive empowerment, providing sustained training and support to overcome reticence and resistance. In contrast, the manager at Metalfab framed his situation as a misfit with prescribed best practice: substantive empowerment is too difficult to realize in such a large factory. This took continuous flow off the table for them, because of the difficult of managing this without empowered workers.

In sharp contrast with Metalfab Plus, the plant manager at Second Tier Specialist demonstrated just such a dedicated and sustained approach to developing a true continuous flow system, in which workers manage the scheduling via *kanban*. Their entire operation has been restructured into three cells. Currently, the teams in the cells decide issues such as what the cell needs to spend money on or what it needs to do in terms of fixturing. The following comment illustrates a perspective that workers are capable of self-management in the interests of the firm. Management is working on devolving responsibilities to free up the:

> cell leader's time, to be looking at how do we do training for the employees, how do we do brainstorming, problem solving analysis, root cause analysis, those sorts of things, team building, having team meetings that just involve the people

out there on the factory floor. Instead of chasing all the jobs, like the cell leaders currently do, there's other people in the cell that will be doing that.

In order to facilitate their transformation, the plant manager embraced a joint union-management committee, with help from the international union, the International Association of Machinists (IAM) and its High Performance Work Organization Department (HPWO). He was working closely with the union leadership to implement changes and bring the workforce on board. In the plant manager's words:

Before me the process was dictated from above. Now I let them know what we need help in and we work together. So it's going over much better than the dictated approach which was going on before I got here, and that was very clumsy and met with a lot of resistance from the shop floor, which I fully understand. The company did a crappy job of implementing *kaizen* in the first place. First it was *kamikaze kaizen*, where they would swoop in and look at a particular machining center and people wouldn't know in advance; they'd pick people the day of the event and it was a multiple-day event.

Now they are taking a longer-term approach, working in a methodical and sustained way to train the workforce to embrace lean and develop a culture of continuous improvement. In his words:

Now what we do is we focus in from value-stream mappings on where we need to target to get the biggest bang for the buck for the *kaizen* activities. If we have the people with the skills internally then we just do it ourselves. I'm in the process of challenging each cell leader to perform X amount of *kaizen* events in their cell, but that's again just really getting rolling at this point. We're still in the process of educating people on the different lean tools and how to implement them. This is where the [IAM] HPWO group can help us.

A first step is cross training and moving to broader job descriptions. The plant manager expressed disappointment with union defense of their detailed job descriptions, while also noting he believes the process has to be negotiated rather than imposed:

I've been very frustrated in our joint union-management team meetings because we're getting too hung up on [narrow job classifications] and we're losing sight of where we're trying to head. But in respect to the union I realize that

> it's a very difficult step to get over. And it's very non-traditional in where we're heading. We have to go through that together.

This plant manager demonstrates high aspiration levels in response to numerous obstacles, including worker resistance flowing from a history of negative experiences with top-down, rushed directives and management fads of the month. In contrast to Metalfab Plus, the manager at Second Tier took a long-term perspective on substantive empowerment. The plan is to get to seven flexible job classifications, but "We're not quite ready to do that yet." As discussed in Chapter 5, this manager estimated that it would take several years before the teams would be self-driven: "We won't get there for 3 or 4 years."

Now, the emphasis on peer pressure is certainly about discipline, at minimum about ensuring sufficient effort, and may have the consequence of shifting conflict from the labor-management relation to a worker-worker relation. But my interpretation of the evidence—including the evidence from workers presented in Chapters 6 and 7—is that the strategic orientation of this manager is to prioritize substantive empowerment and not to focus on quantitative work intensification. The evidence suggests he is attempting a real devolution of responsibilities to workers, beyond having them engage in peer pressure: he had taken substantial steps toward multiskilling his workforce, including training in problem solving and leadership.

While it might be objected that one can reasonably expect peer pressure as such to lead to work intensification, the data on Custom Seats in Chapter 6 suggests that things are not so simple; they were struggling with low productivity after the move to team-based incentive pay. As James Barker's (1993) classic study showed, realizing team self-discipline itself is an ideological process requiring a negotiated consensus around a host of contested issues and competing visions, including but not limited to what is considered an appropriate level of effort. Further, the manager at Systems explicitly rejected the fordist-taylorist logic of maximizing output, noting that his focus is no longer from "an efficiency standpoint *of the machine* and how much a person can produce. Instead, the whole goal in the future . . . is move the people to where the work is, have them as highly trained and able to run different machines, perform different operations."

The final comparison is between LV Gaskets and Deep Stampings. *LV Gaskets* is an autonomous lean (substantive empowerment) factory, a nonunion shop with 300 production workers who make gaskets for heavy equipment makers such as Caterpillar, John Deere, Mack Trucks, Cummins, and International Trucks. They are a mid-volume, make-to-stock operation that sells parts through their catalog. Their primary operations include metal fabrication and assembly.

Deep Stampings is a lean standardization (nominal empowerment) factory, a nonunion shop with 300 production workers who make deep-drawn metal stampings for the automotive sector (around 75% of their business) and other sectors including mobile phones. They are a high-volume, engineer-to-order operation that sells directly to customers. Their primary operations are stamping, with secondary operations (vibing, washing, and packing), and some limited assembly.

These two companies are similar in terms of being metalworking operations with around 300 production workers, including a smaller number of skilled workers (die setters and toolmakers, respectively) and a majority of semiskilled workers (operators and assemblers, operators and finishers, respectively).

Gaskets had been organized on focused factory principles for around two decades, where each focused factory includes all the processes needed for a narrow range of products and customers. In that sense it's similar to a cell, but without continuous flow. Production is organized into five focused factories, which are largely autonomous though they share a single maintenance department. Each focused factory is organized into teams consisting of between fifteen to thirty people per shift.

The plant manager at LV Gaskets framed substantive participation in terms of individual-level autonomy because it was consistent with his company's corporate policy of participatory management:

> Employees know their own 25 square feet, which was sort of a "Don't mess with them; they probably know the best way to do it." You know, it doesn't mean because you're an industrial engineer you're really going to be able to go in and say, "Matt, you ought to do it this way." You know, Matt may not be at all comfortable doing it that way.

Because of their emphasis on individual-level autonomy, they have not standardized processes across individuals and cells, and still have a lot of nonstandard processes. While they have not emphasized standardization, and have not implemented *kanban* control, they are regularly using value-stream mapping as a tool for ongoing continuous improvement, including shopfloor employees:

> We've actually identified five value streams for this year. We're working well through the first one. . . . We're well underway on the second one; third one probably within a month or so we'll get into that. Whether we'll make all five or not by the end of the year, I don't really know, but that's kind of the goal that's out there.
>
> *Who's involved in the value-stream mapping exercises?*
>
> Everybody.
>
> *Everybody. The shopfloor employees too?*
>
> Yeah. Oh, yeah.

He went on to explain how they assemble teams based on volunteers, and they in general they have plenty of volunteers:

> Normally we go for a group of volunteers, and then we'll choose from the group of volunteers. We haven't . . . so far we've had plenty of people who are willing to participate, we haven't had to twist any arms. Well, I guess that's not true, we've twisted an arm or two versus, you know, for where we needed a particular expertise kind of thing.
>
> *To get the right person, uh-huh.*
>
> But other than that, it's basically volunteer.
>
> *And it . . . something where every employee has the opportunity to volunteer?*
>
> Yep.

In addition to value-stream mapping, they are engaging in extensive continuous improvement activities, again with substantial participation from production workers:

> Basically what we do is, we'll put a team together, we'll decide what the *kaizen* is going to be on, okay? We do basically two types of *kaizen*: we do a 5S *kaizen* and we do a production *kaizen*. . . . A team is normally 7 to 10 people. We try to get somebody from all of the shifts in the plant. . . . We'll get everybody sat down, we'll do some brainstorming and suggest that, "Okay, this is the area we're looking at." . . . We'll try and generate some distinct goals as to what we want to do: you know, generate x number of ideas, or save x number of dollars or, you know, whatever it might be.
>
> Once we get that all kind of laid out then it goes one of a couple directions. If it's a 5S *kaizen*, the people get out on the floor and just start getting involved and, you know, start cleaning and throwing things away and labeling things and that sort of thing. If it's a production *kaizen*, we may do everything from videotaping the operation so that they can study it, and just having people kind of hang out there for a while that they're not familiar with the operation.
>
> Hopefully we come back with a bunch of ideas of where we want to go. The *kaizen* leader is normally the trainer or one of the operating committee people, and they just kind of keep it on track and on focus and say, okay—*kaizen* in particular tend to begin to take on a life of their own if you don't keep them constrained in some way, shape or form. And so that's really the role that that *kaizen* leader tends to play.

Along with the full-time trainer the teams include a "Lean Deployment Manager." The rest of the members are volunteers from the shopfloor. He estimated a ratio of: "70 percent on-the-floor people and 30 percent supervisors." In terms of participation levels:

> I don't have any solid numbers but I would guess that it's probably somewhere around 35% of the people. Volunteers tend to, they tend to grow as you get more involved. Initially it's tough to find somebody because nobody knows what it is and, you know, they don't want to be the guinea pigs kind of thing. And then a couple people do it and say, "Hey, well, it was really kind of a good time. I got to talk about this and talk about that." And then more people go, "Oh, okay, well maybe I'd like to do it too."

Management is working to increase that number, and hopes to have widespread participation of workers in these problem-solving groups.

Deep Stampings provides a sharp contrast with Gaskets in terms of approach to worker participation and lean production. On the latter,

Stampings had a sustained focus on using lean tools to standardize processes, whereas Gaskets did not due to their focus on allowing individual autonomy. As discussed in Chapter 5, it was difficult for me to decide whether to code Stampings as a lean-enough or lean standardization case based on my one interview there. This was one my first interviews and I was still developing my understanding of lean. I opted to code Stampings as a lean standardization case because, according to my reading, they have a systematic focus on using lean tools to standardize processes and realize some degree of ongoing improvement in workflow and process standards. But I am uncertain about this categorization; further probing may reveal Stampings to be a lean-enough case, given that there are open questions about the frequency with which they use value-stream mapping and the extent to which they have implemented or plan to implement demand-driven continuous flow.

The following extended discussion with the plant manager at Stampings illustrates their emphasis on standardization. In the discussion, among other key points, the manager also explained that they have not emphasized batch size reduction because their processes are too variable:

> What impresses me about them [Autoliv] is, they actually had a gentleman from Toyota live in their plant for like three years, and taught them the Toyota Production System. And they are the only customer I've seen that actually does it, actually—you read all about it; they do it. So, you know, they walk the talk, which is, you know, has a lot of credence then. And then because of that, now they're taking it to the next step and they of course have dubbed it the Autoliv Production System, and now they're trying to train their suppliers, their key suppliers, on that. So they've been in here more so from an inventory, *kanban*, visual management, that standpoint, than really a quality standpoint, really trying to, you know, teach us lean manufacturing and those kinds of things. But they've, you know, they were probably in here for a while every six weeks, pretty consistently.
>
> *So it was inventory,* kanban, *like this kind of plant layout . . .*
>
> Lean manufacturing, 5-S was a big part of it . . .
>
> *Cells?*
>
> We had cells. I mean where it makes sense, we have cells. So that really wasn't part of it. Really, the way they look at it, they have what they call their House of APS. The foundation is 5-S: you've got to have your place organized, clean, got to know where things are, that type of thing. We have, you know, done fairly

well, still got a ways to go, but I think we've made pretty decent progress in that regard. And then you start to get into the other, you know, parts of the house. That's where we struggle because, you know, what Autoliv has done, in my mind, is they have done an excellent job of reducing variation with everything in their process: not just quality, but production. I mean, and if you think about it, that is the key to make lean manufacturing work.

Our process still has a tremendous amount of variation compared to—I mean they can sit there and say, "Yeah, I'm going to get, I need 100 parts an hour," and they'll get 101 one hour and 98 the next and 103 . . . I mean and they've really got it down. Their process is different, they're more of an assembly place. Our processes is, yeah, we're supposed to get 1,000 parts an hour and we don't get any for the first hour and we get 500 for the second, and then we get 2,000 for the third. It's, you know, something we've got to work on, but we are . . . So it's more difficult to lean out your inventories if you can't count on that, you know, kind of steady beat. . . .

Cells only make sense when the volumes dictate it. So we really just look at, if there's enough volume to justify putting a washer next to a press, putting a vibe next to a press, then we'll go ahead and do it

The foregoing discussion raises two key issues. First, given that most of their parts were made within a single stamping operation (which generally includes multiple stations/dies), they *do* have less opportunity for regular use of value-stream mapping to continuously improve process flow and eliminate bottlenecks. However, as we will see below, they still have plenty of room for continuous improvement in terms of both 5S, setup reduction, and production issues.

Second, the manager invoked a misfit in terms of his local context being too difficult to use some lean tools: inventory reduction is difficult due to their variable processes; cells are often inappropriate due to insufficiently high volumes. It is common to see highly variable production as a difficult context in which to implement lean. But my sample includes factories which have implemented a high-involvement, lean-as-system approach in similarly variable contexts, including make-to-order factories (Inspired Castings, Second Tier Specialist, Custom Seats) and a job shop (Mini Metalfab). Further, as discussed in more detail in the following chapter, my sample includes factories implementing cells in low-volume contexts (including Industrial Pumps, Inspired Castings, Second Tier Specialist, and Custom Seats). This suggests that the Stampings manager's invocation of difficulty is a reflection of a moderate aspiration level, likely in conjunction with a taylorist orientation (see below) and a focus on other production and strategic issues.

In the following discussion, the manager described having persistent problems with changeover and production, attributing this to the complexity of their tools:

> I mean we have to get better, but the parts we make, our niche is very complex, multi-station, tool/parts. So, you know, you read the trade journals where people are changing over in three minutes and all that.
>
> *Yeah.*
>
> We will never do that. Our tools are too complex. There have been occasions where we've been able to do a changeover in a half an hour. That's excellent for the type of tooling we have. The problem is we haven't done it consistently and we haven't been able to do it across the board.
>
> *Um-hmm. But you don't have day-long tool changeovers, do you?*
>
> Some of our, what we call our eyelet-style presses where you're actually putting in each punch and die for each station individually, those can take up to a day, those are just slow changeover presses.
>
> *And then you think that the setup, the changeover time, isn't one of the big cost drivers out there then with this process or . . . ?*
>
> Oh, I . . . no, I think it's a huge cost driver. No, I think that if we could get our changeover times down and get them consistent, it has a huge ripple effect with what we could, and should, be able to do, in terms of taking inventory and waste out of the process. It's huge.
>
> But yeah, we have an issue with setups, we also have an issue with production; I mean, it's both. We can get a good setup and then, you know, muddle through production; that's just as painful, you know.

I asked him to elaborate on the production problems. He continued:

> Many times you can have a job that comes out running, you go in a week later, same material, haven't done anything to the tool, and the part's out of print. And you go from there. It doesn't make sense, but it's the nature of the beast.
> *It just, does it depend on the variation in the material that goes through, or . . . ?*

> Like I said, we can even have the same material. I mean sometimes they'll save a partial of the coil they were running, just because, okay, we're going to start back up with a known, and . . .
>
> *Heat, humidity?*
>
> I mean you've got a lot, you've got coolants, you've got a lot of variables. But, yeah, you just kind of scratch your head.

We have seen in this chapter how other managers would deal with these persistent problems by substantively empowering the operators to engage in problem solving and decision making, and by systematically running quick changeover *kaizen* events, including operators, to develop their capabilities. In contrast, this manager left such responsibilities to individual toolmakers, which he described as the "troubleshooters, problem solvers" in the company. These "toolmakers spend a huge chunk of the time at the press, so they're looking, you know, at how they can do things differently, better, make their life easier."

By not doing *kaizen* events and or using any other type of offline team engaging production workers in problem solving, the management at Stampings is satisficing. They achieved limited, scattershot continuous improvement by relying heavily on their production toolmakers. But they simply had not engaged, and did not plan to engage production workers in problem solving. When I asked if "the teams or anything else increased the amount of input that the workers can give into the production process," the manager replied:

> Maybe a little bit. Again, our, how do I say it? We work pretty hand-in-hand with our toolmakers out there. And some, we only have one scheduler for all our presses. So they aren't afraid to come in and talk to him and say, "Hey, it would be a lot easier if you'd run this first and this second," or, "Why are we running so few? Can't we run some more?" or, "My tool's not ready, can we . . . ?" I mean they're always in here. So I don't think that's really changed, I mean that communication has always been there.

While some toolmakers gave their input, he noted that they prioritized standardization but without a sustained focus on continuous improvement:

> And again, when I, yeah. And when I say, I mean just like everything else, you've got your good toolmakers and your average toolmakers. So usually the good toolmakers are the ones you're pulling back in to the design phase and picking their brain and getting their input. So it's not everybody, it's the good ones. . . . Actually it's a good thing and a bad thing because our designers will complain that we'll, every toolmaker wants things different. And it is a problem. I mean we need to kind of hold our ground and say, "No, this is the standard, this is how we're going to do it."

The foregoing data suggest this manager sees workers through a traditional fordist-taylorist lens, suggesting a taylorist logic is driving the satisficing. He had not considered training his operators in problem solving, using lean tools like root-cause analysis, the Five Whys, and so on. Beyond the "good toolmakers," this manager simply did not attempt to develop a culture of worker-driven continuous improvement or even to engage the operators—the bulk of the workforce—in substantive participation.

His explanation for not substantively empowering his operators was that some workers do not *want* the responsibility:

> You know, if you have a sharp operator who has an aptitude and an interest and maybe has been here awhile, and depending if the toolmaker is willing to mentor that person, you know, they'll let them do more. They'll look over their shoulder. But you have other operators, they just want to operate, you know, "Just let me do my job. I could care less about how that tool works or what you do," and that works too.

The observation is sound in the sense that, as shown in Chapter 7, some workers find the "opportunity to participate" a stressful obligation they do not want. However, managers in several other factories from my sample experienced similar reticence (and resistance) from workers but forged ahead with training to develop a culture of problem solving and continuous improvement. While a taylorist orientation plays a role here, the comparison with the learning-lean approach suggests a key role for moderate aspiration levels, in which the Stampings manager received bottom-up feedback—worker reticence—and framed the situation as one in which the workers do not want to be empowered. The fact that he did not lament this situation, like others did, suggests that a taylorist logic may be reinforcing his moderate aspiration levels.

In sum, management at Stampings is satisficing with a hybrid approach, focusing on lean tools to standardize processes, but being content with some fordist practices using shopfloor labor in a taylorist way, with mainly semiskilled workers not involved in cross training or problem solving. Offline teams in particular could be very useful here: convening teams, including production workers, to engage in problem solving around setup reduction and production problems.

Conclusion

Managers face competing pressures regarding whether to substantively empower their workers or not. I presented evidence demonstrating that in four factories, managers found it highly beneficial to substantively empower their workers, broadly throughout their workforce via cross training and the devolution of problem-solving and decision-making authority. These managers reporting that doing so was difficult for several reasons, including worker reticence and resistance (in this chapter and in Chapter 7), but they persisted, suggesting high aspiration levels. Such persistence included disciplined, methodical, patient management in order to overcome resistance and reticence.

I also presented evidence showing that in four other factories, managers did not attempt to implement substantive empowerment broadly throughout their workforce, instead relying either on managers or a small number of enthusiastic workers to achieve a limited degree of continuous improvement. There are two main factors that lead managers to forego substantive empowerment: their cognitive orientation (thinking in terms of the logic of fordism-taylorism) and moderate aspiration levels.

The cases of Complex Iron Castings and Custom Blinds illustrate a top-down process, in which cognitive orientation exerts an influence independent from aspiration level. In these cases, the managers presented clearly taylorist views of workers and this logic as such shaped their interpretation of their situation.

But the analysis of Metalfab Plus and Deep Stampings suggests that these cognitive orientations and aspiration levels often work in combination, reinforcing each other. In both cases, there is evidence of a bottom-up process, in which managers satisficed in response to stimuli from their local situation: lack of discipline, engagement, or interest from the workers, and the difficulty of overcoming this. But in both cases the manager also expressed a fordist-taylorist view of workers. Unfortunately, I don't have sufficient data to disentangle these factors. I return to this issue in the concluding chapter.

9

Workplace Regimes: Valorization Logics and Organizational Logics

Chapter 3 discussed the critical distinction between the labor process and the valorization process. The valorization question concerns how to ensure sufficient effort and output from labor, while the labor process question concerns how to organize the overall production process. Of course, this is an analytical distinction and in practice the two processes are deeply intertwined. Chapters 7 and 8 focused on the valorization process, the latter showing that some managers blend the currently dominant institutional logic of best practice regarding valorization (substantive empowerment) with the formerly dominant logic (traditional taylorism) to produce hybrid practice: nominal empowerment.

This chapter focuses on holistic analysis of workplace regimes, including the labor process and the valorization process. Because the previous two chapters focused on the valorization process, the present chapter emphasizes the broader labor process. Again, as in Chapter 8, we see interaction effects between valorization strategy and organizational strategy (most notably in the cases of Second Tier Specialist and LV Gaskets).

Chapter 5 documented two prominent logics of the postfordist labor process. The dominant institutional logic of best practice is what I call *lean-as-system*, which consists of the entire package of principles and practices from the House of Lean (Figure 4.2). The two distinguishing features of this approach are: sophisticated use of value-stream mapping (VSM) throughout the factory *on a regular basis* to drive continuous improvement; and use of true continuous flow production throughout the factory, where operations in a flow loop are scheduled by a single pacemaker or trigger point, which sends a signal to upstream operations to build, both within cells and via *kanban* signals for parts feeding or leaving cells.

The hybrid logic is what I call the *lean-as-toolbox* approach, which results either from a top-down process of blending the fordist logic with the lean logic or a bottom-up process of satisficing in response to the difficulty of implementing lean-as-system. These factories adopt most or all of the

Management Divided. Matt Vidal, Oxford University Press. © Matt Vidal (2022).
DOI: 10.1093/oso/9780198795278.003.0009

basic lean practices (inventory and batch reduction, quick changeover, 5S, quality at source, visual management, point of use storage, total productive maintenance, and standardized work), but without continuous flow and with limited, irregular use of value-stream mapping, typically only for a single major restructuring effort.

In this chapter I explain the variation in approaches to lean organization. After some analytical considerations, I begin with a case study of a supplier development project at Metalfab Plus, in which supplier development engineers from a major industrial customer—a world-class leader in lean production—worked with lean experts from the Wisconsin Manufacturing Extension Partnership (WMEP) to train Metalfab in using value-stream mapping to implement cellular production on a pull system for a product family. This provides an overview of a highly sophisticated value-stream mapping process, which I use as a comparison point for the analysis that follows.

After the case study, I match establishments again (as in Chapter 8) on key factors in order to highlight schema-driven (top-down) and aspiration-driven (bottom-up) cognitive processes. On the former, I present one matched pair (see Table 9.1). The case of Tubefab illustrates a schema-driven process in which a fordist logic of maximizing machine uptime influences the manager's approach. However, this manager also displays moderate aspiration levels on other issues, suggesting that cognitive orientation and aspiration level may reinforce each other in leading to a lean-as-toolbox approach.

On aspiration levels, I present two matched pairs (Table 9.1). LV Gaskets and Hydraulic Systems are both cases of autonomous lean, where an emphasis on individual autonomy precludes the adoption of standardized work. Both cases illustrate an aspiration-driven process in which managers claimed that adopting true continuous flow was a poor fit for their factory due to its complexity, and further that regular use of value-stream mapping and formal programs for continuous improvement are too difficult given how busy there were trying to satisfy existing customers. In both cases, I present matched factories where managers were pushing ahead with a lean-as-system approach despite having similar levels of complexity, similarly demanding environments and experiencing several obstacles and setbacks. The comparisons provide evidence that the managers not implementing lean-as-system are satisficing, based on moderate aspiration levels, invoking misfit and difficulty as a rationale for their moderate aspiration levels.

Table 9.1 Organization logics with factory cases matched on key characteristics

Factory	Characteristics	Factory	Characteristics
Top-down process: Adopt dominant logic of lean-as-system		**Top-down process: Adopt hybrid logic of lean-as-toolbox**	
Second Tier Specialist	Employment: 80 Technology: Machining, assembly Strategy: Make-to-order Volume: Low to mid	Tubefab	Employment: 150 Technology: Metal forming, assembly Strategy: Make-to-order and engineer-to-order Volume: Mainly high, but also low and mid
Bottom-up process: High aspiration level		**Bottom-up process: Moderate aspiration level**	
Designer Railings	Employment: 90 Technology: Metal fabrication, assembly Strategy: Make-to-stock Volume: Mid	LV Gaskets	Employment: 300 Technology: Metal fabrication, assembly Strategy: Make-to-stock Volume: Mid
Custom Seats	Employment: 220 Technology: Sewing, upholstery, Assembly Strategy: Make-to-stock, make-to-order, engineer-to-order Volume: High and low	Hydraulic Systems	Employment: 90 Technology: Machining, fabrication, assembly Strategy: Engineer-to-order Volume: Low

Note: "Employment" refers to the number of production workers.

Analytical Considerations

As in Chapter 8, my analytical strategy is to present matched cases, in which factories are matched as closely as possible on relevant technical, market, and organizational factors. Again, this controls for such factors to highlight the role of cognitive orientation (logic of practice) and managerial aspiration level in producing variation. This is critical for managerial aspiration level, given that managers are unlikely to articulate a moderate aspiration level as a factor in their decision making. Managers with moderate aspiration levels are likely rationalize their deviation from widely agreed best practice by framing that practice as a poor fit with their context.

The goal for the labor process/organization question is to match factories in terms of the objective fit of lean-as-system with a particular factory context. The key factors here are product volume (high/mid/low), product mix (high/low), and product strategy (engineer-to-order, make-to-order, or make-to-stock). A high-mix, low-volume context is broadly understood by practitioners to be an extremely challenging context within which to implement true continuous flow, due to the broader range of parts used and products made. Similarly, engineer- or make-to-order contexts are understood to be difficult contexts due to a broader range of products. Engineers and managers widely agree that the easiest context in which to implement lean-as-system is high-volume, low-mix, make-to-stock. In addition to the managers below, the engineer from Industrial Pumps explained:

> And I think we still struggle with that mental aspect of it too, that we could pull things through the shop. But everybody still gets really stuck on the fact that our, we don't make maybe more than two of the exact same part number in any one day. And people just feel that, because we're not, you know, making 50 identical lawnmowers all day, but you know, there's a little bit of difference to everything that we do and a lot of shared resources, I think that right now we've had just that mental hurdle to get over.

Table 9.1 provides details in the matched cases. The top panel lists factories that illustrate a top-down process in which the logic adopted by management shapes interpretation of the local situation. The bottom panel lists those that illustrate a bottom-up process in which managers with moderate aspiration levels satisfice in response to feedback from the local situation.

The table shows variation across the two work organization strategies within the following matched factors:

- Second Tier Specialist (lean-as-system) versus Tubefab and Hydraulic Systems (lean-as-toolbox) matched on employment levels, technology, strategy, and volume;[1]
- Second Tier Specialist and Designer Railings (lean-as-system) versus Tubefab and Hydraulic Systems (lean-as-toolbox) matched on employment levels, technology, and volume;
- Second Tier Specialist and Custom Seats (lean-as-system) versus Tubefab and Hydraulic Systems (lean-as-toolbox) on strategy and volume;
- Designer Railings (lean-as-system) versus LV Gaskets (lean-as-toolbox) on technology, strategy, and volume;

[1] I treat make-to-order and engineer-to-order as effectively identical with regard to the fit of lean work organization, both presenting a broader range of parts and products than make-to-stock. I treat mid- and low-volume as effectively identical for the same reason.

- Designer Railings and Custom Seats (lean-as-system) versus LV Gaskets (lean-as-toolbox) on strategy and volume;
- Custom Seats (lean-as-system) and LV Gaskets (lean-as-toolbox) on employment levels, strategy, and volume.

Most importantly, the analysis reveals:

- Lean-as-system being adopted across product strategy and volume, including in four high-mix, low-volume factories (Second Tier Specialist, Tubefab, Custom Seats, and Hydraulic Systems).

I begin with a case study on value-stream mapping. I then turn to the analysis of the factories in the top panel of Table 9.1, focusing on matched cases that demonstrate competing logics of work organization. Finally, I turn to the bottom panel, focusing on matched cases that show variation in aspiration levels.

A Case Study on Value-Stream Mapping

As discussed in Chapter 4, I observed Metalfab Plus for a twenty-month period over 2003–04, including interviews with four managers, six workers, participation in a half-day "Lean 101" training for workers, and nineteen hours of observation (over eight sessions) of a supplier development project, run by a large industrial customer and the WMEP. In order to maintain anonymity, I will not describe the products produced by the industrial customer who ran the supplier development project at Metalfab. But the customer is a global leader in its industry, a household-name company with net revenue of over $20 billion in 2004, from sales in North and South America, Europe, Asia, and Africa. I will call this company Global OE. In addition to observing the supplier development project, on separate occasions I interviewed the following three individuals from Global OE: the corporate-level (global) supplier development process lead; a manager, supplier development; and an engineer, supplier development.

Metalfab Plus had achieved "partner" status with Global OE, meaning the former consistently met the top standards of the latter for quality, delivery, and price. Yet, the supplier management team was convinced that Metalfab Plus had—like many of their suppliers—achieved this performance through inefficient, non-lean methods. I quoted the supplier development manager in Chapter 4 describing how suppliers can achieve quality by adding inspectors rather than using lean methods to devolve quality control to production workers; delivery by adding stock rather than doing just-in-time production; and price by buying the business.

Metalfab had been doing strong and steady business until they lost the business of a major customer—$20 million annually—who re-sourced to China. This shock made them reassess their situation. They brought in a new production manager with experience in lean production but, beyond that, decided not to seek the help of outside consultants or customers. The plant was reorganized based on lean principles to improve the workflow.

Recall from Chapter 8 that management at Metalfab Plus considered its lean re-layout to be "90% complete," and did not plan to do more value-stream mapping. However, after I had completed that interview, but was still observing this company, the team at Global OE insisted on running a supplier development project inside Metalfab plus to show them how to do value-stream mapping and implement a true pull system for a product family Metalfab made for Global EO.

After the engineers from Global OE had assessed what Metalfab had done, they concluded that Metalfab didn't have any systematic analysis of what the best flow for the shop should be—even after the supplier had *completed* its own lean reorganization. From the perspective of the external engineers, the managers at the supplier hadn't even considered what would be a good balance for given sets of machines that could run product families. They essentially did their restructuring based on hunches and intuition, without having conducted a systematic analysis of data on their processes. In the words of the engineer in charge of the project, the supplier management team was "shooting from the hip." They did not even have a well-defined problem, beyond a basic understanding of the need to rationalize their plant layout.

Metalfab conducted a single, major restructuring, which they had considered near complete. But in the meetings I observed, the external engineers stressed that value-stream mapping should be an ongoing process; my fieldnotes from observing the project include the following quotes taken down from the engineers: "Once you get to a future state, start again." And: "A value stream manager is key for maintaining the vision. Simply doing setup reduction or 5S will not get you there. The future state becomes the current state and you map a new future state—always be pushing the envelope."

The value-stream mapping that Metalfab did was informal and not data-based. This was in sharp contrast to the systematic mapping process that the external engineers walked them through. This process took several months of weekly meetings by a cross-functional team. The team diagnosed process flows, based on part families, using a tool called Pareto analysis, from which they concluded that 20% of the process flows make up 50% of their total volume; the remaining 670 process flows they identified make up the other 50% of their volume.

A major part family was then picked to be used for a current-state map of the value stream, from sales all the way to shipping. The shopfloor operations included a laser cutter, press brakes, and welding. Based on empirical analysis, the current-state map divided the full value stream into value-added time, necessary non-value-added time, and unnecessary value-added time. A future-state map was then created, based on further data analysis and deliberation.

Table 9.2 presents an internal memo from the customer to the supplier, dated June 30, 2004, showing that this process took five months from the current-state map to the formal list of recommendations for improvement. The reason this process took so long was due to the depth of data analysis and discussion that went into the list of recommendations. They created a future-state map and then set about doing intensive data analysis and discussion around how to realize that future state. The team met every week for five months. The meetings to create the current-state and future-state value streams were eight hours each, supplemented by statistical analysis outside the meetings, and additional weekly meetings that often ran two hours or more.

The external engineers told me, on background, that management at Metalfab failed to fully appreciate the lessons and tools in which they were trained. Metalfab management had plans to install in a new laser, which involved a massive capital expense, including cutting a space in the concrete floor to install the laser; once the laser was in, that is where it would stay. Against the protestations of the external engineering team, senior management went ahead with purchasing and installing the laser before the mapping team was able to fully assess their product flows and organizational capacity, which would allow them to see where and how such a laser could be best utilized.

The mapping team subsequently found that the over-utilization of Metalfab's two existing lasers was due largely to their forecasting system over-scheduling the lasers, resulting in bottlenecks downstream at the press

Table 9.2 Memo from value-stream mapping project at Metalfab Plus

Activity	End Date
Develop project charter	10/15/2003
Current process map	01/15/2004
Document baseline	02/15/2004
Conduct analyses	04/30/2004
List of recommendations for improvement	06/30/2004
Finalize project implementation plan	07/31/2004
Complete implementation	09/30/2004
Confirm results	12/31/2004

brakes. In short, the problem was not with a lack of laser capacity—as Metalfab management had concluded—but with scheduling problems creating bottlenecks at other operations, problems which would not be solved, and could be exacerbated, by purchasing and permanently installing the new laser without having completed the value-stream mapping analysis.

Management at Metalfab saw their key strategic priorities in terms of product market strategy, which led to satisficing on operational strategy. According to the company president, "as part of the strategy . . . we've tried to focus on those things that we think there is a high probability they will never go offshore; partly because of size, partly because of volume." The other part of the strategy was to offer their customers additional services, including quick-turn prototyping and assembly.

To be sure, the president, who came from an accounting background, was thinking strategically at a high level for the organization, balancing competing goals. In view of this, his approach to lean could be seen as pragmatic. But he and his team saw lean as a toolbox rather than a system, resulting in what is objectively—compared with Second Tier Specialist (a machine shop), Designer Railings (a fabrication shop), and Mini Metalfab (a job shop)—a satisficing approach.

In a meeting presenting the findings from the analysis of the current-state value-stream map, the team of external engineers noted that just sixteen of 393 process flows accounted for 51% of the laser run hours. Their value-stream analysis of a single process flow found that for each of the three parts of a foot pedal, unnecessary non-value-added time constituted over 98% of the process. After presenting these data and beginning to work on the future-state value-stream map, the president asked: "From a strategy standpoint are we pushing for too much?"

In a separate interview, the engineer from Global OE reported that in his experience, it is common for suppliers to fail to embrace "lean thinking" after the supplier development project has been completed:

> We've tried to do the technology transfer and tried to help them out and, in a lot of cases, the projects were very successful and we met all the goals or very close to all the goals. The problem comes when the OEM's presence leaves. The focus on the project or the particular metrics or whatever it may be goes away and it becomes business as usual.
>
> So because we've had a lot of experience with those types of projects—not all of them are like that but there's certainly a good many of them—all of the executives [in his company] were concerned about sustainability. The assumption, and it's a good assumption, is that lean improvements are not sustainable without a certain level of cultural change. If you're going to take a small company or a company that's not doing lean manufacturing and you want to move them into the realm of lean manufacturing, clearly, um, there needs to be a cultural change. There's a lot of things in terms of sustainability that deal with culture.

He went on to elaborate how even if supplier management seems to understand lean thinking during the supplier development project, they often revert to more traditional practices:

> I know it happens, is that once we leave, maybe it's supervision, maybe it's a lack of focus, but the all of a sudden you come back and you see mounds of inventory between each station, *even within a cell*. And the whole idea behind that concept it you reduce the in-process inventory so you can move stuff through quicker, and you reduce the batching.
>
> And it's that kind of stuff that I can say is more typical. Not the fact that they're going to rearrange their factory back into a traditional environment, but they don't operate within a lean, what's called a lean management style—where supervisors or cell leaders allow non-lean practices to happen within the infrastructure that's placed by the OEM or the consultant or whatever it may be.

Compared with managers I observed adopting lean-as-system (discussed in depth below), managers at Metalfab Plus had moderate aspiration levels. Again, this is not meant as a criticism of the Metalfab managers; running a manufacturing concern with 450 production workers is exceptionally difficult, and they were making incremental improvements. As the plant manager said:

> It's always something different. So you don't have one focal point: Tell me what the priority is, what should I be doing? You've got five different people pulling you in different directions. It gets to be quite confusing.

This is completely understandable: manufacturing managers are being pulled in multiple directions, facing competing pressures of all sorts. The point is not to criticize managers for having moderate aspiration levels, but to acknowledge variation in aspiration levels, and the satisficing and relative inefficiency that results under capitalist management.

Schema-Driven Divergence on Work Organization: Lean vs Fordist Logics

Chapter 4 showed that in the American manufacturing field a highly specified model of lean production, called the House of Lean (Figure 4.2), has been adopted by leading companies, consultants, associations, and state agencies. The House of Lean is widely understood to constitute a *package* of complementary practices, which only produces world-class performance when implemented as a package. This is what I refer to as the lean-as-system approach. But some managers continue to think partially in terms of the fordist logic, resulting in a hybrid logic of practice I call lean-as-toolbox. In Chapter 3 I theorized the latter process as one in which conceptual schema associated with a formerly dominant logic continue to exert a powerful influence on managerial cognition.

In this section I illustrate the role of fordist schema in shaping divergence from the dominant logic of lean-as-system, comparing the two factories from the top panel of Table 9.1 As we have seen, *Second Tier Specialist* (a lean-as-system factory) is a union shop with around eighty production workers that make industrial cylinders for the automotive and hydraulics industries. It is a low- to mid-volume factory. Most of their work is make-to-order, with about half of their cylinders being custom designed and half coming from previously made designs.

Tubefab (a lean-as-toolbox factory) is a nonunion shop with around 150 production workers that make mufflers for the automotive and outdoor power equipment industries. Its volumes range from high (around 300,000 per year) to mid to low (1000 per year). The mufflers need to be price-competitive but they still require skilled welders able to do light-gauge sheet metal welding, in addition to semiskilled press operators and assemblers. Most of their work is make-to-order, with about half of their mufflers being custom-designed (by an engineering center at a different location) and half made according to customer designs.

While Second Tier has a higher proportion of skilled workers (machinists) versus a smaller proportion at Tubefab (light-gauge sheet metal welders), the two factories face very similar work organization issues in terms of both being make-to-order shops producing complex subassemblies, with a mix of custom and to-print work. The Second Tier case illustrates a plant manager seeing the substantive empowerment of his workforce to be a necessary step for implementing true continuous flow.

In a low-volume, high-mix context, the plant manager at Specialist has adopted a lean-as-system approach, organizing his entire factory into three cells. By contrast, the plant manager at Tubefab implemented some assembly cells but maintained functional departments for stamping presses and tube fabrication. His explanation for doing so reveals a fordist orientation, seeing dedicated cells as being justified only where there are sufficiently high volumes:

> Well, generally if you have a product that you can't dedicate a cell to, you know if you . . . we have families of mufflers that, they're similar enough that maybe they can run down the same line and they use the same crimping die, but all the rest of the fixturing is different. You know all the line really does for you is get the part from one person to another. It really doesn't slow you down or speed you up. If the balance is good on the line, it really doesn't hurt you that much. There's products we've run faster on a line than we have in a cell. But you know, that's not the norm but it's feasible. *Generally we take a look at the volume and we say, "Okay, can this family justify a cell full time and does it give us an advantage? And what advantage does it give us?"* And if it can, great, and then we move in that direction; and if it can't, we don't.

When discussing the issue further, he explicitly invoked the fordist principle of maximizing output on individual machines (to achieve economies of scale) as a primary source of efficiency:

> To feed a cell that runs continuously—like our highest volume cell, it runs continuously at about 140 parts an hour—to make every component, there's one, two, three, four, five; there's five pressed components in there. So that's only 900 parts an hour that you need to make. It's not even that, it's only 700 parts an

> hour that you need to make. And generally straight-sides can run 1,200 to 2,000 parts an hour depending on the size of the part. *So you're only utilizing that press to half capacity*. You know, so unless you had, say, one press feeding two cells somehow, it would be a challenge, you know.

The plant manager at Systems provides a sharp contrast. The following comment illustrates a lean-as-system logic, which replaces the traditional mass production of maximizing machine uptime with the principle of just-in-time production (to achieve economies of scope and flexibility):

> In the past you would have measures such as *optimum up time on a machine*, you know, how much is that machine running. Who gives a shit? Do what needs to be done to get the orders out, don't make extra inventory unless you absolutely need it, because you can't replenish those particular parts within the lead times you need to get your product to your customer. It's a moot—train your workers so they move to where the work is and perform the work you need, don't have them doing work that doesn't need to be done right now.

Now, the manager at Tubefab did note that setting up cells that are directly fed by their 400-ton straight-side presses would be both expensive and "a logistical nightmare" to move. But he was clear that he only saw cells as justified if they are sufficiently high volume that they can be fed by a press running at full capacity.

The manager at Specialist implemented cells at volumes much lower than the Tubefab manager did. Because the low-volume, high-mix context is so dynamic, implementing continuous flow production there requires both high aspiration levels from management but also a highly committed, substantively empowered workforce. As we saw in Chapter 8, after past management pushed a top-down, "dictated approach" he called "*kamikaze kaizen*," which provoked widespread resistance from the workforce, he substantively involved the workers from the get-go, taking a methodical and dedicated approach to educating and training his workers in lean tools and practices.

Systems used value-stream mapping as an ongoing tool to direct their continuous improvement activities: "we focus in from value stream mappings on where we need to target to get the biggest bang for the buck for the *kaizen* activities." Their *kaizen* events were multi-day events including cross-shift teams of workers, focusing on a range of activities, including *kanban* systems for true pull production:

> A *kaizen* event is typically a multiple-day event. It may not all get completed within that time period, three for four days. But at least you're identifying everything that needs to get done, itemize the tasks. You have a goal you're trying to solve, e.g. maybe we're setting up a *kanban* system for the raw inventory for Cell 2, or we might be doing a setup reduction on a LC30 or LC40 [CNC lathes]. It's very specific and you know what you're trying to do, you're trying to reduce your setup times by 50%. And you get a group of people from first and second shift, hopefully, to work together for that event.

Chapters 7 and 8 noted that this manager experienced overt resistance to lean, cross training, and devolved responsibilities from a large faction of workers. Yet, despite this, he had succeeded in reorganizing the entire factory on continuous-flow principles and was systematically working toward having continuous improvement driven by empowered teams, illustrating both an embrace of the logic of lean-as-system and the high aspiration levels needed to adopt high-involvement lean. He focused on building a culture of worker-driven continuous improvement to make possible factorywide just-in-time pull systems in a low-volume, high-mix factory.

In contrast, the manager at Tubefab adopted a lean-as-toolbox approach, alongside a strategy of nominal empowerment. He noted that they do some *kaizen* events, but these are driven by management with limited participation from workers. The only people he sent to lean training events (run by the Wisconsin Manufacturing Extension Partnership) were: "a continuous improvement coordinator, and/or a manufacturing manager that went to them." The following comment on employee involvement suggests a largely taylorist view of workers. The primary emphasis for getting input from workers was a suggestion program, not *kaizen* events:

> We've had a suggestion box for years that we never used, for whatever reason. Over the past few years we've really tried to emphasize, we have a safety team, we have a quality council, we have *kaizen* teams that we try to get people to volunteer for, a variety of things like that. Right now we're in the midst of releasing, hopefully today actually at the supervisor meeting we're going to roll out a new employee input program, kind of like a, it's kind of like a suggestion form, but it's definitely more formalized where they have to put their name on it for one, some of their co-workers and supervisors in the area, they have to kind of make them aware of it, and then we have a very structured feedback system so that within six days we'll have feedback to them.

> So it's kind of a more advanced version of a suggestion box that, you know, people can't just write down whatever and throw it in the box and, you know, then complain about when it doesn't get done. This is, it requires them to kind of, "Okay, yes, I'm the one making this suggestion, I think it's a good idea." And it holds us accountable for our feedback timeframe. So yeah, we are in the midst of, I guess, adding a more formalized suggestion program.

While Specialist used value-stream mapping as a regular basis for their continuous improvement, Tubefab saw it primarily as a basis for their limited approach to implementing cells. The following comment suggests that part of the issue is a moderate aspiration level, noting that it is theoretically possible be very difficult in practice:

> *Have you done value-stream mapping out there and looked at the whole flow?*
>
> On certain products we've done it. We haven't done it on every product we have. We've picked product families and done some, like on that international bracket family, we did a map. And there we definitely, the move is to get, we'd like to get some presses over in assembly because we could dedicate them to doing those press operations and you could probably justify it because it doesn't take a large press. In some cases it makes a lot of sense; in others, you know, *I think it makes theoretical sense, but when you start looking at all the real life issues that you have out in the plant of how do you move a press and dedicate it to this one cell, you get into some other issues.*

The Tubefab case shows that managers may be committed to or influenced by interpretative frames associated with the formerly dominant logic, shaping the way they frame the local situation. Here the role of cognitive orientation (the fordist schema of maximizing uptime) and aspiration level (the difficulty of implementing the lean-as-system logic) reinforce each other. The Tubefab manager had realized substantial performance improvements with his lean-enough approach: on one product family that he provided me data for, PPMs—defect parts per million, a key quality measure for large volume producers—had gone from about 1500 to around 100 and on-time delivery had gone from below 90% to about 98%. So there was little pressure for him to alter his practices to become closer in line with the postfordist logic of best practice. He articulated a clear rationality justifying his approach, but it was a partially fordist rationality. And a taylorist orientation toward labor reinforced this rationality.

Aspiration-Driven Divergence on Work Organization: High versus Moderate Aspiration Levels

In this section I compare the factories from the bottom panel of Table 9.1, first Designer Railings and LV Gaskets, then Custom Seats and Hydraulic Systems. In the first comparison, I also bring in some data from Metalfab Plus, which provides an instructive comparison on crude versus sophisticated value-stream mapping.

Designer Railings (a lean-as-system factory) is a nonunion shop with ninety production workers that make handrails. It is a mid-volume company that sells through a catalog to a dispersed base of large architectural and construction firms as well as mom-and-pop stores. The primary operations are metal fabrication and assembly, with secondary operations in polishing and welding. Their catalog has around 8000 parts in it and, according to the plant manager they "are, like most manufacturers, classic 80/20 . . . probably 80% of our volumes" are made up of "probably 10% of our parts" (i.e. around 800 parts).

LV Gaskets (a lean-as-toolbox factory) is a nonunion shop with 300 production workers that make gaskets. It is a mid-volume company that sells out of a catalog to the heavy equipment industry (e.g. John Deere, Caterpillar, Mack Trucks). The primary operations are metal fabrication and assembly, with secondary operations in roll coating and screen printing. Their catalog has thousands of parts, and again according the factory manager, "the 80/20 rule always applies in manufacturing to one extent or another," in their case "maybe the 80/20 is 600 part numbers."

Railings and Gaskets face effectively identical issues regarding work organization because they are both mid-volume metal fabricators who sell make-to-stock subassemblies through catalogs, with most of their business consisting of around 600–800 parts.

The plant manager at Designer Railings described how they got the cycle time on one product down from weeks to under a minute using continuous flow:

> We made that just a study in how to—it was our first manufacturing cell. It used to be we cut the product over in the saws and we bent it over in the benders, and we flattened it over in the press department, and then we sent it back to get it trimmed over here, and you know, then it was reworked over there, kind of thing. And you know, it was a 10 or 12 step process that we got down, that took literally weeks to get through the shop.

And we got it to the point where we cut it, we bent it, we flattened it, we trimmed it and we put it in a box, almost as fast as I just said that. It was: pull the pipe through the die, hit the thing that cuts it off, stick it in the bender, bend one side, flip it, stick it in the bender, bend the other side, and flip it, flatten it, trim, trim, pull. We got it down to less than a minute a piece. And it was continuous flow. And that's been phenomenally successful.

In the following set of extended quotes, the manager illustrates having embraced the logic of lean-as-system: using value-stream mapping as an ongoing tool for discovering bottlenecks, improving flow, and reducing lead time. First, he described the regular use of value-stream mapping, which they do both on the shopfloor and in the office:

Yeah. We have been using WMEP [Wisconsin Manufacturing Extension Partnership] for initiatives in lean manufacturing, whether that's, you know, we did some 5S training initially through them that we now do regularly on our own, through value stream mapping. We've done some of that through WMEP. We, when we moved, we used them extensively to help value, doing some value flow analysis on our paperwork and how we lay out our offices, to reduce some of that kind of blather.

And that was really very helpful because we were, we did make significant gains there that, to be honest, we've managed to—you know, we concentrated a lot on the shop, but we have probably done as much—you know, we have 137 or 138 employees today. Ninety of them are shop floor support people in some way, shape or form; that means that there's another, you know, 48 or so that are office. And we have probably worked as hard in the office to improve our productivity as we have out in the shop.

He went on to describe their ongoing efforts at using value-stream mapping to improve flow and shorten lead times:

We have, and I'll give you a great example. We make, it's a very simple product, but we make rings of different sizes for architectural shapes. And in the past it has been wound and cut in pipe and it's been pressed, or flattened in the press department, and then it went to the welding department and they welded it. And we're setting that up as a cell, where it's all going to be done in, as soon as this piece of equipment gets rebuilt. Because we found a piece of equipment where we can automatically weld them—actually we inherited a piece of equipment. One of our engineers figured out we could alter it to use for this. And we'll

> knock 80% of the labor out of that and two weeks of lead time out of it. And all we had to do is get this big piece, it should be back in a few weeks.
>
> So we'll take that out of the flow. *And that's what we've really been doing, we've been identifying things that will work that way*, getting them engineered properly, and then moving that stuff in place and taking that, that whole family of whatever it is, out of the flow to simplify everything else.

Some of their most successful continuous improvement initiatives have been worker-driven:

> We have a variety of levels of success there. We have ones that are supervisor-driven, we have ones that are worker-driven. We have a very successful inventory—our inventory control has improved by leaps and bounds. It still has a way to go, but we are much better off today than we were a year ago, and phenomenally better off today than we were two years ago. And that's been largely two shop floor guys that we called in and said, would, you know, what's the most frustrating thing you do? "Control this fucking inventory," you know. "Go solve it. Go solve it. Create a team, we'll help you, be part of it, but we want you to take care of it."

However, this manager discussed several ongoing challenges. The following series of quotes suggest a high aspiration level, as he experienced several problems but continued to push forward with a lean-as-system approach. One area where they were having major problems was in terms of trying to implement pull systems and scheduling more generally. He said they have always struggled with scheduling:

> We have always, we've never had a very good philosophy about scheduling. And it has always been done departmentally. And a year, roughly a year ago, maybe a year and a quarter ago, we drug three people, three of our good people together and said, "We're going to,"—we never had a production control, never had it; it was always left to the individual department supervisors. Which led to all sorts of firefighting. And so what we've been working on for the last year is just getting a handle over what we do and how we do it and why we do it that way.

But his plan was to continue cellularizing and working on *kanban* systems to develop true pull systems throughout the shop. He described a system for a stock product line that was "almost a *kanban*" and he intended to turn into a real *kanban* system:

We don't call it *kanban*, but it's almost *kanban* because what we do is, the computer tells us when we've reached a reorder point, and it automatically generates an order.

Kind of a virtual kanban.

It's a virtual *kanban*.

Um-hmm.

The discipline of running that, however, has not been good.

Right.

And so what we're trying to do is take that virtual *kanban* and move it to the cell. Because it is, you know, we have a planner code system. So the planner code for that product line is out there. If we maintain it properly, in terms of where you trigger, how many do you make, how does that effect inventory turns and stuff like that, I think we can actually make it into a real *kanban* without any intervention. That's, we're in the middle of doing some of that kind of work down there, because we have a, it's a place where we have a huge opportunity to improve.

Another problem has been resistance from supervisors and reticence from the workforce:

Getting the whole workforce on board has been a challenge. We haven't, we've got a, we have a lot of people that have never worked anywhere else, and they don't understand the realities of what's going on in the world. And as those people turn over and so forth, we—because they retire—we're replacing them with people that are much better in tuned to what's going on in the world and what's expected in the real world workplace. It's been a huge cultural issue for us. And some of our older line supervisory and salespeople just have a real hard time understanding the need to do things by process and procedure. The customer's right.

Despite these challenges, however, the manager was clear in his intention to continue implementing continuous flow principles throughout the factory and to continue working on developing *kanban* inventory control and pull production systems. The following comment illustrates his high aspiration level, that continuous improvement really needs to be understood as an ongoing process:

There are plenty of people out there that want to change if they're allowed to; if they're allowed to have the input, if they're allowed to do, you know, to take on, to make the mistakes, okay?

Um-hmm.

And, you know, my most successful people are people that let their people do that, and when the people make mistakes, which they're going to do, okay, because they haven't done it before, go, "Hey, that's part of the deal. Let's . . ." You know, it's like I said earlier, somebody's expecting a *kaizen* to solve all problems for all times. And the fact is, it's just one step in the process.

Right. And it's really getting the workers to understand that it's continuous improvement.

That's right. You know, there's all the wonderful watchwords, you know, it's a journey not a goal, it's—but if it's true, you know, and you talk about, you know, we'll make it better and then we'll make that better, and we'll make that better, you've got to get the first better.

While facing effectively identical operational issues, the plant manager at LV Gaskets viewed lean as a toolbox rather than a system. They had "been working on lean, you know, really off and on for 15 years." While they have improved workflow, in the following extended discussion that manager explained why he thought continuous flow was not a good fit with his factory context—impractical due to its complexity, to a batch-shop mentality, and to demands of running the business:

Are you trying to get towards a one-piece flow type operation, or are they still doing batches?

No, we're in a, we're trying to cut our batch sizes. We're using master planning to alleviate some of that, to reduce some of the work-in-process. *You know one-piece flow, to a large extent here, is a dream.* Primarily because we're in a situation where—oh, I'm going to guess—let's say I've got 8,000 pieces of tooling, okay? I've got presses that were purchased anywhere from 1945 to 2004. Standardization is not something that we're at all familiar with here. So as a result, you could only do so much with single-minute exchange of dies and things like that. *So, a one-piece flow isn't practical for us.*

We were making things, we were making a lot of things five years ago in monthly batches that we're now making in weekly batches, you know, to reduce that. We've done a lot with our setups and things like that. . . .

Right. I guess I should have maybe said continuous flow rather than one-piece, because I know that's always kind of a dream in most shops. The idea being that, with continuous flow, that if you can schedule based on the pull of the product through the, you know, then you only have to schedule it at one point in a continuous flow loop.

In the operation, yeah.

And if you can do that, then you can cut out queue times and cut down lead-times.

Well, yes, we are working towards that. We're not very good at it at this point in time. There's always a, you know, a batch shop mentality in an operation like this that's been around this long, and people don't feel secure when they don't see inventory. So some of it simply becomes a mindset change as much as anything else. You know, and you walk through it and everything goes well for a few weeks, and then everything goes well for a few months, and then you have a hiccup and people will all come back and say, "See, I told you we should have more inventory."

Right. Right.

And then they want to fall back to the way they were doing it in the past. So, it becomes somewhat of a battle to implement that and get people thinking along that line.

Um-hmm.

It's also a lot better in the textbook than it is, you know, in reality.
Right.

I'm sure you've done the continuous flow experiment they do with all of the lean manufacturing and things like that.

The Lean 101, um-hmm.

It looks good and it works well, but you know, right in the middle of it you're not stopping because you've got to make 300 of something else.

These issues are certainly daunting. But the fact that Designer Railings had implemented continuous flow in an effectively identical context suggests that the Gaskets manager's invocation of a poor fit is a rationalization based on a moderate aspiration level.

There were two other factors that operated alongside a moderate aspiration level, producing a self-reinforcing set of orientations leading to satisficing on lean. First, this manager was skeptical of too much standardization, based on his experience. Second, his valorization approach entailed high levels of individual autonomy. On the former, he explained that in his experience, standardization is impractical:

> I actually got my start in the business [as] the rate setter on the floor. You know, I went out and said, "This is how many pieces you've got to make." And, you know, that was all very standardized work. We used a system called MTM: methods, time, measurement; predetermined time cycles and all the rest of it. It didn't work then, doesn't work now. Doesn't work in the Toyota Production System. Tour a Toyota plant, you'll see standardization to the extent of, you know, this is what's done at this station, you've got this much time to get it done, and you know, you pull the cord if you're having a problem with something, and that sort of thing. But watch two people put doors on, and you'll see they're not really doing it exactly the same way

On autonomy, he explained, approvingly, that his company's corporate policy is to allow high levels of individual autonomy. I quoted him in the last chapter stating that "Employees know their own 25 square feet." He went on to explain that in his experience this policy was beneficial: "that's some of the entrepreneurial style that has been good for [the corporation] over the years and has kept a lot of people in [it]. We've got a lot of long-term employees in [the corporation], probably much more so than a lot of big companies."

As discussed in Chapter 3, standard work is seen as a foundation of lean. While standard work and other forms of process standardization limit individual autonomy, if workers are offered substantive participation in group problem solving and decision making this is a form of collective autonomy. Because Gaskets allowed high levels of individual autonomy, this precluded the adoption of standard work, which provides a basis for process improvement; if there is not a standard for each task and process, then they cannot be systematically improved.

If standard work instructions are for standardizing task execution, value-stream mapping is for standardizing processes, by providing a systematic accounting of all processes involved in a product family and rationalizing the workflow. We saw in the case of Metalfab Plus above, that the engineers from their industrial customer who assessed Metalfab's operations and processes said the latter had an informal approach to value-stream mapping based on hunches and intuitions rather than systematic data analysis. This assessment seems to apply to how Gaskets conducted their value-stream mapping.

As the following extended quote illustrates, Gaskets spent two days on a current-state map and then launched immediately into implementation, without having developed a future-state map, or without having done detailed data analysis and deliberation around that future state:

Now, in terms of reorganizing the factory and moving from, maybe to focused factories and then maybe to more cellular type . . . you do value-stream mapping exercises and that type of thing?

Yeah, we do. We've got—we've actually identified five value streams for this year. We're working well through the first one. We've got some capital appropriations that are up for review and things like that, which you know, kind of always slows the process down. We're well underway on the second one; third one probably within a month or so we'll get into that. Whether we'll make all five or not by the end of the year, I don't really know, but that's kind of the goal that's out there.

Who's involved in the value-stream mapping exercises?

Everybody.

Everybody. The shop floor employees too?

Yeah. Oh, yeah. Normally we set up, or we choose a team for the value stream. The first value stream was largely management because it was new processes to us. You know we've done process mapping and things like that in the past, but never really taken that beyond the process mapping to the value streaming. And we had an individual from [the parent corporation] in to walk us through the first value stream. We had basically all of my operating committee in the training, and then we chose about three I think, out of that group, in the operating group . . .

The operating committee is . . .

Operating committee is basically department heads: the HR, the plant controller, the purchasing manager, the quality manager, myself; we've got two area managers, one that handles the production side and one that handles what we call production services side, which is the planning and the customer service and things like that. And then we had a couple of production leaders and then we also had three or four production, people off the production floor who were involved: two or three that were actually involved in it and one that was totally uninvolved in it to ask the pertinent, "Why do we do this?" questions, you know.

Right. And so that was, so your first one then was your operating committee mostly.

Well, it was a good—all of the training was the operating committee and some selected production leaders. That was about two days' worth of training. And then we spent about two days doing the value stream map itself. And then out of that came eight task forces to address eight separate issues.

Is that, so you do a current state map and these, is the task force to look at like . . . .

Yeah, the task force then kind of puts the future state together, because, normally—well, at least in our limited experience I guess—what tends to end up happening is that you don't really know what the future state is.

Um-hmm.

You know, I guess we could put some very empty, hollow dream together and make it the future state, but the future state develops and it develops out of the work that those people who took the present state map and juggled it and moved things and changed things and introduced a new process of thinking about it I guess.

Again, this approach contrasts with the one I observed run by engineers from a world-class multinational prime contractor at Metalfab Plus, where they used detailed data analysis of factory processes, and months of meetings, to flesh out a future-state map.

Now, Gaskets and Metalfab realized considerable performance improvements by using lean as a toolbox and were maintaining strong and steady business. My interpretation of the Gasket manager's invocation of the complexity and uniqueness of his factory, which precluded standardization and the systematic creation of future-state value-steam maps, is that it reflects a moderate aspiration level rationalized in terms of a misfit. This was reinforced by his embrace of the logic of individual autonomy for workers and associated skepticism toward standardization.

The second matched pair involves Custom Seats, a high-involvement lean factory, and Hydraulic Systems, an autonomous lean factory. *Custom Seats* (a lean-as-system factory) is a union shop with 220 production workers that make seats for the recreational vehicle and lawn and garden industries. The factory is split into two sides, one with make-to-stock, high-volume, repetitive products, and another with make-to-order and engineer-to-order, low-volume, high-mix products. On the low-volume side, there are up to "400 product numbers, some of which [individual workers] may only see once a year." The seats are high-quality products which require skilled sewers—it takes "12 weeks minimum to train a sewer"—along with more semi-skilled workers doing upholstery, MIG welding, and assembly.

Hydraulic Systems (a lean-as-toolbox factory) is a union shop with ninety production workers that make large hydraulic pumps and systems for the hydraulic industries (e.g. press manufacturers) and heavy equipment industries. It is an engineer-to-order, low-volume, high mix factory. The pumps and systems are high-quality products that require skilled CNC machinists along with semi-skilled workers in fabrication and assembly.

While some of the primary operations are different in the two factories—sewing and upholstery versus machining and fabrication—they face largely identical work organization issues because they are both engineer-to-order, low-volume, high-mix producers of complex subassemblies that include both skilled and semiskilled operations producing components for final assembly in house.

Hydraulic Systems (like LV Gaskets) has done less standardization because it operates a regime of substantive participation including a high level of individual autonomy. The manager was not planning to implement a continuous flow system. In contrast, the managers at Custom Seats described in detail their ongoing efforts to implement continuous flow in their low-volume, high-mix area, despite encountering substantial problems.

The following discussion illustrates the high aspiration levels of the Seats managers in the face of multiple difficulties and problems. Manager A noted that the goal is to have it "all brought into one continuous flow environment, in theory." He then elaborated on their efforts to realize this despite the complexity of it all. After that, Manager B explained how they were on the fourth attempt at implementing continuous flow production in the high-mix, low-volume area. Both display high aspiration levels:

> Manager A: But we've cellularized both those areas [for high-volume, repetitive products] and we've created, we were able to find commonality of product families that large numbers of, chunks of those, fit with that. Okay, this is this product family; this is this product family. And we created standard work and work instructions that make, help us distribute the work amongst the four positions differently, depending on what we're producing. And it also helps us do a better job of being timely with the components that need to come into the area and which ones need to go out.
>
> As we continue to set foot on that [low-volume] side of the wall we're starting to get into some products now that aren't as repetitive. And that's the area where we're going to face some of the same challenges that [Manager B] faces in the P&A [after-market, parts-and-accessories] area, where you're doing large numbers of . . . and small quantities. *And you know, the complexity in bringing all that together: get it in, get it built, get it out; now get the next one in, get . . . Bringing it all together is really taking an army of support. It's really, we're really struggling with that.* We're really not good at that yet.
>
> Manager B: We have gone through a number of, on the P&A side, a number of renditions of attempts to solve the issue of high mix, low volume. And I'd say we're probably, in the last 18 months, two years, *we're probably on our fourth version of trying something different. And what that is is really just a continuous improvement process* that says, okay, we got together as a team, we looked at some, we put something out there, how's this working? Try it. Jeez, that didn't work. Well, like, what didn't work about it? Get back together again, look at something else, make an adjustment here, make an adjustment there, or in some cases revamp the whole thing. And we've seen some pretty good improvements, and we've had some failures.

We have seen managers at Tubefab and LV Gaskets suggest they cannot do continuous flow production due to the complexity of their operations. But the manager at Seats described continuing to implement continuous flow despite the problems of complexity in a high-mix, low-volume context.

Manager A subsequently explained how they have achieved a literal single-minute exchange of die in their repetitive areas and are now trying to apply the same concepts in their high-mix, low-volume areas. They used a company-specific acronym for their *kaizen* events in order to not use Japanese terms, to make it feel less alien to their workforce. These

> events have, in the repetitive environments, created something that I would describe as SMED, if you've heard this acronym, Single Minute Exchange of Die. We can take a glue fixture off an XR-210 bench, pull the pin, pull it out, slide it up on the shelf, grab the other one, slide it in, put the pin in and we're there, we're rocking. It's literally that fast.
>
> We've tried to apply those types of concepts in other areas. The issue of setup that I'm describing though is in the non-repetitive environment, where it's, you know, you're only going to make six of these, and you're probably not going to make them again for nine months, and where the hell is that fixture and how—let's see, what part did that use? And we lose a lot of time with that, and there's a lot of that stuff going on back there

The managers at Custom Seats were remarkable for their high aspiration levels and persistent efforts at trying to implement a truly lean system based on demand-driven continuous flow with genuine, worker-driven continuous improvement. The manager at Hydraulic Systems provides an instructive contrast. Whereas the Seats managers had proactively embraced the House of Lean as a complementary system, the Systems manager took a more reactive approach, seeing lean as a toolbox. To be sure, Systems realized substantial performance improvements, but the following discussion suggests that the plant manager had a moderate aspiration level.

The manager at Systems explained how they initially turned to lean out of necessity, cutting back on staff and figuring out how to keep up quality and output with fewer staff. He took a few lean classes, but largely did lean restructuring in an informal, unsystematic manner, based on local knowledge and hunches. Thus, in the following extended discussion, he described an informal approach to value-stream mapping and continuous improvement:

> *Now you had also mentioned that you guys started this restructuring towards cells and stuff some 12 years ago or more. Did you start . . .*
>
> 10, 12 years ago.
>
> *Did you bring consultants in then, or did you do it on your own?*

On our own.

You did.

Yeah.

So you were able to do, back then, even value-stream mapping in terms of . . .

Yeah, we didn't call it that then, but we'd look for, eliminated waste, we would just say . . .

Were you influenced then by this lean movement at that time? Were you influenced by lean production and stuff?

Oh, I think so, yeah. I went to the seminars and all that. I think that became part of it. Really what it came down to be is that we kept getting leaner, just because we had to. Part of what happens as you cut back people, overhead, you've still got to get the same amount of work done, you get leaner because you find ways to keep your quality up, to keep your product going out the door. So what happens, as you had, as every supervisor retired or production control retired or purchasing, we didn't replace them. So we got it built in, you know.

And now, so in terms of getting these workers to contribute their ideas and this type of thing, I mean do you do kaizen *events? How do you, what is the most effective way?*

Yeah, we probably, we've used *kaizen*. I don't know if it's the strict definition of *kaizen*, but like when we did setup reduction, we called that . . .

Right. So I mean continuous improvement so that, you know . . .

Right. It's not the *kaizen* event where you, in one week we're going to move this machine to get it down to, you know, that type of thing. But it is a non-process-improvement where we . . . and we get suggestion programs, and a lot of it is just talking to the guys. You know if they see you make the changes, you know, we had suggestion programs where there was some compensation, you know, like, yeah, you win credits to get company logo items and that, and then you may have a drawing and you win fifty bucks. It worked for some people, but what works better is just that you respond to their ideas, which is more effective.

He called it a pull system because some orders are triggered by customer demand but it is not a true pull system, with production organized in a continuous-flow loop connected by *kanban* signals. They do have some cells with internal continuous flow, but the scheduling is done based via a material requirements planning (MRP) system that sends orders to the cells and work centers. They do not use *kanban* and hence do not have a continuous flow supplying the cells:

And now are you guys doing just-in-time out there, and trying to do any of this lean stuff?

Oh, yeah, we've done a lot of that. We've set up a lot of cells, we, you know as you walk through the plant, we've got a lot of cells set up. And we do have a pull system, a production system. What we really, a large portion of what we do is we use—I used to call it a push system—but we'll order materials and even release a certain number of the orders based on a forecast. . . .
It's a flexible manufacturing system, and now it becomes a pull system. So the actual orders, as far as the work-in-process, as we schedule in the plant, is a pull system for the ship date. So the aftermarket and that we'll have a certain amount of orders issued, but then what gets worked on in the plant gets pulled through per order.

And where is, in your cellular system then where is the trigger at? Is it right, do you have like a final good supermarket at the end that triggers it, or do you have, is it really a customer order . . . ?

It will be a customer order will trigger. We don't have a *kanban*, per se. It's just the customer order—I don't even know if I'd call that electronic *kanban*—but it's customer order will trigger it. You know when we've got an MRP and that, when they sell that pump or that valve or whatever, that gets loaded, they explode the bill of material, that will have a ship date. So then it goes from there and it goes back: these are parts I need and when I need them, and it schedules every work center they need.

As the manager went on to explain, the individuals in the cells have individual autonomy to do the scheduling within the cells, as opposed to a truly continuous flow system where the entire production process is scheduled via a single pacemaker or trigger point sends a signal to upstream processes in the flow loop:

But what it is, is now those two individuals that are in that cell, they can run all the operations. So they just move to whatever machine, you know, this batch or . . .

Right. And do they get to work it out between themselves . . .

They do it all; they schedule themselves. They know this is what we need from production-control based on the customer order, and then we shuffle up the deck and say, "Alright, these are the ones we've got to work on."

Okay. And then do you have them doing, are they more involved in these, you know, like problem-solving type activities than they used to be?

Oh, it's worked great for us. You know they become, if there's a problem with the cylinder, they're there, they inspect them, they know those. So right, if any issue comes up with those parts, they become a very key part.

He decided against implementing continuous flow/pull system because it would be too difficult in his factory, given complexity and the demands of running the business.

It's difficult for me at times: heard it, seen it. I've seen it work. I've seen it work at John Deere, up at Horicon. I mean, but when something stops, and getting the resources to fix that problem, ours is, we're so, with the number of products, you know and then like operators moving around, it's much more difficult. You know like when that person has that particular problem there, we focus resources on that statement. It isn't, like you say, they're not interdependent, you know, because it's not a continuous flow.

Again, the comparison with Custom Seats, and with Second Tier Specialist—which is similar to Systems in being a low-volume, make/engineer-to-order operation doing machining and assembly—suggests that the Systems manager is invoking a misfit as a rationale for a moderate aspiration level.

Although the Systems manager gave his workers a high level of individual autonomy, he was not systematically involving them in formal continuous improvement activities. He explained that they are simply too busy to dedicate the time to this:

> When you're on ten hours and Saturdays and you've got to get that part out, and I've got the guys sitting there in a meeting telling me, you know, it gets difficult. From a management standpoint to put the time into communications and to facilitate the program. . . . Now if we were to slow down, which I don't want to happen, we'd be able to get more of the 5Ss and setups and we'd spend more time talking and we'd get these ideas. But when you're rocking and you're busy, even for that worker, he's out there running that machine and he's making parts, he isn't really taking a step back as much saying, "Wait a minute, this is a better way of doing it."

Now, given that this factory is "rocking and busy," they did not experience external pressure to become leaner, there was a certain rationality to the manager's position. According to the manager, they were highly competitive due to their reputation for quality, which was surely a result of their strategy of training workers and allowing individual autonomy. Nonetheless, Custom Seats was also rocking and busy, yet they did not use this as a reason to hold off on substantive empowerment or dial back their efforts to implement lean-as-system. The Systems manager illustrates a bottom-up process in which the manager experienced significant performance improvements by adopting lean as a toolbox, and did not feel external pressure to attempt to implement the more advanced but difficult lean practices.

Conclusion

This chapter focused on holistic analysis of workplace regimes, organizational and valorization (labor utilization) strategies. The chapter presented three matched pairs, demonstrating in each case that one manager claimed that implementing continuous flow was not practical for his factory context, while another manager in an effectively identical context persevered in implementing continuous flow despite ongoing problems and difficulties.

The chapter suggested two ways in which a strategy on one question can influence the strategy on another question. On the one hand, implementing lean-as-system—true continuous flow and regular use of value-stream mapping to drive continuous improvement—is exceptionally difficult without a substantively empowered workforce with formal channels for input into problem solving and decision making. This was illustrated by Second Tier Specialist, whose manager explicitly noted that he saw substantive empowerment to be a necessary step for implementing true continuous flow. The latter seems to be the case particularly for low-volume, high-mix contexts, in which substantively empowered workers can manage the problems that routinely arise in such dynamic and changing environment.

On the other hand, implementing a high level of individual autonomy precludes the adoption of standard work and process standardization. This was clearest in the case of LV Gaskets. Here, the manager's embrace of the logic of individual autonomy seemed to engender or be associated with a skepticism toward standardization in general, and hence a skepticism toward core elements of lean, perhaps generating, and at least reinforcing, satisficing on work organization.

It is also noteworthy that in both cases of autonomous lean—LV Gaskets and Hydraulic Systems—although the plant managers allowed high levels of individual autonomy, neither had adopted the formal channels for employee involvement via regular use of *kaizen* events or value-stream mapping to drive continuous improvement. Perhaps the reason why they didn't feel pressure to formalize continuous improvement is due to their high levels of individual autonomy, which provide a certain level of continuous improvement. Nonetheless, given their rejection of standardized work, they will struggle to realize organization-wide learning. Systematic organization-wide learning requires standardization. Without standardized tasks and processes, what is learned in one problem-solving event cannot be diffused throughout organizational practice.

Finally, like Chapter 8, this chapter also suggested interaction between cognitive orientation and aspiration levels. This was clearest in the case of Tubefab, where a lean-as-toolbox approach was clearly driven in part by fordist thinking, yet the hybrid approach generated performance improvements that satisfied his aspiration level. As such, there was little pressure to adopt a more thorough approach to lean, even though this would surely improve performance.

PART IV
CONCLUSION

10
Capitalist Management and Routine Inefficiency

The central thesis of this book is that in response to contradictory pressures regarding labor management, many managers satisfice. Managers face conflicting pressures between harnessing the creativity and abstract cognitive capabilities of workers versus ensuring workforce discipline to realize sufficient levels of output. Management is divided, experiencing conflicting pressures and competing strategies. Substantively empowering workers via cross training on enlarged tasks with enriched responsibilities, including participation in problem solving and decision making, would often enhance organizational capabilities and considerably improve organizational performance. Yet managers often settle for an approach based on job rotation among narrow tasks, without worker participation in problem solving or decision making.

While my empirical case is the manufacturing sector in the United States, as I suggested in Chapter 1, contradictory pressures to fully utilize or develop the capabilities of labor while also ensuring workforce discipline are likely to be experienced across a wide range of occupations, from routinized occupations, such as production and administrative support, to semiautonomous occupations, including education, healthcare, software engineering, and social services. The balance and precise nature of conflicting pressures and strategies will vary across occupations but may include pressures to use workers for manual versus abstract cognitive labor power, to provide minimal training versus substantial training, or to standardize work versus allowing discretion and autonomy.

In this book I have demonstrated that within the manufacturing sector, global best practice for work organization and human resource management consists of lean production (implemented as a complementary package of practices) and the substantive empowerment of labor. In the face of resistance and reticence from alienated workers, and concerned with securing sufficient output, many managers satisfice, settling for lean-enough regimes based on selective and partial adoption of lean practices,

Management Divided. Matt Vidal, Oxford University Press. © Matt Vidal (2022).
DOI: 10.1093/oso/9780198795278.003.0010

without substantive worker empowerment, thus sacrificing capabilities for dynamic efficiency and continuous improvement.

My analysis is based on three years of fieldwork, during which I interacted with 486 people from fifty-nine organizations over a total of 332 hours. I conducted in-depth interviews with 109 individuals in thirty-one manufacturing firms across Wisconsin, Michigan, and Illinois. I conducted an additional 169 hours of direct observation, including observation of two union suppliers over fifteen months, and observation of a nonunion supplier over twenty months.

Through inductive analysis, I developed a theory I call organizational political economy. The foundation of the theory is Marx's historical materialism, into which I integrate concepts and ideas from organization theory. My analysis—the empirical findings, the theoretical framework, and the method—makes contributions in five areas. These contributions are not limited to manufacturing contexts but have broad implications for the sociology of work, human resource management, organization theory, and the sociology of markets.

In this concluding chapter, I discuss the five contributions. First, I theorize labor management within capitalism as inherently contradictory, and I operationalize the concept of contradiction for empirical analysis. Second, I develop a cultural-satisficing model of agency, including a novel operationalization of the concept of satisficing. Managerial approaches differ due to competing orientations, which are rooted in institutional logics, and to managerial satisficing in response to contradictory pressures and competing priorities.

Third, I introduce the concept of permissive competition. I advance the idea that there is one best way to organize production, and I marshal extensive evidence to support this, from previous research and from the study presented in this book. I find widespread variation in managerial approaches and present quantitative and qualitative data suggesting that the typical factory is a relatively inefficient imitator rather than a highly efficient innovator.

Fourth, I introduce the concept of *routine* politics of production. Many managers in postfordist American manufacturing are more interested in the qualitative improvement of operational routines than with quantitative work intensification. Most workers are interested in making their work meaningful and in helping their organization to be successful, but they are skeptical of management due to their alienation within the capitalist employment relation. Workers often conflict with managers over competing visions of efficiency, the focus of this contestation being workplace routines.

Finally, I introduce the concept of routine inefficiency to highlight how organizational inefficiency is routine in two senses: it is based in routines, and it is regular and commonplace. After summarizing the main contributions, I discuss the politics of lean management and work intensification, and the implications for unions and policymakers. I conclude by discussing the implications for future research, focusing in particular on the sociology of (in)efficiency.

Labor Management Within Capitalism is Inherently Contradictory

Marx's early formulations of historical materialism, in *The German Ideology* (Marx and Engels [1846] 1996: 42–8) and the 1859 Preface to *A Contribution* to the Critique of Political Economy (Marx [1859] 1978), were teleological, based on an improbably unilinear vision of historical development and change. These early formulations can also be interpreted in technologically determinist ways. But by 1857–8, writing in the *Grundrisse* ([1857–8] 1993: 495), Marx had moved beyond a unilinear, teleological theory. Contemporary approaches—based on Marx's own writings—appreciate agency, contingency, and variation, theorizing historical development in terms of multiple, complex determinations and multilinear chronology (Blackledge 2019; Lin 2019).

As discussed in Chapter 1, the Lakatosian hard core of historical materialism is the insistence on the fundamental importance of the interaction between the forces of production (labor power, divisions of labor, management models, and fixed capital) and relations of production (ownership and control over the productive forces). This framework continues to inspire fascinating and illuminating historical research (Heller 2019; Hobsbawm 2007; Wickham 2007).

My theory of organizational political economy is based on two key elements of historical materialism. First, the proposition that historical development, including the capitalist economy and the capitalist labor process, is animated by the material contradiction between the forces and relations of production. Second, the proposition that the nature of this contradictory relation evolves across stages, including broad historical modes of production, and developmental stages within capitalism.

The forces and relations of production are contradictory insofar as the relations of production can develop but also constrain the development or deployment of the productive forces. One key way in which this contradictory relation is manifest within capitalism is via contradictory pressures and experiences within the production process, which consists of both a labor process and a valorization process (Marx [1867] 1990). As human *techniques* for producing useful goods and services, labor processes (including cognitive labor) are constituent of the forces of production. As power relations for extracting surplus value from labor, specific to capitalism, valorization processes are a manifestation of the relations of production.

Following from this dual character of capitalist production, managers have dual, contradictory roles (Marx [1867] 1990, [1894] 1981). They play a productive role in coordination, including planning the division of labor and developing human resources, and an unproductive role in maintaining workforce discipline to ensure sufficient output. Managers experience contradictory pressures regarding which roles to emphasize: deploying and developing labor to harness its full potential versus ensuring workforce discipline.

Labor process theory has conflated the labor process and the valorization process, theorizing the overriding concern of managers within the labor process as establishing, maintaining, and increasing control over labor (Braverman 1974; R. Edwards 1979; P. K. Edwards 1986; Thompson 2010; Thompson and van den Broek 2010). But the problem of securing sufficient labor effort—the valorization problem—is only part of the problem of labor management. Managers must also determine issues regarding the organization and management of the broader labor process: the overall division of labor, the use of technology (beyond and addition to concerns with ensuring workforce discipline), the scale and scope of production, workflow, production control, quality control, problem solving, and continuous improvement.

While managers face any number of competing demands, a fundamental contradiction they face flows from their dual role in the labor process: the need to discipline workers versus the need to harness their creativity. This is the management contradiction. My study illustrates how managers experience demands to discipline labor through standardized work and prioritizing manual labor, keeping them at their machines or stations and emphasizing physical output. Yet they also experience demands to harness the creativity of labor through upskilling and empowering workers to contribute cognitive labor to problem solving and decision making.

It is exceedingly difficult to strike a balance between these two competing pressures. As such, management is divided.

The experience of workers in the capitalist labor process is also contradictory. The workforce contradiction consists of the dual experience of workers as, on the one hand, possessing sophisticated capabilities and skills (from training and education inside and outside of the workplace) and being asked to contribute to problem solving and decision making while, on the other hand, being objectively alienated insofar as they have submitted to the authority of capitalist management and have experience with various combinations of incompetent management, disrespectful management, being treated like a commodity, mind-numbingly boring work, intense work, dangerous work, management rejecting their ideas, and so on.

Building on the work of Paul Adler (1990, 2007), I offered an interpretation of Marx as theorizing a process of productive socialization (*Vergesellschaftung*) that occurs alongside shorter-term processes of degradation and immiseration. Productive socialization is the upgrading of the capabilities of humans and technology over time, based on the progressive accumulation of scientific and technical knowledge, both within the labor process and within broader society through various educational institutions. An illustrative example is semiskilled workers primarily responsible for narrow, simple tasks yet using computers and engaging in sophisticated forms of coordination within lean factories.

A Cultural-Satisficing Model of Agency

The assumption that humans maximize utility maintains a strong hold on social science despite its manifest lack of realism—and a track record of failed predictions from the macroeconomy down to the behavioral economics lab. This assumption largely afflicts institutional theory as a whole. Thus, one of the foundational statements of sociological institutionalism explicitly proposed: "Organizations that incorporate societally legitimated rationalized elements in their formal structures maximize their legitimacy and increase their resources and survival capabilities" (Meyer and Rowan 1977). If organizations decouple their formal structure from their actual practice this is because they are maximizing both external legitimacy and internal efficiency. Similarly, arguments around the fit of practices with organizational contingencies are implicitly based on a maximizing assumption: management models and practices vary in how they are implemented because managers are making rational, maximizing adaptations to make practices fit local cultural, technical, or political contingencies (Ansari et al. 2010).

The maximizing assumption also afflicts labor process theory, with classical contributions theorizing managers as maximizers of labor control and the extraction of surplus value (Braverman 1974; R. Edwards 1979; Friedman 1977; Gordon 1976). As noted in Chapter 3, I am aware of only two references to satisficing within labor process theory (Delbridge 2003; Elger and Smith 2005).

Against these heroic visions of maximizing managers and an economy uniformly populated by highly efficient organizations, I submit that sociology and organization theory should reject the assumption that actors maximize and, in its place, make satisficing the default assumption. Toward this end, I develop a cultural-satisficing model of agency that provides a novel operationalization of the concept of satisficing. To do so I draw from institutional theory and behavioral theory. But first I briefly note how the theory is consistent with historical materialism.

Marx's theory of human society is a social constructionist approach that is realist and modernist rather than relativist and post-modernist (Berger and Luckmann 1966; Vidal and Peck 2012). To be sure, Marx saw the material relations of society as foundational. But he also saw cultural-cognitive institutions—what he referred to as ideology—as foundational, arguing that they *preexist* individuals and provide the basis for individual consciousness. Indeed, Marx articulated one of the pithiest statements of the realist social constructionist position:

> Men make their own history, but they do not make it just as they please; they do not make it under circumstances chosen by themselves, but under circumstances directly encountered, given and transmitted from the past. The *tradition* of all the dead generations weighs like a nightmare on the brain of the living.
>
> (Marx [1852] 1994: 15, emphasis added)

For Marx, human consciousness is constituted through ideology, understood in the broadest sense (Nicolaus 1968; Therborn [1980] 1999). The point of the base/superstructure metaphor and similar formulations was to emphasize how cultural and political institutions are *co-produced* as part of human economic activity, the substructural core of which is human labor (within a class structure) (Vidal and Peck 2012).

As argued in Chapter 3, the theory of institutional logics is complementary with historical materialism: logics are cultural meaning systems rooted in material practice. Roger Friedland and Robert Alford's (1991: 259) original theory of institutional logics was partly inspired by Gramscian theories of "class conflict as simultaneously culturally and materially generated through institutional contradictions." Although Patricia Thornton and colleagues (2012) did not retain any acknowledgment of class, their development of the theory provided important microfoundations.

The core model comes from the behavioral approach of Herbert Simon and collaborators, who theorized agency in terms of two elements: a person's definition of the situation and her aspiration level (Cyert and March [1963] 1992; March and Simon [1958] 1993; Simon [1947] 1961). Building on this foundation, and theorizing institutional logics as the primary source of how a situation is defined, William Ocasio and collaborators (Ocasio 2011; Thornton et al. 2012) developed a model of top-down and bottom-up information processing. Individuals understand and frame any situation via both top-down attentional processes and bottom-up, environmental stimuli. Institutional logics provide a central source of top-down attention processing, as discussed in the following section.

Ocasio (2011) and Thornton et al. (2012) suggested that a core bottom-up process is selective attention to environmental stimuli. I propose that aspiration levels are central to how environmental feedback is processed. As discussed in Chapter 3, the literature on aspiration levels has emphasized how they tend to adjust over time to the level of achievement (Cyert and March [1963] 1992; Levinthal and March 1981; March and Simon [1958] 1993). But I theorize aspirations as generally being stable, based on my reading of the empirical and theoretical literature. Commitment to existing interpretive frames engenders resistance to change and stabilizes aspirations. Extended experience with a given practice leads to psychological investment and strong commitment to previously made decisions.

I operationalize the concept of stable aspiration levels by developing a theoretical framework and methodological approach that allows me to question the assumption that any adaptation a manager makes is maximizing. Theoretically, I draw from the finding that individuals often rationalize poor performance in order to maintain the appearance of competence and avoid cognitive dissonance (Milliken and Lant 1991; Staw et al. 1983). I suggest that satisficing managers are likely to rationalize deviation from best practice by framing that practice as a poor fit with their organizational context. Methodologically, I match cases on technical, market, and organizational factors in order to demonstrate the role of unacknowledged aspiration levels.

I find that managers frame effectively identical situations differently, leading some to adopt best practice and others to reject it by framing it as a misfit with their context. I interpret the latter to be a rationalization of satisficing. The analysis is consistent with the theory suggesting that aspiration levels vary across the population (see Chapter 3) and with empirical data showing wide variation in organizational performance, with only a small proportion of firms achieve world-class performance (Chapter 4, and below). The typical manager should be expected to have moderate aspiration levels and therefore we should expect that organizations investing high levels of authority in individual managers will be relatively inefficient imitators.

Institutional Logics of Best Practice, One Best Way, and Permissive Competition

In Chapters 1 and 3, I theorize growth stages from marxist theory (Aglietta [1976] 2000; Gramsci [1929–35] 1999) using the theory of institutional logics. Cornerstone institutional logics (Thornton et al. 2012) of a society get elaborated in distinct ways within growth stages, which consist of settled organizational fields, many, though not all of which are based around cornerstone logics (in pure or hybrid form). Many fields become settled around a dominant logic of best practice for an extended period until it is destabilized by some force, such as an economic crisis or a new, competing practice (Fligstein 1990). Yet, formerly dominant logics may continue to hold some influence in a field to the extent that alternative visions, goals, templates, or understandings continue to exist, albeit outside of mainstream practice and discourse.

The fordist stage of American capitalism lasted roughly from the 1920s through the 1960s, during which the cornerstone logics of fordist mass production and the taylorist division of labor constituted best practice within and beyond the manufacturing field. After a period of transition during the 1970s and 1980s, there began to be settlement around a series of postfordist institutions. Within the US manufacturing field, I have documented a remarkable degree of agreement among management practitioners that best practice for work organization and labor management is constituted by the combination of two dominant institutional logics, respectively: an approach to lean I call lean-as-system and substantive empowerment via multiskilling and participation in problem solving and decision making. In Chapter 2, I presented a review of previous findings showing robust support for the idea that this combination is in fact superior in terms of dynamic efficiency, flexibility, and learning capability. There are demonstrably many ways to profitably organize production, but critics of a single best way simply have not provided any compelling evidence or theory that distinct models produce comparable performance levels.

Throughout the rest of the book I have presented extensive qualitative data showing that managers with the highest aspiration levels did adopt this combination of lean as a system of complementary practices along with broad levels of substantive empowerment among their workforce. At the same time, other managers adopted suboptimal practices in terms of work organization and/or employee involvement, due either to thinking according to a fordist-taylorist logic or to moderate aspiration levels. I return to managerial satisficing in the sections below on Routine Politics of Production and Routine Inefficiency.

In order to theorize how markets permit widespread relative inefficiency, I developed a theory of permissive competition. If we adopt the realistic assumption that aspiration levels vary across the population and therefore most managers are satisficers, then we would expect the majority of organizations in any particular sector to consist of middling performers. This expectation is borne out by the applied economics literature, which documents widespread technical inefficiency (Angeriz et al. 2006; Caves and Barton 1990; Frantz 1988; Green and Mayes 1991). As discussed in detail in Chapter 4, a survey of 3000 factories from the same population as my case study (Luria 1996) found the majority of factories clustered in the middle of the distribution, with the difference between the middling performers and top performers being vast: the top 10% outperform the median in value added per employee by 160%.

In such a context, while the worst performers will eventually drive themselves out of business, the small number of top performers cannot drive out the large number of middling performers (Winter 1964). This constitutes the basic foundation of permissive competition: to the extent that markets contain widespread variation across technologies (including operational strategies and management systems), inputs and outputs, world-class firms will not be able to drive out satisficing competitors.

In addition, I suggested two further factors that facilitate and encourage permissive competition. First, a competitive field is permissively institutionalized when the dominant institutional logics are normative in nature, without enforcement mechanisms to compel their adoption. Second, the existence of technical and relational embeddedness and complexity in supply networks further attenuates competitive pressures. Once a long-term contract is granted and so long as the targets are being met, ongoing relations between purchasing managers and supplier factories, along with possible asset specificities associated with making complex parts, mean that suppliers who are relatively inefficient in operational terms can still satisfy their industrial customers.

Routine Politics of Production

Existing theory frames the labor process as a battle over effort and autonomy. Managers are theorized to focus on maximizing labor control and hence exploitation (Ackroyd and Thompson 1999; P. K. Edwards 1986; Thompson and Smith 2009b, 2009a), and lean is seen as inherently a system of work intensification (Carter et al. 2011, 2013a, Carter et al. 2013b; Danford 1999; Graham 1995; Parker and Slaughter 1995; Rinehart et al. 1997; Stewart et al. 2009). Workers are theorized as being concerned primarily with trying to secure autonomy and reasonable effort levels in the face of managerial attempts to extend control over labor (Ackroyd and Thompson 1999; P. K. Edwards 1986; Thompson and Smith 2009b).

This near-exclusive emphasis on effort and autonomy has limited the development of labor process theory. My empirical findings lead me to conclude that many managers in postfordist American manufacturing are interested in qualitative improvement of operational routines rather than quantitative work intensification. I have documented workers both trying to make work meaningful *and* being interested in helping the organization be successful, without expressing concerns over autonomy as such.

These findings require a broader understanding of managerial and worker interests, moving beyond the imputation of interests based on an implicit or explicit rational choice analysis, toward a theory in which managerial and worker orientations are variables to be explained. The cultural-satisficing model of agency provides the theoretical framework for this. The theory of labor process contradictions, specifically that managers face distinct, sometimes conflicting pressures to both develop and discipline, provides a framework for contributing to explanations of technical change, rather than simply cataloguing an ever-growing list of control mechanisms and regimes.

Managerial strategic orientations are more likely to be shaped by institutional logics of best practice in the field, due to the demands of their role as managers, whereas the strategic orientations of workers are more often—though by no means universally—rooted in local workplace custom and practice. I begin this discussion with workers because worker alienation and the workforce contradiction constitute one of the foundational factors shaping routine politics of production.

Working inductively from my empirical data, I developed and operationalized a theory of alienation to help explain the workforce contradiction, namely, workers resisting or being reticent toward their own partial empowerment (in the form of cross training and opportunities for participation in problem solving and decision making). On the one hand, workers have experience with management either never asking for their ideas or asking for their ideas and then rejecting them. Further, workers regularly experience bad management, management fads of the month, and aborted or failed initiatives. These experiences are the direct result of the objective alienation of the labor of workers to the authority of capitalist management. As a result, workers develop a distrust of and skepticism toward management.

On the other hand, consistent with the work of Hugh Willmott (1990) and Randy Hodson (2001), in response to their alienation workers attempt to make work meaningful, realize a purpose, or feel pride by working hard and producing high-quality output, but they do so according to their own understandings of best practice regarding efficiency and quality, and of the proper distribution of responsibilities. My findings documented how many workers continue to be influenced by the logic of fordist-taylorism. This logic, which conflicts with postfordist managerial initiatives, was enshrined in union contracts for decades and remains influential within local workforce culture. As argued in Chapter 1, fordism and taylorism were cornerstone logics of the fordist growth stage, exerting influence across multiple organizational fields, and they continue to do so today.

As a result of contradictory experiences, pressures, and cultural logics, many workplaces are split into competing factions, including oppositional factions and collaborationist factions. Routine politics of production are politics of contestation over routines but, as Theo Nichols and Peter Armstrong (1976) astutely observed long ago, workers are often internally divided due to contradictions in their experiences and in ideological currents within and beyond the workplace.

Their contradictory experiences—often framed through particular ideological narratives or institutional logics—lead many workers, rightfully so, to be skeptical of managerial attempts to upskill and empower them. They are being asked to take on increasingly managerial responsibilities without any commensurate increase in managerial rights. Such empowerment is real but limited and precarious: limited to contributions for process improvement; precarious because management continues to be the ultimate authority, ready to exercise a veto or remove worker empowerment at any time.

Turning to management, I have documented a group of managers in the upper tiers of the manufacturing supply chain—subsystems, subassemblies, and complex parts—who are primarily interested in upgrading routines and operational systems to improve organizational capability (quality), not with increasing effort levels as such (quantity). These managers were concerned with effort, but focused on the problem of cognitive effort, including worker contributions to problem solving and decision making, and more generally around the problem of getting workers to embrace, or at least accept and enact, new routines and practices.

On the effort (valorization) question, I presented evidence demonstrating that in some factories, managers found it highly beneficial to substantively empower their workers, broadly throughout their workforce, via cross training and the devolution of problem-solving and decision-making authority. Yet, some managers do not substantively empower their workers because they continue to be influenced (in a top-down process) by the logic of taylorism. Other managers acknowledge that substantive empowerment would be ideal, but in the face of competing pressures and severe tensions regarding valorization strategy, including multiple, competing demands on their time, resistance and reticence from alienated workers, and pressures to keep workers at their machines or stations, they satisfice. Being content with existing performance, (in a bottom-up process) these managers settle for good enough by failing to devolve responsibility *and* train workers to provide skills for, and facilitate contributions to, problem solving and decision making.

Finally, on the broader work organization (labor process) question, I documented how some managers adopt the logic of *lean-as-system*, which consists of the entire package of principles and practices from the House of Lean (Figure 4.2). Other managers, however, adopted a hybrid logic of *lean-as-toolbox*, selectively adopting some of the basic lean tools but not adopting lean as a comprehensive package of practices including true continuous-flow production and regular use a value-stream mapping to drive continuous improvement. Again, such outcomes result either from a top-down process of blending the fordist logic with the lean logic or a bottom-up process of satisficing in response to the difficulty of implementing lean-as-system. I discuss the interaction between satisficing and managerial orientation in the section below on Future Research.

Routine Inefficiency

We have seen that the statistical evidence documents widespread technical inefficiency, with the average factory being a mediocre performer compared with a small number of truly high-performance factories. The theory of routine politics of production is an attempt to explain this state of affairs.

The two sets of competing logics—on work organization and labor utilization—can be combined to produce four different types of lean (Figure 5.1). In my qualitative sample of twenty-two supplier factories, only eight adopted the approach I call high-involvement lean, which includes substantive worker empowerment within a lean-as-system approach. If anything, this qualitative sample is likely biased *toward* such factories insofar as factories taking a low-road approach to labor management may be less likely to agree to allow a researcher inside their organization to examine their operations.

In manufacturing, only with a lean-as-system approach can managers institutionalize learning routines in the form of regular use of value-stream mapping and regular, systematic, formal use of *kaizen* events. And while a certain level of continuous improvement can be driven by dedicated managers and engineers, the most effective way to ensure true continuous improvement and the generation of ideas throughout the organization is through the substantive empowerment of workers so that they have formal channels for participation in problem solving and decision making.

Nine of the factories adopted the *lean-enough* type: lean-as-toolbox with nominal empowerment (i.e. job rotation with consultative participation). A lean-enough regime can generate substantial performance improvements but does not provide the capabilities for dynamic efficiency and organizational learning. Three factories adopted the *lean standardization* type, which results from a combination of lean-as-system with consultative participation. By adopting lean-as-system, this approach may be able to achieve dynamic efficiency and true continuous improvement, but because managers have adopted consultative participation, continuous improvement is entirely management-driven. Two factories adopted the *autonomous lean* type, which results where management adopts lean-as-toolbox and substantive participation in the form of individual worker autonomy. The emphasis on individual autonomy limits the process standardization necessary for lean-as-system.

Given the stability of managerial aspirations and strong forces of organizational inertia, I expect the lean-enough, autonomous lean, and lean standardization types to be stable configurations. The former two are inferior in terms of dynamic efficiency and organizational learning. The lean standardization approach is expected to be higher performance and to facilitate more continuous improvement due to adopting lean as a system. If the management team is competent and dedicated enough to driving continuous improvement, a lean standardization approach may approximate the performance levels of high-involvement lean.

The Politics of Lean and Work Intensification

We saw in Chapter 1 that within the American labor movement, there have been movements for workers' control and union-management cooperation since the beginning of the twentieth century. There have also been competing factions within the broader movement, from business unionism to militant, class-oriented unionism.[1] And we saw throughout several chapters that these factions are mirrored within the workplace. It is no surprise that the same divisions also find expression within academia.

Among the most prominent and influential critics of lean production are scholars who work closely with or are otherwise aligned with oppositional factions in the labor movement (e.g. Carter et al. 2011; Moody 1997; Parker 1985; Parker and Slaughter 1995; Stewart et al. 2009). These scholars do important work and I agree with them that capitalism is an economic system based in class antagonism. In the face of high concentrations of power by business owners, business managers, and managers in the public sector, unions are essential for workplace democracy, countervailing power, and indeed for social progress within capitalism. Militant opposition is an important, often-necessary, and appropriate tool for organized labor.

[1] For a comparative analysis of three distinct orientations within the labor movements of Western Europe and North America—oppositional, class-based; integrative, social democratic; and market-oriented, business unionism—see Richard Hyman (2001).

But I disagree with these scholars on two points: that the employer-employee relation is always, in every respect, zero-sum; and that lean management is primarily and universally a management model for work intensification and work degradation. Kim Moody (1997: 3) summarized the former point as follows: "there is no 'win-win' solution to the age-old conflict between employer and employee." This position is well motivated by the experience of untold millions of workers who have experienced being underpaid and overworked, being treated like a commodity and not a human being, working jobs that are boring or otherwise not intrinsically rewarding, and subjected to bad management.

Dismissing lean as more of the same, nothing more than taylorism on steroids, however, misses an important development: in the postfordist era there are real movements toward the empowerment of labor within the capitalist labor process, as part and parcel of the development of the forces of production, though these are necessarily limited within capitalism, due to the private ownership of the means of production and the concentration of power this entails.

If there are movements toward empowerment and democracy within capitalist firms, unions and workers can fight to increase and expand those, rather than resist them. Indeed, unions can push for more direct and institutionalized forms of power, such as the formal Labor-Management Partnership of companies like Second Tier Specialist, driven and facilitated by the International Association of Machinists (IAM) union. This explicitly does not entail foregoing militancy. According to a representative from the IAM's High Performance Work Organization (HPWO) Department, who worked on the Labor-Management Partnership at Specialist: "The HPWO process at IAM doesn't eliminate adversarial elements, but we need more tools in our toolbox. If companies want to take us on, we can do that. We have over 100 years of experience doing so. But if they want to work together, we can do that too."

The employer-employee relation will always have an irreducible element of antagonism. No amount of empowerment within the capitalist employment relation will overcome this immanent antagonism. But there is room for labor to make material improvements within the capitalist employment relation. As such, labor unions, workers, and other worker advocates (including academics) should focus on making lean more participatory, using the acknowledgement of the need for teamwork and employee involvement within lean discourse and practice as a basis for asserting the need for workers to be more involved in organizational decision making at all levels.

I do not mean to suggest that we can rely on enlightened management or that there is blame to be laid at the feet of conservative workers who think of work, labor, and management in fordist terms. The capitalist employment relation is a relation of asymmetrical power. The contradictions of the labor process, along with competitive pressures, encourage continued deskilling and disempowerment despite decades of advocacy of the high-involvement model of human resource management within and beyond business schools. Organized labor, adversarial tactics, and militancy play an essential and indispensable role, for worker dignity and the extension of democracy within the workplace.

Union demands should go beyond what most lean advocates suggest: in the US context, this entails pushing and organizing for labor-management partnerships with institutionalized decision-making rights over business strategy and other high-level decisions (see Chapter 6 for a discussion of power sharing within the IAM HPWO program). This requires a strong union ready and willing to engage in militant tactics.

If critics use lean as a symbol for all that is wrong with postfordist work organization, then it simply becomes a chaotic concept that obscures more than it illuminates. It does not seem helpful to equate lean with the entire range of contemporary management practices harmful to workers, as Moody (1997: Ch. 5) does: outsourcing, downsizing, ideological cooptation through labor-management partnerships, whipsawing union factories in collective bargaining, work casualization, and part-time work. These practices are distinct from and not directly related to the Toyota Production System, which is what managers, consultants, and most others understand lean to be.

More broadly, many critics see lean as primarily and fundamentally a system designed to cut costs through deskilling and work intensification. But quantitative work intensification is a structural tendency inherent to the capitalist employment relation as such. Work intensification is a strategy which is encouraged by competitive pressures; lean is a package of tools which can be used to intensify work or to improve organizational capabilities without work intensification.

At the level of the labor process, managers process competitive pressures through specific cognitive frames, which again can focus attention on work intensification as a key strategy or may deemphasize intensification in favor of other forms of process improvement. If a sector is either highly competitive with low profit margins (e.g. auto assembly) or highly labor intensive (e.g. textile production), then managerial attention is likely to be focused on work intensification. But where competitive pressures are moderated—as in supplier sectors producing systems (Tier 1), subassemblies (Tier 2), and complex parts (some lower tiers)—managers can adopt strategies of, and institutional logics may focus attention on, forms of process improvement not based on work intensification. Lean offers several ways of increasing dynamic efficiency that are not based on work intensification. I submit that the core of lean production—what makes it distinctive, more than taylorism on steroids—is a set of principles and practices for process control and the qualitative improvement of operational routines.

The auto assembly sector requires special comment, given that (a) this is the context in which many who see intensification as inherent to lean have conducted their research (Carter et al. 2013b; Fucini and Fucini 1990; Graham 1995; Parker and Slaughter 1995; Rinehart et al. 1997; Stewart et al. 2009) and (b) the literature does appear to suggest that in the postfordist era, intensification is nearly universal here. These studies suggest that the goal of having workers work for fifty-seven seconds of every minute has become standard in auto assembly, yet as far as I am aware this is an explicit metric only in auto assembly. This is a form of work intensification as such. Why, then, does such a metric exist in this subsector?

Recall from Chapter 2 that the average cost of downtime for auto assembly plants in 2006 was $22,000 per minute (Warner Communications 2006). This, along with high volumes due to the continuing importance of economies of scale in auto assembly, generates intense pressure to prioritize uptime. Further, auto assembly has razor thin profit margins. As shown in Tables 10.1 and 10.2, based on the best available data on US firms, of twenty-three manufacturing subsectors, only three had net margins below 4% in both 2005 and 2019: Auto & Truck, Auto Parts, and Rubber & Tires. Against an average net margin of over 8% in both years, the auto sector is consistently a low-margin sector. Within auto assembly, the combination of low margins, astronomical downtime costs, and economies of scale have focused managerial attention on throughput as a key metric and work intensification as a priority. This has been facilitated by a dramatic reduction in the bargaining power of labor under combined forces of union decline and employer whipsawing (Greer and Hauptmeier 2016). In contrast, suppliers (who generally supply across end-use sectors), are more able to focus on other lean metrics, such as flexibility and continuous improvement, due to higher margins, lower volumes, and less dependence on scale economies.

Table 10.1 Operating and net profit margins, selected manufacturing subsectors, 2005

Industry Name	# of Firms	After-tax Operating Margin	Net Margin
Machinery	134	6.36%	19.71%
Drugs (Pharmaceutical)	306	17.52%	14.38%
Semiconductor Equip	14	13.18%	13.20%
Semiconductor	121	12.76%	12.85%
Telecom. Equipment	122	12.18%	12.56%
Beverage (Alcoholic)	22	12.45%	11.92%
Household Products	26	11.71%	10.69%
Beverage (Soft)	19	11.93%	10.36%
Electrical Equipment	91	36.65%	9.75%
Steel	26	8.53%	8.60%
Total Market	***7094***	***8.17%***	***7.78%***
Healthcare Products/Medical supplies	261	7.89%	7.21%
Shoe	22	6.70%	7.16%
Metal Fabricating	41	6.89%	6.09%
Food Processing	110	6.04%	5.86%
Computers/Peripherals	138	5.33%	5.69%
Furn/Home Furnishings	36	5.06%	4.14%
Auto & Truck	29	5.34%	3.49%
Apparel	60	6.09%	3.34%
Aerospace/Defense	70	4.97%	3.29%
Office Equipment & Services	27	4.73%	2.51%
Electronics (General)	175	2.94%	2.23%
Auto Parts	58	3.17%	1.63%
Rubber & Tires	13	2.45%	0.82%
Total Market (without financials)	—	—	—

Source: Aswath Damodaran, "Operating and Net Margins by Industry Sector," 2005, http://pages.stern.nyu.edu/~adamodar/New_Home_Page/dataarchived.html#returns. Last visited on December 22, 2020.
Notes: Damodaran uses aggregate categories that do not exactly correspond to the NAICS coding system. I attempted to include all of the manufacturing subsectors included in his data. I spot checked the lists of firms used for each of his industry estimates, and all of the industries in my Tables 10.1 and 10.2 appear to include only companies within the Manufacturing sector (NAICS 31–3), with the exception of "Total Market," which is average of all sectors, and "Furn/Home Furnishings," which includes some companies whose primary NAICS code is in Wholesale Trade (NAICS 42) and Retail Trade (NAICS 44–5), along with several furniture and home furnishings manufacturers (NAICS 31–3). The 2005 data (Table 10.1) only have after-tax operating margin, while the 2019 data (Table 10.2) only have pre-tax operating margin. Tables are sorted by net margin.

The real culprit is not lean but capitalist competition. The oligopolistic nature of competition during the fordist period attenuated competitive pressures on management. A return to intensified competition in the postfordist period is the primary source of work intensification. The first

Table 10.2 Operating and net profit margins, selected manufacturing subsectors, 2019

Industry Name	# of firms	Pre-Tax Operating Margin	Net Margin
Semiconductor	72	28.36%	19.42%
Beverage (Soft)	34	20.89%	18.50%
Drugs (Pharmaceutical)	267	26.54%	18.38%
Semiconductor Equip	39	21.09%	15.92%
Computers/Peripherals	48	17.29%	12.83%
Telecom. Equipment	91	22.14%	12.55%
Shoe	11	13.30%	10.48%
Machinery	120	14.52%	9.62%
Healthcare Products/Medical supplies	242	17.09%	9.27%
Electrical Equipment	113	14.72%	8.89%
Beverage (Alcoholic)	21	22.57%	7.94%
Total Market	***7053***	***11.78%***	***7.71%***
Aerospace/Defense	77	11.82%	7.25%
Total Market (without financials)	***5878***	***12.19%***	***6.35%***
Steel	32	8.13%	5.98%
Apparel	51	11.48%	5.87%
Electronics (General)	153	9.92%	5.70%
Furn/Home Furnishings	35	7.53%	5.15%
Office Equipment & Services	22	9.42%	4.91%
Household Products	127	18.23%	4.73%
Auto Parts	46	7.60%	3.05%
Auto & Truck	13	3.82%	3.04%
Food Processing	88	12.35%	1.31%
Rubber & Tires	4	5.66%	1.26%
Metal Fabricating	—	—	—

Source: Aswath Damodaran, "Operating and Net Margins by Industry Sector," 2019, http://pages.stern.nyu.edu/~adamodar/New_Home_Page/dataarchived.html#returns. Last visited on December 22, 2020.
Notes: See the notes for Table 10.1.

basis of quantitative work intensification under lean is speeding up the line or using time/motion study to increase performance standards. But line speedup and time/motion study are management practices as old as the assembly line itself. The second basis of quantitative work intensification under lean is the use of value-stream mapping to eliminate non-value-added steps in the production process. But again, process mapping was developed at the beginning of the fordist era.

I interviewed fifty-two workers across twelve companies who had implemented lean production. I found only one worker who complained of quantitative intensification making his job more difficult and reducing his job satisfaction. Twelve workers said they experienced quantitative or qualitative work intensification but found this to have improved their job, making it less boring or more challenging, and thirty-nine workers did not experience any work intensification.

Much of what is discussed in the literature is relative work intensification in relation to a prior system that many workers apparently find boring. Working in a factory will always be hard work, but people vary in their orientations toward which particular practices they find boring. As I have shown elsewhere (Vidal 2007), workers' assessments of work conditions can change over time. Without downplaying the negative health effects that extreme forms of work intensification can cause, it is important to remember that individual work practices are not uniformly experienced by workforces.

Implications for Practitioners

I hope the research presented in this book, and perhaps future research based on my framework, provides evidence that workers, their unions, and other advocates can use to push managers in the direction of substantive empowerment. Efficiency is the language of capitalists and their managers; workers and their unions can use the language of efficiency, flexibility, and learning to push managers toward a high-involvement approach to lean.

Among my cases, the high-involvement lean factory that I believe to be the most dynamically efficient and flexible, with the best capability for continuous improvement, was Second Tier Specialist. As shown in Chapters 8 and 9, the plant manager at Specialist embraced a joint union-management committee, with help from the international union, the IAM, and its HPWO Department. This labor-management partnership, facilitated by resources from the international union, helped the organization to forge a highly efficient and flexible system where continuous improvement truly was driven by a dedicated, highly skilled workforce.

The implications of my analysis for policymakers are clear and straightforward. Policymakers should advocate unionization and revise labor law to facilitate unionization, not simply as a matter of economic democracy but also as a matter of economic efficiency. Unions fighting for a high-involvement approach to lean can push satisficing managers to develop more dynamically efficient organizations based on the substantive empowerment of their workers. Finally, policymakers should learn from the experiences of Germany and Scandinavia. Formal institutions of codetermination—such as having worker representation on company boards and in local works councils, alongside unions, as in Germany—and formal institutions for corporatist coordination and worker participation, as in Scandinavia, make high-involvement workplace regimes much more likely (Benders et al. 2018; Ingvaldsen 2013; Jürgens 2004; Krzywdzinski 2017; Smith and Vidal 2021).

Future Research

My analysis suggests several promising avenues for future research, including some issues which the analysis finds to be central but has, in some respects, only scratched the surface of. I begin with the more straightforward avenues and then discuss the more difficult issues that emerge from my analysis. After that I conclude by offering some broader reflections for a sociology of the market rooted in organizational analysis.

First, my theory needs to be tested with quantitative data, ideally with a random sample survey. The framework readily lends itself to statistical analysis. A survey could be fielded in one or more countries, in one or more sectors, testing the model of four types of lean production and their performance effects. The model is precise enough to suggest measures for the two approaches to work organization (lean-as-system versus lean-as-toolbox) and the two approaches to employee involvement (substantive versus nominal empowerment).

To be clear about what my theory predicts: my reading of the secondary literature on Toyota suggests that it operates a lean standardization approach, in which the dominant form of participation is consultative. The theory suggests that if another firm were able to master the lean-as-system approach while adopting substantive empowerment, it would outperform Toyota.

Second, the interaction between labor process strategy and valorization strategy needs to be analyzed in more depth. The most appropriate approach is probably a case study that gathers quantitative performance data over time. In particular, there are two working hypotheses that need more empirical analysis. Based on the cases of Metalfab Plus and Deep Stampings discussed in Chapter 8, nominal empowerment limits the ability to realize the efficiency and flexibility possible with a lean-as-system regime. Based on the cases of LV Gaskets and Hydraulic Systems discussed in Chapter 9, high levels of individual autonomy limit the ability to realize high levels of standardization necessary for learning lean.

Third, moving beyond the performance issues, my analysis demonstrates the utility of an institutional logics approach for understanding the question of why managers facing effectively identical technological, organizational, and competitive/institutional contexts adopt different strategies and practices regarding work organization and labor management. However, there is much more that we need to understand about the reasons why certain institutional logics resonate with some managers but not others.

One critical issue that my analysis leaves open is the question of to what extent managers and workers adopt logics in a conscious or unconscious way. More broadly, what is the balance between deliberative versus habitual behavior? These questions derive from institutional theory, but they are critical for understanding labor process dynamics. If a manager believes that most workers cannot or should not be given responsibility for decision making, it matters whether this belief is based in an unconscious assumption, which would make it highly resistant to change, or whether it is conscious and hence more amenable to revision based on experience and/or reason. Are those who manage workers according to the logic of traditional taylorism driving on autopilot, acting out of habit, whereas those who substantively empower their workers doing so out of deliberative cognition? Similar questions apply to the orientations of workers and competing factions within the workplace, of course, with important implications for labor process dynamics and for class analysis.

Within the academic literature, in the same year that Paul DiMaggio and Walter Powell (1991:14) doubled down on the "neoinstitutional rejection of intentionality," emphasizing the "taken-for-granted nature of most human behavior," Christine Oliver (1991: 148) emphasized how organizations may attempt to strategically avoid, defy, manipulate, or balance institutional demands. Subsequently, the institutional literature has taken the path suggested by Oliver, emphasizing strategic discretion in responding to institutional pressures and demands, assuming maximizing agents (e.g. Ansari et al. 2010; Fiss and Zajac 2004; Goodrick and Salancik 1996). But the question of unconscious assumptions and habitual behavior remains central to understanding the nature of the cultural and institutional bases of human behavior in general—and more specifically to questions of labor management.

I suspect that sociologists have not pursued the question of unconscious assumptions and habitual behavior because the most appropriate method for providing direct evidence on these is the experiment. This territory is ripe for organizational sociologists to explore. But these questions are also important for understanding the dynamics of and possibilities for politics of production, and as such I hope sociologists of work will also focus research on the logics underlying managerial decisions and practices, including trying to tease out the conscious and unconscious bases of the orientation and practice of both managers and workers. Even without conducting experiments, sociologists and other scholars of work and organizations can be creative in asking similar questions through qualitative research.

Fourth, I hope labor process researchers will be inspired to dig deeper into workplace culture using the framework I have developed. My findings are suggestive of the critical role of local culture and ideology within each workplace. I document divergent reactions to identical practices, including variation within and across workplaces.

The standard labor process interpretation would be to see worker opposition as a legitimate form of resistance against managerial attempts to maximize exploitation and control. But I think this is too crude. To be sure, lean is often implemented with a primary goal of increasing quantitative work intensification, and more broadly, workers within capitalism routinely experience bad management, anti-unionism, wage theft, wage stagnation, and assaults on their dignity. Militant opposition to these things is legitimate and necessary. That being said, my analysis suggests that the oppositional factions in lean organizations tend to be based on a fordist-taylorist understanding of the proper roles of managers and workers, a logic which is more regressive than that of substantive empowerment. In any case, sociologists of work should take variation in worker orientations as a central object of analysis and try to understand the cultural and institutional basis of competing factions within workplaces.

Fifth, the analysis of aspiration levels and the evidence on satisficing needs substantially more research. This line of analysis is exceptionally difficult due to the fact that individuals are likely unwilling, and perhaps unable to admit that they have moderate aspiration levels. Managers are likely to rationalize satisficing as a rational adaptation to fit their local context.

As with the difficulty of gathering direct evidence on unconscious assumptions, the difficulty of measuring aspiration levels is likely why institutional theory has in general, explicitly or implicitly, adopted a maximizing model. The maximizing assumption can be easily imputed without being measured. It is not so with satisficing, given the hypothesis of variation across individuals. I have offered an attempt to tackle this difficult methodological problem by matching cases on key characteristics. Future researchers will have to be creative if they want to make variable aspiration levels a core component of the analysis of managerial strategy.

Sixth, there remain open questions about the interaction between cultural logics and satisficing. Some of my cases clearly showed managerial orientation, based on a particular logic, shaping behavior independently of aspiration levels. But the analysis of Metalfab Plus and Deep Stampings in Chapter 8, and of Tubefab in Chapter 9, suggests that cognitive orientations and aspiration levels often work in combination, reinforcing each other. These cases showed a bottom-up process, in which managers satisficed in response to stimuli from their local situation: lack of discipline, engagement, or interest from the workers, and the difficulty of overcoming this. But these managers also expressed a fordist-taylorist view of workers. Future research could examine the extent to which a moderate aspiration level shapes cognitive orientation and vice versa.

Finally, my analysis suggests that sociologists should make inefficiency a subject of analysis to develop a more realistic sociology of markets. The analysis also suggests that a theory of organizations is a necessary element of a sociology of markets. The findings in this book accord with an extensive body of research in the sociology of work and organization theory, reviewed in Chapters 2 and 3, which documents variation in internal organizational dynamics and suggests that organizations differ substantially in their capacities to efficiently and effectively respond to environmental pressures. Yet, despite all this research, theories of the market in both economics and sociology generally do not accord a role for internal organizational processes in shaping the operation of markets.

Neil Fligstein (2002) identified three main approaches within the sociology of markets. Efficiency approaches of network economic sociology focus on the role of embedded social relations in promoting efficiency (Uzzi 1996). Power approaches of political economy examine interlocking directorates and attempts by elites to reproduce existing economic structures (Useem 1984). And effectiveness approaches of institutional sociology, focused on problems of organizational legitimation and survival, concentrate on how organizations seek to satisfy external constituencies (Meyer and Rowan 1977). None of these approaches to the sociology of markets have questioned the assumptions that managers maximize or that markets ensure high levels of efficiency, nor considered efficiency as a dependent variable. Since Fligstein wrote that paper, institutional logics theory has emerged as a leading approach to the sociology of markets, one that sees what happens inside of organizations as central to the operation of markets. But so far institutional logics scholars have not considered the question of organizational (in)efficiency as an important one.

The analysis in this book suggests that even in the highly competitive manufacturing sector, organizations commonly and consistently implement suboptimal strategies and allow relatively inefficient routines to persist. Organizational inefficiency is doubly routine: in the sense that it is embedded in operational routines (procedures and patterns of activity that form the basis of organizational capability); and in the sense of being regular and commonplace. The pressures for efficiency are generally quite blunt at the level of organizational routines, and managerial satisficing and organizational inertia ensure the reproduction of inefficient routines. A key theoretical implication is that we cannot properly understand market competition without taking seriously what happens inside organizations. The organization is central to the operation of the market.

I hope my plea to make organizational inefficiency a central object of analysis appeals to sociologist of work and organizational sociologists who are critical of neoclassical economic theory and are frustrated with its hegemony throughout the social sciences. Sociologists have offered a partial alternative to rational choice theory with their theories of how institutions and culture shape competing rationalities, along with value-driven behavior. But the core of rational choice theory is the assumption of maximizing behavior. This assumption is not only unrealistic but arguably insidious insofar as it provides the basis for any number of efficiency-based theories of firms and markets, which in turn provide legitimacy for anything a private actor does inside a firm or in the market, whatever the impact on workers, their families, communities, and the environment.

Finally, I hope marxists will take up this call to conduct further research on the capitalist production of inefficiency as a basis for deepening the critique of capitalism. The primary justification for capitalism is that it drives efficiency and innovation. Demonstrating that capitalist management is systematically producing routine inefficiency, failing to ensure the most efficient use of human resources, offers a direct criticism of the raison d'être of capitalism. Management despotism is no longer justifiable based on appeals to efficiency. Worker participation in decision making at all organization levels can tip the balance from an overemphasis on profits and short-termism, and the satisficing this entails, to an emphasis on efficiency, long-term orientation, and sustainability.

In the postfordist world, my study suggests, the best way to ensure the diffusion of best practice regarding dynamic efficiency and organizational learning is to substantively empower workers to engage in decision making within the organization. This need not be limited to the forms of participation documented in my study. As Adler (2019) has shown, deeper forms of participation that can generate "collaborative strategizing" include democratic determination of top-level goals and democratic participation in organizational decision making beyond continuous improvement of organizational routines and processes. Such empowerment will necessarily be limited within the capitalist employment relation.

So long as management and work organization remain capitalist, management will remain divided. The most dedicated managers with the highest aspiration levels will forge ahead in pursuing world-class, dynamically efficient organizations via the systematic, substantive empowerment of their workforce. But others—surely the majority—will satisfice, settling for good enough in the face of the contradictions of capitalist management. In the age of flexibility and rapid technical change, the contradictions of the capitalist employment relation systematically encourage managerial satisficing, leading to widespread underdevelopment and underutilization of human resources.

References

Abernathy, Frederick H., et al. (1999), *A Stitch in Time: Lean Retailing and the Transformation of Manufacturing—Lessons from the Apparel and Textile Industries* (Oxford: Oxford University Press).

Abo, Tetsuo (ed.), (1994), *Hybrid Factory: The Japanese Production System in the United States* (Oxford: Oxford University Press).

Ackroyd, Stephen and Thompson, Paul (1999), *Organizational Misbehaviour* (London: SAGE).

Adler, Paul (1993), "The Learning Bureaucracy: New United Motor Manufacturing Inc.," *Research in Organizational Behavior*, 15, 111–94.

Adler, Paul S. (1990), "Marx, Machines, and Skill," *Technology and Culture*, 31 (4), 780–812.

Adler, Paul S. (1999), "Hybridization: Human Resource Management at Two Toyota Transplants," in Jeffrey K. Liker, W. Mark Fruin, and Paul S. Adler (eds.), *Remade in America: Transplanting & Transforming Japanese Management Systems* (New York: Oxford University Press), 75–116.

Adler, Paul S. (2007), "The Future of Critical Management Studies: A Paleo-Marxist Critique of Labour Process Theory," *Organization Studies*, 28 (9), 1313–45.

Adler, Paul S. (2019), *The 99 Percent Economy: How Democratic Socialism Can Overcome the Crisis of Capitalism* (New York: Oxford University Press).

Adler, Paul S. and Cole, Robert E. (1993), "Designed for Learning: A Tale of Two Auto Plants," *Sloan Management Review*, Spring, 85–94.

Adler, Paul S. and Cole, Robert E. (1993), "Designed for Learning: A Tale of Two Auto Plants," *Sloan Management Review*, 34 (3), 85–94.

Adler, Paul S., Goldoftas, Barbara, and Levine, David I. (1999), "Flexibility versus Efficiency? A Case Study of Model Changeovers in the Toyota Production System," *Organization Science*, 10 (1), 43–68.

Aglietta, Michel ([1976] 2000), *A Theory of Capitalist Regulation: The U.S. Experience* (London: Verso).

Alchian, Armen A. (1950), "Uncertainty, Evolution, and Economic Theory," *Journal of Political Economy*, 58 (3), 211-21.

Althusser, Louis ([1971] 2001), "Ideology and Ideological State Apparatuses (Notes towards an Investigation)," in Louis Althusser (ed.), Lenin and Philosophy and Other Essays (New York: Monthly Review Press), 85–126.

Amin, Ash (1994), "Post-Fordism: Models, Fantasies and Phantoms of Transition," in Ash Amin (ed.), *Post-Fordism: A Reader* (Oxford: Blackwell), 1–39.

Anderson, Perry (1974), *Passages from Antiquity to Feudalism* (London: New Left Books).

Angeriz, Alvaro, McCombie, John, and Roberts, Mark (2006), "Productivity, Efficiency and Technological Change in European Union Regional Manufacturing: A Data Envelope Analysis Approach," *The Manchester School*, 74 (4), 500–25.

Ansari, Shahzad M., Fiss, Peer C., and Zajac, Edward J. (2010), "Made to Fit: How Practices Vary As They Diffuse," *Academy of Management Review*, 35 (1), 67–92.

Appelbaum, Eileen and Batt, Rosemary (1994), *The New American Workplace: Transforming Work Systems in the United States* (Ithaca, NY: ILR Press).

Appelbaum, Eileen, et al. (2000), *Manufacturing Advantage* (Ithaca: Cornell University Press).

Armstrong, Peter (1984), "Competition between the Organizational Professions and the Evolution of Management Control Strategies," in Kenneth Thompson (ed.), *Work, Employment and Unemployment: Perspectives on Work and Society* (Milton Keynes: Open University Press), 97–120.

Au, Wayne (2011), "Teaching under the New Taylorism: High-Stakes Testing and the Standardization of the 21st Century Curriculum," *Journal of Curriculum Studies*, 43 (1), 25–45.

Bacon, Nicholas and Blyton, Paul (2000), "High Road and Low Road Teamworking: Perceptions of Management Rationales and Organizational and Human Resource Outcomes," *Human Relations*, 53 (11), 1425–58.

Barker, James R. (1993), "Tightening the Iron Cage: Concertive Control in Self-Managing Teams," *Administrative Science Quarterly*, 38 (3), 408–37.

Barker, James R. (1999), *The Discipline of Teamwork: Participation and Concertive Control* (Thousand Oaks, CA: SAGE).

Barron, John M., Black, Dan A., and Loewenstein, Mark A. (1987), "Employer Size: The Implications for Search, Training, Capital Investment, Starting Wages, and Wage Growth," *Journal of Labor Economics*, 5 (1), 76–89.

Baum, Joel A. C. and Dahlin, Kristina B. (2007), "Aspiration Performance and Railroads' Patterns of Learning from Train Wrecks and Crashes," *Organization Science*, 18 (3), 368–85.

Becker, Howard S. (2001), "The Epistemology of Qualitative Research," in Robert M. Emerson (ed.), *Contemporary Field Research: Perspectives and Formulations* (Long Grove, IL: Waveland), 317–30.

Becker, Markus C. (2004), "Organizational Routines: A Review of the Literature," *Industrial and Corporate Change*, 13 (4), 643–78.

Beer, Michael, et al. (1985), *Human Resource Management: A General Manager's Perspective: Text and Cases* (New York: Free Press).

Benders, Jos and Van Bijsterveld, Mark (2000), "Leaning on Lean: The Reception of a Management Fashion in Germany," *New Technology, Work and Employment*, 15 (1), 50–64.

Benders, Jos, van Grinsven, Marlieke, and Ingvaldsen, Jonas A. (2018), "The Persistence of Management Ideas: How Framing Keeps 'Lean' Moving," in Andrew Sturdy, et al. (eds.), *The Oxford Handbook of Management Ideas* (Oxford: Oxford University Press), 271–85.

Berger, Peter L. and Luckmann, Tomas (1966), *The Social Construction of Reality: A Treatise in the Sociology of Knowledge* (New York: Doubleday).

Bernhardt, Annette, et al. (2008), *The Gloves-off Economy: Workplace Standards at the Bottom of America's Labor Market* (Ithaca, NY: Cornell University Press).

Besharov, Marya L. and Smith, Wendy K. (2014), "Multiple Institutional Logics in Organizations: Explaining Their Varied Nature and Implications," *Academy of Management Review*, 39 (3), 364–81.

Binder, Amy (2007), "For Love and Money: Organizations' Creative Responses to Multiple Environmental Logics," *Theory and Society*, 36 (6), 547–71.

Blackledge, Paul (2019), "Historical Materialism," in Matt Vidal, et al. (eds.), *The Oxford Handbook of Karl Marx* (New York: Oxford University Press), 37–56.

Bonacich, Edna and Appelbaum, Richard P. (2000), *Behind the Label: Inequality in the Los Angeles Apparel Industry* (Berkeley: University of California Press).

Bouville, Gregor and Alis, David (2014), "The Effects of Lean Organizational Practices on Employees' Attitudes and Workers' Health: Evidence from France," *The International Journal of Human Resource Management*, 25 (21), 3016–37.

Boxall, Peter and Winterton, Jonathan (2018), "Which Conditions Foster High-Involvement Work Processes? A Synthesis of the Literature and Agenda for Research," *Economic and Industrial Democracy*, 39 (1), 27–47.

Boyer, Robert (1988), "Technical Change and the Theory of 'Régulation', " in Giovanni Dosi, et al. (eds.), *Technical Change and Economic Theory* (London: Pinter Publishers Limited), 67–94.

Boyer, Robert (1997), "How Does a New Production System Emerge?," in Robert Boyer and Jean-Pierre Durand, *After Fordism* (London: Macmillan Press), 1–63.

Boyer, Robert (1998), "Hybridization and Models of Production: Geography, History, and Theory," in Robert Boyer, et al. (eds.), *Between Imitation and Innovation: The Transfer and Hybridization of Productive Models in the International Automobile Industry* (Oxford: Oxford University Press), 23–56.

Boyer, Robert, et al. (eds.) (1998), *Between Imitation and Innovation: The Transfer and Hybridization of Productive Models in the International Automobile Industry* (Oxford: Oxford University Press).

Boyer, Robert (1998), "Hybridization and Models of Production: Geography, History, and Theory," in Robert Boyer, et al. (eds.), *Between Imitation and Innovation: The Transfer and Hybridization of Productive Models in the International Automobile Industry* (Oxford: Oxford University Press), 23–56.

Boyer, Robert (2000), "Is a Finance-Led Growth Regime a Viable Alternative to Fordism? A Preliminary Analysis," *Economy and Society*, 29 (1), 111–45.

Boyer, Robert and Durand, Jean-Pierre (1997), *After Fordism* (London: Macmillan Press).

Boyer, Robert and Saillard, Yves (eds.) (2002), *Régulation Theory: The State of the Art* (London: Routledge).

Boyer, Robert and Saillard, Yves (2002a), "A Summary of Régulation Theory," in Robert Boyer and Yves Saillard (eds.), *Régulation Theory: The State of the Art* (London: Routledge), 36–44.

Boyer, Robert and Saillard, Yves (eds.) (2002b), *Régulation Theory: The State of the Art* (London: Routledge).

Braverman, Harry (1974), *Labor and Monopoly Capital: The Degradation of Work in the Twentieth Century* (New York: Monthly Review Press).

Brecher, Jeremy (1997), *Strike!* (Boston: South End Press).

Brenner, Robert ([1976] 1985), "Agrarian Class Structure and Economic Development in Pre-Industrial Europe," in T. H. Aston and C. H. E. Philpin (eds.), *The Brenner Debate: Agrarian Class Structure and Economic Development in Pre-Industrial Europe* (Cambridge: Cambridge University Press), 10–63.

Brenner, Robert ([1998] 2006), *The Economics of Global Turbulence* (London: Verso).

Burawoy, Michael (1982), *Manufacturing Consent: Changes in the Labor Process under Monopoly Capitalism* (Chicago: University of Chicago Press).

Burawoy, Michael (1987), *The Politics of Production* (New York: Verso).

Callinicos, Alex (2009), *Making History: Agency, Structure, and Change in Social Theory* (Chicago: Haymarket).

Carter, Bob, et al. (2011), "'All They Lack is a Chain': Lean and the New Performance Management in the British Civil Service," *New Technology, Work and Employment*, 26 (2), 83–97.

Carter, Bob, et al. (2013), "'Stressed out of my box'": Employee Experience of Lean Working and Occupational Ill-Health in Clerical Work in the UK Public Sector," *Work, Employment & Society*, 27 (5), 747–67.

Carter, Bob, et al. (2013a), "Taxing Times: Lean Working and the Creation of (In)Efficiencies in HMRC," *Public Administration*, 91 (1), 83–97.

Carter, Bob, et al. (2013b), "Taxing Times: Lean Working and the Creation of (In)efficiencies in HMRC," *Public Administration*, 91 (1), 83–97.

Carter, Bob, et al. (2013b), "Stressed out of my box': Employee Experience of Lean Working and Occupational Ill-Health in Clerical Work in the UK Public Sector," *Work, Employment & Society*, 27 (5), 747–67.

Caves, Richard E. and Barton, David R. (1990), *Efficiency in U.S. Manufacturing Industries* (Cambridge, MA: MIT Press).

Clarke, Simon (1992), "What in the F—'s Name is Fordism," in Nigel Gilbert, Roger Burrows, and Anna Pollert (eds.), *Fordism and Flexibility: Divisions and Change* (London: The Macmillan Press Ltd), 13–30.

Cohen, Sheila (1987), "A Labour Process to Nowhere," *New Left Review*, 165, 34–50.

Cotton, John L., et al. (1988), "Employee Participation: Diverse Forms and Different Outcomes," *The Academy of Management Review*, 13 (1), 8–22.

Cotton, John L. (1993), *Employee Involvement: Methods for Improving Performance and Work Attitudes* (London: SAGE).

Cressey, Peter and MacInnes, John (1980), "Voting for Ford: Industrial Democracy and the Control of Labour," *Capital & Class*, 4 (2), 5–33.

Crowley, Martha, et al. (2010), "Neo-Taylorism at Work: Occupational Change in the Post-Fordist Era," *Social Problems*, 57 (3), 421–47.

Cyert, Richard M. and March, James G. ([1963] 1992), *A Behavioral Theory of the Firm* (Second Edition. Cambridge, MA: Blackwell).

Danford, Andy (1999), *Japanese Management Techniques and British Workers* (London: Mansell).

Dassbach, Carl H. A. (1996), "Lean Production, Labor Control, and Post-Fordism in the Japanese Automobile Industry," in William C. Green and Ernest J. Yanarella (eds.), *North American Auto Unions in Crisis: Lean Production as Contested Terrain* (Albany, NY: State University of New York Press), 19–40.

Davidson, Neil (2004), "Asiatic, Tributary or Absolutist?," *International Socialism* Online only (3 November).

Dedoussis, Vagelis and Littler, Craig R. (1994), "Understanding the Transfer of Japanese Management Practices: The Australian Case," in Tony Elger and Chris Smith (eds.), *Global Japanization? The Transnational Transformation of the Labour Process* (London: Routledge), 175–95.

Delbridge, Rick (2003), *Life on the Line in Contemporary Manufacturing: The Workplace Experience of Lean Production and the "Japanese" Model* (Oxford: Oxford University Press).

Delery, John E. and Doty, D. Harold (1996), "Modes of Theorizing in Strategic Human Resource Management: Tests of Universalistic, Contingency, and Configurational Performance Predictions," *Academy of Management Journal*, 39 (4), 802–35.

Deming, W. Edwards (1982), *Quality, Productivity and Competitive Position* (Cambridge, MA: MIT Press).

Dennis, Pascal (2015), *Lean Production Simplified: A Plain-Language Guide to the World's Most Powerful Production System* (University Park, IL: Productivity Press).

Digman, John M. (1990), "Personality Structure: Emergence of the Five-Factor Model," *Annual Review of Psychology*, 41, 417–40.

DiMaggio, Paul (1997), "Culture and Cognition," *Annual Review of Sociology*, 23, 263–87.

DiMaggio, Paul J. and Powell, Walter W. (1983), "The Iron Cage Revisited: Institutional Isomorphism and Collective Rationality in Organizational Fields," *American Sociological Review*, 48 (2), 147–60.

DiMaggio, Paul J. and Powell, Walter W. (1991), "Introduction," in Walter W. Powell and Paul J. DiMaggio (eds.), *The New Institutionalism in Organizational Analysis* (Chicago: The University of Chicago Press), 1–38.

Djelic, Marie-Laure (1998), *Exporting the American Model: The Postwar Transformation of European Business* (Oxford: Oxford University Press).

Doellgast, Virginia (2012), *Disintegrating Democracy at Work: Labor Unions and the Future of Good Jobs in the Service Economy* (Ithaca, NY: ILR Press).

Dohse, Knuth, Jürgens, Ulrich, and Malsch, Thomas (1985), "From 'Fordism' to 'Toyotism'? The Social Organization of the Labor Process in the Japanese Automobile Industry," *Politics and Society*, 14 (2), 115–45.

Duncan, Ewan and Ritter, Ron (2014), "Next Frontiers for Lean," *McKinsey Quarterly*, *2*, 82–89.

Edwards, Paul K. and Scullion, Hugh (1982), *The Social Organization of Industrial Conflict: Control and Resistance in the Workplace* (Oxford: Blackwell).

Edwards, P. K. (1986), *Conflict at Work* (Oxford: Blackwell).

Edwards, R. (1979), *Contested Terrain: The Transformation of the Workplace in the Twentieth Century* (London: Heinemann).

Elger, Tony (1979), "Valorisation and 'Deskilling': A Critique of Braverman," *Capital & Class*, 3 (1), 58–99.

Elger, Tony and Smith, Chris (eds.) (1994), *Global Japanization: The Transnational Transformation of the Labour Process* (London: Routledge).

Elger, Tony and Smith, Chris (2005), *Assembling Work: Remaking Factory Regimes in Japanese Multinationals in Britain* (Oxford: Oxford University Press).

Esser, Josef and Hirsch, Joachim (1994), "The Crisis of Fordism and the Dimensions of a 'Post-Fordist' Regional and Urban Structure," in Ash Amin (ed.), *Post-Fordism: A Reader* (Oxford: Blackwell), 71–97.

Eurofound (2013), *Work Organisation and Employee Involvement in Europe* (Luxembourg: Publications Office of the European Union).

Fantasia, Rick, Clawson, Dan, and Graham, Gregory (1988), "A Critical View of Worker Participation in American Industry," *Work and Occupations*, 15 (4), 468–88.

Fiss, Peer C. and Zajac, Edward J. (2004), "The Diffusion of Ideas over Contested Terrain: The (Non)adoption of a Shareholder Value Orientation among German Firms," *Administrative Science Quarterly*, 49 (4), 501–34.

Fligstein, Neil (1985), "The Spread of the Multidivisional Form among Large Firms, 1919–1979," *American Sociological Review*, 50, 377–91.

Fligstein, Neil (1990), *The Transformation of Corporate Control* (Cambridge, MA: Harvard University Press).

Fligstein, Neil (2002), "Agreements, Disagreements, and Opportunities in the 'New Sociology of Markets,'" in Mauro F. Guillén, et al. (eds.), *The New Economic Sociology: Developments in an Emerging Field* (New York: Russell Sage Foundation), 61–78.

Fligstein, Neil and Goldstein, Adam (2010), "The Anatomy of the Mortgage Securitization Crisis," in Michael Lounsbury and Paul M. Hirsch (eds.), *Markets on Trial: The Economic Sociology of the US Financial Crisis* (Bingley: Emerald), 27–58.

Forrant, Robert (2000), "Between a Rock and a Hard Place: US Industrial Unions, Shop-Floor Participation and the Lean, Mean Global Economy," *Cambridge Journal of Economics*, 24, 751–69.

Frantz, Roger (1988), *X-Efficiency: Theory, Evidence and Applications* (Boston, MA: Kluwer Academic Publishers).

Freyssenet, Michel, et al. (eds.) (1998), *One Best Way? Trajectories and Industrial Models of the World's Automobile Producers* (Oxford: Oxford University Press).

Friedland, Roger and Alford, Robert R. (1991), "Bringing Society Back in: Symbols, Practices, and Institutional Contradictions," in Walter W. Powell and Paul DiMaggio (eds.), *The New Institutionalism in Organizational Analysis* (Chicago: University of Chicago Press), 232–66.

Friedman, Andrew L. (1977), *Industry and Labour: Class Struggle at Work and Monopoly Capitalism* (London: The Macmillan Press Ltd.).

Friedman, Andrew L. (1987), "The Means of Management Control and Labour Process Theory: A Critical Note on Storey," *Sociology*, 21 (2), 287–94.

Fucini, Joseph J and Fucini, Suzy (1990), *Working for the Japanese: Inside Mazda's American Auto Plant* (New York: The Free Press).

Gavetti, Giovanni (2005), "Cognition and Hierarchy: Rethinking the Microfoundations of Capabilities' Development," *Organization Science*, 16 (6), 599–617.

Glyn, Andrew, et al. (2007), "The Rise and Fall of the Golden Age," in Stephen A. Marglin and Juliet B. Schor (eds.), *The Golden Age of Capitalism: Reinterpreting the Postwar Experience* (Oxford: Clarendon Press), 39–125.

Goodrick, Elizabeth and Salancik, Gerald R. (1996), "Organizational Discretion in Responding to Institutional Practices: Hospitals and Cesarean Births," *Administrative Science Quarterly*, 41 (1), 1–28.

Gordon, D., Edwards, R., and Reich, M. (1982), *Segmented Work, Divided Workers: The Historical Transformation of Labor in the United States* (Cambridge: Cambridge University Press).

Gordon, David M (1976), "Capitalist Efficiency and Socialist Efficiency," *Monthly Review*, 28 (3), 19–39.

Gorz, André (1968), *Strategy for Labor: A Radical Proposal*, trans. Martin A. Nicolaus and Victoria Ortiz (Beacon Press).

Gorz, André (1976), "Technology, technicians and class struggle," in André Gorz (ed.), *The Division of Labour: The Labour Process and Class Struggle in Modern Capitalism* (Hassocks: The Harvester Press), 159–89.

Gospel, Howard F. (1992), *Markets, Firms and the Management of Labour in Britain* (Cambridge: Cambridge University Press).

Graham, Laurie (1995), *On the Line at Subaru-Isuzu: The Japanese Model and the American Worker* (Ithaca, NY: Cornell University Press).

Gramsci, Antonio ([1929–1935] 1999), *Selections From the Prison Notebooks*, trans. Quintin Hoare and Geoffrey Nowell Smith (New York: International Publishers).

Green, Alison and Mayes, David (1991), "Technical Inefficiency in Manufacturing Industries," *The Economic Journal*, 101 (406), 523–38.

Green, Francis (2006), *Demanding Work: The Paradox of Job Quality in the Affluent Economy* (Princeton: Princeton University Press).

Greenwood, Royston, et al. (2011), "Institutional Complexity and Organizational Responses," *The Academy of Management Annals*, 5 (1), 317–71.

Greer, Ian and Hauptmeier, Marco (2016), "Management Whipsawing: The Staging of Labor Competition Under Globalization," *ILR Review*, 69 (1), 29–52.

Greve, Henrich R. (1998), "Performance, Aspirations, and Risky Organizational Change," *Administrative Science Quarterly*, 43 (1), 58–86.

Grinyer, Peter and McKiernan, Peter (1990), "Generating Major Change in Stagnating Companies," *Strategic Management Journal*, 11, 131–46.

Guillèn, Mauro F. (1994), *Models of Management: Work, Authority, and Organization in a Comparative Perspective* (Chicago: University of Chicago Press).

Gustavsen, Bjørn (2007), "Work Organization and 'the Scandinavian Model'," *Economic and Industrial Democracy*, 28 (4), 650–71.

Hall, Stuart (1986), "The Problem of Ideology: Marxism without Guarantees," *Journal of Communication Inquiry*, 10, 28–44.

Hall, Stuart and Jacques, Martin (1990), *New Times: The Changing Face of Politics in the 1990s* (London: Lawrence & Wishart).

Hannan, Michael T. and Freeman, John (1984), "Structural Inertia and Organizational Change," *American Sociological Review*, 49 (2), 149–64.

Haveman, Heather A. (1993), "Follow the Leader: Mimetic Isomorphism and Entry Into New Markets," *Administrative Science Quarterly*, 38 (4), 593–627.

Heller, Henry (2019), "Class and Class Struggle," in Matt Vidal, et al. (eds.), *The Oxford Handbook of Karl Marx* (New York: Oxford University Press), 57–76.

Helper, Susan and Kiehl, Janet (2004), "Developing Supplier Capabilities: Market and Non-market Approaches," *Industry and Innovation*, 11 (1/2), 89–107.

Herrigel, Gary (2004), "Emerging Strategies and Forms of Governance in the Components Industry in High Wage Regions," *Industry and Innovation*, 11 (1–2).

Herrigel, Gary and Sabel, Charles F. (1999), "Craft Production in Crisis: Industrial Restructuring in Germany in the 1990s," in Pepper D. Culpepper and David Finegold (eds.), *The German Skills Machine: Sustaining Comparative Advantage in a Global Economy* (New York: Berghahn Books), 77–114.

Herzberg, Frederick (1968), "One More Time How Do You Motivate Employees," *Harvard Business Review*, 46, 53–62.

Hirschhorn, Larry (1990), *Beyond Mechanization: Work and Technology in a Postindustrial Age* (Cambridge, MA: MIT Press).

Hobsbawm, Eric (2007), "Marxist Historiography Today," in Chris Wickham (ed.), *Marxist History-Writing for the Twenty-first Century* (Oxford: Oxford University Press), 180–7.

Hodgson, Geoffrey M. (1997), "The Ubiquity of Habits and Rules," *Cambridge Journal of Economics*, 21 (6), 663–84.

Hodson, Randy (2001), *Dignity at Work* (Cambridge: Cambridge University Press).

Hounshell, David A. (1984), *From the American System to Mass Production, 1800–1932: The Development of Manufacturing Technology in the United States* (Baltimore: The Johns Hopkins University Press).

Huselid, Mark A. (1995), "The Impact Of Human Resource Management Practices On Turnover, Productivity, And Corporate Financial Performance," *Academy of Management Journal*, 38 (3), 635–72.

Hyman, Richard (2001), *Understanding European Trade Unionism: Between Market, Class and Society* (London: Sage).

Ichniowski, Casey, et al. (1996), "What Works at Work: Overview and Assessment," *Industrial Relations*, 35 (3), 299–333.

Ichniowski, Casey, Shaw, Kathryn, and Prennushi, Giovanna (1997), "The Effects of Human Resource Management Practices on Productivity: A Study of Steel Finishing Lines," *The American Economic Review*, 87 (3), 291–313.

Ilhara, Ryoji (2007), *Toyota's Assembly Line: A View from the Factory Floor* (Victoria: Trans-Pacific Press).

Ingvaldsen, Jonas A. (2013), "Democratic Lean? Work Systems in Norwegian Industry," PhD (Norwegian University of Science and Technology).

Jacoby, Sanford M. (1983), "Union-Management Cooperation in the United States: Lessons from the 1920s," *Industrial and Labor Relations Review*, 37 (1), 18–33.

Jacoby, Sanford M. (1997), *Modern Manors: Welfare Capitalism Since the New Deal* (Princeton, NJ: Princeton University Press).

Janoski, Thomas and Lepadatu, Darina (eds.) (2021), *The Cambridge International Handbook of Lean Production: Diverging Theories and New Industries around the World* (Cambridge: Cambridge University Press).

Jensen, Michael C. and Meckling, William H. (1976), "Theory of the Firm: Managerial Behavior, Agency Costs, and Ownership Structure," The Journal Financial Economics, 3 (4), 305–60.

Jessop, Bob (1989), "Conservative Regimes and the Transition to Post-Fordism: The Cases of Great Britain and West Germany," in Mark Gottdeiner and Nicos Komninos (eds.), *Capitalist Development and Crisis Theory: Accumulation, Regulation and Spatial Restructuring* (New York: St Martin's Press), 261–99.

Jessop, Bob (1992), "Fordism and Post-Fordism: a Critical Reformulation," in M. Storper and A.J. Scott (eds.), *Pathways to Industrialization and Regional Development* (London: Routledge). 42–62.

Jessop, Bob (2012), "The World Market, Variegated Capitalism and the Crisis of European Integration," in Petros Nousios, Henk Overbeek, and Andreas Tsolakis (eds.), *Globalisation and European Integration* (London: Routledge), 91–111.

John, Oliver P. and Srivastava, Sanjay (2001), "The Big Five Trait Taxonomy: History, Measurement, and Theoretical Perspectives," in Lawrence A. Pervin and Oliver P. John (eds.), *Handbook of Personality: Theory and Research* (Second Edition. New York: The Guilford Press), 102–38.

Juran, J. M. and Gryna, Frank M. ([1970] 1993), *Quality Planning and Analysis* (New York: McGraw Hill Higher Education).

Jürgens, Ulrich (2004), "An Elusive Model—Diversified Quality Production and the Transformation of the German Automobile Industry," *Competition & Change*, 8 (4), 411–23.

Jürgens, Ulrich and Krzywdzinski, Martin (2016), *New Worlds of Work: Varieties of Work in Car Factories in the BRIC Countries* (Oxford: Oxford University Press).

Kalirajan, K. P. and Shand, R. T. (1999), "Frontier Production Functions and Technical Efficiency Measures," *Journal of Economic Surveys*, 13 (2), 149–72.

Kamata, Satoshi (1982 [1973]), *Japan in the Passing Lane: An Insider's Account of Life in a Japanese Auto Factory*, trans. Tatsuru Akimoto (New York: Panteon Books).

Kenney, Martin and Florida, Richard (1993), *Beyond Mass Production: The Japanese System and Its Transfer to the U.S.* (Oxford: Oxford University Press).

Kern, Horst and Schumann, Michael (1992), "New Concepts of Production and the Emergence of the Systems Controller," in Paul Adler (ed.), *Technology and the Future of Work* (New York: Oxford University Press), 111–48.

Klein, Janice A. (1991), "A Reexamination of Autonomy in Light of New Manufacturing Practices," *Human Relations*, 44 (1), 21–38.

Kluge, Norbert (2005), "Corporate Governance with Co-determination—A Key Element of the European Social Model," *Transfer: European Review of Labour and Research*, 11 (2), 163–77.

Knoke, David and Kalleberg, Arne L. (1994), "Job Training in U.S. Organizations," *American Sociological Review*, 59 (4), 537–46.

Kochan, Thomas A., Lansbury, Russell D., and MacDuffie, John Paul (1997), "Conclusion: After Lean Production?," in Thomas A. Kochan, Russell D. Lansbury, and John Paul MacDuffie (eds.), *After Lean Production: Evolving Employment Practices in the World Auto Industry* (Ithaca, NY: ILR Press), 303–24.

Korczynski, Marek (2009), "Understanding the Contradictory Lived Experience of Service Work: The Customer-Oriented Bureaucracy," in Marek Korczynski and Cameron Lynne Macdonald (eds.), *Service Work: Critical Perspectives* (London: Routledge), 73–90.

Kraatz, Matthew S. and Block, Emily S. (2008), "Organizational Implications of Institutional Pluralism," in Royston Greenwood, et al. (eds.), *The SAGE Handbook of Organizational Institutionalism* (London: SAGE), 243–75.

Krafcik, John F. (1988), "Triumph of the Lean Production System," *Sloan Management Review*, 30 (1), 41–52.

Krzywdzinski, Martin (2017), "Accounting for Cross-Country Differences in Employee Involvement Practices: Comparative Case Studies in Germany, Brazil and China," *British Journal of Industrial Relations*, 55 (2), 321–46.

Landes, David S. (1986), "What Do Bosses Really Do?," *The Journal of Economic History*, 46 (3), 585–623.

Langlois, Richard N. and Foss, Nicolai J. (1999), "Capabilities and Governance: The Rebirth of Production in the Theory of Economic Organization," *Kyklos*, 52, 201–18.

Lant, Theresa K. (1992), "Aspiration Level Adaptation: An Empirical Exploration," *Management Science*, 38 (5), 623–44.

Lant, Theresa K. and Montgomery, David B. (1987), "Learning from Strategic Success and Failure," *Journal of Business Research*, 15 (6), 503–17.

Lapavitsas, Costas (2009), "Financialised Capitalism: Crisis and Financial Expropriation," *Historical Materialism*, 17 (2), 114–48.

Lapavitsas, Costas (2011), "Theorizing Financialization," *Work, Employment & Society*, 25 (4), 611–26.

Lawler, Edward E., III(1992), *The Ultimate Advantage: Creating the High-Involvement Work Organization* (San Francisco: Jossey-Bass).

Lazonick, William (1990), *Competitive Advantage on the Shop Floor* (Cambridge, MA: Harvard University Press).

Lazonick, William and O'Sullivan, Mary (2000), "Maximizing Shareholder Value: A New Ideology for Corporate Governance," *Economy and Society*, 29 (1), 13–35.

Leibenstein, Harvey (1966), "Allocative Efficiency vs. 'X-Efficiency,'" *The American Economic Review*, 56 (3), 392–415.

Levine, David I. and Tyson, Laura D'Andrea (1990), "Participation, Productivity, and the Firm's Environment," in Alan S. Blinder (ed.), *Paying for Productivity: A Look at the Evidence* (Washington, D.C.: Brookings Institution), 183–243.

Levinthal, Daniel and March, James G. (1981), "A Model of Adaptive Organizational Search," *Journal of Economic Behavior & Organization*, 2 (4), 307–33.

Levitt, Barbara and March, James G. (1988), "Organizational Learning," *Annual Review of Sociology*, 14 (1), 319–38.

Liker, Jeffrey K. (2004), *The Toyota Way: 14 Management Principles from the World's Greatest Manufacturer* (New York: McGraw-Hill).

Liker, Jeffrey K., Fruin, W. Mark, and Adler, Paul S. (1999a), "Bringing Japanese Management Systems to the United States: Transplantation or Transformation?," in Jeffrey K. Liker, W. Mark Fruin, and Paul S. Adler (eds.), *Remade in America: Transplanting and Transforming Japanese Management Systems* (Oxford: Oxford University Press), 3–35.

Liker, Jeffrey K., Fruin, W. Mark, and Adler, Paul S. (1999b), *Remade in America: Transplanting and Transforming Japanese Management Systems* (Oxford: Oxford University Press).

Liker, Jeffrey K. and Meier, David P. (2007), *Toyota Talent: Developing Your People the Toyota Way* (New York: McGraw-Hill).

Lin, Chun (2019), "Asia and the Shift in Marx's Conception of Revolution and History," in Matt Vidal, et al. (eds.), *The Oxford Handbook of Karl Marx* (New York: Oxford), 699–719.

Lipietz, Alain (1987), *Mirages and Miracles: Crisis in Global Fordism* (London: Verso).

Lipietz, Alain (1988), "Accumulation, Crises, and Ways Out," *International Journal of Political Economy*, 18 (2), 10–43.

Lipietz, Alain (1992), *Towards a New Economic Order: Postfordism, Ecology and Democracy*, trans. Malcolm Slater (Cambridge: Polity Press).

Lipietz, Alain (1997), "The Post-Fordist World: Labour Relations, International Hierarchy and Global Ecology," *Review of International Political Economy*, 4 (1), 1–41.

Littler, Craig R. (1982), *The Development of the Labour Process in Capitalist Societies* (London: Heinemann).

Lofland, John, et al. (2005), Analyzing Social Settings: A Guide to Qualitative Observation and Analysis (Fourth edn.; Belmont, CA: Wadsworth).

Lounsbury, Michael (2001), "Institutional Sources of Practice Variation: Staffing College and University Recycling Programs," *Administrative Science Quarterly*, 46 (1), 29–56.

Lounsbury, Michael (2007), "A Tale of Two Cities: Competing Logics and Practice Variation in the Professionalizing of Mutual Funds," *Academy of Management Journal*, 50 (2), 289–307.

Lowe, James, Delbridge, Rick, and Oliver, Nick (1997), "High-Performance Manufacturing: Evidence from the Automotive Components Industry," *Organization Studies*, 18 (5), 783–98.

Luria, Dan, et al. (2005), *'Full-Utilization Learning Lean' in Component Manufacturing: A New Industrial Model for Mature Regions, & Labor's Stake in Its Success* (Sloan Industry Studies Working Paper WP-2006-03, Alfred P. Sloan Foundation).

Luria, Daniel (1996), "Why Markets Tolerate Mediocre Manufacturing," *Challenge*, 39 (4), 11–16.

Luria, Daniel (1996), "Why Markets Tolerate Mediocre Manufacturing," *Challenge*, July–August, 11–16.

MacDuffie, John Paul (1995), "Human Resource Bundles and Manufacturing Performance: Organizational Logic and Flexible Production Systems in the World Auto Industry," *Industrial and Labor Relations Review*, 48 (2), 197–221.

MacDuffie, John Paul and Pil, Frits K. (1997), "Changes in Auto Industry Employment Practices: An International Overview," in Thomas A. Kochan, Russell D. Lansbury, and John Paul MacDuffie (eds.), *After Lean Production: Evolving Employment Practices in the World Auto Industry* (Ithaca, NY: ILR Press), 9–42.

Mallet, Serge (1975), *The New Working Class*, trans. Andrée Shepherd and Bob Shepherd (Nottingham: Spokesman Books).

March, James G. and Simon, Herbert A. ([1958] 1993), *Organizations* (Second Edition. Cambridge, MA: Blackwell).

Marglin, Stephen A. (1974), "What Do Bosses Do?: The Origins and Functions of Hierarchy in Capitalist Production," *Review of Radical Political Economics*, 6 (2), 60–112.

Marschall, Daniel and Scully-Russ, Ellen (2010), "Joint Union–Management Workforce Development Model," in David Finegold, et al. (eds.), *Transforming the U.S. Workforce Development System: Lessons from Research and Practice* (Ithaca, NY: ILR Press), 205–36.

Marsh, Robert M. (1992), "The Difference between Participation and Power in Japanese Factories," *Industrial and Labor Relations Review*, 45 (2), 250–57.

Martin, Stephen (1993), "Endogenous Firm Efficiency in a Cournot Principal-Agent Model," *Journal of Economic Theory* 59 (2), 445–50.

Marx, Karl ([1867] 1965), *Capital: A Critique of Political Economy, Vol. 1* (Moscow: Progress Publishers).

Marx, Karl ([1844] 1978), "Economic and Philosophic Manuscripts of 1844," in Robert C. Tucker (ed.), *The Marx-Engels Reader* (New York: W. W. Norton & Company), 66–125.

Marx, Karl ([1859] 1978), "Preface to A Contribution to the Critique of Political Economy," in Robert C. Tucker (ed.), *The Marx-Engels Reader* (New York: W. W. Norton & Company), 3–6.

Marx, Karl ([1894] 1981), *Capital, Vol. 3* (London: Penguin).

Marx, Karl ([1867] 1990), *Capital, Vol. 1*, trans. Ben Fowkes (London: Penguin).

Marx, Karl ([1857–8] 1993), *Grundrisse: Foundations of the Critique of Political Economy*, trans. Martin Nicolaus (London: Penguin).

Marx, Karl ([1852] 1994), *The Eighteenth Brumaire of Louis Bonaparte* (New York: International Publishers).

Marx, Karl and Engels, Frederick ([1846] 1996), *The German Ideology: Part One, with Selections from Parts Two and Three and Supplementary Texts* (New York: International Publishers).

Marx, Karl and Engels, Friedrich ([1848] 1978), "Manifesto of the Communist Party," in Robert C. Tucker (ed.), *The Marx-Engels Reader* (Second Edition. New York: W. W. Norton & Company), 469–500.

Masami, Nomura (1994), "The Myths of the Toyota System," *AMPO Japan-Asia Quarterly Review*, 25 (1), 18–25.

Mathews, John (1989), *The Age of Democracy: The Politics of Post-Fordism* (Melbourne: Oxford University Press).

Maurice, Marc, Sellier, François, and Silvestre, Jean-Jacques (1986), *The Social Foundations of Industrial Power: A Comparison of France and Germany* (Cambridge, MA: MIT Press).

Maurice, Marc, Sorge, Arndt, and Warner, Malcolm (1980), "Societal Differences in Organizing Manufacturing Units: A Comparison of France, West Germany, and Great Britain," *Organization Studies*, 1 (1), 59–86.

McKay, Steven C. (2006), *Satanic Mills or Silicon Islands? The Politics of High-Tech Production in the Philippines* (Ithaca, NY: ILR Press).

Meyer, John W. and Rowan, Brian (1977), "Institutionalized Organizations: Formal Structure as Myth and Ceremony," *American Journal of Sociology*, 83 (2), 340–63.

Mezias, Stephen J., Chen, Ya-Ru, and Murphy, Patrice R. (2002), "Aspiration-Level Adaptation in an American Financial Services Organization: A Field Study," *Management Science*, 48 (10), 1285–300.

Miles, Raymond E. (1965), "Human Relations or Human Resources?," *Harvard Business Review*, (July–August).

Milkman, Ruth (1991), *Japan's California Factories: Labor Relations and Economic Globalization* (Los Angeles: Institute of Industrial Relations, University of California).

Milkman, Ruth (1997), *Farewell to the Factory: Auto Workers in the Late Twentieth Century* (Berkeley: University of California Press).

Miller, Kathrine I. and Monge, Peter R. (1986), "Participation, Satisfaction, and Productivity: A Meta-Analytic Review," *Academy of Management Journal*, 29 (4), 727–53.

Milliken, Frances J. and Lant, Theresa K. (1991), "The Effect of an Organization's Recent Performance History on Strategic Persistence and Change: The Role of Managerial Interpretations," in Paul Shrivastava, Anne S. Huff, and Jane Dutton (eds.), *Advances in Strategic Management*, 7; Greenwich, CT: JAI Press), 129–56.

Minssen, Heiner (2006), "Challenges of Teamwork in Production: Demands of Communication," *Organization Studies*, 27 (1), 103–24.

Mishina, Kazuhiro (1998), "Making Toyota in America: Evidence from the Kentucky Transplant, 1986–1994," in Robert Boyer, et al. (eds.), *Between Imitation and Innovation: The Transfer and Hybridization of Productive Models in the International Automobile Industry* (Oxford: Oxford University Press), 99–127.

Misumi, Jyuji (1984), "Decision-Making in Japanese Groups and Organizations," in Bernhard Wilpert and Arndt Sorge (eds.), *International Perspectives on Organizational Democracy* (2; New York: John Wiley & Sons), 525–39.

Monden, Yasuhiro (1983), *Toyota Production System: Practical Approach to Production Management* (Norcross, GA: Industrial Engineering and Management Press).

Montgomery, David (1979), *Workers' Control in America* (Cambridge: Cambridge University Press).

Moody, Kim (1997), *Workers in Lean World: Unions in the International Economy* (London: Verso).

Nelson, Richard R. and Winter, Sidney G. (1982), *An Evolutionary Theory of Economic Change* (Cambridge, MA: Harvard University Press).

Nichols, Theo and Armstrong, Peter (1976), *Workers Divided: A Study in Shopfloor Politics* (Glasgow: Fontana).

Nicolaus, Martin (1968), "The Unkown Marx," *New Left Review*, I/48 (March-April), 41–61.

Nigam, Amit, Huising, Ruthanne, and Golden, Brian (2016), "Explaining the Selection of Routines for Change during Organizational Search," *Administrative Science Quarterly*, 61 (4), 551–83.

Noble, David F. (1986), *Forces of Production: A Social History of Industrial Automation* (Oxford: Oxford University Press).

Nyland, Chris (1998), "Taylorism and the Mutual-Gains Strategy," *Industrial Relations: A Journal of Economy and Society*, 37 (4), 519–42.

Ocasio, William (2011), "Attention to Attention," *Organization Science*, 22 (5), 1286–96.

Ohno, Taiichi (1988), *Toyota Production System: Beyond Large-Scale Production* (New York: Productivity Press).

Oliver, Christine (1991), "Strategic Response to Institutional Processes," *Academy of Management Review*, 16 (1), 145–79.

Oliver, Nick, et al. (1994), "World Class Manufacturing: Further Evidence in the Lean Production Debate," *British Journal of Management*, 5, S53–S63.

Oliver, Nick and Wilkinson, Barry (1992), *The Japanization of British Industry: New Developments in the 1990s* (Oxford: Blackwell).

Orsburn, Jack D., et al. (1990), *Self Directed Work Teams: The New American Challenge* (Homewood, Il: Business One Irwin).

Osterman, Paul (1994), "How Common is Workplace Transformation and Who Adopts It?," *Industrial and Labor Relations Review*, 47 (2), 173–88.

Osterman, Paul (1995), "Skill, Training, and Work Organization in American Establishments," *Industrial Relations: A Journal of Economy and Society*, 34 (2), 125–46.

Pache, Anne-Claire and Santos, Filipe (2010), "When Worlds Collide: The Internal Dynamics of Organizational Responses to Conflicting Institutional Demands," *Academy of Management Review*, 35 (3), 455–76.

Palloix, Christian (1976), "The Labour Process: From Fordism to Neo-Fordism," in Conference of Socialist Economists (ed.), *The Labour Process & Class Struggle* (London: stage 1), 46–67.

Parker, Mike (1985), *Inside the Circle: A Union Guide to QWL* (Boston: South End Press/Labor Education and Research Project).

Parker, Mike and Slaughter, Jane (1995), "Unions and Management by Stress," in Steve Babson (ed.), *Lean Work: Empowerment and Exploitation in the Global Auto Industry* (Detroit: Wayne State University Press), 41–53.

Peck, Jamie and Tickell, Adam (2000), "Searching for a New Institutional Fix: the *After-*Fordist Crisis and the Global-Local Disorder," in Ash Amin (ed.), *Post-Fordism: A Reader* (Oxford: Blackwell), 280–315.

Pfeffer, Jeffrey (1998), *The Human Equation: Building Profits by Putting People First* (Boston: Harvard Business School Press).

Pil, Fritz K. and MacDuffie, John Paul (1996), "The Adoption of High-Involvement Work Practices," *Industrial Relations*, 35 (3), 423–55.

Piore, Michael J. and Sabel, Charles F. (1984), *The Second Industrial Divide: Possibilities for Prosperity* (New York: Basic Books).

Purdy, Jill M. and Gray, Barbara (2009), "Conflicting Logics, Mechanisms of Diffusion, and Multilevel Dynamics in Emerging Institutional Fields," *Academy of Management Journal*, 52 (2), 355–80.

Scott, W. Richard (2008), *Institutions and Organizations: Ideas and Interests* (Third Edition. Los Angeles: SAGE).

Rinehart, James, Huxley, Christopher, and Robertson, David (1997), *Just Another Car Factory? Lean Production and Its Discontents* (Ithaca, NY: Cornell University Press).

Rothstein, Jeffrey S. (2016), *When Good Jobs Go Bad: Globalization, De-Unionization, and Declining Job Quality in the North American Auto Industry* (New Brunswick: Rutgers University Press).

Sabel, Charles F. (1982), *Work and Politics: The Division of Labor in Industry* (Cambridge: Cambridge University Press).

Sandberg, Åke (ed.), (1995), *Enriching Production: Perspectives on Volvo's Uddevalla Plant as an Alternative to Lean Production* (Aldershot: Avebury).

Schneiberg, Marc (2007), "What's on the Path? Path Dependence, Organizational Diversity and the Problem of Institutional Change in the US Economy, 1900–1950," *Socio-Economic Review*, 5 (1), 47–80.

Schneiberg, Marc and Soule, Sarah A. (2005), "Institutionalization as a Contested, Multilevel Process: The Case of Rate Regulation in American Fire Insurance," in Gerald F. Davis, et al. (eds.), *Social Movements and Organization Theory* (Cambridge: Cambridge University Press), 122–60.

Schonberger, Richard J (1982), *Japanese Manufacturing Techniques: Nine Hidden Lessons in Simplicity* (New York: The Free Press).

Shaikh, Anwar (1987), "The Falling Rate of Profit and the Economic Crisis in the US," in Robert Cherry, et al. (eds.), *The Imperiled Economy: Macroeconomics from a Left Perspective* (New York: Union for Radical Political Economists), 115–26.

Shingo, Shigeo (1988), *Non-Stock Production: The Shingo System of Continuous Improvement* (Portland, OR: Productivity Press).

Simon, Herbert ([1947] 1961), *Administrative Behavior* (Second Edition. New York: Macmillan).

Simon, Herbert A. (1955), "A Behavioral Model of Rational Choice," *Quarterly Journal of Economics*, 69 (1), 99–118.

Simon, Herbert A. (1991), "Organizations and Markets," *Journal of Economic Perspectives*, 5 (2), 25–44.

Sjöström, Tomas and Weitzman, Martin L. (1996), "Competition and the Evolution of Efficiency," *Journal of Economic Behavior & Organization*, 30 (1), 25–43.

Smith, Chris (1987), *Technical Workers: Class, Labour and Trade Unionism* (Basingstoke: Macmillan).

Smith, Chris (1989), "Flexible Specialisation, Automation and Mass Production," *Work, Employment & Society*, 3 (2), 203–20.

Smith, Chris and Meiksins, Peter (1995), "System, Society and Dominance Effects in Cross-National Organisational Analysis," *Work, Employment & Society*, 9 (2), 241–67.

Smith, Chris and Vidal, Matt (2021), "The Lean Labor Process: Global Diffusion, Societal Effects, Contradictory Implementation," in Thomas Janoski and Darina Lepadatu (eds.), *The Cambridge International Handbook of Lean Production: Diverging Theories and New Industries around the World* (Cambridge: Cambridge University Press), 150–75.

Smith, Tony (2000), *Technology and Capital in the Age of Lean Production* (Albany, NY: SUNY Press).

Smith, Vicki (1997), "New Forms of Work Organization," *Annual Review of Sociology*, 23, 315–39.

Sorge, Arndt (1991), "Strategic Fit and the Societal Effect: Interpreting Cross-National Comparisons of Technology, Organization and Human Resources," *Organization Studies*, 12 (2), 161–90.

Spencer, David A. (2000), "Braverman and the Contribution of Labour Process Analysis to the Critique of Capitalist Production—Twenty-Five Years on," *Work, Employment & Society*, 14 (2), 223–43.

Staw, Barry M., McKechnie, Pamela I., and Puffer, Sheila M. (1983), "The Justification of Organizational Performance," *Administrative Science Quarterly*, 28 (4), 582–600.

Stewart, Paul, et al. (2009), *We Sell Our Time No More: Workers' Struggles Against Lean Production in the British Car Industry* (London: Pluto).

Storey, John (1985), "The Means of Management Control," *Sociology*, 19 (2), 193–211.

Strang, David and Michael W. Macy, (2001), "In Search of Excellence: Fads, Success Stories, and Adaptive Emulation," *American Journal of Sociology*, 107 (1), 147–82.

Streeck, Wolfgang (1996), "Lean Production in the German Automobile Industry: A Test Case for Convergence Theory," in Suzanne Berger and Ronald Dore (eds.), *National Diversity and Global Capitalism* (Ithaca, NY: Cornell University Press), 138–70.

Sugimori, Y., et al. (1977), "Toyota Production System and Kanban System Materialization of Just-in-Time and Respect-for-Human System," *International Journal of Production Research*, 15 (6), 553–64.

Taylor, Phil and Bain, Peter (1999), "'An Assembly Line in the Head': Work and Employee Relations in the Call Centre," *Industrial Relations Journal*, 30 (2), 101–17.

Therborn, Göran ([1980] 1999), *The Ideology of Power and the Power of Ideology* (London: Verso).
Thomas, Robert J. (1994), *What Machines Can't Do: Politics and Technology in the Industrial Enterprise* (Berkeley: University of California Press).
Thompson, Paul (1983), *The Nature of Work: An Introduction to Debates on the Labour Process* (London: The Macmillan Press).
Thompson, Paul (1990), "Crawling from the Wreckage: The Labour Process and the Politics of Production," in David Knights and Hugh Willmott (eds.), *Labour Process Theory* (London: Macmillan), 95–124.
Thompson, Paul (2003), "Disconnected Capitalism: Or Why Employers Can't Keep Their Side of the Bargain," *Work, Employment & Society*, 17 (2), 359–78.
Thompson, Paul (2010), "The Capitalist Labour Process: Concepts and Connections," *Capital & Class*, 34 (1), 7–14.
Thompson, Paul and van den Broek, Diane (2010), "Managerial Control and Workplace Regimes: An Introduction," *Work, Employment & Society*, 24 (3), 1–12.
Thompson, Paul and Newsome, Kirsty (2004), "Labor Process Theory, Work, and the Employment Relation," in Bruce E. Kaufman (ed.), *Theoretical Perspectives on Work and the Employment Relationship* (Urbana-Champaign: Industrial Relations Research Association), 133–62.
Thompson, Paul and Smith, Chris (2009a), "Labour Power and Labour Process: Contesting the Marginality of the Sociology of Work," *Sociology*, 43 (5), 913–30.
Thompson, Paul and Smith, Chris (2009a), "Waving, Not Drowning: Explaining and Exploring the Resilience of Labor Process Theory," *Employee Responsibilities and Rights Journal*, 21 (3), 253–62.
Thompson, Paul and Smith, Chris (2009b), "Waving, Not Drowning: Explaining and Exploring the Resilience of Labor Process Theory," *Employee Responsibilities and Rights Journal*, 21 (3), 253–62.
Thompson, Paul and Smith, Chris (2009b), "Labour Power and Labour Process: Contesting the Marginality of the Sociology of Work," *Sociology*, 43 (5), 913–30.
Thornton, Patricia A. (2004), *Markets from Culture: Institutional Logics and Organizational Decisions in Higher Education Publishing* (Stanford, CA: Stanford Business Books).
Thornton, Patricia A. and Ocasio, William (1999), "Institutional Logics and the Historical Contingency of Power in Organizations: Executive Succession in the Higher Education Publishing Industry, 1958–1990," *American Journal of Sociology*, 105 (3), 801–43.
Thornton, Patricia A., Ocasio, William, and Lounsbury, Michael (2012), *The Institutional Logics Perspective: A New Approach to Culture, Structure, and Process* (Oxford: Oxford University Press).
Timmermans, Stefan (2005), "From Autonomy to Accountability: The Role of Clinical Practice Guidelines in Professional Power," *Perspectives in Biology and Medicine*, 48 (4), 490–501.
Tolliday, Steven (1998), "The Diffusion and Transformation of Fordism: Britain and Japan Compared," in Robert Boyer, et al. (eds.), *Between Imitation and Innovation: The Transfer and Hybridization of Productive Models in the International Automobile Industry* (Oxford: Oxford University Press), 57–95.
Tolliday, Steven, et al. (1998), "Introduction: Between Imitation and Innovation: The Transfer and Hybridization of Productive Models in the International Automobile Industry," in Robert Boyer, et al. (eds.), *Between Imitation and Innovation: The Transfer and Hybridization of Productive Models in the International Automobile Industry* (Oxford: Oxford University Press), 1–19.

Tolliday, Steven and Zeitlin, Jonathan (1992), "Introduction: Between Fordism and Flexibility," in Steven Tolliday and Jonathan Zeitlin (eds.), *Between Fordism and Flexibility: The Automobile Industry and its Workers* (Providence, RI: Berg), 1–25.

Trist, Eric (1981), "The Sociotechnical Perspective," in A. van den Ven and W. Joyce (eds.), *Perspectives on Organizational Design and Performance* (New York: Wiley), 19–75.

Trusson, Clive, Hislop, Donald, and Doherty, Neil F. (2018), "The Role of ICTs in the Servitisation and Degradation of IT Professional Work," *New Technology, Work and Employment*, 33 (2), 149–70.

Tsutsui, William M. (1996), "W. Edwards Deming and the Origins of Quality Control in Japan", *Journal of Japanese Studies, 22* (2), 295–325.

Turner, Lowell (1991), *Democracy at Work: Changing World Markets and the Future of Labor Unions* (Ithaca, NY: Cornell University Press).

Useem, Michael (1984), *The Inner Circle* (New York: Oxford University Press).

Uzzi, Brian (1996), "The Sources and Consequences of Embeddedness for the Economic Performance of Organizations: The Network Effect," *American Sociological Review*, 61 (4), 674–98.

Vallas, Steven Peter (1993), *Power in the Workplace: The Politics of Production at AT&T* (Albany, NY: SUNY Press).

Veblen, Thorstein. *The Theory of Business Enterprise*. New Brunswick: Transaction Publishers, [1904] 1996.

Vidal, Matt (2007), "Lean Production, Worker Empowerment, and Job Satisfaction: A Qualitative Analysis and Critique," *Critical Sociology*, 33 (1–2), 247–78.

Vidal, Matt (2012), "On the Persistence of Labour Market Insecurity and Slow Growth in the US: Reckoning with the Waltonist Growth Regime," *New Political Economy*, 17 (5), 543–64.

Vidal, Matt (2013), "Postfordism as a Dysfunctional Accumulation Regime: A Comparative Analysis of the USA, the UK and Germany," *Work, Employment & Society*, 27 (3), 451–71.

Vidal, Matt (2014), "Incoherence and Dysfunctionality in the Institutional Regulation of Capitalism," in Marco Hauptmeier and Matt Vidal (eds.), *Comparative Political Economy of Work* (Basingstoke: Palgrave Macmillan), 73–97.

Vidal, Matt (2015), "Fordism and the Golden Age of Atlantic Capitalism," in Stephen Edgell, Heidi Gottfried, and Edward Granter (eds.), *Sage Handbook of the Sociology of Work and Employment* (London: Sage), 283–305.

Vidal, Matt (2017), "Lean Enough: Institutional Logics of Best Practice and Managerial Satisficing in American Manufacturing," *Socius*, 3, 1–17.

Vidal, Matt (2019a), "Geriatric Capitalism: Stagnation and Crisis in Western Capitalism," in Matt Vidal, et al. (eds.), *The Oxford Handbook of Karl Marx* (New York: Oxford University Press), 581–606.

Vidal, Matt (2019b), "Work and Exploitation in Capitalism: The Labor Process and the Valorization Process," in Matt Vidal, et al. (eds.), *The Oxford Handbook of Karl Marx* (New York: Oxford University Press).

Vidal, Matt (2019c), "Contradictions of the Labour Process, Worker Empowerment and Capitalist Inefficiency," *Historical Materialism*, 20 (2), 170–204.

Vidal, Matt and Peck, Jamie (2012), "Sociological Institutionalism and the Socially Constructed Economy," in Trevor Barnes, Jamie Peck, and Eric Sheppard (eds.), *The Wiley-Blackwell Companion to Economic Geography* (Oxford: Wiley-Blackwell), 594–611.

Wagner, John A. (1994), "Participation's Effects on Performance and Satisfaction: A Reconsideration of the Evidence," *Academy of Management Review*, 19 (2), 312–30.

Walker, C.R. (1950), "The problem of the repetitive job", *Harvard Business Review*, 28 (3), 54–58.

Warhurst, Chris (1997), "Political Economy and the Social Organisation of Economic Activity: A Synthesis of Neo-Institutional and Labour Process Analyses," *Competition & Change*, 2, 213–46.

Warhurst, Christopher (1998), "Recognizing the Possible: The Organization and Control of a Socialist Labor Process," *Administrative Science Quarterly*, 43 (2), 470–97.

Warner Communications (2006), "New Survey of Auto Industry Manufacturing Executives Shows Stopped Production Costs an Average $22,000 Per Minute," *Nasdaq Global Newswire*, March 27.

Wellins, Richard S., Byham, William C., and Wilson, Jeanne M. (1991), *Empowered Teams: Creating Self-Directed Work Groups That Improve Quality, Productivity, and Participation* (San Francisco: Jossey-Bass).

Westphal, James D., Gulati, Ranjay, and Shortell, Stephen M. (1997), "Customization or Conformity? An Institutional and Network Perspective on the Content and Consequences of TQM Adoption," *Administrative Science Quarterly*, 42 (2), 366–94.

Wever, Kirsten S., Batt, Rosemary, and Rubinstein, Saul (1996), "Innovation in Isolation: Labor-Management Partnerships in the United States," *The Economic and Labour Relations Review*, 7 (1), 67–87.

Whitford, Josh (2005), *The New Old Economy: Networks, Institutions, and the Organizational Transformation of American Manufacturing* (Oxford: Oxford University Press).

Wickham, Chris (1984), "The Other Transition: From the Ancient World to Feudalism," *Past & Present*, (103), 3–36.

Wickham, Chris (1985), "The Uniqueness of the East," *The Journal of Peasant Studies*, 12 (2–3), 166–96.

Wickham, Chris (ed.), (2007), *Marxist History-Writing for the Twenty-First Century* (Oxford: The British Academy/Oxford University Press).

Williams, Karel, Haslam, Colin, and Williams, John (1992), "Ford Versus Fordism: The Beginning of Mass Production?," *Work, Employment and Society*, 6 (4), 517–55.

Williamson, Oliver E. (1985), *The Economic Institutions of Capitalism: Firms, Markets, Relational Contracting* (New York: Free Press).

Willmott, Hugh (1990), "Subjectivity and the Dialectics of Praxis: Opening up the Core of Labour Process Analysis," in David Knights and Hugh Willmott (eds.), *Labour Process Theory* (Basingstoke: Macmillan), 336–78.

Winter, Sidney G. (1964), "Economic 'Natural Selection' and the Theory of the Firm," *Yale Economic Essays*, 4 (1), 225–72.

Winter, Sidney G. (2000), "The Satisficing Principle in Capability Learning," *Strategic Management Journal*, 21 (10–11), 981–96.

Wolff, Edward N. (2003), "What's Behind the Rise in Profitability in the US in the 1980s and 1990s?," *Cambridge Journal of Economics*, 27 (4), 479–99.

Womack, James, Jones, Daniel, and Roos, Daniel (1990), *The Machine that Changed the World* (New York: Rawson Associates).

Wright, Erik Olin (1978), *Class, Crisis, and the State* (London: Verso).

Index

Index

f refers to figures, *t* refers to tables